NAGARJUNIANA

BUDDHIST TRADITION SERIES

VOLUME 2

NAGARJUNIANA

Studies in the Writings and Philosophy of Nāgārjuna

CHR. LINDTNER

MOTILAL BANARSIDASS PUBLISHERS
PRIVATE LIMITED • DELHI

*Reprint: Delhi, 1990, **2011***
First Indian Edition: Delhi, 1987
First Published: 1982

ISBN: 978-81-208-0288-9 (Cloth)
ISBN: 978-81-208-0395-4 (Paper)

MOTILAL BANARSIDASS
41 U.A. Bungalow Road, Jawahar Nagar, Delhi 110 007
8 Mahalaxmi Chamber, 22 Bhulabhai Desai Road, Mumbai 400 026
203 Royapettah High Road, Mylapore, Chennai 600 004
236, 9th Main III Block, Jayanagar, Bangalore 560 011
Sanas Plaza, 1302 Baji Rao Road, Pune 411 002
8 Camac Street, Kolkata 700 017
Ashok Rajpath, Patna 800 004
Chowk, Varanasi 221 001

Printed in India

By Jainendra Prakash Jain at Shri Jainendra Press,
A-45 Naraina, Phase-I, New Delhi 110 028
and Published by Narendra Prakash Jain for
Motilal Banarsidass Publishers Private Limited,
Bungalow Road, Delhi 110 007

Foreword

The flood of modern books and articles on Buddhism has its pearls and its 'fool's gold'. Lindtner's *Nagarjuniana* must be classified as a pearl. It is a tireless and resourceful attempt to ferret out what Nāgārjuna is talking about, by way of his own works in Sanskrit and in the Tibetan renditions. Lindtner discovers that Nāgārjuna is faithful to Buddhist tradition as he knows it, but as a reformer. The author has frank, even biting, criticisms of some previous attempts to translate Nāgārjuna's works. This might invite criticism in return. Whatever be in store in this matter, this series on Buddhist Traditions is proud to include Lindtner's book

New Delhi ALEX WAYMAN
6 August 1986

Preface

These studies in the writings and philosophy of the Buddhist patriarch Nāgārjuna could not have achieved their present form had I not been able to benefit from the co-operation and support of a number of friends, students, colleagues and library staffs here and abroad.

To all of them, too numerous to mention individually, it is a pleasure to acknowledge my sincere gratitude and tender my best thanks.

In particular I would like to mention the names of four *svayūthyas:* Per K. Sørensen, Ole Holten Pind, Harish Gaonkar and Torvald Olsson with whom I have enjoyed indulging in the study of Madhyamaka texts and in discussions concerning problems of Indian philology and philosophy. Professors J. W. de Jong, V. V. Gokhale and M. Hahn, Dr. M. Hara and Mr. A. Saito all provided me either with indispensable suggestions, papers or copies of manuscripts.

I most heartily thank Mrs. Else Pauly who read the proofs, and, above all, Dr. Eric Grinstead who, readily and generously as always, *inter alia* rendered unfailing support *in rebus sinicis* and in reading my manuscript. Finally I cannot be reticent about the deep and obvious debt my work owes to that of scholars who have done so much, in various respects, to clear the perilous *madhyamā pratipad* before me. Suffice it to mention the names of Erich Frauwallner, Poul Tuxen, Jacques May, Étienne Lamotte and Louis de La Vallée Poussin, still the unsurpassed master of Buddhist studies.

C. L.

Preface to the Third Indian Reprint

Almost thirty years have elapsed since this study of the various works ascribed - rightly or wrongly - to the famous Buddhist ācārya Nāgārjuna - was first published in Denmark. The author is, of course pleased to see that yet another - the third Indian reprint is now called for. The book thus seems to have proved its usefulness.

To trace the Buddhist and Indian sources of these texts was an important task for me. As in the case of any other philosopher, Nāgārjuna's religious or philosophical way of thinking had to be traced to its sources and seen on a historical background as far as possible. It is seldom the case that new ideas simply drop down from the blue sky. The task of a philologist is not unlike that of a detective. He looks at the words and ideas, and traces them to the sources from which their meaning is to be derived.

Some twelve or fifteen years ago I discovered - to my own great surprise - that the Greek text of the New Testament showed unmistakable direct influence from some of the very same Buddhist canonical texts originally composed in the Sanskrit language that had inspired Nāgārjuna (*www.jesusisbuddha.com*). It is a simply fact that can be verified by any scholar who takes the trouble - and the precious time - to learn Greek and Sanskrit.

Eventually, yet another question arose - namely the question of the sources of the Buddhist sources. Little by little, there was another surprise in stock for a philologist taking almost nothing for granted. Some of the early Buddhist canonical texts transmitted to us in the Sanskrit language must have had Greek sources - just like early Buddhist art.

There is , of course, no Buddha if there is no Dharma. If the Dharma - i.e., the body of teachings concerning the five skandhas, the Middle Path, etc. - could be traced back to Greek or Hellenistic sources, what, then, becomes of the Buddha himself? Was he a real historical person - or merely a mythical figure, like all the previous Buddhas and Bodhisattvas?

To my mind, there is no longer any doubt whatsoever, that the king of the Śākyas, just like the king of the Jews, is but a mythical figure, exactly as Zeus and Apollo, Sarapis and Mithras, or Indra and Agni.

Buddhism, in other words, is to a large extent a Indian version of Greek Hellenism and syncretism. In the final analysis, we are dealing with various forms and expressions of solar theology with very old roots. Sometimes, these roots were, for various reasons, forgotten. Surely, Nāgārjuna can be studied from various points of view.

My hope now is that my old book can serve a purpose that I hardly had in mind when it was first published, namely that of opening a small door to a vast field of new research: ancient Indian Buddhism as an Eastern form of Hellenistic religious wisdom. Nāgārjuna is interesting in himself, but, in a broader perspective, even more so as a representative of old ways of thinking.

When dealing with Nāgārjuna and Mahāyāna there are, indeed, several "fundamental concepts". If one concept can be regarded as more fundamental than any other, it is perhaps that of *Prajñā*. This concept is philosophical as well as religious. For Nāgārjuna, *Prajñā* is a Mother - and when we then start searching for the original identity of Mother Wisdom in the broader Hellenistic landscape where we are obliged to search, we will - as I intend to show elsewhere - end up with the daughter of Zeus - Pallas Athena, also known as Pronoia - reflected in Sanskrit Prajñā.

Once this identification has been made on a purely comparative textual basis, we shall find the validity of our discovery confirmed by the independent evidence provided by Buddhist art and Hellenistic coinage. Coins with the image of the daughter of Zeus must have been familiar to all Buddhists from the third century before the - likewise - mythical Christ.

In due course, further research will be able to distinguish different kinds of Hellenistic influence in different Buddhist sources, Pythagorean, etc.

Christian Lindtner, November 2010

Contents

Introduction

1) Spurious and dubious

Even though a steadily increasing amount of papers and books about Nāgārjuna and the Madhyamaka school testify to a widespread interest in this branch of Mahāyāna Buddhism,[1] Indologists have still not laid the solid foundation required for real progress in these studies in particular. Only a small – though important – fraction of his works are available in modern editions and reliable translations,[2] while more than one hundred of the most varied texts transmitted under Nāgārjuna's name still lie in Chinese and Tibetan versions, and even in Sanskrit manuscripts, without having been analysed let alone critically edited.[3]

It is only when a genuine and intelligible kernel of text has been extracted from this *rudis indigestaque molis* that the two main tasks awaiting the scholar in this field may be taken up: The first will be the endeavour to understand the ideas and the personality of Nāgārjuna from his own works against his own background (mainly Buddhist), the next, to trace the immense impact – for I am certain that it will prove to have been so – that his efforts exercised on the subsequent development not only inside but also outside the Buddhist fold.[4]

In a previous work[5] I have attempted to assign all the texts and

1. Suffice it to mention Murti (1966); Robinson (1967); Streng (1967). – General bibliographical surveys may be found in Potter (1970), pp. 480-484; Regamey (1950), pp. 55-58; Streng (1967), pp. 237-245; Nakamura (1977), pp. 77-94. – Good selective bibliographies in May (1959), pp. 23-45; Lamotte (1970), pp. lxi-lxviii; (1976), p. xvii-xix; (1980) pp. xii-xv. – The most recent survey of Madhyamaka is by May in Hōbōgirin, pp. 470-493 (s.v. *Chūgan*).
2. Viz. MK, VV, PK, and, in part RĀ, see below.
3. The Chinese translations are conveniently registered in the *Fascicule annexe* to Hōbōgirin, Tōkyō 1978; the Tibetan e.g. in the index volume to the *Tibetan Tripiṭaka, Peking edition,* Tōkyō 1962.
4. Here I have only pointed out a few instances where Nāgārjuna's influence is obvious, see pp. 278-281.
5. *Nāgārjuna – Ægte og Uægte. En analyse og sammenfatning af Nāgārjunas autentiske*

fragments (to the extent I have come across such in the commentatorial literature) attributed to Nāgārjuna to three classes, viz. works 1) correctly attributed, 2) wrongly attributed to him, and 3) those which may or may not be genuine.

The following internal and external criteria of authenticity were applied: I took my *point d'appui* in a close study – with careful regard to the commentaries[6] – of the doctrine and style of *Mūlamadhyamakakārikā* (MK)[7] which I axiomatically, but in accordance with a unanimous and, for all we know, reliable Indian, Chinese and Tibetan tradition[8] regard as his *magnum opus*. Those among the remaining works which agree with MK in regard to a) style, b) scope, c) doctrine, and – turning to the external criteria – *in addition* explicitly are ascribed to Nāgārjuna by the testimony of 'trustworthy witnesses', viz. Bhavya (Bhāvaviveka), Candrakīrti, Śāntarakṣita and Kamalaśīla, I recognize as genuine.[9] Works that are

værker og fragmenter udskilt blandt samtlige på sanskrit, tibetansk og kinesisk under hans navn overleverede skrifter. København 1978. (Unpublished). It is now superseded by the present work.

6. Namely *Akutobhayā* (TP, No. 5229); *Buddhapālitavṛtti* (TP, No. 5242), *Prajñāpradīpa* (TP, No. 5253) by Bhavya, *Prajñāpradīpaṭīkā* (TP, No. 5259) by Avalokitavrata and *Prasannapadā* (ed. La Vallée Poussin) by Candrakīrti. I have only resorted to the commentaries extant in Chinese (Taishō, Nos. 1564, 1567) occasionally, as they seldom are of much use from a philological point of view.
7. Sanskrit text in *Mūlamadhyamakakārikās (Mādhyamikasūtras) de Nāgārjuna avec la Prasannapadā Commentaire de Candrakīrti*. Publié par Louis de La Vallée Poussin. St.-Pétersbourg 1903-13. – There is a separate edition of *Nāgārjuna, Mūlamadhyamakakārikāḥ* by J.W. de Jong, Adyar 1977. As modern versions of MK (by Inada and Streng) are most unreliable one still has to consult MK as translated together with the *Prasannapadā* by Stcherbatsky, Schayer, Lamotte, de Jong and May, see de Jong, *IIJ*, XX, p. 25. A recent attempt by M. Sprung, *Lucid Exposition of the Middle Way: The Essential Chapters from the Prasannapadā of Candrakīrti*. London 1979, again suffers from the author's insufficient philological outfit.
8. I.e. colophons as well as the testimony of commentators (Indian) and »historians« (Chinese and Tibetan).
9. Buddhapālita is absent from this list as he only refers to MK (cf. my remarks in *IIJ*, XXIII, p. 154). I have consulted all the extant works of Candrakīrti (for a brief account of which see *AO*, XL, pp. 87-92) and Bhavya (see *WZKS*, XXVI (1982)). Among the many works of Śāntarakṣita and his pupil Kamalaśīla the former's *Madhyamakālaṃkāravṛtti* and *Tattvasiddhi* and the latter's *Madhyamakālaṃkārapañjikā*, *Madhyamakāloka* as well as *Bhāvanākrama* (I & III) have proved most profitable. True, we cannot prove that these

provable as unauthentic (e.g. if they quote from a source later than Nāgārjuna, always allowing for cases of interpolation) belong to the second class, while texts from which I have in vain tried to extract decisive criteria, external or internal, come within the third.

Summing up, I found that apart from MK twelve other texts must thus be considered genuine. They will be analysed, edited or translated on the following pages in this order subsequent to a review of MK: *Śūnyatāsaptati* (ŚS), *Vigrahavyāvartanī* (VV), *Vaidalyaprakaraṇa* (VP), **Vyavahārasiddhi* (VS), *Yuktiṣaṣṭikā* (YṢ), *Catuḥstava* (CS), *Ratnāvalī* (RĀ), *Pratītyasamutpādahṛdayakārikā* (PK), *Sūtrasamuccaya* (SS), *Bodhicittavivaraṇa* (BV), *Suhṛllekha* (SL) and **Bodhisaṃbhāra[ka]* (BS).

Decidedly spurious are **Mahāprajñāpāramitopadeśa*,[10] *Abudhabodhakaprakaraṇa*,[11] *Guhyasamājatantraṭīkā*,[12] **Dvādaśadvāraka*,[13] *Prajñāpāra-*

authorities possessed any objective means of deciding what Nāgārjuna wrote and what he did not write. However, we do know that all of them were very learned and meticulous in dealing with their texts, and that even a slight misquotation etc. on their part would be certain to expose them to the censure of lurking *svayūthyas*. On the other hand I never accept the testimony of other (usually later) authors unless its credibility can be established independently.

10. Cf. May, *Chūgan*, p. 482.
11. TP, No. 5238. This is a small but very readable *prakaraṇa* demonstrating *pudgaladharmanairātmya*. It does however, betray itself by quoting (without naming any source) *Catuḥśataka*, XIII, 2; BV, 18; MK, V, 6; PK, »7«; *Bhavasaṃkrānti* »8«. An *Abodhabodhaka* ascribed to Advayavajra (TP, No. 3145) is nothing but another recension of the very same text!
12. As pointed out by G. Tucci, *Opera Minora*, I, p. 214 a quotation from Maitreya occurs in this *ṭīkā*. – I find it quite likely that the author of this work is identical with the author of *Pañcakrama* (ed. La Vallée Poussin, Gand 1896), a work which is already cited in *Madhyamakaratnapradīpa*, ca. 570, see *WZKS*, XXVI (1982). – As a mere working hypothesis I would at present suggest that this 'Nāgārjuna II', i.e. the *tāntrika* or *siddha* flourished ca. 400 A.D. He may also have been responsible for numerous *sādhanas* and other more or less tantric works transmitted under the name of Nāgārjuna (see. e.g. B. Bhattacharya, *Sādhanamālā*, I-II, Baroda 1968). As a discussion of this complex question has no direct bearing on the 'real' Nāgārjuna it must be postponed for future research.
13. Usually referred to as *Dvādaśanikāyaśāstra*, *Dvādaśamukhaśāstra* or *Dvādaśadvāraśāstra* i.e. Taishō, No. 1568, but there is seldom any reason to attach much weight to the Chinese *lùn* in titles etc. – Some observations on this text by May, *Chūgan*, pp. 488-489; Robinson (1967), p. 32. Cf. also sToṅ pa ñid kyi sgo bcu gñis pa, No. 595 in the lDan dkar ma Catalogue. – While there can be

mitāstotra[14] and *Svabhāvatrayapraveśasiddhi.*[15]

The third group, i.e. the dubious texts, may be divided into those that are *perhaps* authentic: *Mahāyānaviṃśikā,*[16] *Bodhicittotpādavidhi,*[17]

no doubt that (nearly) all the verses were originally composed by Nāgārjuna (MK, ŚS) there are in my opinion several good reasons for maintaining that the author of the commentary (most probably identical with the compiler of the verses) is *not* Nāgārjuna but rather *Piṅgala. Here I must postpone further remarks to a later occasion.

14. See *IIJ*, XXIII, p. 182, n. 94.
15. Edited and translated by La Vallée Poussin, *MCB,* II, pp. 147-161. – First of all the doctrine of *svabhāvatraya* (already attested in the *Laṅkāvatāra*) is refuted by Nāgārjuna in his BV, 28, q.v. Moreover, the existence of *paratantrasvabhāva* endorsed by *Svabhāvatrayapraveśasiddhi* (also called *Trisvabhāvanirdeśa*) is repeatedly refuted by Bhavya, Candrakīrti etc. who never quote this work, sometimes, and perhaps correctly, ascribed to Vasubandhu.
16. The Sanskrit text was edited and translated by G. Tucci, *Minor Buddhist Texts, Part I,* pp. 195-207. Further ref. Nakamura (1977), p. 83, n. 38. – I have come across quotations from this work ascribed to Nāgārjuna in *Caryāmelāyanapradīpa* (TP, No. 2668, 95a) and *Tattvasārasaṃgraha* (TP, No. 4534, 92a, 100a), q.v. Atiśa also ascribes this work to Nāgārjuna, *Bodhimārgadīpapañjikā* (TP, No. 5344, 324b), but Bhavya etc. never quote it. Still it shows great similarity to YṢ. RĀ, BV etc. as far as style and doctrine is concerned, so it may be authentic. – Here are some emendations to Tucci's edition made in the light of the Tibetan and Chinese translations, q.v.: 3a, read *pārāvāram ivotpannāḥ,* cf. CS, III, 11. Note that Tib. wrongly has *tshul bźin* for *tshu bźin.* – 6a, Tucci has *ṣaḍgatir yaś ca saṃsāraḥ svargaś* which is impossible. Read with Tib. and Chin. *ṣaḍgatayaś ca saṃsāre svarge.* – 6d, Tucci has *jarāvyādhir apīyatām* with the note that Ms. has °*rapībhyatām,* or *rapītyatām.* However, this is, as Tib. and Chin. show, not to be counted as 6d but as 7b. Due to haplography (originally 6c and 7a must have ended with *duḥkham!* v. Tib. and Chin.), the scribe left out two *pādas.* In 7b we find ... *mi rtag ñid,* so Tucci's Ms. apparently has *anityatām.* – »11a«, read *bhāvato.* – »12b«, Tucci reads *karuṇādhīramānasāḥ,* but Tib. has *sñiṅ rje'i dbaṅ gyur* ... which is a common idea (cf. CS, I, 1; II, 1 etc.). So read *karuṇādhīnamānasāḥ* (Tucci probably misread Ms.). – »14« read, of course, *tattvārtha*° with Tib. and Chin. – »15a«, Tucci reads *tena,* »therefore«, but with Tib. *de dag* read *te na,* cf. YṢ, 5. – »17a«, read *māyāvī,* and in »18b« perhaps *māyākārasamutthitam,* cf. *Caryāmelāyanapradīpa, loc. cit.: sgyu ma'i rnam par yaṅ dag 'byuṅ.*
17. A brief but interesting ritual text (TP, Nos. 5361, 5405, nearly identical). – It prescribes a sevenfold rite for a bodhisattva (cf. *Upālipariprcchā,* p. 98, n. 7; BS, 48 with ref.): *vandanā, pāpadeśanā, puṇyānumodanā, śaraṇagamana, ātmatyāga, bodhicittotpāda* and *pariṇāmanā.* The final paragraph is noteworthy as it alludes to the same *āgama* as the prose introduction to BV. Moreover it ends with three *praṇidhānas* the first of which is identical with RĀ, V, 83. The second recalls RĀ, V, 80. – A Danish translation of this will be found in C. Lindtner

Dvādaśakāranayastotra,[18] *(Madhyamaka-)Bhavasaṃkrānti,*[19] **Nirālambastava,*[20] *Śālistambakārikā,*[21] *Stutyatītastava,*[22] *Dānaparikathā,*[23] *Cittavaj-*

et al., Buddhismen. København 1982, pp. 102-105.

18. Only extant in Tibetan (TP, No. 2026) in 14 stanzas. Clearly a Madhyamaka text (speaks of *puṇyajñānasaṃbhāra, upāyakauśalya* etc.) relating the Buddha's *dvādaśakāra,* cf. BV, 91-92; CS, II, 23. Perhaps the same author as the *Aṣṭamahāsthānacaityastotra,* v. H. Nakamura in *Indianisme et bouddhisme,* Louvain-la-Neuve, 1980, pp. 259-265.
19. The edition by N. A. Sastri (see ref. Nakamura (1977), p. 84) is useful but far from definitive. The transmission of this text is more complex than that of any other work ascribed to Nāgārjuna. Apart from the versions published by Sastri one must consult the *Bhavasaṃcara* ascribed to Nāgārjuna, and the *Nirvikalpaprakaraṇa* ascribed to Āryadeva both of which contain many similar or identical verses. – Verse »6« is attributed to Nāgārjuna in Bhavya's *Madhyamakaratnapradīpa,* 352a. Incidentally the same verse is discussed by Williams, *JIP,* VIII, p. 27. – In Sanskrit I have come across a quotation (no source given) in *Ādikarmapradīpa* (ed. La Vallée Poussin), p. 196: *dānaśīlakṣamāvīryadhyānādīn sevayet sadā* I *acireṇaiva kālena prāpyate bodhir uttamā* II; cf. RĀ, II, 25; IV, 80, 98-99.
20. Known from a quotation in Dharmendra's *Tattvasārasaṃgraha,* TP, No. 4534, 102b: *bsam byed bsam gtan bsam bya dag* II *spaṅs pa bden pa mthoṅ ba yin* II *'di kun rtog pa tsam ñid do* II *gaṅ gis rtogs pa de grol 'gyur* II. Atiśa ascribes this verse to Nāgārjuna in *Bodhimārgadīpapañjikā,* TP, No. 5344, 329b: *kun tu rtogs pas ma btags śiṅ* II *yid ni rab tu mi gnas la* II *dran med yid la byed pa med* II *dmigs med de la phyag 'tshal lo* II. The three verses found in *Pañcakrama* (ed. La Vallée Poussin), p. 36 ending in *nirālamba namo 'stu te* may be from the same source (note that the previous verses are extracted from CS, II, 18-19!).
21. Only in Tibetan (TP, No. 5466 and No. 5485). 70 verses, originally probably *anuṣṭubh.* 47d missing in TP. This is simply a very faithful versification of the *Śālistambasūtra,* one of Nāgārjuna's basic *āgamas,* cf. *svavṛtti* to VV, 54; May (1959), p. 267, n. 967. According to *Ratnapradīpa,* 342a, Nāgārjuna composed a *sa lu ljaṅ pa'i mdo'i 'grel pa* (**Śālistambasūtravṛtti*); possibly this refers to these kārikās. Anyhow it hardly refers to the *Śālistambakaṭīkā* also attributed to Nāgārjuna – as this must be a rather late work inasmuch as it deals with the four *anubandhas,* not attested in early Madhyamaka.
22. Only Tibetan (TP, No. 2020). Sanskrit reconstruction by Patel, *IHQ,* VIII, pp. 689-705. The most philosophical of all the hymns attributed to Nāgārjuna apart from CS, I and III. I have not seen any quotations from this hymn which is quite possibly authentic.
23. Only in Tibetan (TP, No. 5661). A collection of 13 verses (various metres) forming a sermon on one of the distinctive *pāramitās* of an *upāsaka* often praised by Nāgārjuna (BS, SL, RĀ, SS, *passim*). Belongs to the same genre as several other products of the early Madhyamaka school, e.g. Mātṛceṭa's *Caturviparyayakathā.* No quotations known to me. Cf. also *Traité,* pp. 650-769.

rastava,[24] *Mūlasarvāstivādiśrāmaṇerakārikā,*[25] **Daśabhūmikavibhāṣā,*[26] **Lokaparīkṣā,*[27] *Yogaśataka,*[28] *Prajñādaṇḍa,*[29] *Rasavaiśeṣikasūtra*[30] and

– The *Svapnacintāmaṇiparikathā,* in 32 verses, also belongs to this group of dubious texts.

24. The Tibetan version edited with a French translation by La Vallée Poussin, *Le Muséon,* N.S.XIV, pp. 14-16. I found verse 3 in *Ādikarmapradīpa,* p. 200: *cittena labhyate bodhiś cittena gatipañcakam | na hi cittād ṛte kiṃ cil lakṣaṇaṃ sukhaduḥkhayoḥ ||* (Tib. *rim thob* must be corrupt.)

25. Only Tibetan (TP, No. 5629). 50 kārikās based on the *Vinayavibhaṅga* on the *Bhikṣuprātimokṣasūtras* of the Mūlasarvāstivādins. – Recalling how influential the Vinaya of this school must have been in the early centuries A.D. (cf. *Traité,* III, p. xviii) in the Madhyamaka milieu it is not unlikely that Nāgārjuna should have compiled a *summa* of monastic rules. It would tally excellently with RĀ, V, 1, 34, q.v., and also be consistent with the *samuccaya*-genre, a favourite of Nāgārjuna's. There is a possible allusion to this work in *Ratnapradīpa,* 350 a, which speaks of the *śikṣās ... slob dpon klu sgrub kyi źal sna nas ji ltar bkod pa rnams ...*

26. Only Chinese (Taishō, No. 1521), cf. *Vimalakīrtinirdeśa,* p. 76; Ramanan (1966), p. 340, n. 61) Nakamura (1977), p. 82; *Traité,* III, p. xliv (with ref.) – Though, like **Mahāprajñāpāramitōpadeśa* etc., this commentary is apparently unknown to Indo-Tibetan tradition there are in my opinion several reasons to render it likely that it is authentic: The very early Chinese evidence; quotations from **Bodhisaṃbhāra*; the Amitābha doctrine set forth here tallies with SL, 121 (cf. RĀ, III, 99); *Daśabhūmikasūtra* is known to have been used by Nāgārjuna elsewhere (PK; RĀ, V, 41-60; SS, 249 b). – All this certainly deserves a discussion more thorough than I am prepared to undertake at present. – Cf. J. Eracle, *Le Chapitre de Nāgārjuna sur la Pratique Facile, suivi du Sūtra qui loue la Terre de Pureté,* Bruxelles 1981 (not seen).

27. Only known to me from a quotation in *Prajñāpradīpa,* 114b: *'di ni yod ñid 'gog pa ste || med ñid yoṅs su 'dzin pa min || nag po min źes smras pa na || dkar po yin źes ma brjod bźin ||.* According to Avalokitavrata (*loc. cit.,* Źa *fol.* 96a) its source is Nāgārjuna's *'jig rten brtag pa źes bya ba'i gtan* (read: *bstan*) *bcos, *Lokaparīkṣā.* I.e. *astitvapratiṣedha* does not necessarily imply *nāstitvaparigraha.* Thus one can deny that something is *kṛṣṇa* without necessarily affirming that it is *śukla.* In other words (see Avalokitavrata, *loc. cit.*) a Mādhyamika is allowed to express *paramārthataḥ* a *prasajyapratiṣedha* of *astitva,* without, however, advocating *nāstitva* by way of a *paryudāsa.* – Other verses attributed to Nāgārjuna occur e.g. *Ekasmṛtyupadeśa* (TP, No. 5389, 26a); *Madhyamakālaṃkāravṛtti* (TP, No. 5285, 72b = TP, No. 5274, 383a); *Caryāmelāyanapradīpa* (TP, No. 2668, 95a) – to mention only a few of the most interesting verses which I have failed to identify in the extant works.

28. A summary of therapeutic formulas (*yoga*) composed in various metres and closely following the classical doctrine of medicine (*aṣṭāṅga*). Recently two useful editions (including the Tibetan version) have appeared: B. Dash (1976), *Tibetan Medicine with special reference to Yoga Śataka,* Dharamsala; and J.

Bhāvanākrama;[31] and those most probably *not genuine: Akṣaraśataka,*[32] *Akutobhayā (Mūlamadhyamakavṛtti),*[33] *Āryabhāṭṭaraka-Mañjuśrīparamār-*

Filliozat (1979), *Yogaśataka: Texte médical attribué à Nāgārjuna,* Pondichéry. (Note that there are two Mss. in The Royal Library, Copenhagen, not collated. Rask and Tuxen collections.) – *Yogaśataka* is commonly (but not exclusively) ascribed to Nāgārjuna, see Filliozat, *op.cit.*, pp. iv-xix, who discusses the question of authenticity. Here I would only call attention to three pieces of evidence in favour of the authenticity of *Yogaśataka:* RĀ, III, 46 speaking of *triphala, trikaṭuka, ghṛta, madhu, añjana* etc.: *'bras bu gsum daṅ tsha ba gsum* || *mar daṅ sbraṅ rtsi mig sman daṅ* || *dug sel chu rar bźag bgyi źiṅ* || *grub pa'i sman daṅ sṅags kyaṅ bgyi* ||. BS 79 and SS, 251b recommend that a bodhisattva cultivates *vidyāsthāna* etc. which include *cikitsā.* Finally *Ratnapradīpa* (337b) reports that Nāgārjuna mastered *gso ba (cikitsā)* etc. – For other medical texts etc. see Dash (1976), pp. 9-17.

29. The Tibetan version (260 verses, various metres) was edited and translated by W.L. Campbell, *The Tree of Wisdom,* Calcutta 1919. Recently 255 verses were translated by Tarthang Tulku, *Elegant Sayings,* Emeryville 1977. – Note that vv. 76, 108 and 196 recall RĀ, II, 41; IV, 49, 8, q.v. – Atiśa's *Satyadvayāvatāra,* 25 is nearly identical with 140. – *Prajñādaṇḍa* and other *nīti* texts ascribed to Nāgārjuna in Tibetan versions have been discussed by S.K. Pathak, *The Indian Nītiśāstras in Tibet,* Delhi 1974, q.v.
30. Contrary to what one might expect this is not an alchemic tract but rather a »biochemical«, see N.E. Muthuswami (ed.), *Rasavaiśeṣikasūtraṃ Narasiṃhakṛtabhāṣyopetam,* Trivandrum 1976. – Filliozat (1979), pp. x-xiii has discussed the question of authenticity.
31. Only Tibetan (TP, No 5304). 55 *anuṣṭubh.* The most salient features of this text advocating full-fledged *māyāvāda* is that a large number of its stanzas also occurs in the *Laṅkāvatārasūtra* (e.g. 1-4 ~ X, 7-10; 53-55 ~ X, 255-257 etc.) with several interesting variants. The third verse is quoted *Tattvasārasaṃgraha,* 102 b, as from Nāgārjuna's **Nirālambastava* (cf. n. 20 above), the fourth also occurs as *Madhyamakabhavasamkrānti,* »15«. It certainly deserves a separate treatment, preferably along with the many other (if not always unambiguous) points of agreement between early Madhyamaka and the *Laṅkāvatārasūtra.*
32. Only Tibetan and Chinese, see EOB, I, p. 360; V. V. Gokhale, *Aksaraśatakam. The Hundred Letters,* Heidelberg 1930. – The Chinese (Taishō, *No. 1572) attributes it to* Āryadeva, the Tibetan (TP, 5234, *sūtra,* and TP, 5235, *vṛtti*) and Atiśa, *Bodhimārgadīpapañjikā,* 324a to Nāgārjuna. – If the *sūtras* and the *vṛtti* have the same author (which is most likely the case), and the quotation of *Sāṃkhyakārikā,* 9 in the *vṛtti* (see W. Liebenthal, *Satkārya in der Darstellung seiner buddhistischen Gegner,* Stuttgart-Berlin 1933, p. 25) is not a late interpolation it cannot possibly have been composed by Nāgārjuna or Āryadeva. Liebenthal, *loc. cit.*, instead suggests »Vasu«, perhaps correctly. See also Robinson (1967), p. 33. – A new edition by Mr. Holten Pind will appear in *Indiske Studier* V.
33. See Nakamura (1977), p. 78, and May (1979), p. 481 who summarizes some

thastuti,[34] *Kāyatrayastotra*,[35] *Narakoddharastava*,[36] *Niruttarastava*,[37] *Vandanāstava*,[38] *Dharmasaṃgraha*,[39] *Dharmadhātugarbhavivaraṇa*,[40] **Ekaślokaśāstra*,[41] *Īśvarakartṛtvanirākṛti*,[42] *Saitvārādhanastava*,[43] **Upāyahṛda-*

of the arguments against the authenticity of the *Akutobhayā*. – In my opinion the same Sanskrit original must be supposed behind the Tibetan version (TP, No. 5229) and the Chinese, i.e. *Zhōng lùn* (Taishō, No. 1564). The latter is quite free in its rendering of verses as well as commentary. In spite of the fact that there is a good Indian tradition in support of Nāgārjuna as the author of *Akutobhayā* (see *IIJ*, XXIII, p. 212, n. 18; *WZKSO*, VII, p. 37; *Bodhimārgadīpapañjikā*, 324 b; *Akutobhayā*, 114a, etc.) I consider it spurious, not only because its prose compares rather poorly with that of the *svavṛttis* to VP, ŚS and VV but especially because Āryadeva's *Catuḥśataka*, VII, 9 is quoted ad MK, XXVII, 24, in the Tibetan version as well as in the Chinese (so correct Robinson's remark (1967), p. 31 that XXVII, 25 has »no counterpart in the Sanskrit«. It must have had, not in MK but in the *vṛtti* quoting *Catuḥśataka*). At present we must accept the obscure *Piṅgala to have composed the commentary, cf. May (1979), p. 481. He was certainly not identical with Āryadeva.

34. TP, No. 2023. Simply another recension of *Paramārthastava* (CS, IV).
35. Four verses in the *sragdharā* metre, see A. von Staël Holstein: 'Bemerkungen zum Trikāyastava', *Bulletin de l'Académie impériale des sciences de St.-Petersbourg*, XI, pp. 837-835; G. N. Roerich, *The Blue Annals*, Calcutta 1949, pp. 1-2; D. S. Ruegg (1969), p. 49. – Ascribed to Nāgārjuna in Jñānaśrīmitra's *Sākārasiddhiśāstra*, p.503, but the *trikāya*-doctrine is hardly compatible with the *kāyadvaya* of YṢ, 60; RĀ, III, 10, 12. Moreover the style is very loose, rather unlike Nāgārjuna. – Several extracts in *JRAS* (1906), pp. 943-977.
36. I have edited and translated this hymn *AO*, XL, pp. 146-155. – It has nothing to do with Nāgārjuna. (*Corrigenda:* 4c, *yās*°; 6a, °*rūḍha;* 15a, °*rājā*. – Prof. de Jong kindly makes the following suggestions: 1a, read *dāridrya*°?; 2b, is *anātha*° an old corruption for *ananta*°?; 4, cf. *Dharmasamuccaya*, XIII, 13; 13c, seems corrupt. Read *rājāhaṃ me tadā mānas*?).
37. Only Tibetan (TP, No. 2021) Eight verses, too poor to be genuine.
38. Only Tibetan (TP, No. 2027). Also eight poor verses.
39. Cf. Murti (1960), p. 91, n. 5. Though certainly a Mahāyāna text there is nothing particularly Nāgārjunian about it.
40. TP, No. 5602. – Discussed and reconstructed into Sanskrit by S. K. Pathak, *IHQ*, XXXIII, pp. 246-249. Cf. BV, 59-63 (note).
41. A literal version of the Chinese (Taishō, No. 1573) is found in L. de La Vallée Poussin, *Catalogue of the Tibetan Manuscripts from Tun-Huang in the India Office library*, London 1962, No. 595; *raṅ gi ṅo bo ñid myi rtag* ‖ *de bźin ṅo bo ṅo bo myed* ‖ *raṅ bźin ṅo bo ñid myed pas* ‖ *de phyir stoṅ daṅ myi rtag gsuṅs* ‖.
42. Also called *Viṣṇor ekakartṛtvanirākaraṇam*. Discussed and translated by G. Chemparathy: 'Two early Buddhist refutations of the existence of Īśvara as the creator of the universe', *WZKSO*, XXII-XIII, pp. 85-100 (with ref.). Text and translation also in H. C. Gupta (transl.), *Papers of Th. Stcherbatsky*,

ya,[44] **Aṣṭādaśaśūnyatāśāstra*,[45] *Dharmadhātustava*,[46] *Yogaratnamālā*,[47] etc.

Calcutta 1969, pp. 3-16.

43. Nine verses in Tibetan (TP, No 2017) and Sanskrit (*vasantatilakā*) edited by S. Lévi under Aśvaghoṣa's name: 'Autour d'Aśvaghoṣa', *JA*, CCXV, pp. 264-66. – According to the Tibetan colophon (which ascribes it to Nāgārjuna) it is a *bsdus pa* of a part of *Bodhisattvapiṭaka* called *tshva chu kluṅ*. – The style of this nice little hymn recalls Mātṛceṭa more than anyone else.

44. There is a Chinese version (Taishō, No. 1632) 'retranslated' into Sanskrit by G. Tucci, *Pre-Diṅnāga Buddhist texts on logic from Chinese sources*, Baroda 1929. – Its authenticity was impeached by H. Ui, cf. Nakamura (1977), p. 85. – At least two circumstances render its genuineness dubious in my mind: It appears unlikely that Nāgārjuna, whose predilection for arguing merely by way of *prasaṅga* is well-known, should recommend conventional rules of debate in order to vindicate the Dharma. And again, why does the **Upāyahṛdaya* never figure in the subsequent Svātantrika-Prāsaṅgika controversy in which its tenets would certainly have entitled it to play a decisive role if authentic? If, on the other hand, we assume that it fell into oblivion in India at an early date it is quite possible that Nāgārjuna composed it »from a desire to defend the Saddharma« (*loc.cit.*, 23b 19-20), i.e. on the *saṃvṛti*-level (cf. *ibid.*, 25a 4 ff. where a *satyadvaya*-theory is implicit). Moreover we here find the same disdainful attitude towards *vāda* usually motivated by various *kleśas* (*ibid.*, 23b 6ff. Here the *pūrvapakṣa* is, of course, rhetorical).

45. See the arguments advanced by Ramanan (1966), p. 34 (with n. 55).

46. Extant in Tibetan, 101 verses (TP, No. 2010) and Chinese, 87 verses (Taishō, No. 1675). They are not different works (as Nakamura, *op.cit.*, p. 84 apparently thinks), the Chinese being merely a free version. – Discussed and paraphrased by D. S. Ruegg: 'Le *Dharmadhātustava* de Nāgārjuna', *Études Tibétaines dédiées à la Mémoire de Marcelle Lalou*, Paris 1971, pp. 448-471, q.v. – It is attributed to Nāgārjuna by Bhavya, quoting 91-96 and 101 (*op.cit.*, 358a and 361a). It must also be noticed that several sūtras asserting the existence of *dharmadhātu* or *tathāgatagarbha* as *nitya*, *dhruva*, *śiva* and *śāśvata* (cf. CS, II, 22) are also known from quotations in Nāgārjuna's SS. In this *stava* (or *stotra*) we also find a *prima facie* 'positive ontology': *dharmadhātu* is *niyatasthāna* (1), *saṃsārahetu* (2), *anutpanna, aniruddha* (8), *prabhāsvara, viśuddha* (9), *sāra* (15), *bīja* (17), *anātman* (24, here 'without gender'), *dhruva* (35) etc. It is not merely *śūnya* (22). – It would be a glaring inconsistency for the author of MK, ŚS, VV etc. to express himself thus *paramārthataḥ*. On the other hand I do not think we can exclude that Nāgārjuna wrote this hymn *saṃvṛtitaḥ*, or *neyārtha* (cf. CS, III, 57) with the motive *sattvāvatārataḥ* (cf. CS, II, 21-22).

47. See most recently P. Kumar (ed.), *Nāgārjuna's Yogaratnamālā*, Delhi 1980. It is a collection of verses dealing with various matters such as *vaśīkaraṇa, vidveṣakaraṇa, uccāṭana, piśācīkaraṇa, āveśavidhāna, vandhyāputrajanma, dīpena kāṇīkaraṇa* and similar whimsical – not to say criminal – devices which in the opinion of Nāgārjuna would certainly secure their author a place of honour in Avīci. – Worthy of a more serious interest are the extracts from *Rasaratnākara*

The fact that my desire to treat all the works ascribed to Nāgārjuna in one way or another – κατὰ τὴν ὕλην οἱ λόγοι ἀπαιτητέοι – has thus made the present work rather wide in its scope, does, needless to say, inevitably entail that numerous details or points of minor significance are tacitly passed by. This could not be otherwise. Nobody could be more aware of how much still remains to be done by future research than I am. However, I may say that I have done my best to clarify, or at least to indicate all points affording genuine problems, textual or philosophical. For misunderstandings and omissions I can, of course, only crave the reader's indulgence.

2) A preliminary summary

It will be convenient for the reader when studying the texts and for the editor when annotating them, if I anticipate the results of the detailed analysis of each of the genuine texts and provide a synthetic survey (*saṃkṣepa*) of the religious and philosophical persuasions of Nāgārjuna.[48]

edited by P. C. Ray, *A History of Hindu chemistry*, Calcutta 1909, vol. II, pp. *3-*17. The author is an alchemist with a high opinion of his sacred vocation (III, 4): *prajñāpāramitā niśīthasamaye svapne prasādīkṛtam* | *nāmnā tīkṣṇamukhaṃ rasendram amalaṃ nāgārjunaproditam* ||. Perhaps this line which apparently does not belong to the *Rasaratnākara* but rather to the *Kakṣāpuṭa* (sometimes ascribed to Nāgārjuna, cf. Tucci, *op.cit.*, p. 214) reveals the true identity of this namesake: *śrīśailaparvatasthāyī siddho nāgārjuno mahān* | *sarvasattvopakārī ca sarvabhāgyasamanvitaḥ* || (*ibid.*, p. *12). – On *Rasaratnākara* cf. also M. Eliade, *Yoga: Unsterblichkeit und Freiheit*, Frankfurt 1977, p. 430; *Traité*, p. 383.

The remaining works ascribed to Nāgārjuna are mainly *sādhanas* etc. or other texts the form or content of which, at least from a first perusal, appear too insipid and unworthy of the author of the thirteen works I consider genuine.

48. Lamotte, *Vimalakīrtinirdeśa*, pp. 40-51 and May, *TP*, LIV, pp. 339-342 (cf. Hōbōgirin, *Chūgan*, p. 474) have attempted to summarize 'la position du *Mādhyamika*' in six fundamental theses, or essential elements, q.v. – As many of Nāgārjuna's authentic works have not been taken into account full justice has not been done to the ethical, epistemological and psychological (religious) aspects of his thought, nor has an attempt to demonstrate the inherent unity of these aspects been made. In my *saṃkṣepa* I take it for granted that a philosopher faces four fundamental problems: the ontological, the epistemological, the psychological and the ethical. This division reflects a distinctly Occidental approach, which, historically speaking, ultimately

The best starting point for such an exposition is the theory of two truths (*satyadvaya*): a relative or conventional truth (*saṃvṛti-satya*) which serves as the means for obtaining the absolute or ultimate truth (*paramārthasatya*).[49]

α) The ultimate goal of all endeavours is the *summum bonum* of one self and of others: abolition of rebirth, or Nirvāṇa.[50] It implies the attainment of buddhahood, or a double body (*kāyadvaya*).[51] – This may be considered from four angles:

1) *Ontologically:* All phenomena (*dharma*) are empty (*śūnya*) since they lack own-being (*svabhāva*) inasmuch as they, empirically and logically, only occur in mutual dependence (*pratītyasamutpanna*).[52]
2) *Epistemologically:* The ultimate truth (*tattva*) is the object of a cognition without an object (*advayajñāna*),[53] thus only an object metaphorically speaking (*upādāya prajñapti*).[54]
3) *Psychologically:* It is the abolishment of all the passions (*kleśa*), primarily desire (*rāga*), hatred (*dveṣa*) and delusion (*moha*).[55]
4) *Ethically:* It implies freedom from the bonds of *karma* but subjection to the altruistic imperatives of compassion (*karuṇā*).[56]

hails from Xenocrates's tripartition of philosophy into logic, cosmology and ethics (according to Sextus Empiricus, *Adv. Mathematicos*, VII, 16). I am mainly indebted to the clear exposition by H. Høffding, *Filosofiske Problemer*, København 1902, (English translation: *The problems of philosophy*, New York, 1905), and *Den menneskelige Tanke, dens Former og dens Opgaver*, København 1910 (German translation: *Der menschliche Gedanke, seine Formen und seine Aufgaben*, Leipzig 1911). These two are not at all outdated: the latter may even be claimed to be one of the most substantial philosophical works ever written in Danish. – Below (pp. 249-277) I have set myself to describe the unity of Madhyamaka *vistareṇa*.

49. To Nāgārjuna the theory of *satyadvaya* is above all a pedagogical device. – I have collected the most instructive texts on this theme in a paper: 'Atiśa's Introduction to the Two Truths, and its sources', in *JIP*, IX, pp. 161-214.
50. SL, 104; RĀ, I, 4.
51. RĀ, III, 12-13; YṢ, 60.
52. VV, 22; MK, XXIV, 18; YṢ, 19 etc.
53. CS, II, 3; III, 37-39; YṢ, 1; MK, XXV, 24; RĀ, I, 98 etc.
54. MK, XXII, 11; XXIV, 18; cf. May (1959), p. 161, n. 494 (ref.).
55. ŚS, 73; MK, XVIII, 5; XXV, 2.
56. CS, I, 1 (with ref.); MK, XXVII, 30.

β) The conventional Buddhist means ([*saṃ*]*vyavahāra*) devised for the fulfilment of this objective may be classified variously, but most briefly and comprehensively under the heading of the two collections of enlightenment (*bodhisaṃbhāra*):[57]

1) Collection of merit (*puṇyasaṃbhāra*). – It comprises the four perfections (*pāramitā*): Liberality (*dāna*) and good morals (*śīla*)[58] are mainly for the benefit of others whereas patience (*kṣānti*) and energy (*vīrya*) are for one's own good.[59] Their practice presupposes faith (*śraddhā*) in the 'law' of *karma* and results in the attainment of the physical body (*rūpakāya*) of a Buddha.[60] Along with the pursuit of meditation (*dhyāna*), the fifth *pāramitā*, this constitutes temporal happiness (*abhyudaya*).[61]
2) Collection of cognition (*jñānasaṃbhāra*). – It consists in ecstatic meditation (*dhyāna*) surpassed by insight into the emptiness (*śūnyatā*) of all phenomena (*dharma*), or wisdom (*prajñā*).[62] This is the non plus ultra or ultimate good (*naiḥśreyasa*) of all living beings.[63] It amounts to the attainment of a 'spiritual body' (*dharmakāya*).[64]

In other words, cognition of emptiness and display of acts of compassion are – to the chosen few – the two means of realizing enlightenment.[65]

57. RĀ, III; BS, *passim*.
58. RĀ, IV, 81, 99 etc.
59. RĀ, IV, 81 etc.
60. RĀ, I, 6; III, 12.
61. RĀ, I, 24; IV, 98; I, 4; III, 30.
62. Nāgārjuna hardly defines *prajñā* (cf. RĀ, V, 37) and *jñāna* and their mutual relationship. However, it seems fairly consistent with his usage (and Buddhist in general) to claim that *prajñā* is a discursive, intellectual understanding presupposing analysis or experience of phenomena, whereas *jñāna* is the intuitive knowledge gradually developed by exercising *prajñā*. Thus a Buddha hardly employs *prajñā*, but always enjoys *jñāna* of everything (cf. also May (1959), p. 104, n. 252 (with ref.). In brief: *prajñā* is *sādhana*, *jñāna* is *sādhya*.
63. RĀ, I, 4, 45; III, 30.
64. RĀ, III, 12.
65. RĀ, IV, 96: *śūnyatākaruṇāgarbham ekeṣāṃ bodhisādhanam*. Cf. *Prasannapadā*, p. 360; Bu-ston, I, p. 111. These two aspects of *bodhicitta* form the theme of BV, q.v.

With this scheme in mind I trust the reader will be able to interpret each of Nāgārjuna's statements within their proper context.

Like Indian hagiographers in general the ancient anonymous authors of Nāgārjuna legends did not share our curiosity to understand the personality of this remarkable individual. So for a portrayal of the man we are referred to the conclusions we may draw from observations of his genuine works.[66]

Only blurred outlines of a shadowy figure are still visible, to my eye at least. – Nāgārjuna was first of all an ardently devoted Mahāyānist and a staunch propagator of his faith (especially evidenced by his *Sūtrasamuccaya, Catuḥstava* and *Ratnāvalī*).[67] His learning was extensive and not confined to the various branches of Buddhist lore.[68] Though he even attempted to make proselytes of Brahmin logicians (*Vaidalyaprakaraṇa*),[69] his main concern, however,

66. For »biographical« accounts of Nāgārjuna, see Ramanan (1966), pp. 25-30; K.S. Murty, *Nāgārjuna,* New Delhi 1978, pp. 38-67; M. Walleser, *The life of Nāgārjuna from Tibetan and Chinese sources,* Delhi 1979 (rep.); May, *Chūgan,* p. 478 (ref.); É. Lamotte, »Der Verfasser des Upadeśa und seine Quellen«, *Nachrichten der Akademie der Wissenschaften in Göttingen. I. Philologisch-historische Klasse.* 1973, Nr. 2, pp. 3-5. One can only subscribe to the Belgian master's statement that: »Dieser Mischung an sagenhaften Überlieferungen, in denen sich unterschiedlos Wahres, Falsches und Zweifelhaftes widerspiegeln, steht die moderne Kritik ratlos gegenüber. Sie hat nur einige Arbeitshypothesen vorbringen können.« (*ibid.*, p. 4). Accordingly I shall only take these traditions into account when they coincide with the evidence, however scanty, to be gleaned from the author's own writings, above all RĀ.
67. To be sure, the strange question posed by A. K. Warder, 'Is Nāgārjuna a Mahāyānist', in M. Sprung (ed.), *The Problem of Two Truths in Buddhism and Vedānta,* Dordrecht 1973, pp. 78-88 has been rejoined by May, *Chūgan,* p. 473. One may add that the term *gandharvanagara* (MK, VII, 34; XVII, 33; XXIII, 8) does not occur in the ancient *āgamas* (cf. *Traité,* p. 370, n. 1). Moreover MK, XIII, 8 is inspired by *Kāśyapaparivarta* (cf. *Traité,* p. 1227), and MK, XXIV, 8 by *Akṣayamatinirdeśa* (cf. P. L. Vaidya, *Études sur Āryadeva et son Catuḥśataka,* Paris 1923, p. 21, n. 6). So even in MK alone the Mahāyāna background is indisputable.
68. It is noteworthy that on the *vyavahāra*-level Nāgārjuna endorses polymathy, cf. BS, 79, 103.
69. We have no reason to believe that such attempts proved very successful. Whatever the reason – lack of time or interest – it was left for Nāgārjuna's most brilliant pupil Āryadeva to refute the doctrines of Sāṃkhya and Vaiśeṣika (cf. RĀ, I, 61 and *Laṅkāvatārasūtra,* X, 723).

was to reform the dogmatic attitude (*dṛṣṭiparāmarśa*) of Abhidharma by propagating his conviction of the emptiness of all phenomena. This was the scope of his fundamental work *Mūlamadhyamakakārikā* and its supplements *Śūnyatāsaptati* and *Vigrahavyāvartanī* meeting some of the objections which inevitably rain upon a radical innovator.[70] – His commitment to the cause of instructing the lay public had several outcomes: *Suhṛllekha* and *Ratnāvalī* are, each in its own way, introductions to Buddhism. They are addressed to a king.[71] His **Bodhisaṃbhāra[ka]* and *Bodhicittavivaraṇa* are manuals in the theory and practice of Mahāyāna for the benefit of monks and laymen. These facts tally well with the tradition that Nāgārjuna had close connections at court and held responsible monastic offices.[72] It is thus quite probable that he played a decisive role in the foundation of monasteries etc. in Nāgārjunakoṇḍā.[73] – Of his character we only catch occasional glimpses of self-assurance and sarcasm as well as humility and compassion. His writings are, on the whole, characterized by a lucid and elegant diction, thus differing significantly from those e.g. of his pupil Āryadeva.[74]

70. ŚS and VV are, as Candrakīrti observes (cf. *IIJ*, XXIII, p. 177, n. 4), elaborations of respectively MK, VII, 34 and I, 3. It is in fact only in this perspective that the motives behind the objections raised and the topics introduced become quite intelligible. Along with YṢ and, possibly, VS these writings are intended to establish the ontological and epistemological tenets of Mahāyāna by way of *yukti*.
71. Perhaps a Śātavāhana, see É. Lamotte, *Histoire du bouddhisme indien, des origines à l'ère Śaka*, Louvain 1958, p. 379; K.S. Murty (1978), pp. 62-65. Also S. Dietz, »Der Autor des Suhṛllekha«, to appear in the *Proceedings of the Csoma de Körös Symposium, Velm/Wien, Sept. 13th-19th, 1981.*
72. *Ibid.*
73. *Ibid.*, p. 64; K.K. Murthy, *Nāgārjunakoṇḍā: A Cultural Study*, Delhi 1977. – References to caityas, stūpas, vihāras, buddha-images etc. are found RĀ, II, 77; III, 3134; 39, 41, 92; IV, 10-11, 17; V, 65; BS, 111, 113, 136, 150-151. It would certainly prove worthwhile to compare this evidence closely with the archaeological remains of Nāgārjunakoṇḍā and Amarāvatī. Also BS, 79, 103 (*śilpa*).
74. His verses are usually simple as far as syntax, metre, vocabulary and style are concerned. They differ distinctly from that of a predecessor such as Aśvaghoṣa, or a successor such as Āryadeva or Mātṛceṭa. His prose (VV, VP, ŚS) seems modelled on that of Patañjali's *Mahābhāṣya* (cf. L. Renou, *Histoire de la langue sanskrite*, Paris 1956, p. 135; K. Bhattacharya *et al.*, *The Dialectical method of Nāgārjuna*, Delhi 1978, p. 8) and differs totally e.g. from that of the *Arthaśāstra* of Kauṭilya (cf. Renou, *loc.cit.*, p. 136).

In the sequel I shall deal with the thirteen genuine works one by one, first six mainly dialectical works (MK, ŚS, VV, VP, VS and YṢ) and then the remaining chiefly didactic texts (CS, RĀ, PK, SS, BV, SL and BS), thus roughly following the prescriptive distinction between *yukti* and *āgama*.

The reader may find it convenient in advance to consult my essay on the unity of Nāgārjuna's thought (below pp. 249-277).

I. Mūlamadhyamakakārikā prajñā nāma (MK)

As indicated by its very title, 'The fundamental verses on the Middle (Way)' called 'Wisdom',[75] the large number of important commentaries by renowned teachers, and, thirdly, by its very thorough and radical treatment of the cardinal concepts (*dharma*) of Buddhist systematic soteriology (Abhidharma), MK may suitably be labelled the *chef d'œuvre* among Nāgārjuna's dialectical tracts.[76]

For a correct understanding of MK three main issues require clarification, viz. the subject-matter and composition of the work, its aim and, thirdly, the method employed for its achievement.

α) Let us first review the twenty-seven chapters (448 verses) of the Sanskrit *textus receptus*[77] compared with the recensions now only available within the body of four Indian commentaries transmitted in Tibetan versions.[78] Each *prakaraṇa* forms a critical examination (*parīkṣā*) of:

75. Also known as *Mādhyamikasūtra*, *Mādhyamikaśāstra* (cf. May (1959), p. 7) or, especially among Tibetans, *rtsa ba śes rab*, **Mūla-prajñā*, or **Mūlaprakaraṇa* (e.g. *Śūnyatāsaptativṛtti*, TP, No. 5268, Ya *fol.* 309a, 312a, 325a, 329a etc.). – The standard edition is that of La Vallée Poussin (see n. 7 above), supplemented by de Jong, 'Textcritical notes on the Prasannapadā', *IIJ*, XX, pp. 25-59, 217-252. – As no satisfactory English version of the kārikās alone exists one must refer to those incorporated in one of the commentaries (cf. May (1959), pp. 8-10; n. 6-7 above), or R. Gnoli, *Nāgārjuna, Le stanze del cammino di mezzo* ... Torino 1961, pp. 39-139. A Danish version (with Sanskrit) in my *Nāgārjunas filosofiske Værker*, København 1982.

76. Along with ŚS, VV, VP, VS and YṢ, MK may, to adopt the convenient Tibetan 'classification tripartite, qui est à la fois formelle et synchronique' (D. S. Ruegg, *loc.cit.*, p. 449) be said to form the **yuktikāya*, in which it is its 'backbone'. The hymns, of course, form the **stavakāya*, the remaining texts the **kathākāya* (i.e. expositions, or sermons, mainly, but not exclusively, *yathāgamam*).

77. As edited by La Vallée Poussin with the addenda of J. W. de Jong, v. above n. 75.

78. See n. 6 above for the list. – The titles of the twenty-seven *prakaraṇas* are identical in *Akutobhayā*, *Buddhapālitavṛtti*, *Prajñāpradīpa* and *Prajñāpradīpavṛtti*, and they have been adopted here.

I The conditions (*pratyaya*), in 16 verses
II Change, or movement (*gatāgatagamyamāna*), in 25 verses
III The sense-fields (*āyatana*), in 9 verses
IV The skandhas, or aggregates (*skandha*), in 9 verses
V The elements (*dhātu*), in 8 verses
VI Affection and the (person) affected (*rāgarakta*), in 10 verses
VII Origination, duration and decay (*utpādasthitibhaṅga*), in 34 verses
VIII Action and agent (*karmakāraka*), in 13 verses
IX Grasper and grasping (*upādātrupādāna*), in 12 verses
X Fire and fuel (*agnīndhana*), in 16 verses
XI Birth and death (*saṃsāra*), in 8 verses
XII Suffering (*duḥkha*), in 10 verses
XIII The real (*tattva*), in 8 verses
XIV Combination (*saṃsarga*), in 8 verses
XV Being and non-being (*bhāvābhāva*), in 11 verses
XVI Bondage and release (*bandhanamokṣa*), in 10 verses
XVII Action and its results (*karmaphala*), in 33 verses
XVIII The self and phenomena (*ātmadharma*), in 12 verses
XIX Time (*kāla*), in 6 verses
XX Cause and effect (*hetuphala*), in 24 verses
XXI Coming to be and passing away (*saṃbhavavibhava*), in 21 verses
XXII The Buddha (*tathāgata*), in 16 verses
XXIII The perverted views (*viparyāsa*), in 20 verses
XXIV The noble truths (*āryasatya*), in 40 verses
XXV Extinction (*nirvāṇa*), in 24 verses
XXVI The twelve sectors (*dvādaśāṅga*), in 12 verses, *and*
XXVII The dogmas (*dṛṣṭi*), in 30 verses.

Though it remains uncertain whether these titles are authentic or not, they are anyhow appropriate and ancient.[79] As to the wording

79 *Prasannapadā* differs thus: II: *gatāgata*°; III: *cakṣurādi*°; VII: *saṃskṛta*°; XI: *pūrvāparakoṭi*°; XIII: *saṃskāra*°; XV: *svabhāva*°; XVIII: *ātma*°; XX: *sāmgrī*°. – As far as the number of verses is concerned *Prasannapadā* III, 7 (cf. *IIJ*, XX, p. 40), XII, 6 and XXIII, 20 are absent in the four other commentaries. So unless it is supposed that Candrakīrti had access to better Mss than his predecessors – which I find unlikely – these three verses as well as the titles of

of the 448 verses, it is, if not identical, at least very close to the text as it left the hand of its author (or his scribe).[80]

the eight chapters mentioned are probably Candrakīrti's own innovations. Clearly it influenced the separate Tibetan version of the kārikās (TP, No. 5224), q.v. – I append some remarks on a few kārikās. Comparing the commentaries there only seems to be one really significant v.l. (in XXVII, 19 d): – I, 3: *hi* is used as a technical term to indicate something which is logically or empirically obvious, in no need of further elaboration, cf. I, 7; II, 6, 19, 22; III, 2; VI, 3, 4; VII, 9, 10, 28, 30; VIII, 7, 8; IX, 2; XI, 1; XII, 2, 7, 8, 10; XV, 2, 3, 4, 8; XVII, 22; XVIII, 7, 10; XIX, 1; XX, 14, 19; XXI, 3, 4, 5, 14, 15; XXIII, 1, 4, 23, 24; XXIV, 21, 34; XXV, 4, 5, 6, 8, 12; XXVI, 6; XXVII, 3, 6, 9, 10, 15. It provides the *saṃvṛti*-basis for arguments *paramārthataḥ*. – For *pratyayādiṣu* cf. XXIII, 9 and Pāṇ. III, 3, 37. – I, 4 cf. XXI, 6. – I, 5 *kila* (as in *Abhidharmakośabhāṣya* etc.) indicates an opponent's opinion only provisionally acceptable, cf. RĀ, IV, 50. – II, 1 *tāvat* always indicates the first of two (equally absurd) alternatives. – II, 2d Buddhapālita read *yasya* for *yataḥ* for which Bhavya rightly criticizes him. – III, 6d Buddhapālita takes *te* as *tava* (hardly convincing). – VII, 13d for *jāte* cf. *niruddhe* I, 9d. – VII, 29c perhaps *tadaiva* for *tadaivaṃ?* – VII, 31cd same *dṛṣṭānta* in the apparatus to *Mahābhārata*, XII, 173, 27, q.v. – XII, 5d Candrakīrti has *kutaḥ* and in 8d (= 7d) *katham*. The other commentators vice versa. – XIII, 6c read *kasyātha* for *kasya cid*. The Mss read *kasyārtha*. In MK, XVI, 6 and XXVI, 2 *atha* is also left untranslated in Tib.! – XX, 7d read *yac* for *yaś*. – XXI, 7b all Tibetan versions point to °*syāpi* rather than °*syāsti*. – (XXI, 8 Candrakīrti reverses the order of *pādas* ab and cd against the previous commentators (*Prasannapadā*, p. 417, 1 is a quotation from *Akutobhayā*, 91b 3!). – XXI, 11 nearly verbatim *Laṅkāvatārasūtra*, X, 36, q.v. – XXI, 12 identical with *Catuḥśataka*, XV, 14. – XXIII, 8cd = XVII, 33cd. – XXIII, 10c Candrakīrti has *pratītya śubham* but the previous commentators read *pratītyāśubhaṃ*. – XXIII, 11c again Candrakīrti has *pratītyāśubhaṃ* against *pratītya śubhaṃ*. – XXIII, 13cd Candrakīrti has *nānityaṃ ... viparyayaḥ* against *na nityaṃ ... 'viparyayaḥ*. – XXIII, 14a Candrakīrti has *anitye nityam*, in b as in 13b, in c *anityam* against *anitye 'nityam* in a, in b as in 13 d and in c *nānityam*, in d perhaps *aviparyayaḥ* (or *naviparyayaḥ*) for *na viparyayaḥ*. – XXIV, 18 Professor Wayman's interpretation of this important verse in *JAOS*, LXXXIX, pp. 141 ff. does not make any sense. – XXV, 13b, 14b Candrakīrti reads *katham* but the previous commentators read *yadi* (cf 11b, 12b). – XXVII, 19d Candrakīrti's *saṃsāraḥ* seems to be a gloss. The previous commentators have *rtag par gyur na*, i.e. *śāśvataḥ*. (The wording of the kārikās included in the various commentaries was also discussed by S. Yamaguchi, *Chūkan Bukkyō Ronkō*, Tokyo 1965, pp. 3-28, which was, however, not available to me.) – I have edited MK anew in *Indiske Studier* II.

80. An account of the textual transmission of MK etc. (along the lines, *mutatis mutandis*, of e.g. L. D. Reynolds & N. G. Wilson, *Scribes and Scholars*, Oxford 1974, or H. Hunger *et al*, *Die Textüberlieferung der antiken Literatur und der Bibel*, Zürich 1961) would certainly prove highly instructive. However, the paucity

Each chapter is mainly concerned with (but by no means strictly confined to) one of these basic topics:[81]

of sources, at least as far as early Mādhyamika is concerned, warrants no such attempt. Still we may note that at least the kārikās, then as now, were meant to be learnt by heart, cf. *svādhyāya*, PK, 5. But naturally in the case of sūtras, commentaries etc. the oral transmission was supported by a written, cf. RĀ, III, 38: *thub dbaṅ gsuṅ daṅ des byuṅ ba'i* ‖ *gźuṅ rnams bri daṅ glegs bam ni* ‖ *snag cha dag daṅ smyu gu daṅ* ‖ *sṅon du 'gro ba sbyin par mdzod* ‖; cf. *Traité*, p. 752; *Upālipariprcchā*, p. 95. – Our knowledge of how books (*pustaka*) were copied, corrected, circulated, preserved and quoted is regrettably fragmentary. – However, the fact that MK was transmitted virtually without variants or corruptions for many centuries within the body of different commentaries the earliest of which, *Akutobhayā*, is hardly more than a century younger than the *Mūla*, must surely inspire us with confidence in the *textus receptus*. Though I believe that this rule on the whole also applies to the twelve other authentic works it is by no means universal: Texts such as *Bhavasaṃkrānti* and *Mahāyānaviṃśikā* are in many cases so contaminated or hopelessly corrupt that we can never hope to reconstruct an archetype but only, at best, one intelligible recension among others in *their* own right.

81. Here I confine myself to a summary of the observations set forth at length in the introduction to my Danish translation of MK (cf. also *IIJ*, XXIII, pp. 153-154). MK is addressed to monks thoroughly conversant with the Abhidharma of the most influential of all comtemporary schools: Sarvāstivāda. Other less influential schools are occasionally introduced and criticized (cf. May (1959), p. 111, n. 278). It would be misleading, as some modern authorities have done, to claim that Nāgārjuna also had non-Buddhists (Sāṃkhya, Vaiśeṣika) in mind, though, of course, many of his arguments *also* – indirectly – apply to them (as Bhavya more than other commentators is never loth to point out). The purpose of MK (ŚS, VV) is to train Ābhidhārmikas in *prajñāpāramitā*, i.e. to make them realize *pudgaladharmanairātmya* by understanding the Buddha's doctrine of *pratītyasamutpāda* in the sense of *śūnyatā* through *cintā* and *bhāvanā*. (The first aspect of *prajñā*, *śruti*, Nāgārjuna treats in SS, SL etc.) The twenty-seven chapters are arranged in a number of 'clusters': *I-VII* refute the fundamental notions of Abhidharma: I-II those of causality and movement, III-V *sarvaṃ yad asti*, viz. *skandhādi*, VI *sahabhāva*, VII *saṃskṛtalakṣaṇa*, with an excursion against Sāṃmitīya. *VIII-X* refute various aspects of *pudgalavāda*. *XI-XIII* may have been intended to refute the notion of *bhāva* in a more general sense. *XIV-XVII* elaborate II, VI and specific Buddhist notions not discussed previously. *XVIII* is in a sense the culmination of MK. Here for once, the author reveals his own opinion about *tattva* and *tattvāvatāra*. *XIX-XXI* abruptly bring back the criticism of Sarvāstivāda. They elaborate I. *XXII-XXV* show that *all* Buddhist concepts are empty *in the ultimate sense*. Not even the most sacred is spared. Thus, at first, the final chapters *XXVI-XXVII* dealing with traditional Buddhist ideas *in a relative sense* may seem to form a curious anticlimax. In my

a) Specific Abhidharmic or canonical Buddhist concepts (*dharma*): I, III, IV, V, VII, XVII, XXIII, XXIV, XXV, XXVI, XXVII.

b) Various aspects of the belief in the existence of *ātman:* VIII, IX, X, XII, XVI, XVIII, XXII.

c) Common-sense notions underlying all realistic ('positivistic') views concerning *dharmas* and *ātman:* II, VI, XI, XIII, XIV, XV, XIX, XX, XXI.

β) The scope of Nāgārjuna's criticism is not to disavow the practical value of traditional Buddhist concepts but to demonstrate that the right attitude to be adopted towards them is one of pragmatic relativism and not one of stubborn dogmatic absolutism.[82] He wants to reform, not to reject Buddhist tradition.[83]

γ) The procedure adopted for this purpose – as Nāgārjuna informs us in stray verses in MK[84] – begins with the relentless demand for own-being (*svabhāva*):[85] To be real (*sat*) implies being permanent (*nitya*), independent (*nirapekṣa*), numerically one (*eka*) and self-created (*svayaṃkṛta*). However, neither experience nor logic warrants our assumption of the existence of real entities (*bhāva*). Hence Nāgārjuna has the game in his hands when showing the absurdities

opinion the author appended them with a very specific purpose, namely in order to show the orthodoxy of his *śūnyavāda:* One can only understand the *dvādaśāṅga* and the warnings against *dṛṣṭis* by means of *śūnyatā*.

82. Thus, according to Nāgārjuna, the Saddharma was taught *sarvadṛṣṭiprahāṇāya,* MK, XXVII, 30. Similarly XIII, 8; CS, I, 23; III, 52 etc. All *dṛṣṭis* being due to *astīti/nāstīti* (cf. MK, XV, 10) they can only be abolished by realizing their *parasparāpekṣikī siddhi*, or *śūnyatā*.

83. Not only is Nāgārjuna intent on being an orthodox Buddhist (BS, 130) but in the cases where he writes according to *āgama* and we are able to check his use of sources he proves to represent them very meticulously, see, above all, SL, BS and SS *passim*.

84. A number of 'axiomatic aphorisms' scattered more or less at random in MK indicate the logical premises from which Nāgārjuna reduces his opponent to an absurd position: MK, I, 1, 3; II, 1, 21; IV, 6, 8, 9; V, 8; VI, 4; VII, 34; IX, 5; X, 10, 11, 16; XI, 1; XIII, 1, 8; XIV, 4cd, 5, 6, 7; XV, 1, 2, 10; XXI, 6, 12; XXII, 12, 15, 16; XXIII, 1; XXIV, 8, 9, 10, 11. They were later formulised as the four *mahāhetu* (cf. CS, I, 13; III, 9 notes); *infra*, p. 273.

85. On this term May (1959), p. 124, n. 328; de Jong: 'The problem of the absolute in the Madhyamaka school', *JIP*, II, pp. 2 3.

implicit (*prasaṅga*) in all the claims of a realistic attitude. Moreover, since positive existence is unfounded, non-existence (*abhāva*), i.e. the negation or destruction of existence (*bhāva*),[86] must, of course, also be unwarranted. Thus Nāgārjuna proceeds along the middle way (*madhyamā pratipad*) empty of extremes towards his intangible goal: the unorigination of all phenomena.[87]

86. RĀ, I, 72: *vināśāt pratipakṣād vā syād astitvasya nāstitā* ...
87. E.g. the initial stanzas of MK; RĀ, IV, 86. For *anutpāda* in Mahāyāna sūtras, *Vimalakīrtinirdeśa,* pp. 408-413; Hōbōgirin, s.v. *Chūdō*.

II. Śūnyatāsaptati (ŚS)

This text is in 73 verses (originally composed in the *āryā* metre like VV and PK) accompanied by a commentary from the author's own hand (*svavṛtti*). It is ascribed to Nāgārjuna by Bhavya,[88] Candrakīrti,[89] and Śāntarakṣita.[90] Testimonies anterior to these are found in *Akutobhayā*[91] and **Dvādaśadvāraka*.[92] Later on it is also referred to e.g. by Atiśa.[93]

I have seen no references or allusions to the *svavṛtti*, but as its prose-style (i.e., to be sure, in Tibetan) is quite similar to that of the commentaries on VV and VP, there is no good reason to impeach its authenticity.[94]

The doctrine and scope of ŚS do not differ from that of MK in comparison with which it may be said to form an appendix,[95] as it partly summarizes its verses, partly introduces new topics and elaborates old ones.[96] Like MK it reveals no strict underlying struc-

88. *Ratnapradīpa*, 33a: *dbu ma'i rtsa ba rtsod pa bzlog* || *ston ñid bdun cu rigs drug cu* || *rnam par 'thag pa la sogs pas* || *dṅos rnams skye med śes par bya* ||.
89. **Madhyamakaśāstrastuti* (ed. de Jong), 10: *dṛṣṭvā Sūtrasamuccayaṃ parikathāṃ Ratnāvalīṃ Saṃstutī abhyasyāticiraṃ ca Śāstragaditās tāḥ Kārikā yatnataḥ* | *Yuktyākhyām atha Ṣaṣṭikāṃ sa Vidalāṃ tāṃ Śūnyatāsaptatiṃ yā cāsāv atha Vigrahasya racitā Vyāvartanī, tām api* || ...
90. 58 is quoted *Madhyamakālaṃkāravṛtti*, 72b.
91. 19-21 are quoted with indication of source 90b.
92. 8 is quoted – very freely – from the **Saptatiśāstra* 160a 22, and 19 without indication of source 164b 27.
93. *Bodhipathapradīpa* (ed. Eimer), 1. 205.
94. Cf. my remarks on his prose, above n. 74. It differs markedly from that of e.g. *Akutobhayā*, tediously dull as it often is, or *Akṣaraśatakavṛtti* (cf. above n. 32), already more condensed in its style. On the other hand it is very close to that of Buddhapālita. – The verses of ŚS were *āryās*, as Parahita states ad 18-20, 32, 36-37, 54-55, 63 and 68-69.
95. Cf. above n. 70. – Having stated that ŚS and VV both are *dbu ma las 'phros pa* Candrakīrti goes on quoting MK, VII, 32 and adds that *ston pa ñid bdun cu pa ni de la brgal ba dan lan btab par gyur pa'i phyir de las 'phros pa yin par mnon no* (*Yuktiṣaṣṭikāvrtti*, TP, No. 5265, Ya *fol.* 2b). This is, incidentally, also the opinion of *Śūnyatāsaptativivṛtti*, TP, No. 5269, Ya *fol.* 381b, q.v.
96. Thus 29 is a summary of MK, XIX. 33-44 elaborate MK, XVII, and 45-54

ture of composition, but it may, as I have ventured, be divided into at least seven paragraphs.

For the study of ŚS I have had the following sources at my disposal:[97]

Sigla

K *Śūnyatāsaptatikārikā,* trans. by Gźon nu mchog, Gñan Dhar ma grags and Khu lo.
TP, No. 5227, Tsa *fol.* 27a-30b; TN, No. 3218, Tsa *fol.* 24a-26a.

V *Śūnyatāsaptativṛtti,* trans. Jinamitra and Ye śes sde.
TP, No, 5231, Tsa *fol.* 126a-138a; TN, No. 3222, Tsa *fol.* 116b-128b.

C *Śūnyatāsaptativṛtti,* trans. Abhayākara and Dhar ma grags.
TP, No. 5268, Ya *fol.* 305-381b; TN, No. 3259, Ya *fol.* 295a-375b.

P *Śūnyatāsaptativivṛtti,* trans. Parahita and Gźon nu mchog.
TP, No. 5269, Ya *fol.* 381b-425a; TN, No. 3260, Ya *fol.* 357a-420b.

The translations of the kārikās included in C and P sometimes differ considerably – and sometimes unhappily – from that given in V, and more often agree with K than with the one in V.[98] As editions and translations of V, C and P are expected I shall confine myself to an edition of K adding the kārikā version transmitted in V. Though I have consulted C and P my translation of the kārikās strictly follows the *svavṛtti* which must, of course, remain the final

supplement MK, IV. These are only the most obvious instances beyond all doubt. – Acc. to C, 306a ŚS is a **saṃkṣepa* of MK.

97. For information about the Indian and Tibetan translators etc. I must refer to J. Naudou, *Les bouddhistes kaśmīriens au Moyen Âge,* Paris 1968, *passim.* – Possibly the Sanskrit text of Candrakīrti's commentary (C) is still extant, see G. N. Roerich, *The Blue Annals,* Calcutta 1949, p. 342. (Note that C does not include verses 53 and 67, but P has all 73 stanzas.)

98. The variants are of some interest for the light they shed on the technique of translating Sanskrit into Tibetan. As they hardly ever affect the sense, and a separate edition of C is expected I have only referred to C occasionally. P has not been of much use for the present purpose. – V does not seem to have been known to C and P.

authority in questions of interpretation.[99]

Here is the briefest possible survey of ŚS. It summarizes the analysis given in the introduction to my Danish rendering of the verses with the author's own commentary and must be supplemented by consulting the notes.

1-6: The dharmas only exist *vyavahāravaśāt* (i.e. *saṃvṛtitaḥ*) as *yukti* shows that *paramārthataḥ* everything is *anutpanna*.

7-26: All entities (*bhāva*) are *pratītyasamutpanna*, or *śūnya*. So *nirvāṇa* is simply *anutpāda*.

27-32: Various aspects of *bhāva* refuted as being relative.

33-44: Karma is also *śūnya* according to orthodox Buddhism.

45-57: Refutation of the five skandhas, above all *rūpa*.

58-66: *avidyā* vanishes when it is understood, as shown, that there really is no *bhāva* etc. whatsoever.

67-73: Thus *paramārtha* is simply *śūnyatā, anutpāda* etc. However, since it is not generally realized, one must resort to *saṃvṛti* with *śraddhā* in order to achieve it oneself.[100]

99. See my Danish translation (based on TP, TD and TN) referred to n. 75. – I regret that the Japanese translation (*Daijō Butten,* XIV) by Ryūshin Uryūzu was not accessible to me.
[I may here add that having collated K and V in TD I deemed that the *variae lectiones,* disregarding scribal errors, may be accounted for as results of emendation and contamination. Hence they have been eliminated from the apparatus. A similar editorial licence has clearly affected the transmission in case of the verses of VV and YṢ. – I have not collated the other texts in TD.]

100. In my view it would be very naive to interpret the introduction of e.g. *śraddhā* in ŚS (cf. RĀ, I, 4-6; SS, 175b ff.) or the stress laid on *vāda* in VV as signs of a development in the thought of Nāgārjuna. Of course, facing new charges, he had to lend new nuances to his standpoint, but I do not think that his fundamental belief in *śūnyatā*, once formed, ever underwent any decisive change.

Śūnyatāsaptati-kārikā ||

sToṅ pa ñid bdun cu pa'i tshig le'ur byas pa ||

1. K/V

| gnas pa'am skye 'jig yod med dam || dman pa'am mñam daṅ khyad par can |
| saṅs rgyas 'jig rten sñad dbaṅ gis || gsuṅ gi yaṅ dag dbaṅ gis min |

| gnas pa'am skye 'jig yod med dam || dman pa'am mñam pa'am khyad par can |
| saṅs rgyas 'jig rten bsñad dbaṅ gis || gsuṅ gis yaṅ dag dbaṅ gis min |

2. K/V

| bdag med bdag med min bdag daṅ || bdag med min pas brjod 'ga'aṅ med |
| brjod bya mya ṅan 'das daṅ mtshuṅs || dṅos po kun gyi raṅ bźin stoṅ |

| bdag med bdag med min bdag daṅ || bdag med min pas brjod 'ga'aṅ med |
| brjod par bya ba'i chos rnams kun || mya ṅan 'das mtshuṅs raṅ bźin stoṅ |

3. K/V

| gaṅ phyir dṅos rnams thams cad kyi || raṅ bźin rgyu rkyen tshogs pa 'am |
| so so'i dṅos po thams cad la || yod min de phyir stoṅ pa yin |

| gaṅ phyir dṅos po thams cad kyi || raṅ bźin rgyu rkyen tshogs pa 'am |
| so so rnams la 'am thams cad la || yod min de'i phyir stoṅ pa yin |

The Septuagint on Emptiness

1. Though the Buddhas have spoken of duration (*sthiti*), origination (*utpāda*), destruction (*bhaṅga*), being (*sat*), non-being (*asat*), low (*hīna*), moderate (*sama*) and excellent (*viśiṣṭa*) by force of worldly convention (*lokavyavahāravaśāt*), [they] have not done [so] in an absolute sense (*tattvavaśāt*).

2. Designations (*abhidhāna*) are insignificant (*na kiṃ cit*) as self (*ātman*), non-self (*anātman*) and self-non-self (*ātmānātman*) do not exist, [because] all expressible things (*abhidheyabhāva*) are, like Nirvāṇa, empty of own being (*svabhāvaśūnya*).

3. Since all things all together lack substance (*svabhāva*) either in causes or conditions (*hetupratyaya*) [or their] totality (*sāmagrī*) or separately, therefore they are empty (*śūnya*).

1. Or, in the words of MK, XXIV, 8: *dve satye samupāśritya buddhānāṃ dharmadeśanā;* cf. VV, 28; YṢ, 30-33. For *vyavahāra* in general, v. May (1959), p. 221, n. 760. – Here **lokavyavahāravaśāt* = *kāryavaśāt* of YṢ, 33, q.v.
2. This verse about *tattva* (i.e. *paramārtha* etc.) summarizes MK, XVIII, 1-7, q.v.
3. Similar reason for *anutpāda* VV, 1; 21; MK, I; XX. – Due to the fact that things lack *svabhāva* they are termed *śūnya*, VV, *passim*.

4. K/V

| yod phyir yod pa skye min te || med phyir med pa skye ma yin |
| chos mi mthun phyir yod med min || skye ba med pas gnas 'gag med |

| yod pa yod phyir skye ma yin || med pa med pa'i phyir ma yin |
| chos mi mthun phyir yod med min || skye ba med phyir gnas 'gog med |

5. K/V

| gaṅ źig skyes de bskyed bya min || ma skyes pa yaṅ bskyed bya min |
| skyes pa daṅ ni ma skyes pa'i || skye bźin pa yaṅ bskyed bya min |

| skyes pa bskyed par bya ba min || ma skyes pa yaṅ bskyed bya min |
| skye ba'i tshe yaṅ bskyed bya min || skyes daṅ ma skyes pa yi phyir |

6. K/V

| 'bras bu yod par 'bras ldan rgyu || med de la 'aṅ rgyu min mtshuṅs |
| yod min med pa'aṅ min na 'gal || dus gsum rnams su 'thad ma yin |

| 'bras yod 'bras daṅ ldan pa'i rgyu || de med na ni rgyu min mtshuṅs |
| yod min med pa min na 'gal || dus gsum rnams su'aṅ 'thad ma yin |

7. K/V

| gcig med par ni maṅ po daṅ || maṅ po med par gcig mi 'jug |
| de phyir rten ciṅ 'brel 'byuṅ ba'i || dṅos po mtshan ma med pa yin |

| gcig med par ni maṅ po daṅ || maṅ po med par gcig mi 'jug |
| de phyir brten nas dṅos po rnams || byuṅ ba mtshan ma med pa yin |

4 Kb med pa : med pas NP
5 Kc skyes pa : skyed pa NP
6 Vc min : yin NP

4. Being (*sat*) does not arise since it exists. Non-being (*asat*) does not arise since it does not exist. Being and non-being (*sadasat*) do not arise due to [their] heterogeneity (*vaidharmya*). Consequently they do not endure or vanish.

5. That which has been born (*jāta*) cannot be born (*notpādya*), nor can that which is unborn (*ajāta*) be born. But that which is [now said] to be born (*utpadyamāna*) [is, in fact, partly] born (*jāta*) [partly] unborn (*ajāta*) [and] cannot be born (*utpādya*) either.

6. A cause (*hetu*) has an effect (*phalavat*) when there is an effect (*phala*), but when there is no [effect] the [cause] amounts to no cause (*ahetu*). It is inconsistent (*viruddha*) that [the effect] neither exists nor does not exist. It is illogical that [the cause is active] in the three periods (*kāla*).

7. Without one (*eka*) there are not many (*aneka*). Without many (*aneka*) one (*eka*) is not possible. Therefore things that arise dependently (*pratītyasamutpanna*) are indeterminable (*animitta*).

4. This refutes the three hypothetically possible subjects of origination, *sat* etc. (really there are four *koṭis,* see e.g. CS, III, 23) as does MK, VII, 20; CS, I, 13 etc.

5. Refutation of *utpāda* as the first of the three *saṃskṛtalakṣaṇa,* cf. MK, VII, 1-2. – This verse corresponds to **Dvādaśadvāraka*, 26 (Taishō, No. 1568, 167a 23-24) which may, however, have read **jātājātavinirmukta* (cf. MK, II, 1) in *pāda* c.

6. Again *utpāda* is absurd because the notion of *hetu* (i.e. to *utpāda*) is untenable. See MK, XX; RĀ, I, 47: *prāgjātaḥ sahajātaś ca hetur ahetuko 'rthataḥ | prajñapter apratītatvād utpatteś caiva tattvataḥ* ||

7. Things (*bhāva*) are also empty because they cannot be indicated (*animitta*) in terms of numbers (*saṃkhyā*) since numbers also are *pratītyasamutpanna.* Here the concept of *eka/aneka* seems quite concrete, so that *eka* = *kṣaṇa* or *paramāṇu,* cf. RĀ, I, 67-71.

8. K/V

| rten 'byuṅ yan lag bcu gñis gaṅ || sdug bsṅal 'bras can de ma skyes |
| sems gcig la yaṅ mi 'thad ciṅ || du ma la yaṅ 'thad ma yin |

| rten 'byuṅ yan lag bcu gñis gaṅ || sdug bsṅal 'bras can de ma skyes |
| sems gcig la yaṅ mi 'thad la || du ma la yaṅ mi 'thad do |

9. K/V

| rtag min mi rtag min bdag daṅ || bdag min gtsaṅ min mi gtsaṅ min |
| bde min sdug bsṅal ma yin te || de phyir phyin ci log rnams med |

| mi rtag rtag min bdag med pa || bdag min mi gtsaṅ gtsaṅ ma yin |
| sdug bsṅal bde ba ma yin te || de phyir phyin ci log rnams med |

10. K/V

| de med phyin ci log bźi las || skyes pa'i ma rig mi srid la |
| de med 'du byed mi 'byuṅ źiṅ || lhag ma rnams kyaṅ de bźin no |

| de med na ni phyin ci log || bźi las skyes pa'i ma rig med |
| de med na ni 'du byed rnams || mi 'byuṅ lhag ma'aṅ de bźin no |

11. K/V

| ma rig 'du byed med mi 'byuṅ || de med 'du byed mi 'byuṅ źiṅ |
| phan tshun rgyu phyir de gñis ni || raṅ bźin gyis ni ma grub yin |

| ma rig 'du byed med mi 'byuṅ || de med 'du byed mi 'byuṅ bas |
| de gñis phan tshun rgyu phyir yaṅ || raṅ bźin gyis ni ma grub yin |

8 Kb 'bras can N : 'bral can P
9 Ka rtag min P : brtag min N
10 Vb bźi : gźi NP
11 Vd yin : min NP
11 Kc gñis : ñid NP; Vd yin : min NP

8. The [first of the] twelve dependently arising members (*dvādaśāṅga*), which results in suffering (*duḥkhaphala*), is unborn (*ajāta*): it is not possible in one mind (*ekacitta*) and it is not possible in many (*aneka*) either.

9. Permanent is not (*na nitya*), impermanent is not (*nānitya*), non-self is not (*nānātman*), self is not (*nātman*), impure is not (*nāśuci*), pure is not (*na śuci*), pleasure is not (*na sukha*) and suffering is not (*na duḥkha*). Therefore the perverted views do not exist (*na viparyāsa*).

10. Without these, ignorance (*avidyā*) based on these perverted views is not possible. Without this [ignorance] the formative forces (*saṃskāra*) do not arise and the remaining [ten members] similarly.

11. Ignorance (*avidyā*) does not occur without the formative forces (*saṃskāra*) [and] without it the formative forces (*saṃskāra*) do not arise. Since [they] are caused by one another (*anyonyahetutaḥ*) they are not established with own-being (*svabhāva*).

8. Nor can *citta* (*sems*) be called *eka* or *bhinna* (i.e. *aneka*) because, as we shall see, its 'content' i.e. *duḥkha* due to *avidyādi* is in fact *ajāta*. – This verse is 'quoted', **Dvādaśadvāraka*, 2 (160a 22-23).

9-10. The four *viparyāsas* (see MK, XXIII) do not exist in themselves. Hence *avidyādi* which is based on them does not exist either.

12. K/V

| gaṅ źig bdag ñid raṅ bźin gyis || ma grub de gźan ji ltar bskyed |
| de phyir gźan las grub pa yi || rkyen gźan dag ni skyed byed min |

| gaṅ źig bdag ñid raṅ bźin gyis || ma grub de gźan ji ltar bskyed |
| de lta bas na pha rol po || ma grub rkyen gźan bskyed byed min |

13. K/V

| pha ni bu min bu pha min || de gñis phan tshun med min la |
| de gñis cig car yaṅ min ltar || yan lag bcu gñis de bźin no |

| pha bu ma yin bu pha min || de gñis phan tshun med min la |
| de gñis cig car yaṅ min ltar || yan lag bcu gñis de bźin no |

14. K/V

| ji ltar rmi lam yul brten pa'i || bde sdug de yi yul med pa |
| de bźin gaṅ źig la brten nas || gaṅ źig rten 'byuṅ daṅ 'di med |

| rmi lam yul brten bde sdug daṅ || yul de'aṅ med ltar brten nas gaṅ |
| byuṅ ba de yaṅ de bźin med || brten nas gaṅ yin de yaṅ med |

15. K/V

| gal te dṅos rnams raṅ bźin gyis || med na dman mñam khyad 'phags daṅ |
| sna tshogs ñid ni mi 'grub ciṅ || rgyu las kyaṅ ni mṅon 'grub min |

| gal te dṅos rnams raṅ bźin gyis || med na dnam mñam khyad 'phags ñid |
| yod min sna tshogs ñid mi 'grub || rgyu las mṅon par grub pa'aṅ med |

16. K/V

| raṅ bźin grub na rten 'byuṅ gi || dṅos po med 'gyur ma brten na |
| raṅ bźin med par ga la 'gyur || dṅos po yod daṅ dṅos med kyaṅ |

| raṅ bźin grub rten dṅos mi 'gyur || ma brten par yaṅ ga la yod |
| raṅ bźin med ñid mi 'gyur źiṅ || raṅ bźin yod pa mi 'jig go |

12 Vb gźan : bźin NP; Kc yi : yis NP
15 Vd grub P : 'grub N

12. That which is unestablished by own-being, how could it create the others? Therefore conditions (*pratyaya*) established by others cannot create the others.

13. A father is not a son, a son is not a father. Neither exists without being correlative (*anyonya*). Nor are they simultaneous (*yugapat*). The twelve members likewise.

14. Just as pleasure (*sukha*) and pain (*duḥkha*) depending upon an object in a dream (*svapnaviṣaya*) do not have [a real] object (*viṣaya*) thus neither that which arises dependently nor that which it arises dependently from exists.

15. *Opponent:* If things (*bhāva*) do not exist by own-being (*svabhāvena*), low (*hīna*), moderate (*sama*), excellent (*viśiṣṭa*) and the manifold world (*citra*) are unestablished (*asiddha*) and cannot even be established through a cause (*hetutaḥ*).

16. *Reply:* If own-being (*svabhāva*) were established (*siddha*), dependently arising things would not occur. If [they were] unconditioned how could own-being be lacking? True being (*sadbhāva*) also does not vanish (*abhāva*).

11-14. Again *avidyādi* are *anutpanna* (i.e. *śūnya*) because they are *pratītyasamutpanna* (in the sense of MK, XXVI, 1-12 and/or PK, 1-5, q.v.), *pitāputravat* (cf. VV, 49-50). Thus *sukha* and *duḥkha* (cf. v. 8) are no more real than experiences in a dream (cf. CS, I, 17; III, 5 etc.).

15-16. In fact all the *laukika-saṃvyavahāra* (see MK, XIV, 6-40; VV, 70; above v. 1) are only possible because they are *pratītyasamutpanna*.

17. K/V

| med la raṅ dṅos gźan dṅos sam || dṅos med 'gyur ba ga la źig |
| des na raṅ dṅos gźan dṅos daṅ || dṅos med phyin ci log pa yin |

| med la raṅ gi dṅos po 'am || gźan dṅos 'jig par ga la 'gyur |
| de phyir gźan dṅos dṅos med daṅ || dṅos daṅ raṅ dṅos log pa yin |

18 K/V

| gal te dṅos po stoṅ yin na || 'gag pa med ciṅ skye mi 'gyur |
| ṅo bo ñid kyis stoṅ pa la || gaṅ la 'gag ciṅ gaṅ la skye |

| gal te dṅos po stoṅ yin na || 'gag par mi 'gyur skye mi 'gyur |
| ṅo bo ñid kyis stoṅ pa la || gaṅ la 'gag ciṅ gaṅ la skye |

19 K/V

| dṅos daṅ dṅos med cig car min || dṅos med med na dṅos po med |
| rtag tu dṅos po'aṅ dṅos med 'gyur || dṅos med med par dṅos mi srid |

| dṅos daṅ dṅos med cig car med || dṅos med med par dṅos po med |
| rtag tu dṅos daṅ dṅos med 'gyur || dṅos daṅ dṅos po med mi 'gyur |

20. K/V

| dṅos po med par dṅos med min || raṅ las min źiṅ gźan las min |
| de lta bas na de med na || dṅos po med ciṅ dṅos med med |

| dṅos po med par dṅos med med || bdag las ma yin gźan las min |
| de lta bas na dṅos po med || de med na ni dṅos med med |

21. K/V

| yod pa ñid na rtag ñid daṅ || med na ṅes par chad ñid yin |
| dṅos po yod na de gñis 'gyur || de phyir dṅos po khas blaṅs min |

| dṅos po yod pa ñid na rtag || med na ṅes par chad pa yin |
| dṅos po yod na de gñis yin || de'i phyir dṅos po khas blaṅs min |

17 Vb 'jig N : 'jog P; V *om.* c, *sed* v. K
18 Vc kyis : kyi NP
21 Vc yin : min NP

17. How could the non-existing (*asat*) have own-being (*svabhāva*), other-being (*parabhāva*) or non-being (*abhāva*)? – Consequently own-being (*svabhāva*), other-being (*parabhāva*) and non-being (*abhāva*) [result from] perverted views (*viparyāsa*).

18. *Opponent:* If things (*bhāva*) were empty (*śūnya*) cessation (*nirodha*) and origination (*utpāda*) would not occur. That which is empty of own-being (*svabhāvena*), how does it cease and how does it arise?

19. *Reply:* Being (*bhāva*) and non-being (*abhāva*) are not simultaneous (*yugapat*). Without non-being (*abhāva*) no being (*bhāva*). Being (*bhāva*) and non-being (*abhāva*) would always be. There is no being (*bhāva*) independently of non-being (*abhāva*).

20. Without being (*bhāva*) there is no non-being (*abhāva*). [Being] neither arises from itself (*svataḥ*) nor from [something] else (*parataḥ*). This being so this [being] does not exist, so there is no being (*bhāva*), and [therefore] no non-being (*abhāva*).

21. If there is being (*sat*) there is permanence (*śāśvata*); if there is non-being (*asat*) there is necessarily (*niyatam*) annihilation (*uccheda*). When there is being (*bhāva*) these two [dogmas] occur. Therefore [one should] not accept being (*bhāva*).

17-20. The various forms of *bhāva* (i.e. *svabhāva, parabhāva, abhāva* and *bhāva* as such) are only conceivable in mutual dependence. They do not occur independently (cf. MK, XV). – For v. 18 in particular cf. MK, XXIV, 1; XXV, 1-2. – *Akutobhayā* ad MK, XXI, 6 quotes 19-21 as from *Śūnyatāsaptati*. **Dvādaśadvāraka,* 20 (164b 27-28) seems to be identical with ŚS, 19.

21. Acceptance of *bhāva* would moreover imply *śāśvatocchedagrāha*, cf. May, *op.cit.*, p. 213, n. 720; *IIJ*, XXIII, p. 179, n. 58 (cf. *ibid.*, p. 178, n. 9); MK, XXI, 14. The verse is quoted *Madhyamakālaṃkāravṛtti,* TP, No. 5285, Sa *fol.* 75a (with *Catuḥśataka,* X, 25; RĀ, I, 60 to the same effect).

22. K/V

| rgyun gyi phyir na 'di med de || rgyu byin nas ni dṅos po 'gag |
| sṅar bźin 'di yaṅ ma grub ciṅ || rgyun chad par yaṅ thal bar 'gyur |

| rgyun gyi phyir na de med de || rgyu byin nas ni dṅos po 'gag |
| sṅa ma bźin du 'di ma grub || rgyun chad pa yi ñes pa'aṅ yod |

23. K/V

| skye 'jig bstan phyir saṅs rgyas kyi || lam bstan ma yin stoṅ ñid phyir |
| 'di dag phan tshun bzlog pa ru || mthoṅ ba phyin ci log las yin |

| skye 'jig gzigs pas mya ṅan 'das || lam bstan stoṅ ñid phyir ma yin |
| 'di dag phan tshun bzlog phyir daṅ || log pa'i phyir na mthoṅ ba yin |

24. K/V

| gal te skye 'gag med yin na || ci źig 'gags pas mya ṅan 'das |
| raṅ bźin gyis ni skye med ciṅ || 'gag med gaṅ de thar min nam |

| gal te skye daṅ 'gag med na || gaṅ źig 'gag phyir mya ṅan 'das |
| gaṅ źig raṅ bźin skye med ciṅ || 'gag med de thar ma yin nam |

25. K/V

| gal te 'gags las myaṅ 'das chad || gal te cig śos ltar na rtag |
| de phyir dṅos daṅ dṅos med dag || mya ṅan 'das par ruṅ ma yin |

| gal te mya ṅan 'das 'gog chad || gal te cig śos ltar na rtag |
| de phyir dṅos daṅ dṅos med min || skye med 'gag pa'aṅ med pa yin |

26. K/V

| gal te 'gog pa 'ga' gnas na || dṅos po las gźan de yod 'gyur |
| dṅos po med phyir 'di med la || dṅos po med phyir de yaṅ med |

| gal te 'gog pa 'ga' gnas yod || dṅos med par yaṅ der 'gyur ro |
| dṅos med par yaṅ de med de || dṅos med med par yaṅ de med |

22 Kb 'gag : 'ga' NP
26 Kd yaṅ : las NP

22. *Opponent:* These [two dogmas] do not occur due to continuity (*saṃtāna*) [which entails that] things (*bhāva*) cease when they have given cause (*hetuṃ dattvā*) [to an effect]. – *Reply:* As before [*vide* 19a] this [continuity] is also unestablished. It also follows that the continuity would be interrupted.

23. *Opponent:* [No!] The Buddha's teaching of the Way (*mārgadeśanā*) aims at showing origination (*utpāda*) and cessation (*nirodha*), not at emptiness (*śūnyatā*)! – *Reply:* To experience the two as mutually excluding (*parasparaviparyaya*) is a mistake (*viparyaya*).

24. *Opponent:* If there is no origination (*utpāda*) and cessation (*nirodha*), then Nirvāṇa is due to the cessation of what? – *Reply:* Is liberation (*mokṣa*) not that by nature (*prakṛtyā*) nothing arises and ceases?

25. If Nirvāṇa [results] from cessation (*nirodha*) [then there is] destruction (*uccheda*). If [Nirvāṇa] were the contrary (*itara*) [there would be] permanence (*śāśvata*). Therefore it is not logical that Nirvāṇa is being (*bhāva*) and non-being (*abhāva*).

26. If a definite cessation (*nirodhaḥ kaś cit*) did abide it would be independent of being (*bhāvād anya*). It does not exist without being (*bhāva*), nor does [cessation] exist without non-being (*abhāva*).

22. The notion of *saṃtāna* does not save one from *śāśvatocchedagrāha*, cf. above, v. 19; MK, XVII; XXI, 15-21. This, of course, is only *paramārthataḥ*, cf. MK, XXVII, 22; *Catuḥśataka*, X, 25.

23-26. As there is no *bhāva* etc. *nirvāṇa* cannot be defined as *(bhāva)nirodha*, or *abhāva*. In fact *utpāda* and *nirodha* are sheer illusions (cf. MK, XXI, 11 and *Laṅkāvatāra*, X, 37; MK, XXV; RĀ, I 42; SL, 105, 123). Thus Nāgārjuna's notion of *nirvāṇa* incurs no *śāśvatocchedagrāha*.

27. K/V

| mtshan gźi las gźan mtshan ñid las || mtshan gźi grub par raṅ ma grub |
| phan tshun las kyaṅ ma grub ste || ma grub ma grub sgrub byed min |

| mtshan gźi las mtshan grub mtshan las || mtshan gźi grub ste raṅ ma grub |
| gcig las gcig kyaṅ ma grub ste || ma grub ma grub sgrub byed min |

28. K/V

| 'dis ni rgyu daṅ 'bras bu daṅ || tshor daṅ tshor ba po sogs daṅ |
| lta po lta bya sogs ci'aṅ ruṅ || de kun ma lus bśad pa yin |

| 'dis ni rgyu daṅ 'bras bu daṅ || tshor bcas tshor ba po sogs daṅ |
| lta po lta bya sogs ci'aṅ ruṅ || de kun ma lus bśad pa yin |

29. K/V

| gnas med phan tshun las grub daṅ || 'chol phyir raṅ ñid ma grub phyir |
| dṅos po med phyir dus gsum ni || yod pa ma yin rtog pa tsam |

| mi gnas phan tshun grub phyir daṅ || 'chol phyir bdag ñid ma grub phyir |
| dṅos po med phyir dus gsum ni || yod pa ma yin rtog pa tsam |

30. K/V

| gaṅ phyir skye daṅ gnas daṅ 'jig || 'dus byas mtshan ñid 'di gsum med |
| de phyir 'dus byas ñid ma yin || 'dus ma byas la'aṅ cuṅ zad med |

| gaṅ phyir skye daṅ gnas daṅ 'jig || 'dus byas mtshan ñid 'di gsum med |
| de phyir 'dus byas 'dus ma byas || ci yaṅ yod pa ma yin no |

28 Vc ci'aṅ : ci yaṅ NP
29 Kb 'chol : 'tshol NP

27. The marked (*lakṣya*) is established from a mark (*lakṣaṇa*) different from the marked (*lakṣya*). It is not established by itself (*na svasiddha*). Nor are the [two] established by each other (*paraspara*) [since] unestablished cannot establish unestablished.

28. In this [manner] cause (*hetu*), effect (*phala*), feeling (*vedanā*), feeler (*vedaka*) etc., seer (*draṣṭṛ*), visible etc. (*draṣṭavyādi*), whatever it may be, are all explained without exception.

29. The three times (*kālatraya*) do not exist (substantially) since they are unfixed (*asthita*), mutually established (*parasparasiddha*), and since they change [and] since they are not self-established [and finally] since there is no being (*bhāva*). They are merely discriminations (*vikalpamātra*).

30. Since the three marks of the conditioned (*saṃskṛtalakṣaṇa*), [i.e.] origination (*utpāda*), duration (*sthiti*) and cessation (*bhaṅga*) do not exist, therefore there is not the slightest conditioned (*saṃskṛta*) nor unconditioned (*asaṃskṛta*) [phenomenon].

27.-28. Again *bhāva* in its various forms cannot be established by means of *lakṣyalakṣaṇa* because they are *asiddha* (v. MK, II, 21). Cf. also MK, IV, 7; V; CS, I 12; **Dvādaśadvāraka,* 18-19 (163c 16-17; 164a 10-11).

29. This refutation of *kāla* summarizes MK, XIX, q.v. **Dvādaśadvāraka*, 25 (166c 21-22); *Catuḥśataka*, XI.

31. K/V

| ma zig mi 'jig źig pa'aṅ min || gnas pa gnas pa ma yin te |
| mi gnas pa la'aṅ gnas ma yin || skyes pa mi skye ma skyes min |

| ma źig mi 'jig źig pa'aṅ min || gnas pa gnas pa ma yin te |
| mi gnas pa yaṅ gnas ma yin || skyes pa mi skye ma skyes min |

32. K/V

| 'dus byas daṅ ni 'dus ma byas || du ma ma yin gcig ma yin |
| yod min med min yod med min || mtshams 'dir sna tshogs thams cad 'dus |

| 'dus byas daṅ ni 'dus ma byas || du ma ma yin gcig ma yin |
| yod min med min yod med min || mtshams 'dir rnam pa 'di kun 'dus |

33. K/V

| bcom ldan bla mas las gnas daṅ || las bdag las kyi 'bras bu daṅ |
| sems can raṅ gi las daṅ ni || las rnams chud mi za bar gsuṅs |

| las gnas pa ni bcom ldan gsuṅs || bla ma las bdag 'bras bu daṅ |
| sems can las bdag bya ba daṅ || las rnams chud za min par gsuṅs |

34. K/V

| las rnams raṅ bźin med gsuṅs te || ma skyes gaṅ de chud mi za |
| de las kyaṅ ni bdag 'dzin skye || de bskyed 'bzin de'aṅ rnam rṭog las |

| gaṅ phyir raṅ bźin med bstan pa || de phyir de ma skyes pa las |
| mi 'jig bdag 'dzin de las skye || de skyed 'dzin de'aṅ rnam rtog las |

32 Kc mtshams : mtshan NP

31. The undestructed (*anaṣṭa*) does not cease, nor does the destructed (*naṣṭa*). The abiding (*sthita*) does not abide, nor does the non-abiding (*asthita*) abide. The born (*jāta*) is not born, nor is the unborn (*ajāta*).

32. Composite (*saṃskṛta*) and non-composite (*asaṃskṛta*) are not many (*aneka*), are not one (*eka*), are not being (*sat*), are not non-being (*asat*) [and] are not being-non-being (*sadasat*). All [possibilities] are comprised within this scheme.

33. *Opponent:* The Lord (*bhagavat*), the Teacher, has spoken of karma's duration, of karma's nature and of karma's result (*phala*) and also of the personal karma of living beings (*sattva*) and of the non-destruction (*avipranāśa*) of karma.

34. *Reply:* Karma is said to lack own-being (*svabhāva*). [Karma] which is unborn (*ajāta*) is not destructed. From that again I-making (*ahaṃkāra*) is born. But the belief (*grāha*) which creates it is due to discrimination (*vikalpa*).

30-32. Now *saṃskṛta* and *asaṃskṛta* cannot be established because their three *lakṣaṇas* (*utpāda, sthiti, bhaṅga*) cannot be established as *eka* or *aneka* etc.: MK, VII and **Dvādaśadvāraka,* IV (162c-163c 13).

35. K/V

| gal te las la raṅ bźin yod || de bskyed lus ni rtag par 'gyur |
| las kyaṅ sdug bsṅal rnam smin can || mi 'gyur de phyir bdag tu 'gyur |

| gal te las ni raṅ bźin 'gyur || de las skyes lus rtag par 'gyur |
| sdug bsṅal rnam smin can mi 'gyur || de phyir las kyaṅ bdag tu 'gyur |

36. K/V

| las ni rkyen skyes yod min źiṅ || rkyen min las skyes cuṅ zad med |
| 'du byed rnams ni sgyu ma daṅ || dri za'i groṅ khyer smig rgyu mtshuṅs |

| las ni rkyen skyes ci yaṅ med || rkyen min skyes pa'aṅ yod min te |
| 'du byed rnams ni sgyu ma daṅ || dri za'i groṅ khyer smig rgyu 'dra |

37. K/V

| las ni ñon moṅs rgyu mtshan can || ñon moṅs 'du byed las bdag ñid |
| lus ni las kyi rgyu mtshan can || gsum ka'aṅ ṅo bo ñid kyis stoṅ |

| las ni ñon moṅs rgyu mtshan can || 'du byed ñon moṅs las bdag ñid |
| lus ni las kyi rgyu mtshan can || gsum ka'aṅ ṅo bo ñid kyis stoṅ |

38. K/V

| las med na ni byed po med || de gñis med pas 'bras bu med |
| de med ñe bar spyod po med || de bas dṅos po dben pa yin |

| las med na ni byed pa med || de gñis med par 'bras bu med |
| de med phyir na za ba po || med pa yin pas dben pa yin |

35 Vb rtag : brtag NP
38 Vd yin : ni NP

35. If karma had own-being (*svabhāva*) the body (*deha*) created by it would be permanent (*nitya*). So karma would not result in suffering (*duḥkha*) and would therefore be substantial.

36. Karma is not born by conditions (*pratyaya*) and by no means by non-conditions (*apratyaya*), for (*hi*) karma-formations (*saṃskāra*) are like an illusion (*māyā*), a city of Gandharvas (*gandharvanagara*) and a mirage (*marīci*).

37. Karma has passions as its cause (*kleśanimittaka*). [Being] passions (*kleśa*) the karma-formations (*saṃskāra*) are of karmic nature (*kleśātmaka*). A body (*deha*) has karma as its cause (*karmanimittaka*), so [all] three are empty of own-being (*svabhāvaśūnya*).

38. Without karma no agent (*kāraka*). Without these two no result (*phala*). Without these no enjoyer (*bhoktṛ*). Therefore things are void (*vivikta*).

33-44. Following is a rather long treatment of karma according to Madhyamaka. 33 summarizes MK, XVII, 1-10, q.v. The remaining verses explain why, *paramārthataḥ*, karma is *śūnya* and how it is *pratītyasamutpanna*. Thus we have: *vikalpa* (cf. below, v. 64) in the form of *ahaṃkāra* (cf. RĀ, I, 27-35) generates *kleśa* (cf. MK, XXIII, 1; XVIII, 5) which, again, gives rise to karma which finally conditions one's *deha* (MK, XVII, 27) i.e. one's rebirth (*janma*, RĀ, I 35; II, 24). This cyclic process (cf. PK, 1-5) can only cease through cognition (*jñāna*, *darśana* etc.) of *tattva*, i.e. *śūnyatā*. – ŚS, 40-42 rec. by La Vallée Poussin, *Prasannapadā*, p. 330, n.l. – The Buddha's *deśanā* (v. 44) varies as it depends upon *sattvāśaya*, MK, XVIII, 6; BV, 98-99; RĀ, IV, 94-96; YṢ, 33.

39. K/V

| las ni stoṅ par yaṅ dag par || śes na de ñid mthoṅ ba'i phyir |
| las mi 'byuṅ ste de med na || las las 'byuṅ gaṅ mi 'byuṅ ṅo |

| yaṅ dag mthoṅ phyir las stoṅ par || legs par rnam par śes na ni |
| las mi 'byuṅ ste las med na || las las gaṅ byuṅ mi 'byuṅ ṅo |

40. K/V

| ji ltar bcom ldan de bźin gśegs || rdzu 'phrul gyis ni sprul pa sprul |
| sprul pa de yis slar yaṅ ni || sprul pa gźan źig sprul gyur pa |

| ji ltar bcom ldan de bźin gśegs || de ni rdzu 'phrul gyis sprul pa |
| sprul pa mdzad la sprul des kyaṅ || sprul pa gźan źig sprul par byed |

41. K/V

| de la de bźin gśegs sprul stoṅ || sprul pas sprul pa smos ci dgos |
| gñis po miṅ tsam yod pa yaṅ || ci yaṅ ruṅ ste rtog pa tsam |

| de la de bźin gśegs sprul stoṅ || sprul pas sprul pa smos ci dgos |
| rtog pa tsam gaṅ ci yaṅ ruṅ || de dag gñi ga yod pa yin |

42. K/V

| de bźin byed po sprul daṅ mtshuṅs || las ni sprul pas sprul daṅ mtshuṅs |
| raṅ bźin gyis ni gaṅ cuṅ zad || yod pa de dag rtog pa tsam |

| de bźin byed po sprul par mtshuṅs || las ni sprul pas sprul daṅ mtshuṅs |
| raṅ bźin gyis ni stoṅ pa yin || rtog tsam gaṅ ci'aṅ ruṅ bar yod |

39 Vd las : la NP
41 Va de la : de las NP
42 Vd ci'aṅ : ci yaṅ NP

39. When one correctly understands that karma is empty (*śūnya*) because the truth is seen (*tattvadarśanāt*), karma does not arise. When [karma] is no more, that which arises from karma arises no more.

40. Just as the Lord Tathāgata magically (*ṛddhyā*) has created a phantom (*nirmitaka*) and this phantom again (*punaḥ*) has created another phantom ...

41. (In that case Tathāgata's phantom is empty – not to mention the phantom [created] by the phantom! Both of them are but names, merely insignificant discriminations (*vikalpamātra*)) ...

42. Thus the agent (*kāraka*) is like the phantom (*nirmitaka*), karma is like the phantom [created] by the phantom. By nature (*svabhāvena*) [they are] insignificant (*yat kiṃ cit*), merely discriminations (*vikalpamātra*).

41. Is this verse a later interpolation?

43. K/V

| gal te las kyi raṅ bźin yod || myaṅ 'das byed po las kyaṅ med |
| gal te med na las bskyed pa'i || 'bras bu sdug daṅ mi sdug med |

| gal te raṅ bźin gyis las yod || mya ṅan 'das las byed po med |
| gal te med na las bskyed pa'i || 'bras bu sdug daṅ mi sdug med |

44. K/V

| yod ces pa daṅ yod med ces || yod daṅ med ces de yaṅ yod |
| saṅs rgyas rnams kyis dgoṅs pa yis || gsuṅs pa rtogs par sla ma yin |

| yod ces pa yod med ces pa'aṅ || yod de yod med ces de'aṅ yod |
| saṅs rgyas rnams kyis dgoṅs nas ni || gsuṅs pa rtogs par sla ma yin |

45. K/V

| gal te gzugs ni raṅ 'byuṅ bźin || gzugs de 'byuṅ las 'byuṅ ma yin |
| raṅ las 'byuṅ min ma yin nam || gźan las kyaṅ min de med phyir |

| gal te gzugs 'byuṅ las byuṅ na || yaṅ dag min las gzugs 'byuṅ 'gyur |
| raṅ gi ṅo bo las ma yin || de med phyir nas gźan las min |

46. K/V

| gcig la bźi ñid yod min ciṅ || bźi la'aṅ gcig ñid yod min pas |
| gzugs ni 'byuṅ ba chen po bźi || rgyur byas nas grub ji ltar yod |

| gcig la'aṅ bźi ni yod min źiṅ || bźi la'aṅ gcig ni yod min na |
| 'byuṅ ba che bźi med brten nas || gzugs ni ji ltar 'grub par 'gyur |

47. K/V

| śin tu mi 'dzin phyir de med || rtags las źe na rtags de'aṅ med |
| rgyu daṅ rkyen las skyes pa'i phyir || rtags med par yaṅ mi rigs so |

| śin tu mi 'dzin phyir gal te || rtags las śe na rtags de med |
| rgyu daṅ rkyen las skyes phyir ro || yod na'aṅ rtags med rigs ma yin |

44 Kc kyis : kyi NP; Kd rtogs par sla : rtog par bla NP
47 Kb źe na rtags : źen na rtag NP; Kd rtags : rtag NP; Vd ma : pa NP

43. If karma possessed own-being (*svabhāva*) there would be no Nirvāṇa nor deeds [of an] agent (*kārakakarma*). If [karma] does not exist the pleasant or unpleasant result (*phala*) created by karma does not exist.

44. 'Is' and 'is not' and also 'is, is not' has been stated by the Buddhas with an intention (*abhiprāyeṇa*). It is not easy to understand!

45. If form (*rūpa*) is material (*bhautika*) in itself, form (*rūpa*) does not arise from the elements (*bhūta*). It is not derived from itself. It does not exist, does it? Nor from anything else. Therefore it does not exist [at all].

46. The four [great elements] are not in one [of the elements] and one of them is not in any of the four [elements]. How can form (*rūpa*) be established with the four great elements (*mahābhūta*) as [its] cause?

47. Since it is not conceived directly [form does, it seems,] not exist. But if [you maintain that it is conceived] through a mark (*liṅga*), that mark, however, does not exist since it is born from causes and conditions (*hetupratyaya*). And it would be illogical [if form could exist] without a mark (*liṅga*).

44. Allusion to *satyadvaya*.
45. Now (45-54) the author refutes the existence of *rūpa* which, *saṃvṛtitaḥ*, is *varṇa* and *saṃsthāna* (see v. 50). – First *rūpa* is unreal because it is neither one with the *mahābhūta* nor different from them. Similarly MK, IV, 1-5.
46. Again the *mahābhūta* cannot be established as *eka* or *aneka* (RĀ, I, 83-89). So *rūpa* cannot be *bhautika*, cf. RĀ, I, 99; CS, I, 5.
47. One cannot infer the existence of *rūpa* from its *liṅga*, i.e., I assume, *bhautika* cannot e.g. be subtle as it is derived from *bhūta* that must be gross. See RĀ, I, 90; *Pañcaskandhaprakaraṇa*, p. 2. – If, on the other hand, *rūpa* really did exist as the Ābhidhārmika contends, it could not be without *liṅga* (i.e. it could not change its *liṅga* under the influence of the *mahābhūta*).

48. K/V

| gal te blo des gzugs 'dzin na || raṅ gi raṅ bźin la 'dzin 'gyur |
| rkyen las skyes pas yod min pas || yaṅ dag gzugs med ji ltar 'dzin |

| gal te gzugs ni 'dzin 'gyur na || bdag gi raṅ bźin ñid 'dzin 'gyur |
| med pa rkyen las skyes pa'i blos || gzugs med ji ltar 'dzin par 'gyur |

49. K/V

| ji skad bśad gzugs skyes pa'i blo'i || skad cig skad cig gis mi 'dzin |
| 'das daṅ ma 'oṅs pa gzugs kyaṅ || de yis ji ltar rtogs par 'gyur |

| gaṅ tshe blo 'byuṅ skad cig pas || gzugs skyes skad cig mi 'dzin na |
| de yis 'das daṅ ma 'oṅs pa'i || gzugs ni ji ltar rtogs par 'gyur |

50. K/V

| gaṅ tshe nam yaṅ kha dog daṅ || dbyibs dag tha dad ñid med pas |
| de dag tha dad 'dzin yod min || gzugs de gcig tu'aṅ grags pa min |

| gaṅ tshe nam yaṅ kha dog dbyibs || tha dad ñid ni yod ma yin |
| tha dad gcig tu 'dzin pa med || de gñis gzugs su grags phyir ro |

51. K/V

| mig blo mig la yod min te || gzugs la yod min bar na med |
| gzugs daṅ mig la brten nas de || yoṅs su rtog pa log pa yin |

| mig blo mig la yod min te || gzugs la yod min bar na'aṅ med |
| mig daṅ gzugs la brten nas de || yoṅs su rtog pa log pa yin |

52. K/V

| gal te mig bdag mi mthoṅ na || des gzugs mthoṅ bar ji ltar 'gyur |
| de phyir mig daṅ gzugs bdag med || skye mched lhag ma'aṅ de bźin no |

| gal te mig bdag mi mthoṅ na || de gzugs mthoṅ bar ji ltar 'gyur |
| de phyir mig daṅ gzugs bdag med || skye mched lhag ma'aṅ de daṅ 'dra |

48 Kb gi : gis NP; Vd par N : pa N
49 Vc yis : yi NP; Kd yis : yi NP; Vd rtogs : rtog NP
52 Ka mi : mig NP

48. If mind (*buddhi*) could grasp form (*rūpa*) it would grasp its own own-being (*svasvabhāva*). How could a [mind] which does not exist as it is born from conditions (*pratyaya*) really conceive absence of form (*rūpābhāva*)?

49. Since one moment of mind (*buddhikṣaṇa*) cannot within [the very same] moment (*kṣaṇa*) grasp a form (*rūpa*) born as explained, how could it understand a past (*atīta*) and a future (*anāgata*) form (*rūpa*)?

50. Since colour (*varṇa*) and figure (*saṃsthāna*) never exist apart (*bhinna*) they cannot be conceived apart (*bhinna*), [for] is form (*rūpa*) not [generally] acknowledged to be one (*eka*)?

51. The sense of sight (*cakṣurbuddhi*) is not inside the eye (*cakṣuḥ*). It is not in form (*rūpa*) or in between. [Therefore] the image (*parikalpa*) depending upon form and eye (*cakṣūrūpa*) is false (*mithyā*).

52. If the eye (*cakṣuḥ*) does not see itself, how can it see form (*rūpa*)? Therefore eye and form are without self (*anātman*). The remaining sense-fields (*āyatana*) similarly.

48. Here I take *buddhi* in the sense of *cakṣurvijñāna* (cf. the use of *ghaṭabuddhi*, VP, 16-19). Since *cakṣūrūpe pratītyaivam ukto vijñānasaṃbhavaḥ* (RĀ, IV, 55) such a *buddhi* is *med pa*, i.e. *śūnya*. So it cannot perceive *rūpa* to which a similar argument applies. Moreover, *buddhi* would have to perceive itself (which is absurd) in order to perceive other things, i.e. *rūpa*, cf. MK, III, 2 (which must be understood in the sense of *Catuḥśataka*, XIII, 16, q.v.); RĀ, IV, 64.

49. Again *buddhi* cannot perceive *rūpa/viṣaya* because being *kṣaṇika* objects are never *sāṃprata*. A *buddhi* which has *atīta* or *anāgata* as its object is, of course, *vyartha*, see RĀ, IV, 56-57.

50. That *rūpaṃ dvidhā varṇaḥ saṃsthānaṃ ca* is well-known, cf. e.g. *Amṛtarasa*, p. 115; *Pañcaskandhaprakaraṇa*, p. 4. Also *Catuḥśataka*, XIII, 7.

51. Similarly *Catuḥśataka*, XIII, 17, q.v.

53. K/V

| mig ni raṅ bdag ñid kyis stoṅ || de ni gźan bdag gis kyaṅ stoṅ |
| gzugs kyaṅ de bźin stoṅ pa ste || skye mched lhag ma'aṅ de bźin no |

| mig de raṅ bdag ñid kyis stoṅ || de ni gźan bdag ñid kyis stoṅ |
| gzugs kyaṅ de bźin stoṅ pa ste || skye mched lhag ma'aṅ de bźin stoṅ |

54. K/V

| gaṅ tshe gcig reg lhan cig 'gyur || de tshe gźan rnams stoṅ pa ñid |
| stoṅ pa'am mi stoṅ mi bsten la || mi stoṅ pa yaṅ stoṅ mi brten |

| gaṅ tshe gcig reg lhan cig 'gyur || de tshe gźan rnams stoṅ pa yin |
| stoṅ pa'aṅ mi stoṅ mi sten te || mi stoṅ pa 'aṅ stoṅ pa min |

55. K/V

| ṅo bo mi gnas yod min pas || gsum 'dus pa yod ma yin no |
| de bdag ñid kyi reg med pas || de tshe tshor ba yod ma yin |

| gsum po yod min mi gnas pa'i || raṅ bźin 'du ba yod min pas |
| de bdag ñid kyi reg pa med || de phyir tshor ba yod ma yin |

56. K/V

| naṅ daṅ phyi yi skye mched la || brten nas rnam par śes pa 'byuṅ |
| de lta bas na rnam śes med || smig rgyu sgyu ma bźin du stoṅ |

| naṅ daṅ phyi yi skye mched la || brten nas rnam par śes pa 'byuṅ |
| de lta bas na rnam śes med || smig rgyu sgyu ma bźin du stoṅ |

53 Kb bdag : dag NP; Kd skye mched : skye med NP
54 Kc pa'aṅ : pa'am NP; Kd stoṅ mi : brten mi NP
55 Kc bdag : dag NP; Vc kyi : kyis NP
56 Kc med : ni NP

53. Eye is empty (*śūnya*) of its own self (*svātman*). It is also empty (*śūnya*) of another's self (*parātman*). Form is likewise empty (*śūnya*). The remaining sense-fields (*āyatana*) similarly.

54. When one [sense-field] occurs simultaneously with contact (*sparśa*), then the others are superfluous (*śūnya*). Empty (*śūnya*) does not depend upon non-empty (*aśūnya*), and non-empty does not depend upon empty.

55. Having no [independent] fixed nature the three cannot come into contact. Since there is no contact (*sparśa*) which has this nature, therefore feeling (*vedanā*) does not exist.

56. Consciousness (*vijñāna*) occurs dependent upon the internal and external sense-fields (*āyatana*). Therefore consciousness (*vijñāna*) is empty (*śūnya*), like mirages and illusions (*marīcimāyāvat*).

52-53. As each of the twelve *āyatanas* is incapable of fulfilling its respective function in itself it lacks *svabhāva,* it is *śūnya,* for *akṛtrimaḥ svabhāvo hi nirapekṣaḥ paratra ca* (MK, XV, 2). Cf. MK, III.

54. The commentaries to this verse are far from exhaustive. But v. RĀ, IV, 52-54. Since each of the six *sparśāyatana* (= *indriya,* ref. CPD, II, p. 129) can only have one object (*artha/viṣaya*) at a time (RĀ, IV, 52; *Catuḥśataka,* XI, 18) this implies that the senses and their respective objects – taken *pratyekam* – must be *vyartha* (RĀ, IV, 54).

55. There can be no *saṃnipāta,* i.e. *sparśa* (MK, XXVI, 5) of *indriya, viṣaya* and *vijñāna,* since, as shown (cf. also MK, XIV) they do not exist by themselves. Hence they cannot come together. Thus it is only *saṃvṛtitaḥ* that one can say *sparśāc ca vedanā saṃpravartate* (MK, XXVI, 5).

57. K/V

| rnam śes śes bya la brten nas || 'byuṅ la śes bya yod ma yin |
| śes bya śes pa med pa'i phyir || de phyir śes pa po ñid med |

| rnam śes rnam śes bya brten nas || 'byuṅ bas yod min śes pa daṅ |
| rnam śes bya med phyir de'i phyir || rnam śes byed pa med pa ñid |

58. K/V

| thams cad mi rtag yaṅ na ni || mi rtag pa yaṅ rtag pa med |
| dṅos po rtag daṅ mi rtag ñid || 'gyur na de lta ga la yod |

| thams cad mi rtag mi rtag pa'am || yaṅ na rtag pa ci yaṅ med |
| dṅos yod rtag daṅ mi rtag ñid || yin na de ltar ga la yod |

59. K/V

| sdug daṅ mi sdug phyin ci log || rkyen las chags sdaṅ gti mug dṅos |
| 'byuṅ phyir chags sdaṅ gti mug daṅ || raṅ bźin gyis ni yod ma yin |

| sdug daṅ mi sdug phyin ci log || rkyen skyes chags sdaṅ gti mug rnams |
| 'byuṅ ste de phyir raṅ bźin gyis || 'dod chags źe sdaṅ gti mug med |

60. K/V

| gaṅ phyir de ñid la chags śiṅ || de la źe sdaṅ de la rmoṅs |
| de phyir rnam par rtog pas bskyed || rtog de'aṅ yaṅ dag ñid du med |

| gaṅ phyir der chags der sdaṅ der || rmoṅs pa de phyir de dag ni |
| rnam rtog gis bskyed rnam rtog kyaṅ || yaṅ dag ñid du yod ma yin |

57 Ka nas : na NP; Va nas : na NP
59 Kb gti mug P : gti mus N

57. Since consciousness (*vijñāna*) arises dependent on a discernible object (*vijñeya*), the discernible does not exist [in itself]. Since [the conscious subject] does not exist without the discernible (*vijñeya*) and consciousness (*vijñāna*), therefore the conscious subject (*vijñātṛ*) does not exist [by himself].

58. [In a relative sense] everything is impermanent, but [in the absolute sense] nothing is permanent (*nitya*) or impermanent (*anitya*). [If there] were being (*bhāva*) then it could be permanent (*nitya*) or impermanent (*anitya*). But how is that [possible]?

59. Since the entities desire (*rāga*), hatred (*dveśa*), and stupidity (*moha*) occur dependently upon perverted views about pleasant and unpleasant (*śubhāśubhaviparyāsa*) therefore desire, hatred, and stupidity do not exist by own-being (*svabhāva*).

60. Since one [may] desire, hate and be infatuated about the very same [thing] therefore [the passions] are created by discrimination (*vikalpa*) and that discrimination is nothing real.

56-57. Refutation of the fifth skandha, its objects and its agent. Similarly CS, I, 10; BV, 26-56; *Catuḥśataka*, XIII, 23. Cf. CS, III, 50.

58. Now (58-61) it is argued that the four *viparyāsas*, the source of *avidyā* (see 10, 62) do not exist *paramārthataḥ*. – Since the concept of *bhāva* is untenable (as shown above 7, 17 ff.) nothing can really be either *nitya* or *anitya* etc. – The verse is quoted *Madhyamakālaṃkāravṛtti*, *loc.cit.*, 72b: *thams cad rtag min mi rtag pa'aṅ* || *ci yaṅ med de rtag de bźin* || *dṅos yod rtag daṅ mi rtag par* || *'gyur na de ni ga la yod* ||.

59-61. The *kleśas* are – *saṃvṛtitaḥ* – born from the *viparyāsas* (MK, XXIII, 1). But as experience shows (cf. BV, 19-20; *Catuḥśataka*, VIII, 2-3) *viparyāsas* must be sheer *vikalpas*. This implies that a *vikalpa* really has no definite object before it. So, *paramārthataḥ*, without an object a *vikalpa* is simply nought.

61. K/V

| brtag bya gaṅ de yod ma yin || brtag bya med rtog ga la yod |
| de phyir brtag bya rtog pa dag || rkyen las skyes phyir stoṅ pa ñid |

| rnam brtag bya gaṅ de yod min || brtag bya med rtog ga la yod |
| de phyir rkyen las skyes pa'i phyir || brtag bya rnam par rtog pa stoṅ |

62. K/V

| de ñid rtogs pas phyin ci log || bźi las byuṅ ba'i ma rig med |
| de med na ni 'du byed rnams || mi 'byuṅ lhag ma'aṅ de bźin no |

| yaṅ dag mthoṅ phyir phyin ci log || bźi las skyes pa'i ma rig med |
| de med phyir na 'du byed rnams || mi 'byuṅ lhag ma'aṅ de bźin no |

63. K/V

| gaṅ gaṅ la brten skye ba'i dṅos || de de med pas de mi skye |
| dṅos daṅ dṅos med 'dus byas daṅ || 'dus ma byas źi mya ṅan 'das |

| gaṅ brten gaṅ skyes de de las || skyes de de med mi 'byuṅ ṅo |
| dṅos daṅ dṅos med 'dus byas daṅ || 'dus ma byas źi mya ṅan 'das |

64. K/V

| rgyu rkyen las skyes dṅos po rnams || yaṅ dag ñid du rtog pa gaṅ |
| de ni ston pas ma rig gsuṅs || de las yan lag bcu gñis 'byuṅ |

| rgyu daṅ rkyen las skyes dṅos rnams || yaṅ dag par ni rtog par gaṅ |
| de ni ston pas ma rig gsuṅs || de las yan lag bcu gñis 'byuṅ |

61 Va rnam P : nam N; Kb yod P : lod N
62 Ka pas : pa'i NP
63 Kd źi (*cf.* C) : 'di NP; Vd śiṅ NP

61. That which is imagined (*pariklp-*) does not exist. Without an imagined object how can there be imagination (*vikalpa*)? So since the imagined and the imagination are born by conditions (*pratyaya-ja*) therefore [they are] empty (*śūnya*).

62. By understanding the truth (*tattva*), ignorance (*avidyā*), which arises from the four perverted views (*viparyāsa*), does not exist. When this is no more the karma-formations (*saṃskāra*) do not arise. The remaining [ten members] likewise.

63. The thing (*bhāva*) arising dependent upon this or that (*tat tat*) does not arise when that is absent. Being (*bhāva*), non-being (*abhāva*), composite and incomposite (*saṃskṛtāsaṃskṛta*) are calm (*śānta*) [and] extinguished (*nirvṛta*).

64. To imagine (*kḷp-*) that things (*bhāva*) born by causes and conditions (*hetupratyaya*) are real (*samyak*) is called ignorance (*avidyā*) by the Teacher (*śāstṛ*). From that the twelve members (*dvādaśāṅga*) arise.

62. Now that *avidyā* has been deprived of its basis, the eleven *aṅgas* based upon *avidyā* also vanish, QED. – Cf. the identification of *avidyā* with *piṇḍasaṃjñā* etc. (= *viparyāsa*) in *Śālistambasūtra*, quoted *Prasannapadā*, p. 562.

63-64. So *avidyā* is simply unawareness of the universal law of *pratītyasamutpāda*, cf. MK, XVIII, 9-11. It is, as *svavṛtti* to 64 says, *brten pa'i dṅos por mṅon par źen pa daṅ lta ba daṅ rtog pa daṅ 'dzin pa*. We may add *bhāvābhāvaparāmarśa*, RĀ, I, 42; *bhāvābhyupagama*, YṢ, 46. See *Dhammasaṅgani*, p. 213 for these equivalents (... *gāha, paṭiggāha, abhinivesa, parāmāsa, vipariyāsaggāha* ...)

65. K/V

| dṅos po stoṅ par de rtogs na || yaṅ dag mthoṅ phyir rmoṅs mi 'gyur |
| de ni ma rig 'gog pa yin || de las yan lag bcu gñis 'gag |

| yaṅ dag mthoṅ phyir dṅos stoṅ par || legs śes ma rig mi 'byuṅ ba |
| de ni ma rig 'gog pa yin || de phyir yan lag bcu gñis 'gag |

66. K/V

| 'du byed dri za'i groṅ khyer daṅ || sgyu ma smig rgyu skra śad daṅ |
| dbu ba chu bur sprul pa daṅ || rmi lam mgal me'i 'khor lo mtshuṅs |

| 'du byed dri za'i groṅ khyer daṅ || sgyu ma smig rgyu chu bur daṅ |
| chu yi dbu ba mtshuṅs pa ste || rmi lam mgal me'i 'khor lo 'dra |

67. K/V

| raṅ bźin gyis ni 'ga' yaṅ med || 'di la dṅos po med pa'aṅ med |
| rgyu daṅ rkyen las skyes pa yi || dṅos daṅ dṅos med stoṅ pa yin |

| raṅ bźin gyis ni dṅos 'ga' med || 'di la dṅos po med pa'aṅ med |
| rgyu daṅ rkyen las skyes pa yi || dṅos daṅ dṅos med stoṅ pa yin |

68. K/V

| dṅos kun raṅ bźin stoṅ pas na || de bźin gśegs pa mtshuṅs med pas |
| rten ciṅ 'brel par 'byuṅ ba 'di || dṅos po rnams su ñe bar bstan |

| dṅos po thams cad raṅ bźin gyis || stoṅ pa yin pas dṅos rnams kyi |
| rten 'byuṅ de ni de bźin gśegs || mtshuṅs pa med pas ñe bar bstan |

65 Kd yan lag : yan yag NP
66 Kb smig : mig NP; Vd mgal : 'gal NP
67 Va 'ga' : 'gags NP
68 Vb kyi : kyis NP

65. But when one, by seeing correctly, has understood that things (*bhāva*) are empty (*śūnya*) one is not infatuated (*mūḍha*). That is the cessation of ignorance (*avidyānirodha*). Thereupon the twelve members (*dvādaśāṅga*) stop.

66. Karma-formations (*saṃskāra*) are like the city of Gandharvas (*gandharvanagara*), illusions (*māyā*), mirages (*marīci*), nets of hair (*keśoṇḍuka*), foam (*phena*), bubbles (*budbuda*), phantoms (*nirmitaka*), dreams (*svapna*) and wheels of firebrand (*alātacakra*).

67. Nothing exists perforce of own-being (*svabhāvena*), nor is there any non-being (*abhāva*) here. Being and non-being born by causes and conditions (*hetupratyaya*) are empty (*śūnya*).

68. Inasmuch as all things are empty of own-being (*svabhāva*) the incomparable Tathāgata has taught this dependent co-origination (*pratītyasamutpāda*) about things (*bhāva*).

65-69ab. When one realizes that *bhāva* etc. are *śūnya*, that they lack *svabhāva* like illusions etc., *avidyā* etc. vanishes. That amounts to *paramārtha*. Cf. MK, XXVI, 11; CS, III, 36ff.

69. K/V

| dam pa'i don ni der zad de || 'jig rten ṅor byas tha sñad dag |
| sna tshogs thams cad rdzogs saṅs rgyas || bcom ldan 'das kyis bden brtags mdzad |

| dam pa'i don ni der zad do || saṅs rgyas bcom ldan 'das kyis ni |
| 'jig rten tha sñad brten nas su || sna tshogs thams cad yaṅ dag brtags |

70. K/V

| 'jig rten pa yi chos bstan mi 'jig ciṅ || yaṅ dag ñid du nam yaṅ chos bstan med |
| de bźin gśegs pas gsuṅs pa ma rig pas || de las dri med brjod pa 'di las skrag |

|'jig rten pa yi bstan mi 'jig || yaṅ dag chos bstan ci yaṅ med |
| de bźin gśegs bśad ma rtogs nas || de phyir sgrub rtogs med 'dir skrag |

71. K/V

| 'di la brten nas 'di 'byuṅ źes || 'jig rten tshul 'di mi 'gog ciṅ |
| gaṅ brten raṅ bźin med pas de || ji ltar yod 'gyur de ñid ṅes |

| 'di brten 'di 'byuṅ źes bya ba'i || 'jig rten sgrub 'di 'gog mi mdzad |
| rten 'byuṅ gaṅ de raṅ bźin med || ji ltar de yod yaṅ dag ṅes |

72. K/V

| dad ldan de ñid tshol la brtson || tshul 'di rigs pas rjes dpog gaṅ |
| rten med chos 'ga' brten pa yi || srid daṅ srid min spaṅs nas źi |

| dad ldan yaṅ dag tshol lhur len || chos bstan gaṅ la'aṅ mi brten gaṅ |
| sgrub 'di rigs pas rjes gñer te || dṅos daṅ dṅos med spaṅs nas źi |

70 Vc bśad ma rtogs : pa bśad rtogs P (rtog N); Vd rtogs : rtog NP
71 Va brten : rten NP
72 Kb dpog : dpogs NP; Kc 'ga' brten : 'gal bstan NP

69. The ultimate meaning (*paramārtha*) consists in that! The perfect Buddhas, the Lords (*bhagavat*) have [only] conceived the entire manifoldness (*citraṃ viśvam*) relying upon the world [as a] convention (*lokavyavahāra*).

70. The worldly norms (*laukikadharma*) are not violated but in reality (*tattvataḥ*) [the Tathāgata] has expressed no teachings about his principles (*dharmadeśanā*). Being ignorant about what the Tathāgata states [fools] are consequently afraid of this spotless preaching (*vimalavacana*).

71. The worldly principle that 'this arises depending upon that' is not violated. But since that which is dependent lacks own-being, how can it exist? That is certain!

72. One with faith (*śraddhāvat*) trying to seek the truth (*tattva*), one who considers this principle (*naya*) logically (*yuktyā*) [and] relies [upon] a supportless norm (*dharma*) overcomes existence (*bhava*) and non-existence (*abhava*) [and becomes] calm (*śānta*).

69cd-73. However, as long as one has not yet realized *paramārtha* one must have *śraddhā* (cf. RĀ, I, 5-6) and rely on *vyavahāra* (cf. MK, XXIV, 8-10; BV, 67). Thus *nirvāṇa*, i.e. *rāgadveṣamohaprahāṇa* (°*kṣaya*) (see SS, 221a 4 quoting *Saṃyuktāgama*, cf. *Saṃyutta*, IV, p. 251ff.), is approached, i.e. attained (cf. MK, XXIV, 10).

73. K/V

| 'di dag rkyen 'di las rig nas || lta ṅan dra ba kun ldog des |
| chags rmoṅs khoṅ khro spaṅs pa'i phyir || ma gos mya ṅan 'das pa thob |

| rkyen ñid 'di pa 'di śes nas || lta ṅan dra ba'i rtog pa ldog |
| chags rmoṅs khoṅ khro spaṅs phyir te || ma gos mya ṅan 'das ñer 'gro |

73. When one understands 'this is a result of that', the nets of bad views (*kudṛṣṭijāla*) all vanish. Then one unsullied (*alipta*) obtains Nirvāṇa by abandoning desire (*rāga*), delusion (*moha*) and hatred (*dveṣa*).

III. Vigrahavyāvartanī (VV)

This text is ascribed to Nāgārjuna by Bhavya,[101] Candrakīrti[102] and Śāntarakṣita,[103] and later testimonies are also known.[104] It is written in the *āryā* metre and provided with a *svavṛtti* in a simple and clear prose, but not without some tiresome pedantry.[105] VV is extant in Sanskrit,[106] Tibetan and Chinese and has often been translated into modern languages.[107]

Like ŚS it was probably composed later than MK,[108] and I agree with Candrakīrti that it, with ŚS, forms an appendix to the *opus magnum.*[109] Its scope is – according to the prevailing rules of debate[110] – to defend Nāgārjuna's thesis that all things are empty,

101. See n. 88.
102. See n. 89; *Prasannapadā,* pp. 16, 29, 59; *Yuktiṣaṣṭikāvṛtti,* 2b.
103. *Madhyamakālaṃkāravṛtti,* 72b (quotes VV, 70).
104. E.g. Atiśa's *Pañjikā* to *Bodhipathapradīpa, pādas* 205-208 (translated in my paper ref. to n. 49).
105. Too many repetitions and too much spelling out. On the other hand this serves to prevent misunderstandings among *vaineyas* about the author's doctrine. Thus the style may to a certain extent be dictated by the notion of *upāyakauśalya* (cf. BS, 17).
106. The critical edition of E. H. Johnston and A. Kunst was recently reprinted with a (revised) English translation by K. Bhattacharya: *The Dialectical Method of Nāgārjuna (Vigrahavyāvartanī),* Delhi 1978. (This supersedes K. Bhattacharya's previous rendering and notes, *JIP,* I, pp. 217-161 and V, pp. 237-241.)
107. The Chinese version (Taishō, No. 1631) was translated by G. Tucci, *Pre-Dinnāga Buddhist Texts on Logic from Chinese Sources,* Baroda 1929. The Tibetan version (also edited by Tucci) was translated into French by S. Yamaguchi: 'Traité de Nāgārjuna: Pour écarter les vaines discussions', *JA,* CCXV, pp. 1-86, with useful notes. – A good Italian version by R. Gnoli, *op.cit.,* pp. 139-156 (kārikās only). – A partial version by E. Frauwallner, *Die Philosophie des Buddhismus,* Berlin 1969, pp. 200-204. – Several modern discussions, most recently by M. Siderits: 'The Madhyamaka Critique of Epistemology', *JIP,* VIII, pp. 307-335.
108. MK, XXIV, 10 cited *ad* VV, 28.
109. See n. 70.
110. Cf. the brief 'Glossary of the significant Nyāya technical terms used in the *Vigrahavyāvartanī*' given by Bhattacharya, *op.cit.,* p. 51 (cf. *JIP,* V, pp. 240-

because they lack own-being, as, for instance, a phantom. This is done on a relative (*saṃvṛtitah*) and absolute (*paramārthataḥ*) level.[111]

The sources are as follows:

Sigla

K *Vigrahavyāvartanīkārikā,* trans. by Jñānagarbha & dPal brtsegs, rev. by Jayānanda and mDo sde dpal.

241). – In the opinion of Bhattacharya (*ibid.*, p. 38, n. 2) Nāgārjuna's opponent is a 'Naiyāyika realist', and in a paper 'On the relationship between Nāgārjuna's *Vigrahavyāvartanī* and the *Nyāyasūtra*-s', *JIES*, V, pp. 265-273 (cf. *op.cit.*, p. 4, n. 15 (not n. '51')) he has discussed this question criticizing some of the views expressed by G. Oberhammer, 'Ein Beitrag zu den Vāda-Traditionen Indiens', *WZKSO*, VII, pp. 63-103. – It is true that VV and *Nyāyasūtra* are 'interdependent' (to use Tucci's expression, *op. cit.*, p. xxvii, q.v.) but it is wrong to regard the 'opponent' in VV as a Naiyāyika (i.e. an exponent of NS in some form). In my opinion he must be an Ābhidhārmika following, of course, the rules of debate prescribed in some Buddhist work on logic such as **Upāyahṛdaya* etc. My main arguments are: a) Together with MK and ŚS, VV forms a unity addressed to the same audience (cf. above, n. 81), viz. Ābhidhārmikas; b) In VV the Buddhist term *āgama* (the third *pramāṇa*) is invariably used, not the corresponding Nyāya term *śabda*; c) The *udāharaṇas* VV, 23 and 27 can only be acceptable to a Buddhist opponent; d) The *svavṛtti* to VV, 54, 55 and 70 only makes sense if the opponent is a Buddhist; e) Nāgārjuna devoted a special work to his controversy with Nyāya, viz. VP (cf. Kajiyama, 'On the relation between the Vaidalyaprakarana and the Nyāyasūtra', *IBK*, V, pp. 192-195). – Future discussions about the relationship between VV and NS are bound to take into account not only VP but also the pertinent evidence found in **Śataśāstra*, or **Śataka* (Taishō, No. 1569), and **Upāyahṛdaya* (cf. above, n. 44).

111. Thus 1-20 give the objections of the Buddhist opponent, real or imaginary. 21-26 are Nāgārjuna's replies *saṃvṛtitaḥ* following the common rules of debate, giving a *pratijñā* etc. 27ff. is Nāgārjuna's standpoint *paramārthataḥ*. The *āgama*-background of this is, I think, *Laṅkāvatārasūtra*, pp. 166-169 (... *pratijñā na karaṇīyā* ... q.v.). The decisive shift of argumentative level (i.e. between *saṃvṛti* and *paramārtha*) is indicated by *athavā* (VV, 28a) which often has a strong adversative force in Nāgārjuna as well as Āryadeva. Often it must (like its short form *atha*) be rendered by 'on the other hand' or better Latin *immo vero*, or *sin autem* (cf. e.g. VV, 2a, 10a, 12a, 15a, 19a, 27a etc. etc.). Apparently this crucial point has escaped modern translators of VV and consequently obscured the inherently clear structure of that work. – The fact that Nāgārjuna is thus ready to argue at both levels also renders the criticism launched at Bhavya (*Prasannapadā*, p. 16, q.v.) in the words of VV, 29-30 out of their proper context somewhat perfidious.

TP, No. 5228, Tsa *fol.* 30b-34a; TN, No. 3219, Tsa *fol.* 26b-29b.

V *Vigrahavyāvartanivṛtti,* trans. by Jñānagarbha & Devendrarakṣita.
TP, No. 5232, Tsa *fol.* 138a-156a; TN, No. 3223, Tsa *fol.* 128b-146b.

S A Sanskrit recension by E.H. Johnston & A. Kunst (see n. 106).

C Chinese trans. by Gautama Prajñāruci.
Taishō, No. 1631, 13b-23a.

S is an excellent piece of work, perhaps 'the possibly nearest approximation of Nāgārjuna's original text'. Still C and K, but particularly V provide variants that cannot be objectively eliminated.

It will not be in vain to offer a critical ed. of K which is the best of all translations of the verses, ancient and modern, and a slightly revised edition of the verses given in S, and, in their turn, based upon the *editio princeps* of Rāhula Sāṅkṛtyāyana.

But first I shall attempt a brief review of the closely-knit and partly implicit arguments since they have not been clearly articulated in the existing translations.[112]

I. *Objections*

N's initial thesis is that all things are empty. The opponent (real or imagined) takes this to mean that N *denies* everything and thus attempts to point out various contradictions in this attitude:

α) If everything, as N claims, is empty, his statements must either be empty – but then they cannot negate own-being (v. 1) – or (*atha*) non-empty (*sasvabhāva*), but this would imply an inconsisten-

112. S. Mookerjee has offered an exposition of the standpoint set forth in VV in *The Nava-Nalanda-Mahavihara Research Publication,* I, Nalanda 1957, pp. 7-41. It also contains a reprint of the Sanskrit text of Johnston and Kunst. – A new edition 'with slight but obvious improvements' of Rāhula Sāṅkṛtyāyana's *editio princeps* is given by P.L. Vaidya, *Madhyamakaśāstra of Nāgārjuna,* Darbhanga 1960, pp. 277-295. (As in the case of MK the version of VV offered by F.J. Streng, *Emptiness: A Study in Religious Meaning,* Nashville 1967, pp. 221-227, is full of mistranslations.)

cy (*vaiṣamikatvam*) and N would have to abandon his initial thesis (*viz.* that *all* things are empty) (v. 2).

β) Again N cannot support this thesis with an example, *śabdavat*, because that would imply the acceptance of something real, i.e. non-empty (v. 3).

γ) Besides N cannot refute the opponent's refutation of N's thesis, because, according to N himself, *everything*, including N's thesis can be negated (v. 4).

δ) Before N can deny things he must accept (some of) the *pramāṇas* thanks to which he obtains his *neganda*, and this implies a self-contradiction (vv. 5-6).

ε) N's standpoint is also antagonistic towards authoritative teachers of Abhidharma. Thus he is in conflict with *āgama* (vv. 7-8).

ζ) If there is an absolute lack of own-being, *what*, then, could be said to lack own-being: of course the term 'lacking own-being' must refer to something manifest. Otherwise (*atha*) own-being must be totally transcendental! (vv. 9-10).

η) Any negation implies that a real negandum is accepted. Otherwise, i.e. if an unreal negandum could be negated, negation would establish itself endlessly without words, which is absurd (vv. 11-12). – Even if the possibility of negation of an unreal negandum be granted, this, however, would have to imply the reality of the misconception of the negandum as real (vv. 13-14), for otherwise, i.e. if there is no misconception etc., there is also no negandum etc.! In other words: own-being exists (vv. 15-16).

θ) Again, N's thesis that all things are empty cannot be proved by the reason he advances, viz. that it is due to their lack of own-being, since, as N himself maintains, there is no own-being to be negated. And of course a reason for one's statements must be advanced, otherwise the opposite standpoint might as well be maintained (vv. 17-18). But, on the other hand, if N feels inclined to accept the reason (*hetu*, gtan tshigs!), viz. existence of own-being, he once again encounters a self-contradiction (v. 19).

ι) Finally there is – N's arguments have boomeranged – no period in which N can negate. – Hence own-being is a fact.[113]

113. I follow S's *svabhāvaḥ san* (in 20d) against R and T but in accordance with C (*loc.cit.*, 14a 11; 17c 7), without actually subscribing to the opinion of the editors that 'C's reading ... is unquestionably correct as giving the opponent's final conclusion.'

II. *Replies*

Before replying to the objections N restates his position: all things are empty (v. 21), because they only exist in mutual dependence (v. 22), as, for instance, a phantom (v. 23). (Note: N argues *saṃvṛtitaḥ* vv. 21-26).

α) Since his statements, like everything else, are empty, he is not at all guilty of inconsistency etc. (v. 24).

β) Again, the example alleged is not acceptable to N. Hence he commits no *dṛṣṭāntavirodha* (vv. 25-26). – A good example would be one which shows how one phantom eliminates another (v. 27). – But even in another sense (*atha vā* = *paramārthataḥ*) the sound adduced in the example does not exist. (It is, of course, empty like everything else.) (v. 28).

γ) N has no thesis (i.e. *paramārthataḥ*). So he cannot possibly contradict his own thesis (v. 29).

δ) No, N accepts no *pramāṇa* (i.e. *paramārthataḥ*) (v. 30), because *pramāṇas* cannot be established (v. 31) by other *pramāṇas* (v. 32), without *pramāṇas* (v. 33) or by themselves, partly because the example (one of N's favourites) to support this thesis is unwarranted (vv. 34-39), partly because it would imply that they were independent of their respective objects (*prameya*) (vv. 40-41). – On the other hand *pramāṇas* cannot be established by *prameyas* (vv. 42-45), nor are they mutually establishing, like a father and his son (vv. 46-50). – So *pramāṇas* cannot be established, QED (v. 51).

ε) All the concepts of Buddhism are also empty, but efficient, which would not be possible if own-being existed (vv. 52-56).

ζ) To N not only the object referred to but also the term referring to it lack own-being (v. 57). – Besides it is absurd, on the opponent's own premises, to speak of an inexistent name (v. 58). – Again, names, like everything else, are, as shown, empty (v. 59). – Of course N does not acknowledge a transcendental form of own-being (v. 60).

η) If the opponent thinks that negation must always have something real as its negandum, he obviously accepts emptiness (v. 61) or else he must give up this thesis (v. 62). – As far as N is concerned he does not negate anything (as this would presuppose the acceptance of *neganda*) (v. 63). – He merely tries to suggest or indicate (*jñāpayate*) the absence of own-being (vv. 64-67).[114]

θ) Similarly there is no own-being lacking as a logical reason to be negated in support of N's thesis (v. 68).

ι) On the contrary! Since there is never any own-being N's 'negations' are valid at any time! (v. 69).

Thus it has been shown that 'emptiness' is quite consistent not only with the demands of logic but also with the practice of Buddhism (v. 70). – A final salutation to the Buddha.[115]

114. If we are to believe Nāgārjuna negation of existence differs *toto caelo* from indication of absence. The former implies previous affirmation of existence (cf. RĀ, I, 72), the latter does not. Cf. the verse from **Lokaparīkṣā* (above, n. 27) to the same effect. – I assume that Nāgārjuna would regard *astitvapratiṣedha* as an *upādāya prajñapti* (cf. MK, XXIV, 18), i.e. as an indication, a concept borrowed (i.e. from common parlance, cf. the usual Japanese rendering *kemyō*, 'borrowed name', v. May, 'On Mādhyamika Philosophy', *JIP*, VI, p. 240), because, according to Nāgārjuna himself, there really is no *astitva* to negate. – On *prajñapti/paññatti*, cf. *JIP*, VIII, pp. 2-14.

115. Cf. CS, I, 22 (with ref.); MK, XXIV, 18; XXVII, 30. – Note that ŚS and VV have no independent initial stanzas of homage like MK (as Candrakīrti observes *Yuktiṣaṣṭikāvṛtti*, 2b) and that only MK and VV have final stanzas of homage which seem to supplement one another well.

Vigrahavyāvartanī-kārikā ||

rTSod pa bzlog pa'i tshig le'ur byas pa ||

1. sarveṣāṃ bhāvānāṃ sarvatra na vidyate svabhāvaś cet |
   tvadvacanam asvabhāvaṃ na nivartayituṃ svabhāvam alam ||

| gal te dṅos po thams cad kyi || raṅ bźin kun la yod min na |
| khyod kyi tshig kyaṅ raṅ bźin med || raṅ bźin bzlog par mi nus so |

2. atha sasvabhāvam etad vākyaṃ pūrvā hatā pratijñā te |
   vaiṣamikatvaṃ tasmin viśeṣahetuś ca vaktavyaḥ ||

| 'on te tshig de raṅ bźin bcas || khyod kyi dam bca' sṅa ma ñams |
| mi 'dra ñid de de yin na || khyad par gtan tshigs brjod par gyis |

3. mā śabdavad ity etat syāt te buddhir na caitad upapannam |
   śabdena hy atra satā bhaviṣyato vāraṇaṃ tasya ||

| de sgra ma 'byin lta bu'o źes || khyod blo sems na de mi 'thad |
| 'di la sgra ni yod pa yis || 'byuṅ bar 'gyur ba de bzlog yin |

4. pratiṣedhapratiṣedho 'py evam iti mataṃ bhavet tad asad eva |
   evaṃ tava pratijñā lakṣaṇato dūṣyate na mama ||

| 'gog pa'i 'gog pa'aṅ de lta źes || 'dod na de yaṅ bzaṅ min te |
| khyod kyi dam bca'i mtshan ñid las || de ltar skyon yod ṅed la med |

5. pratyakṣeṇa hi tāvad yady upalabhya vinivartayasi bhāvān |
   tan nāsti pratyakṣaṃ bhāvā yenopalabhyante ||

| re źig gal te mṅon sum gyis || dṅos rnams dmigs nas bzlog byed pa |
| gaṅ gis dṅos rnams dmigs 'gyur ba || mṅon sum de ni med pa yin |

6. anumānaṃ pratyuktaṃ pratyakṣeṇāgamopamāne ca |
   anumānāgamasādhyā ye 'rthā dṛṣṭāntasādhyāś ca ||

| rjes dpag luṅ daṅ ñer 'jal daṅ || rjes dpag luṅ gis bsgrub bya daṅ |
| dpes bsgrub bya ba'i don gaṅ yin || mṅon sum gyis ni lan btab po |

5a gyis : gyi NP
6d po P : pa N

7. kuśalānāṃ dharmāvasthā idaś ca manyante |
kuśalaṃ janāḥ svabhāvaṃ śeṣeṣv apy eṣa viniyogaḥ ||

| skye bo chos kyi gnas skabs mkhas || dge ba dag gi chos rnams la |
| dge ba'i raṅ bźin yin par ni || sems śiṅ lhag ma rnams la yaṅ |

8. nairyāṇikasvabhāvo dharmā nairyāṇikāś ca ye teṣām |
dharmāvasthoktānām evaṃ anairyāṇikādīnām ||

| gaṅ dag ṅes par 'byin pa'i chos || chos kyi gnas skabs gsuṅs de rnams |
| ṅes par 'byin pa'i raṅ bźin ñid || de bźin ṅes 'byin min la sogs |

9. yadi ca na bhavet svabhāvo dharmāṇāṃ niḥsvabhāva ity evam |
nāmāpi bhaven naivaṃ nāma hi nirvastukaṃ nāsti ||

| gal te chos rnams raṅ bźin med || raṅ bźin med ces bya ba yi |
| miṅ yaṅ de bźin med 'gyur te || gźi med miṅ ni med phyir ro |

10. atha vidyate svabhāvaḥ sa ca dharmāṇāṃ na vidyate tasmāt |
dharmair vinā svabhāvaḥ sa yasya tad yuktam upadeṣṭum ||

| 'on te raṅ bźin yod mod kyi || de ni chos rnams la med na |
| de phyir chos rnams spaṅs pa yi || raṅ bźin gaṅ de bstan par rigs |

11. sata eva pratiṣedho nāsti ghaṭo geha ity ayaṃ yasmāt |
dṛṣṭaḥ pratiṣedho 'yaṃ sataḥ svabhāvasya te tasmāt ||

| gaṅ phyir khyim na bum pa med || ces bya'i 'gog pa yod ñid la |
| mthoṅ ba de phyir khyod kyi yaṅ || 'gog 'di yod la raṅ bźin yin |

12. atha nāsti sa svabhāvaḥ kiṃ nu pratiṣidhyate tvayānena |
vacanenarte vacanāt pratiṣedhaḥ sidhyate hy asataḥ ||

| ci ste raṅ bźin de med na || khyod kyis tshig 'dis ci źig dgag |
| tshig med par yaṅ med pa yi || 'gog pa rab tu grub pa yin |

13. bālānām iva mithyā mṛgatṛṣṇāyāṃ yathājalagrāhaḥ |
evaṃ mithyāgrāhaḥ syāt te pratiṣedhyato hy asataḥ ||

| byis pa rnams kyis smig rgyu la || ji ltar chu źes log 'dzin ltar |
| de bźin khyod kyi yod min la || log par 'dzin pa 'gog byed na |

8d de bźin : raṅ bźin NP
9b evam (*cf.* 57) : eva S : *omm.* NP
12a ci ste : ci de NP; b kyis : kyi NP
13a kyis : kyi NP

14. nanv evaṃ saty asti grāho grāhyaṃ ca tadgrahītā ca |
pratiṣedhaḥ pratiṣedhyaṃ pratiṣeddhā ceti ṣaṭkaṃ tat ||
| de lta na ni 'dzin pa daṅ || gzuṅ daṅ de yi 'dzin po daṅ |
| 'gog daṅ dgag bya 'gog pa po || de drug yod pa ma yin nam |

15. atha naivāsti grāho naiva grāhyaṃ na ca grahītāraḥ |
pratiṣedhaḥ pratiṣedhyaṃ pratiṣeddhāro nanu na santi ||
| ci ste 'dzin pa yod min źiṅ || gzuṅ med 'dzin pa po med na |
| 'o na 'gog daṅ dgag bya daṅ || 'gog pa po yaṅ yod ma yin |

16. pratiṣedhaḥ pratiṣedhyaṃ pratiṣeddhāraś ca yady uta na santi |
siddhā hi sarvabhāvās teṣām eva svabhāvaś ca ||
| gal te 'gog daṅ dgag bya daṅ || 'gog pa po yaṅ yod min na |
| dṅos po kun daṅ de rnams kyi || raṅ bźin ñid kyaṅ grub pa yin |

17. hetoś ca te na siddhir naiḥsvābhāvyāt kuto hi te hetuḥ |
nirhetukasya siddhir na copapannāsya te 'rthasya ||
| khyed la gtan tshigs mi 'grub ste || raṅ bźin med phyir khyod kyi rtags |
| ga la yod de khyod don de || gtan tshigs med phyir 'grub mi 'thad |

18. yadi cāhetoḥ siddhiḥ svabhāvavinivartanasya te bhavati |
svābhāvyasyāstitvaṃ mamāpi nirhetukaṃ siddham ||
| khyod la gtan tshigs med par yaṅ || raṅ bźin bzlog pa grub yin na |
| ṅa la'aṅ gtan tshigs med par ni || raṅ bźin yod pa ñid du 'grub |

19. atha hetor astitvaṃ bhāvāsvābhāvyam ity anupapannam |
lokeṣu niḥsvabhāvo na hi kaś cana vidyate bhāvaḥ |
| ci ste gtan tshigs yod na dṅos || raṅ bźin med ces bya mi 'thad |
| srid na raṅ bźin med pa yi || dṅos 'ga' yod pa ma yin no |

20. pūrvaṃ cet pratiṣedhaḥ paścāt pratiṣedhyam ity anupapannam |
paścāc cānupapanno yugapac ca yataḥ svabhāvaḥ san ||
| gaṅ las raṅ bźin yod min pa'i || 'gog pa gal te sṅa 'gyur źiṅ |
| dgag bya 'phyi źes 'thad min la || phyis daṅ cig car yaṅ mi 'thad |

20d svabhāvaḥ san CS : *svabhāvo 'san NP

21. hetupratyayasāmagryāṃ ca pṛthak cāpi madvaco na yadi |
nanu śūnyatvaṃ siddhaṃ bhāvānām asvabhāvatvāt ||

| ṅa yi tshig ni rgyu rkyen daṅ || tshogs daṅ so so la yaṅ med |
| 'o na dṅos rnams stoṅ grub ste || raṅ bźin med pa ñid phyir ro |

22. yaś ca pratītyabhāvo bhāvānāṃ śūnyateti sā proktā |
yaś pratītyabhāvo bhavati hi tasyāsvabhāvatvam ||

| rten ṇas 'byuṅ ba'i dṅos rnams gaṅ || de ni stoṅ ñid ces brjod de |
| gaṅ źig brten nas 'byuṅ ba de || raṅ bźin med pa ñid yin no |

23. nirmitako nirmitakaṃ māyāpuruṣaḥ svamāyayā sṛṣṭam |
pratiṣedhayeta yadvat pratiṣedho 'yaṃ tathaiva syāt ||

| sprul pa yis ni sprul pa daṅ || sgyu ma yi ni skyes bu yis |
| sgyu mas phyuṅ la 'gog byed ltar || 'gog pa 'di yaṅ de bźin 'gyur |

24. na svābhāvikam etad vākyaṃ tasmān na vādahānir me |
nāsti ca vaiṣamikatvaṃ viśeṣahetuś ca na nigadyaḥ ||

| ṅa yi tshig 'di raṅ bźin med || de phyir ṅa phyogs ma ñams la |
| mi 'dra ñid kyaṅ med pas na || gtan tshigs khyad par brjod mi bya |

25. mā śabdavad iti nāyaṃ dṛṣṭānto yas tvayā samārabdhaḥ |
śabdena hi tac chabdasya vāraṇaṃ naivam etac ca ||

| sgra mi 'byin bya bźin źe na || khyod kyis gaṅ brtsams dpe 'di min |
| de ni sgra yis sgra bzlog la || 'dir ni de lta ma yin no |

26. naiḥsvābhāvyānāṃ cen naiḥsvābhāvyena vāraṇaṃ yadi hi |
naiḥsvābhāvyanivṛttau svābhāvyaṃ hi prasiddhaṃ syāt ||

| gal te raṅ bźin med ñid kyis || ci ste raṅ bźin med pa bzlog |
| raṅ bźin med pa ñid log na || raṅ bźin ñid du rab grub 'gyur |

27. atha vā nirmitakāyāṃ yathā striyāṃ strīyam ity asadgrāham |
nirmitakaḥ pratihanyāt kasya cid evaṃ bhaved etat ||

| yaṅ na kha cig sprul pa yi || bud med la ni bud med sñam |
| log 'dzin 'byuṅ la sprul pa yis || 'gog byed de ni de lta yin |

23b ma yi ... bu yis : ma yis ... bu yi NP
24a 'di raṅ bźin (*et* me tad *pro* etad S?) : ni de bźin NP
25c hi tat *melius quam* tac ca S; d etac ca : evaitat S
27b bud med la N : bu med la P; c yis : yi NP

28. atha vā sādhyasamo 'yaṃ hetur na hi vidyate dhvaneḥ sattā |
saṃvyavahāraṃ ca vayaṃ nānabhyupagamya kathayāmaḥ ||

| yaṅ na rtags 'di bsgrub bya daṅ || mtshuṅs te gaṅ phyir sgra yod min |
| tha sñad khas ni ma blaṅs par || ṅed cag 'chad par mi byed do |

29. yadi kā cana pratijñā syān me tata eṣa me bhaved doṣaḥ |
nāsti ca mama pratijñā tasmān naivāsti me doṣaḥ ||

| gal te ṅas dam bca' 'ga' yod || des na ṅa la skyon de yod |
| ṅa la dam bca' med pas na || ṅa la skyon med kho na yin |

30. yadi kiṃ cid upalabheyaṃ pravartayeyaṃ nivartayeyaṃ vā |
pratyakṣādibhir arthais tadabhāvān me 'nupālambhaḥ ||

| gal te mṅon sum la sogs pa'i || don gyis 'ga' źig dmigs na ni |
| bsgrub pa'am bzlog par bya na de || med phyir ṅa la klan ka med |

31. yadi ca pramāṇatas te teṣāṃ teṣāṃ prasiddhir arthānām |
teṣāṃ punaḥ prasiddhiṃ brūhi kathaṃ te pramāṇānām ||

| gal te khyod kyi don de rnams || tshad ma ñid kyis rab bsgrub na |
| khyod kyi tshad ma de rnams kyaṅ || ji ltar rab tu 'grub pa smros |

32. anyair yadi pramāṇaiḥ pramāṇasiddhir bhavet tad anavasthā |
nādeḥ siddhis tatrāsti naiva madhyasya nāntasya ||

| gal te tshad ma gźan rnams kyis || grub bo sñam na thug pa med |
| de yaṅ daṅ po 'grub min la || bar ma yin źiṅ tha ma'aṅ min |

33. teṣām atha pramāṇair vinā prasiddhir vihīyate vādaḥ |
vaiṣamikatvaṃ tasmin viśeṣahetuś ca vaktavyaḥ ||

| 'on te tshad ma med par yaṅ || de rnams sgrub na smra ba ñams |
| mi 'dra ñid de de yi na || gtan tshigs khyad par smra bar gyis |

34. viṣamopanyāso 'yaṃ na hy ātmānaṃ prakāśayaty agniḥ |
na hi tasyānupalabdhir dṛṣṭā tamasīva kumbhasya ||

| smras pa de ni mi mthun te || mun khuṅ naṅ gi bum pa bźin |
| de la mi dmigs ma mthoṅ bas || me ni raṅ ñid gsal byed min |

28a yaṅ na : gaṅ na NP
31b kyis : kyi NP
34c ma mthoṅ bas V : mthoṅ bas na NP

35. yadi ca svātmānam ayaṃ tvadvacanena prakāśayaty agniḥ |
param iva nanv ātmānaṃ svaṃ paridhakṣyaty api hutāśaḥ ||

| gal te khyod kyi tshig gis ni || me yis raṅ bdag gsal byed na |
| 'o na me yis gźan bźin du || raṅ ñid sreg pa'aṅ byed par 'gyur |

36. yadi ca svaparātmānau tvadvacanena prakāśayaty agniḥ ||
pracchādayiṣyati tamaḥ svaparātmānau hutāśa iva ||

| gal te khyod kyi tshig gis ni || me yis raṅ gźan gsal byed na |
| me bźin du ni mun pa yaṅ || raṅ gźan bdag ñid sgrib par 'gyur |

37. nāsti tamaś ca jvalane yatra ca tiṣṭhati parātmani jvalanaḥ |
kurute kathaṃ prakāśaṃ sa hi prakāśo 'ndhakāravadhaḥ ||

| 'bar byed daṅ ni gaṅ gźan na || me 'dug pa na mun pa med |
| gsal byed de ni mun sel na || ji ltar gsal bar byed pa yin |

38. utpadyamāna eva prakāśayaty agnir ity asadvādaḥ |
utpadyamāna eva prāpnoti tamo na hi hutāśaḥ ||

| me 'byuṅ ñid na gsal byed pa || yaṅ dag min par smra ba ste |
| me 'byuṅ ñid na mun pa daṅ || phrad pa med pa kho na yin |

39. aprāpto 'pi jvalano yadi vā punar andhakāram upahanyāt |
sarveṣu lokadhātuṣu tamo 'yam iha saṃsthito hanyāt |

| yaṅ na me daṅ ma phrad kyaṅ || mun pa sel bar byed na ni |
| 'di na yod pa gaṅ yin pas || 'jig rten kun gyi mun sel 'gyur |

40. yadi svataś ca pramāṇasiddhir anapekṣya tava prameyāṇi |
bhavati pramāṇasiddhir na parāpekṣā svataḥsiddhiḥ ||

| gal te raṅ las tshad ma grub || gźal bya rnams la ma bltos par |
| khyod kyi tshad ma grub 'gyur 'di || raṅ grub gźan la bltos ma yin |

35c svaṃ paridhakṣyaty : saṃparidhakṣyaty S (p. 3)
36a kyi : kyis NP
38a me N : mi P
39d hanyāt : hānyat S
40b la : las NP; d la : las NP

41. anapekṣya hi prameyān arthān yadi te pramāṇasiddhir iti |
na bhavanti kasya cid evam imāni tāni pramāṇāni ||

| gal te gźal bya'i don rnams la || ma bltos khyod kyi tshad ma grub |
| de ltar tshad ma 'di rnams ni || gaṅ gi'aṅ yin par mi 'gyur ro |

42. atha matam apekṣya siddhis teṣām ity atra bhavati ko doṣaḥ |
siddhasya sādhanaṃ syān nāsiddho 'pekṣate hy anyat ||

| 'on te bltos nas de rnams 'grub || 'dod na de la skyon cir 'gyur |
| ma grub gźan la mi bltos pas || grub pa sgrub par byed pa yin |

43. sidhyanti hi prameyāṇy apekṣya yadi sarvathā pramāṇāni |
bhavati prameyasiddhir nāpekṣyaiva pramāṇāni ||

| gal te yoṅs ye gźal bya la || bltos nas tshad ma grub yin na |
| tshad ma rnams la ma bltos par || gźal byar bya ba 'grub par 'gyur |

44. yadi ca prameyasiddhir nāpekṣyaiva bhavati pramāṇāni |
kiṃ te pramāṇasiddhyā tāni yadarthaṃ prasiddhaṃ tat ||

| gal te tshad ma rnams la ni || ma bltos par yaṅ gźal bya 'grub |
| gaṅ phyir de dag de 'grub na || khyod kyi tshad ma grub pas ci |

45. atha tu pramāṇasiddhir bhavaty apekṣyaiva te prameyāṇi |
vyatyaya evaṃ sati te dhruvaṃ pramāṇaprameyāṇām ||

| ci ste khyod kyi tshad ma rnams || gźal bya rnams la bltos nas 'grub |
| de ltar khyod kyi tshad ma daṅ || gźal bya ṅes par ldog par 'gyur |

46. atha te pramāṇasiddhyā prameyasiddhiḥ prameyasiddhyā ca |
bhavati pramāṇasiddhir nāsty ubhayasyāpi te siddhiḥ ||

| 'on te khyod kyi tshad grub pas || gźal bar bya ba 'grub 'gyur la |
| gźal bya grub pas tshad sgrub na || khyod kyi gñis ka'aṅ 'grub mi 'gyur |

43a la : las NP
44d tāni : tani S
46bc gźal P : bźal N; d kyi V : kyis NP

47. sidhyanti hi pramāṇair yadi prameyāṇi tāni tair eva |
sādhyāni ca prameyais tāni kathaṃ sādhayiṣyanti ||

| gal te tshad ma gźal bya 'grub || gźal bya de dag rnams kyis kyaṅ |
| de dag bsgrub par bya yin na || de dag ji ltar sgrub par 'gyur |

48. sidhyanti ca prameyair yadi pramāṇāni tāni tair eva |
sādhyāni ca pramāṇais tāni kathaṃ sādhayiṣyanti ||

| gal te gźal byas tshad ma 'grub || tshad ma de rnams sgrub kyis kyaṅ |
| de dag sgrub par bya yin na || de dag ji ltar sgrub par 'gyur |

49. pitrā yady utpādyaḥ putro yadi tena caiva putreṇa |
utpādyaḥ sa yadi pitā vada tatrotpadayati kaḥ kam ||

| gal te pha yis bu bskyed bya || gal te bu de ñid kyis kyaṅ |
| ci ste pha de bskyed bya na || des na gaṅ gis gaṅ bskyed smros |

50. kaś ca pitā kaḥ putras tatra tvaṃ brūhi tāv ubhāv api ca |
pitṛputralakṣaṇadharau yato bhavati no 'tra saṃdehaḥ ||

| de dag gñis ka'aṅ pha daṅ bu'i || mtshan ñid 'dzin pas de'i phyir |
| de la kho bo the tshom 'gyur || de la pha gaṅ bu gaṅ smros ||

51. naiva svataḥ prasiddhir na parasparataḥ parapramāṇair vā |
na bhavati na ca prameyair na cāpy akasmāt pramāṇānām ||

| tshad ma rnams kyi raṅ ñid kyis || 'grub min phan tshun gyis min pa'am |
| tshad ma gźan gyis ma yin la || gźal byas ma yin rgyu med min |

52. kuśalānāṃ dharmāṇāṃ dharmāvasthāvido bruvīran yat |
kuśalaṃ svabhāvam evaṃ pravibhāgenābhidheyaḥ syāt ||

| chos kyi gnas skabs rab mkhas pa || dge ba yi ni chos rnams kyi |
| dge ba'i raṅ bźin smra ba gaṅ || de ltar rab phye brjod bya yin |

49c ci ste V : ci de NP
50 d la : las NP
52b yi ... kyi : yis ... kyis NP; c smra ba V : chos rnams (*ante* raṅ bźin) NP
53c lta NP *pro* dṅos?

53. yadi ca pratītya kuśalaḥ svabhāva utpadyate sa kuśalānām |
dharmāṇāṃ parabhāvaḥ svabhāva evaṃ kathaṃ bhavati ||
| gal te dge ba'i chos rnams kyi || raṅ bźin 'ga' źig brten skye ba |
| de ni gźan lta de lta na || raṅ gi ṅo bor ji ltar 'gyur |

54. atha na pratītya kiṃ cit svabhāva utpadyate sa kuśalānām |
dharmāṇām evaṃ syād vāso na brahmacaryasya ||
| 'on te dge ba'i chos rnams kyi || raṅ gi ṅo bo de 'ga' la'aṅ |
| ma brten skye na de lta na'aṅ || tshaṅs par spyod pa gnas mi 'gyur |

55. nādharmo dharmo vā saṃvyavahārāś ca laukikā na syuḥ |
nityāś ca sasvabhāvāḥ syur nityatvād ahetumataḥ ||
| rgyu mi ldan pa rtag pa'i phyir || raṅ bźin bcas pa rtag par 'gyur |
| chos daṅ chos ma yin med ciṅ || 'jig rten pa yi tha sñad med |

56. evam akuśaleṣv avyākṛteṣu nairyāṇikādiṣu ca doṣaḥ |
tasmāt sarvaṃ saṃskṛtam asaṃskṛtaṃ te bhavaty eva ||
| mi dge ba daṅ luṅ ma bstan || ṅes 'byin sogs la'aṅ skyon de bźin |
| de bas khyod kyi 'dus byas kun || 'dus ma byas pa ñid du 'gyur |

57. yaḥ sadbhūtaṃ nāmātra brūyāt sasvabhāva ity evam |
bhavatā prativaktavyo nāma brūmaś ca na vayaṃ sat ||
| gaṅ źig raṅ bźin bcas pa źes || miṅ 'dir yod par smra ba la |
| de ltar khyod kyis lan btab kyis || ṅa yis miṅ yod mi smra'o |

58. nāmāsad iti ca yad idaṃ tat kiṃ nu sato bhavaty utāpy asataḥ |
yadi hi sato yady asato dvidhāpi te hīyate vādaḥ ||
| miṅ med ces bya gaṅ yin 'di || ci de yod pa'am med pa yin |
| gal te yod dam med kyaṅ ruṅ || khyod kyis smras pa'aṅ gñis ka'aṅ ñams |

59. sarveṣāṃ bhāvānāṃ śūnyatvaṃ copapāditaṃ pūrvam |
sa upālambhas tasmād bhavaty ayaṃ cāpratijñāyāḥ ||
| dṅos po dag ni thams cad kyi || stoṅ pa ñid ni sṅar bstan pas |
| de phyir dam bcas med par yaṅ || klan ka gaṅ yin de tshol byed |

54b ṅo bo N : ṅo 'o P
55b raṅ bźin bcas pa rtag V : chos rnams thams cad brtag NP
57b 'dir : ni NP; d sat : tat S; yis : yi NP

60. atha vidyate svabhāvaḥ sa ca dharmāṇāṃ na vidyata itīdam I
āśaṅkitaṃ yad uktaṃ bhavaty anāśaṅkitaṃ tac ca II
I 'on te raṅ bźin źig yod la II de ni chos la med do źes I
I dogs 'di rigs pa ma yin mod II dogs pa de ni khyod kyis byas I

61. sata eva pratiṣedho yadi śūnyatvaṃ nanu prasiddham idam I
pratiṣedhayate hi bhavān bhāvānāṃ niḥsvabhāvatvam II
I gal te yod ñid 'gog yin na II 'o na stoṅ ñid rab 'grub ste I
I dṅos rnams raṅ bźin med ñid la II khyod ni 'gog par byed pas so I

62. pratiṣedhayase 'tha tvaṃ śūnyatvaṃ tac ca nāsti śūnyatvam I
pratiṣedhaḥ sata iti te nanv eṣa vihīyate vādaḥ II
I stoṅ ñid gaṅ la khyod 'gog pa'i II stoṅ ñid de yaṅ med yin na I
I 'o na yod pa 'gog yin źes II smras pa de ñams ma yin nam I

63. pratiṣedhayāmi nāhaṃ kiṃ cit pratiṣedhyam asti na ca kiṃ cit I
tasmāt pratiṣedhayasīty adhilaya eṣa tvayā kriyate II
I dgag bya ci yaṅ med pas na II ṅa ni ci yaṅ mi 'gog go I
I de phyir 'gog pa byed do źes II yaṅ dag min te khyod kyis smras I

64. yac cāharte vacanād asataḥ pratiṣedhavacanasiddhir iti I
atra jñāpayate vāg asad iti tan na pratinihanti II
I tshig med par yaṅ med pa yi II 'gog tshig mi 'grub min źe na I
I de la tshig ni med ces par II go bar byed kyi skyes sel min I

65. mṛgatṛṣṇādṛṣṭānte yaḥ punar uktas tvayā mahāṃś carcaḥ I
tatrāpi nirṇayaṃ śṛṇu yathā sa dṛṣṭānta upapannaḥ II
I smig rgyu dpe la khyod kyis kyaṅ II rtsod pa chen po smras pa gaṅ I
I der yaṅ ci nas dpe de 'thad II gtan la dbab pa mñam par gyis I

66. sa yadi svabhāvataḥ syād grāho na syāt pratītya saṃbhūtaḥ I
yaś ca pratītya bhavati grāho nanu śūnyatā saiva II
I gal te 'dzin de raṅ bźin yod II rten nas 'byuṅ bar mi 'gyur ro I
I 'dzin pa gaṅ źig brten 'byuṅ ba II de ñid stoṅ ñid ma yin nam I

61a 'gog P : dgog N
62c źes P : źe N
63c do P : de N
66b rten P : brten N

67. yadi ca svabhāvataḥ syād grāhaḥ kas taṃ nivartayed grāham |
śeṣeṣv apy eṣa vidhis tasmād eṣo 'nupālambhaḥ ||

| gal te 'dzin pa raṅ bźin yod || 'dzin pa de la su yis bzlog |
| lhag ma rnams la'aṅ tshul de bźin || de phyir klan ka de med do |

68. etena hetvabhāvaḥ pratyuktaḥ pūrvam eva sa samatvāt |
mṛgatṛṣṇādṛṣṭāntavyāvṛttividhau ya uktaḥ prāk ||

| smig rgyu'i dpes bzlog bsgrub pa'i tshe || sṅar smras gaṅ yin de daṅ ni |
| sṅa mas gtan tshigs med pa yi || lan btab gyur te mtshuṅs phyir ro |

69. yas traikālye hetuḥ pratyuktaḥ pūrvam eva sa samatvāt |
traikālyapratihetuś ca śūnyatāvādināṃ prāptaḥ ||

| dus gsum gtan tshigs gaṅ yin sṅar || lan btab ñid de mtshuṅs phyir ro |
| dus gsum med kyi gtan tshigs ni || stoṅ ñid smra ba rnams la ruṅ |

70. prabhavati ca śūnyateyaṃ yasya prabhavanti tasya sarvārthāḥ |
prabhavati na tasya kiṃ cin na prabhavati śūnyatā yasya ||

| gaṅ la stoṅ pa ñid srid pa || de la don rnams thams cad srid |
| gaṅ la stoṅ ñid mi srid pa || de la ci yaṅ mi srid do |

yaḥ śūnyatāṃ pratītyasamutpādaṃ madhyamāṃ pratipadaṃ ca |
ekārthāṃ nijagāda praṇamāmi tam apratimabuddham ||

| gaṅ źig stoṅ daṅ rten 'byuṅ dag || dbu ma'i lam du don gcig par |
| gsuṅ mchog mtshuṅs pa med pa yi || saṅs rgyas de la phyag 'tshal lo |

68b sṅar smras gaṅ yin N : smras gaṅ yin pa P
69a sṅar || : sṅar N : pa P; c med kyi P : ched kyi N

IV. Vaidalyaprakaraṇa (VP)

This work, which is in 73 *sūtras* with a *svavṛtti*, is extant only in Tibetan.[116] References to this work are found in Bhavya[117] and Candrakīrti,[118] but I have never noticed any quotation from VP. Judging solely from the text itself, the style and tenets would indicate the same author as for VV, the work where the parallels are closest out of all those ascribed to Nāgārjuna. VP has not received the attention its historical importance and its very enjoyable style entitle it to.[119]

The introductory stanza indicates the scope of VP: 'In order to put an end to the arrogance of those logicians (*tārkika*) who out of conceit of their knowledge are keen to debate, I shall grind them to little pieces.'[120]

Who these sophists are and in what their conceit consists is made clear when Nāgārjuna begins by quoting the following well-known passage, *Nyāya-sūtra* (NS) I.1.1.: *'pramāṇa-prameya-saṃśaya-prayojana-dṛṣṭānta-siddhānta-avayava-tarka-nirṇaya-vāda-jalpa-vitaṇḍā-hetvābhāsa-cchala-jāti-nigrahasthānānām ...'*

116. I have consulted TP, No. 5226 (*sūtras*) and TP, No. 5230 (the *prakaraṇa* proper) both of which were edited (also collating the Narthang and Derge editions) by Y. Kajiyama, *Miscellanea Indologica Kiotensia*, VI-VII, pp. 129-155, who also discussed VP and translated it into Japanese, v. Nakamura (1977), p. 81, n. 24.
117. Cf. n. 88.
118. Cf. n. 89.
119. It is without compare the most lively and amusing of all texts ascribed to Nāgārjuna, full of sophistries as it is. – Historically speaking its quotations from NS are important, cf. also above, n. 110. Some useful remarks in a review by P. M. Williams, *JIP*, VI, pp. 287-290. One may here note that an English translation is forthcoming in *Indiske Studier.*
120. *rtog ge śes pa'i ṅa rgyal gyis* || *gaṅ źig rtsod par mṅon 'dod pa* || *de yi ṅa rgyal spaṅ ba'i phyir* || *źib mo rnam 'thag bśad par bya* ||. Similarly the initial lines of **Upāyahṛdaya*, v. n. 44 above.

In the following 73 sūtras and their commentary Nāgārjuna proposes to split and crush these 16 basic concepts (*padārtha*) one by one:[121]

α) 1. & 2. *padārtha: pramāṇa-prameya* (ss. *1-19*)

N's initial *pratijñā* is that *pramāṇa* and *prameya* are inseparably joined (*miśra*) (s. 1) and therefore they cannot be established (*siddha*) per se (*svataḥ*) (s. 2). – The opponent [= O] allows that they are correlates, but thinks all the same that they can establish each other. – Therefore N must refute the three ways in which this could, hypothetically, come about: neither *sat, asat,* nor *sadasat* can enter into relation. This is of general application, including, of course, *pramāṇa-prameya* (s. 3). – If O insists that everything is established by *pramāṇas* then this must either include the *pramāṇas* as well – but this leads to *anavasthā* – or exclude the *pramāṇas* – but this leads to *pratijñāhāni* (s. 4) [cf. VV v. 2]. – But O persists in maintaining that *pramāṇas* are self-established because they 'illuminate' themselves, *pradīpavat* (s. 5) [cf. NS II.1.19]. N rejoins that the *dṛṣṭānta* is unhappy since a lamp cannot possibly illuminate anything, itself or anything else, whether it is in contact (*prāpta*) with its object or not (ss. 6-10).[122] Besides *pramāṇa-prameya* are *traikālyāsiddha* (s. 11).[123] O's reply, that so is N's *pratiṣedha* (s. 12) [= NS II. 1.12] makes N triumph. If O thinks that N then instead maintains his *pratiṣedha* and O accepts this, he *eo ipso* accepts that *pramāṇa-prameya* are *pratiṣedhya* ('deserve to be negated'); then, in a flash, all disputes (*vivāda*) are settled (s. 14)! [cf. ss. 1-2]. – But actually N accepts neither a *pratiṣedha* nor a *pratiṣedhya* etc., he merely tries to indicate the absence of own-being (s. 15) [cf. VV v. 64]. – O still insists that the *pramāṇas* exist because they

121. Following is an analysis and paraphrase intended to expose the line of arguments – or sophisms! The notes are confined to a minimum. The number of sūtras follows Kajiyama.

122. The Tibetan rendering of s. 8 (... *'jig rten spyod pa po* ...) must be wrong, cf. NS, I, 1, 25: *laukikaparīkṣakānām* ..., so read: *'jig rten daṅ dpyod pa po* ...

123. Cf. NS, II, 1, 8-15; *Laṅkāvatārasūtra,* X, 779; the papers of Bhattacharya and Oberhammer ref. to above, n. 110. It certainly seems that Nāgārjuna here (s. 12) and VV, 20 is aware of the boomerang in NS, II, 1, 12, *pace* Oberhammer (*op.cit.,* p. 70) who concludes that: 'Es kann daher mit Sicherheit gefolgt werden, dass die *traikālyasiddhi*-Diskussion von NS II, 1, 8-15 Nāgārjuna nicht vorgelegen hat.' Possibly Nāgārjuna only knows an earlier recension of NS than the *textus receptus*.

provide correct understanding (s. 16), and when N asks how one can be sure that *prameya* exists independently of *buddhi* [i.e. how one can avoid *esse est percipi*], O claims that the *ghaṭabuddhi* is *pramāṇa* whereas the jar as such (*ghaṭa eva*) is *prameya* (s. 17). But, replies N, O recognises that *buddhi* arises *indriya-artha-saṃnikarṣāt* [= NS I.1.11 & I.1.15], and since the *ghaṭa* must be a specific *pratyaya* beforehand, *buddhi* cannot be *pramāṇa,* and the *ghaṭa* is not *prameya* (s. 18). Besides, O himself [= NS I.1.9, but cf. *ibidem,* II.1.16] categorises *buddhi* as *pramāṇa,* not as *prameya* (s. 19).

β) 3. & 4. *padārtha: saṃśaya* & *prayojana* (ss. *20-23*)

Could N's treatment of *pramāṇa-prameya* not give rise to some doubt (*saṃśaya*)? No, there is nothing to be in doubt about, neither that which is comprehended, which is a fact (*sat*), nor that which is not comprehended, which is null and void (*asat*) (s. 20). – Even if O finds lack of decisive characteristics (*viśeṣa*) [in dubitandum] to be the cause of doubt (s. 21) [cf. NS I.1.23], the same argument also applies here (s. 22). – But may one not be uncertain about a *prayojana*? No, for O himself maintains that: *'yam artham adhikṛtya pravartate tat prayojanam'* [= NS I.1.24] and the object can only be *sat* or *asat,* hence not an object of doubt.

γ) 5. *padārtha: dṛṣṭānta* (ss. *24-30*)

If O objects that there are examples of things that serve a purpose (*prayojana*), like sand, N's refutation remains the same as before (ss. *24-25*). – *Besides there is no* (*dṛṣṭa-*)*anta* because there is no *ādi* or *madhyama* (s. 26). – Still O [cf. NS I.1.25] maintains the possibility of a *dṛṣṭānta* that may be either *sādharmya* or *vaidharmya,* but N rejoins that neither that which is *sādharmya* to what it is supposed to exemplify (e.g. fire of fire) nor that which is *vaidharmya* – whether it be totally or only to some extent – can serve as *dṛṣṭānta* (ss. 27-30).

δ) 6. *padārtha: siddhānta* (s. *31*)

When N claims that everything is *asiddha* he must himself accept *siddha-anta.* No, without a *siddha-ādi* how can he accept a *siddha-anta?* (s. 31).

ε) 7. *padārtha: avayava* (s. *32-48*)

First (ss. 32-39) the five members of the syllogism are refuted in general: Since they are not subject to a whole (*avayavī*) (s. 32), or parts of an independent group (*samūha*) (s. 33) and since they would be identical if they were one with the *avayavī* – for if they were different there would be six – (s. 34), and also because they are *traikālyāsiddha* (s. 35) [cf. NS II. 1.8], therefore the *avayava* are not established. – But O finds that the five *avayava* can operate together, like cotton threads. A single accomplishes nothing, but many combined into one can tether an elephant (s. 36). No, the individual threads are *sādhyasama.* What cannot be achieved by a single *vandhyā* or *jātyandha* cannot be achieved by any number of them (s. 37) [cf. *Mahābhāṣya*, I, p. 31], and even if it be granted that they might do so by working simultaneously, the five *avayava,* however, never occur simultaneously as a single *avayavī* (s. 38). – Besides, before the *avayava* can prove anything they themselves must be proved, viz. by other *avayava* and so on *ad infinitum (anavasthā)* (s. 39).

Next (ss. 40-48) the five *avayava* are refuted one by one: A *pratijñā* is impossible since it is neither identical with nor different from its *hetu* (s. 40). – A *hetu* is impossible since either it must have another *hetu* and so forth *ad infinitum,* or else a *hetu* is present without a *hetu.* But that is absurd and would lead to total confusion (s. 41) [cf. VV vv. 17-18]. So since there is no *pratijñā, hetu* nor *dṛṣṭānta* then the other two *avayava,* viz. *upanayana* and *nigamana,* lapse (s. 42). – Even if a *pratijñā* could be established without a *hetu,* that would mean that the other three members were established without a *hetu* (s. 43). Again, if proof were due to a *hetu,* then a *dṛṣṭānta* would be superfluous (s. 44), and if not, then the *hetu* would be otiose, but in that case *dṛṣṭānta* etc. would be superfluous over again (s. 45). – O's specific *pratijñā,* that *ātman* is *nitya, amūrtatvād ākāśavat,* is refuted (s. 46). – Further, since *pratijñā* and *hetu* can only be denominated successively, a *pratijñā* cannot be a *pratijñā* to its (coexisting) *hetu,* and vice versa (s. 47). – But when N denies all *avayava* it would seem that he implicitly accepts a *pratijñā,* and, *eo ipso,* the four remaining *avayava*? No, since there is no *pratijñā,* for *prati* and *jñā* must be enunciated separately one after the other (s. 48).

ζ) 8. *padārtha: tarka* (s. *49*)

This cannot be sanctioned either as neither the *artha* that is *jñāta* nor the *artha* that is *ajñāta* can be an object of it (s. 49).

η) 9. *padārtha: nirṇaya* (s. *50*)

This is also impossible since *dravya, sat, eka* etc., which would serve to fix something definitely, are neither identical nor different, nor both (s. 50).

θ) 10. *padārtha: vāda* (ss. *51-55*)

N must accept the concept of debate (*vāda*)! No, because *abhidhāna* and *abhidheya* ('the issue under debate') cannot be established as they are neither *eka* nor *aneka* (s. 51). Nor can they alternatively be connected by a definite *nāma-artha-saṃketa* (which would, incidentally – *devānāṃpriya!* – imply that the *artha* of O's 16 *padārthas* [cf. NS I.1.1] should not be taken more seriously than the significance of names such as Devadatta or Indragupta), because the very fact that any word can function as a synonym or homonym of well-nigh anything[124] excludes any definite relationship (*ṅes pa, niyama*) between *nāma* and *artha* (ss. 52-54). Finally they cannot belong to one another. Thus the preconditions of *vāda* are absent (s. *55*).

ι) 11. & 12. *padārtha: jalpa* & *vitaṇḍā* (*s. 56*)

These two concepts are to be refuted in the same manner as *vāda* (s. 56).

κ) 13. *padārtha: hetvābhāsa* (ss. *57-66*)

Everything that N says is *hetvābhāsa* and incapable of refuting anything! No, answers N, neither by being *sādharmya* nor by being *vaidharmya* with the actual *hetu*, can *hetvābhāsa* come into question (s. 57). – If a *hetvābhāsa* is qualified as a *hetu* that is *savyabhicāra* [cf. NS I.2.4] this is wrong, since neither the *hetu* which is *sādhyasādhaka* nor the one which is not, can be classified as *savyabhicāra* (s. 58). – O insists that a *hetu* may be *savyabhicāra* [i.e. in the sense of *anaikāntika;* cf. NS I.2.5]: Thus *amūrtatva* can serve as *hetu*, now to *ākāśa*, now to *karma* (s. 59). No, these are two different types of *amūrtatva*, as it may prove the *nityatva* of one thing, and the *anityatva* of another. Consequently the *hetu* adduced during *dūṣaṇa* and *sādhana* is not in

124. The verse on homonyms also occurs *Abhidharmakośabhāṣya* (ed. P. Pradhan), p. 81 (with v. l. *upadhārayet* in d); *Nyāyabhūṣaṇa* (ed. S. Yogīndrānanda), p. 341: *vāgdigbhūraśmivajreṣu paśvakṣisvargavāriṣu* | *navasv arthesu medhāvī gośabdam avadhārayet* ||.

itself *savyabhicāra* (s. 60). Again, there can be no *hetu* which is *savyabhicāra* in relation to the *sādhya,* for as things occur instantaneously, *sādhana* and *dūṣaṇa* are not concurrent with *sādhya* and *dūṣya* (s. 61). – O now suggests that every *hetu* discarded by N is, if not *savyabhicāra,* contradictory (*viruddha*) at least (s. 62) [cf. NS I.2.4]. No, for how can two utterances be conflicting since it is obvious that when the first statement is being formulated, the second has not yet occurred. They can only be conflicting if they are simultaneous. And yet simultaneous statements cannot be conflicting either, since it is impossible for proponent and antagonist to put forward charge and rebuttal at the same time (s. 63). – O then proposes that a *hetu* which is *kālātīta* [cf. NS I.2.4 & I.2.29] does in fact constitute a *hetvābhāsa;* N disagrees, for a previous basis for something present cannot, by reason of being past, be a basis for anything present which does not occur yet (s. 64). One had better not play fast and loose with past, present and future for all normal intercourse will then be suspended (s. 65)! Besides, since what is previous is past and gone, a *hetu* localised there cannot form the basis for anything in the present time (s. 66).

λ) 14. *padārtha: chala* (s. 67)

All N's statements are simply conscious distortions of the meaning of O's words! (*vacanavighāta;* [cf. NS I.2.10]). Oh no, then any attempt at critical aloofness or disagreement would be distortion (s. 67).

μ) 15. *padārtha: jāti* (s. 68)

The concept of *jāti* is impossible. Without *jāta, ajāta* and *jāyamāna, jāti* is precluded (s. 68).[125]

ν) 16. *padārtha: nigrahasthāna* (ss 69-71)

N is now blamed for having incriminated himself on account of repetition (*punarvacana;* [cf. NS V.2.14 & V.2.15]). But N does not plead guilty, as what is supposed to have been repeated is neither identical with nor different from what it repeats (s. 69). In any case a

125. Same argument as **Dvādaśadvāraka,* 26. – The fact that Nāgārjuna's sophistic reply follows immediately after *chala* lends it a particular finesse (which is, of course, quite lost in its Tibetan garb).

nigrahasthāna does not exist, neither when the charge has been made nor when it has not yet been made (s. 70). As for the third possibility, one is not convicted on any count as long as one is still being prosecuted, any more than one is trussed before the final knot is tied (s. 71).

Now that the 16 *padārthas* have been made the objects of negation (*pratiṣedhya*), *pratiṣedha* is also rendered impossible (s. 72). Hence there is no *abhidhāna* and no *abhidheya* and therefore one cannot distinguish between *nirvāṇa* and *apavarga* (s. 73).[126]

Herewith Nāgārjuna has, as he foretold at the outset, crushed the arrogance of the heretics. It proceeded according to the principles that are known from Nāgārjuna's other works (viz. that ultimately nothing can be conceived as *eka* or *aneka*), but with a wit and virtuosity not met with elsewhere.

126. Nāgārjuna's conclusion is worth citing (Kajiyama, p. 154): *gcig ñid daṅ gźan ñid daṅ gñi ga med pa'i phyir dṅos po thams cad med par khas blaṅs pa yin no* || *de lta bas na dṅos po med par mṅon par brjod par bya ba daṅ* | *mṅon par brjod pa yaṅ med pa yin no* || *de'i phyir mya ṅan las 'das pa daṅ byaṅ grol źes bya ba dag don gźan ñid ni ma yin no* ||. Cf. MK, II, 21; XVIII, 7; ŚS, 2.

V. *Vyavahārasiddhi (VS)

According to the Tibetan historian Bu-ston, Nāgārjuna wrote a work called *THa sñad grub pa* or **Vyavahārasiddhi*, in order 'to show that though there is no *svabhāva* in the ultimate sense (*paramārthataḥ*), still *laukikavyavahāra* is justified *saṃvṛtitaḥ* ...'[127]

The credibility of this has been disputed.[128] I have failed to detect any references to such a title in any of Bhavya's or Candrakīrti's writings or in any other Indian *śāstra* anterior to these. However, in his *Madhyamakālaṃkāravṛtti* Śāntarakṣita quotes six verses[129] the source of which is mentioned by his pupil Kamalaśīla (who adds an exhaustive commentary): They hail from Nāgārjuna's **Vyavahārasiddhi.*[130]

If we consider the content and style of this fragment, it becomes clear not only that it displays very close parallels to other passages in Nāgārjuna's authentic works, but also that one would beforehand have expected the author to express himself in more detail on this topic, clearly of paramount importance to him.[131]

Thus I do not hesitate to accept this fragment as a genuine quotation from Nāgārjuna's lost **Vyavahārasiddhi.*[132]

127. See Bu-ston, I, 51. The Tibetan text is found in Lokesh Chandra (ed.), *The* Collected Works of Bu-ston (Śatapiṭaka Series, LXIV), Ya *fol.* 670: *don dam par raṅ bźin med kyaṅ kun rdzob tu 'jig rten gyi tha sñad 'thad ciṅ grub par ston pa tha sñad grub pa daṅ drug yin no źes gsuṅ ṅo* ||. (Excerpts due to Mr. Per K. Sørensen.)
128. E.g. F. D. Lessing & A. Wayman, *Mkhas grub rje's Fundamentals of the Buddhist Tantras,* The Hague 1968, p. 87, q.v.
129. TP, No. 5285, Sa *fol.* 69b, quoted and translated below.
130. TP, No. 5286, Sa *fol.* 123a-124b. – For Kamalaśīla's reliability as a witness cf. E. Steinkellner, 'Zur Zitierweise Kamalaśīla's', *WZKSO,* VII, pp. 116-150.
131. Cf. in particular MK, XXIV, 36: *sarvasaṃvyavahārāṃś ca laukikān pratibādhase* | *yat pratītyasamutpādaśūnyatāṃ pratibādhase* ||. (Note that Bhavya (*Prajñāpradīpa,* 292b-293a) and Avalokitavrata (*Prajñāpradīpaṭīkā,* 293b) connect 36ab with the previous lines and take 36cd as the protasis of the following verses whereas Candrakīrti (*Prasannapadā,* p. 513) subordinates 36cd to 36ab by taking *yat* as a *kriyāviśeṣaṇa. Akutobhayā* (here adopted by Buddhapālita) and *Zhōng lùn* (*loc.cit.,* 34b 14-17) similarly.)
132. For further evidence see the notes below.

The argument: Though all phenomena, such as *mantras* etc., arise dependently and thus neither are existing nor non-existing, they are none the less efficient. Likewise all interior and exterior phenomena arise dependently, and though they are thus mere metaphorical concepts, Buddha has formulated his *dharmas* with a specific practical purpose (*saṃdhāya*), viz. **nairātmyāvatārataḥ*.[133]

133. See Kamalaśīla ad (5); CS, II, 21.

*Vyavahārasiddhi ||

THa sñad grub pa ||

(1)
| yi ge gcig sṅags gaṅ yaṅ med || yi ge maṅ po gźan yaṅ med |
| yi ge 'gags pa rnams min la || rten nas de ni med pa'aṅ min |

(2)
| de bźin raṅ gi yan lag las || sman ni gud nas mi snaṅ ṅo |
| sgyu ma'i glaṅ po snaṅ ba de || de dag las min gźan yaṅ min |

(3)
| rten ciṅ 'brel par 'byuṅ ba de || yod dam med par su źig 'dod |
| de la dmigs par byed pa yi || mig gi rnam śes byuṅ ba ltar |

Establishment of Convention

(1) One syllable (*akṣara*) is not a spell (*mantra*). On the other hand (*punar*) many (*aneka*) syllables are not a spell either: dependent (*pratītya*) upon syllables that are [therefore] insubstantial (*niruddha*) this [mantra is neither existent] nor non-existent (*asat*).

(2) Likewise no medicine (*auṣadha*) appears independently of its specific ingredients (*svāṅga*). It appears [like] an illusory elephant (*māyāgaja*): It is not [identical with them] nor is it [absolutely] different from them.

(3) It arises in dependent co-origination (*pratītyasamutpanna*)! Who would [be so ignorant as to] maintain that it is existent (*sat*) or non-existent (*asat*)? Actually visual consciousness (*cakṣurvijñāna*) arises [similarly] when it is based upon [eye and form].

1. Kamalaśīla introduces his comment (*Pañjikā*, 123a 5-124b 7) by stating the purport of this text: *sṅags daṅ sman daṅ sgyu ma'i dpes chos thams cad rten ciṅ 'brel par 'gyur ba ñid kyi gtan tshigs kyis don dam par yod pa daṅ med pa ñid las yaṅ dag par 'das par sgrub par byed do.* – For *pāda* c see *ibid.*, 123b 2: *'gags pa źes bya ba ni raṅ gi ṅo bo las ñams pa źes bya'o.* In *pāda* d the *vṛtti* (69b 2) reads *de ni med pa yin* which I have corrected acc. to *Pañjikā* 123b 4: *de ni med pa' 'aṅ min.* So though a mantra being *śūnya* neither is nor is not it is still generally acknowledged to be efficient (cf. *vidyā*, MK, XXIV, 11). – I have edited Kamalaśīla's commentary and discussed VS more fully in 'Nāgārjuna's Vyavahārasiddhi', to appear in the *Proceedings of the Csoma de Kőrős Symposium, Velm/Wien, Sept. 13th-19th, 1981.*
2. Similarly RĀ, II, 10-14 compares *loka* to a *māyāgaja*. They only exist *vyavahārataḥ*, not *paramārthataḥ*. See also CS, III, 29.
3. The notion of *pratītyasamutpāda* excludes *asti* and *nāsti*, cf. e.g. YṢ, 1. – Consciousness (*vijñāna*) being *ālambika/ālambanaka* (*dmigs par byed pa*) only arises *cakṣūrūpe pratītya*, RĀ, IV, 55; ŚS, 56; MK, XXVI, 4) – I take *de la* in *pāda* c as *vyavahārataḥ*, i.e. acc. to Abhidharma, but Kamalaśīla does not gloss it.

(4)
| las daṅ ñon moṅs dbaṅ 'phaṅs pa || len bcas srid las 'byuṅ ba daṅ |
| de bźin du ni gzugs 'byuṅ ba || yod dam med par su źig 'dod |

(5)
| de ltar srid pa'i yan lag kun || tha sñad kyis ni gdags pa ste |
| 'de ltar 'gog la sogs pa yi || chos kun dgoṅs te gsuṅs pa yin |

(6)
| ji ltar sṅags te sṅags min daṅ || ji ltar sman yaṅ sman min pa |
| de ltar rten nas gsuṅs pa de || gñis ka 'grub par 'gyur ma yin |

(4) Projected by the power of [his] karma and passions (*kleśa*) the appropriator (*sopādāna*) arises out of existence (*bhavāt*). Form also arises in the same manner. Who would [be so ignorant as to] maintain that it is existent (*sat*) or non-existent (*asat*)?

(5) Similarly *all* the [twelve] members of existence (*bhavāṅga*) are [simply] conventional designations (*vyavahārataḥ prajñapti*). Consequently all phenomena such as extinction (*nirodhādi*) have [only] been advocated [by the Buddhas] with a specific purpose.

(6) As it [appears to be] a *mantra* without [really being] a *mantra*, and as it [appears to be] a medicine (*auṣadha*) without [really in itself being] a medicine, thus [all phenomena] are stated to be dependent (*pratītya*). Neither of the two [i.e. *hetu* or *phala*] can be established [as existing independently].

4. I.e., as a result of *karmakleśākṣepa* (cf. May, *op.cit.*, p. 253, n. 908; MK, XVII, 27; ŚS, 37) one who is *sopādāna* (i.e. *sāsrava*, *Pañjikā*, 124b 2; cf. MK, XXVI, 7) attains *bhava* (i.e. *pañca skandhāḥ*, MK, XXVI, 8). Similarly all twelve *bhavāṅgas*, see v. 5. – In *pāda* c I understand *gzugs* as *catvāri mahābhūtāny upādāyarūpa* (cf. MK, IV; RĀ, IV, 58, 60) though Kamalaśīla is silent.
5. The twelve *bhavāṅgas* (MK, XXVI; PK, 1-5; BV, 59-63), i.e. *ādhyātmikapratītyasamutpāda*, like all other dharmas, i.e. including *bāhyapratītyasamutpāda*, only exist *saṃvṛtitaḥ* (*vyavahārataḥ*). But they are necessary for understanding *paramārtha* (cf. MK, XXIV, 8-10; YS, 33; ŚS, 1, 69; BV, 67) and it is only for this reason that the Buddha has taught them, or, as Kamalaśīla puts it (124b 6): *bdag med pa la 'jug pa'i phyir skye ba la sogs pa bstan to.*
6. This verse (124b 7): *mjug bsdud do* (*upasaṃharati*). – Note that (124b 7): *gñi ga źes bya ba ni rgyu dan 'bras bu'o*, which I understand in the light of PK, 1-5; RĀ, I, 35-38 etc. see my note to BV, 59-63 for details (five *aṅgas* are *hetu*, seven *phala*).

VI. Yuktiṣaṣṭikā (YṢ)

YṢ, in 61 verses, is one of the most frequently quoted of the texts ascribed to Nāgārjuna, not only by Bhavya,[134] Candrakīrti[135] and Śāntarakṣita,[136] but especially in the later commentatorial literature.[137] Owing to such citations the Tibetan and Chinese translations of this text, now lost in its original language, may be augmented by no less than 12 verses (i.e. as far as I have identified them) in Sanskrit.[138]

The style of YṢ now and then recalls that of MK, RĀ and, especially, CS and BV.[139] It is, on the whole, a collection of aphorisms loosely tied together by a subject-matter in common: *pratītyasamutpāda.*[140] The author sets himself to demonstrate this principle (*naya*) by means of arguments (*yukti*) occasionally supported by references to *āgama.*

The argument: Reality (*tattva*) is beyond all ontological and epistemological dualities (*dvaya*) while the empirical world of origination,

134. Cf. n. 88. – Quotations in *Ratnapradīpa,* 345a, 355a, 363a, 364b.
135. Cf. n. 99. – Quotations e.g. *Madhyamakāvatāra,* pp. 228, 232.
136. *Madhyamakālamkāravṛtti,* 72b, 85b, 76a, 76b, 79b, 82a.
137. From these sources about 20% of YṢ has been saved in Sanskrit, see my notes for details. As virtually every later Mādhyamika cites YṢ now and again the references could easily be multiplied, but I have confined myself to a few of textual import.
138. The Tibetan version of the kārikās (with the variants of Candrakīrti's *vṛtti*) was edited with the Chinese version and translated into Japanese by S. Yamaguchi, *Chūkan bukkyō ronkō,* Tokyo 1965, pp. 29-110. See also Nakamura (1977), p. 81, n. 23. In Sanskrit only 19ab and 39 were known to Yamaguchi. The Chinese version is usually too inaccurate to be of any philological value. A certain idea of it may be had from P. Schaeffer, *Yukti-ṣaṣṭikā, die sechzig Sätze des Negativismus, nach der chinesischen Version übersetzt,* Heidelberg 1923. Few are the verses which say what Nāgārjuna actually had in mind!
139. I have given some of the references in the notes.
140. Cf. *Yuktiṣaṣṭikāvṛtti,* 2b: *rig(s) pa drug cu pa 'di ni dbu ma bźin du 'dir yaṅ gtso bor rten ciṅ 'brel par 'byuṅ ba dpyad pa las brtsams te byas pa'i phyir dbu ma las 'phros pa lta bu ni ma yin no* ||. Thus it is an independent text compared with ŚS and VV.

destruction etc., is illusory and merely due to ignorance (*avidyā*). It subjects mankind to the tyranny of passions (*kleśa*) and endless evil. Buddhism is a practical system solely intended to overcome such *kleśas*.[141]

Our sources are:

Sigla

K *Yuktiṣaṣṭikākārikā*, trans. by Muditaśrī & Ñi ma grags.
TP, No. 5225, Tsa *fol.* 22b-25a; TN, No. 3216, Tsa *fol.* 20b-22b.

V *Yuktiṣaṣṭikāvṛtti*, trans. by Jinamitra, Dānaśīla, Śīlendrabodhi & Ye śes sde.
TP, No. 5265, Ya *fol.* 1-33b; TN, No. 3256, Ya *fol.* 1-34b.

C Chinese trans. by *Dānapāla.
Taishō, No. 1575, 254b-256a.[142]

---

141. Above all 46-48, q.v. are instructive. They are often quoted. Thus *bhāvābhyupagama* → *dṛṣṭi* → *kleśa* → *vivāda*.

142. The following translation of the kārikās strictly adheres to Candrakīrti's commentary. I have refrained from discussing the Chinese version, cf. n. 138.

Yuktiṣaṣṭikā-kārikā ||

Rigs pa drug cu pa'i tshig le'ur byas pa ||

| gaṅ gis skye daṅ 'jig pa dag || tshul 'di yis ni spaṅs gyur pa |
| rten ciṅ 'byuṅ ba gsuṅs pa yi || thub dbaṅ de la phyag 'tshal lo |

1. astināstivyatikrāntā buddhir yeṣāṃ nirāśrayā |
gambhīras tair nirālambaḥ pratyayārtho vibhāvyate |

| gaṅ dag gi blo yod med las || rnam par 'das śiṅ mi gnas pa |
| de dag gis ni rkyen gyi don || zab mo dmigs med rnam par rtogs |

2.

| re źig ñes kun 'byuṅ ba'i gnas || med ñid rnam par bzlog zin gyis |
| rigs pa gaṅ gis yod ñid daṅ || bzlog par 'gyur ba mñan par gyis |

3.

| ji ltar byis pas rnam brtags bźin || dṅos po gal te bden gyur na |
| de dṅos med pas rnam thar du || gaṅ gis mi 'dod rgyu ci źig |

4.

| yod pas rnam par mi grol te || med pas srid pa 'di las min |
| dṅos daṅ dṅos med yoṅs śes pas || bdag ñid chen po rnam par grol |

2d bzlog P : bzlag N

Sixty verses of Arguments

Obeisance (*namaḥ*) to the Buddha (*munīndra*) who has proclaimed dependent co-arising (*pratītyasamutpāda*), the principle (*naya*) by which origination (*utpāda*) and destruction (*vināśa*) are eliminated!

1. Those whose intelligence (*buddhi*) has transcended being and non-being and is unsupported have discovered the profound and inobjective meaning of 'condition'.

2. First of all (*tāvat*) you must reject non-being (*nāstitā*), the source of all faults (*doṣa*). But now listen to the argument (*yukti*) by which being (*astitā*) also is rejected!

3. If things (*bhāva*) were true (*satya*) as fools (*bāla*) imagine, what is the reason that they do not approve of liberation (*vimokṣa*) as non-being (*abhāva*)!

4. One is not liberated by being (*bhāva*), one does not [transcend] the present existence (*bhāva*) by non-being (*abhāva*), [but] by thorough knowledge of being and non-being (*bhāvābhāvaparijñānāt*) the magnanimous (*mahātman*) are liberated.

* I have left the initial stanza of YṢ unnumbered as is also the case with the first eight *pādas* of MK and the final verse of VV. All are noteworthy for stressing the fact that to Nāgārjuna Buddha above all deserves credit for preaching the law of *pratītyasamutpāda*, i.e. *śūnyatā* (cf. MK, XXIV, 18; RĀ, II, 18; CS, III, 1).

1. Sanskrit cited *Sekoddeśaṭīkā* (ed. Carelli), p. 48. – For the thought cf. e.g. RĀ, I, 62. *vibhū-* etc. is very common in the *Laṅkāvatārasūtra*, see Suzuki's *Index*, p. 159 (cf. v. 3 below, and MK, XV, 8).
2. Cf. RĀ, I, 38; 57; MK, XV, 10. – Here the word **yukti* (rigs pa, cf. the title of YṢ) is used in the sense of 'argument', i.e. in contrast to *āgama*. This is in accordance with its use in the *Laṅkāvatāra*, cf. Suzuki's *Index*, p. 143.
3. Closely related to *Laṅkāvatāra*, X, 466, q.v. – If things are real *nirvāṇa*, their annulment must imply *abhāva*, but this is untenable, cf. RĀ, I, 42; MK, XXV, 8.
4. For other def. of *nirvāṇa*, RĀ, I, 42; MK, XVIII, 7-11; XXV, 9; SL, 105; 123; SS, 221a (cf. ŚS, 73).

5. saṃsāraṃ caiva nirvāṇaṃ manyante 'tattvadarśinaḥ I
na saṃsāraṃ na nirvāṇaṃ manyante tattvadarśinaḥ II
I de ñid ma mthoṅ 'jig rten daṅ II mya ṅan 'das par rlom sems te I
I de ñid gzigs rnams 'jig rten daṅ II mya ṅan 'das par rlom sems med I

6. nirvāṇaṃ ca bhavaś caiva dvayam etan na vidyate I
parijñānaṃ bhavasyaiva nirvāṇam iti kathyate II
I srid pa daṅ ni mya ṅan 'das II gñis po 'di ni yod ma yin I
I srid pa yoṅs su śes pa ñid II mya ṅan 'das źes bya bar brjod I

7.
I dṅos po byuṅ ba źig pa la II ji ltar 'gog par brtags pa bźin I
I de bzin dam pa rnams kyis kyaṅ II sgyu ma byas pa'i 'gog pa bźed I

8.
I rnam par 'jig pas 'gog 'gyur gyi II 'dus byas yoṅs su śes pas min I
I de ni su la mṅon sum 'gyur II źig ces pa der ji ltar 'gyur I

9.
I gal te phuṅ po ma 'gags na II ñon moṅs zad kyaṅ 'das mi 'gyur I
I gaṅ tshe 'dir ni 'gags gyur pa II de yi tshe na grol bar 'gyur I

10.
I ma rig rkyen gyis byuṅ ba la II yaṅ dag ye śes kyis gzigs na I
I skye ba daṅ ni 'gags pa'aṅ ruṅ II 'ga' yaṅ dmigs par mi 'gyur ro I

7b brtags N : brtag P
8d ces : śes NP

5. Those who do not see reality (*tattva*) believe in Saṃsāra and Nirvāṇa [but] those who see reality (*tattva*) believe neither in Saṃsāra nor Nirvāṇa.

6. Existence (*bhava*) and Nirvāṇa – these two are not [really] to be found [since] Nirvāṇa [may be] defined as the thorough knowledge of existence.

7. While [the ignorant] imagine that annihilation (*nirodha*) pertains to a created thing (*bhāva*) which is dissolved (*naṣṭa*), the wise (*sat*), however, are convinced that annihilation (*nirodha*) of [something] created (*kṛtaka*) is an illusion (*māyā*).

8. Though [something apparently] is annihilated by being destructed, it is not [destructed] when one thoroughly understands it to be compound (*saṃskṛta*) [for] to whom will it be evident (*pratyakṣa*)? How could one speak of it as dissolved (*naṣṭa*)?

9. *Opponent:* If the aggregates (*skandha*) are not annihilated [then an arhat] is not in Nirvāṇa even though his passions may be extinct (*kṣīṇakleśa*), [but] when [the aggregates] have been annihilated then he becomes liberated.

10. *Reply:* When one sees that which arises conditioned by ignorance (*avidyāpratyaya*) with a correct knowledge (*samyagjñāna*), no origination (*utpāda*) or destruction (*nirodha*) whatsoever is perceived (*upalabhyate*);

5. Sanskrit incorporated in 'Āryadeva's' *Cittaviśuddhiprakaraṇa* (ed. Patel), 24. – For the thought MK, XXV, 19-20. – On *manyante* see Conze (1975), p. 10 ('fancy' etc.).

6. Sanskrit in *Ratnakīrtinibandhāvalī* (ed. Thakur), p. 132 (with *eva* for *etan* in b). See also *Advayavajrasaṃgraha* (ed. Śāstrī), p. 42; *Caryāgīti* (ed. Kværne), p. 102; *Śuklavidarśanā* (ref. May *op. cit.*, p. 237, n. 840); *Jñānaśrīmitranibandhāvali* (ed. Thakur), pp. 389, 464 (with *etan* in b), 555.

7. For *sat* (= *bodhisattva*), cf. RĀ, I, 45. Also CS, I, 2. – That which is *kṛtaka* (*saṃskṛta, kṛtrima*) cannot really be destructed etc., cf. CS, III, 6 sq.

8. See ref. to v. 7.

9. Allusion to the two kinds of *nirvāṇa: nirupadhiśeṣa°*, where *kleśa* and *skandha* are abandoned, and *sopadhiśeṣa°*, where the *skandhas* still remain, see MK, XXV, 1 with commentaries; LVP in *IHQ*, IV, pp. 39-45.

10-12. In other words: *samyagjñāna* (i.e. *tattvajñāna*, cf. CS, III, 47) destroys *avidyā* (cf. MK, XXVI, 11). This is true arhatship (cf. *kṛtakṛtya* etc. PED, p. 77), here and now (PED, p. 320), and there is no difference between *nirvāṇa* and *saṃsāra* (see above, v. 5; MK, XXV, 20; PK, '6').

11.
| de ñid mthoṅ chos mya ṅan las || 'das śiṅ bya ba byas pa'aṅ yin |
| gal te chos śes mjug thogs su || 'di la bye brag yod na ni |

12.
| dṅos po śin tu phra ba la'aṅ || gaṅ gis skye bar rnam brtags pa |
| rnam par mi mkhas de yis ni || rkyen las byuṅ ba'i don ma mthoṅ |

13.
| ñon moṅs zad pa'i dge sloṅ gi || gal te 'khor ba rnam ldog na |
| ci phyir rdzogs saṅs rgyas rnams kyis || de yi rtsom pa rnam mi bśad |

14.
| rtsom pa yod na ṅes par yaṅ || lta bar gyur pa yoṅs su 'dzin |
| rten ciṅ 'brel bar 'byuṅ ba gaṅ || de la sṅon daṅ tha ma ci |

15.
| sṅon skyes pa ni ji ltar na || phyi nas slar yaṅ bzlog par 'gyur |
| sṅon daṅ phyi ma'i mtha' bral ba || 'gro ba sgyu ma bźin du snaṅ |

16.
| gaṅ tshe sgyu ma 'byuṅ źe 'am || gaṅ tshe 'jig par 'gyur sñam du |
| sgyu ma śes pa der mi rmoṅs || sgyu ma mi śes yoṅs su sred |

17.
| srid pa smig rgyu sgyu 'dra bar || blo yis mthoṅ bar gyur pa ni |
| sṅon gyi mtha' 'am phyi ma'i mtha' || lta bas yoṅs su slad mi 'gyur |

18.
| gaṅ dag gis ni 'dus byas la || skye daṅ 'jig pa rnam brtags pa |
| de dag rten 'byuṅ 'khor lo yi || 'gro ba rnam par mi śes so |

11c mjug : 'jug NP
14a rtsom : rtson NP
16d sred N : srid P
18c yi : yis NP

11. This is extinction in this very life (*dṛṣṭadharmanirvāṇa*) and one's task is accomplished (*kṛtakṛtya*). If [however] a difference (*viśeṣa*) occurs here, just before (*anantaram*) the knowledge of the principle (*dharmajñāna*), [then]

12. He who imagines that even the most subtle thing (*sūkṣmabhava*) arises, such an ignorant man does not see what it means to be dependently born (*pratyayotpannārtha*)!

13. *Opponent:* If birth-and-death (*saṃsāra*) has stopped for a monk (*bhikṣu*) whose passions are extinct (*kṣīṇakleśa*), why have the Perfect Buddhas denied that it has a beginning (*ārambha*)?

14. *Reply:* If there was a beginning (*ārambha*) there would certainly (*niyatam*) also be clinging in the form of dogmas (*dṛṣṭikṛtaparigraha*). – How can that which is dependently co-arisen have a first (*pūrva*) and a last (*anta*)?

15. How could that which has generated before later on be negated again? [No, actually] the world, devoid of a previous and final limit (*pūrvapaścimāntarahita*), appears like an illusion (*māyāvat*).

16. When one thinks that an illusion (*māyā*) arises or that it is destructed, one who recognizes the illusion is not bewildered by it but one who does not recognize it longs for it (*paritṛṣ-*).

17. One who, with his intelligence (*buddhi*), comes to see that existence (*bhava*) is like a mirage (*marīci*) [and] illusion (*māyā*), is not corrupted by dogmas [based on] a previous limit or a final limit.

18. Those who imagine that a compound (*saṃskṛta*) possesses origination (*utpāda*) or destruction (*vināśa*) do not understand the movement of the wheel of dependent origination (*pratītyotpādacakra*).

13-18. MK, XI, 1: *saṃsāro 'navarāgro hi* ... (ref. in CPD, s.v. *anamatagga*). Therefore one can only speak of a *bhavacakra* (see PK, 1-5; RĀ, I, 36; II, 7-15) under the law of *pratītyasamutpāda, māyāvat.*

19. tat tat prāpya yad utpannaṃ notpannaṃ tat svabhāvataḥ I
svabhāvena yan notpannam utpannaṃ nāma tat katham II
I de daṅ de brten gaṅ byuṅ de II raṅ gi dṅos por skyes ma yin I
I raṅ gi dṅos por gaṅ ma skyes II de ni skyes źes ji ltar bya I

20.
I rgyu zad ñid las źi ba ni II zad ces bya bar rtogs pa ste I
I raṅ bźin gyis ni gaṅ ma zad II de la zad ces ji ltar brjod I

21.
I de ltar ci yaṅ skye ba med II ci yaṅ 'gag par mi 'gyur ro I
I skye ba daṅ ni 'jig pa'i lam II dgos pa'i don du bstan pa 'o I

22.
I skye ba śes pas 'jig pa śes II 'jig pa śes pas mi rtag śes I
I mi rtag ñid la 'jug śes pas II dam pa'i chos kyaṅ rtogs par 'gyur I

23.
I gaṅ dag rten ciṅ 'brel 'byuṅ ba II skye daṅ 'jig pa rnam spaṅs par I
I śes par gyur pa de dag ni II ltar gyur srid pa'i rgya mtsho brgal I

24.
I so so skye bo dṅos bdag can II yod daṅ med par phyin ci log I
I ñes pas ñon moṅs dbaṅ gyur rnams II raṅ gi sems kyis bslus par 'gyur I

25.
I dṅos la mkhas pa rnams kyis ni II dṅos po mi rtag bslu ba'i chos I
I gsog daṅ stoṅ pa bdag med pa II rnam par dben źes bya bar mthoṅ I

26.
I gnas med dmigs pa yod ma yin II rtsa ba med ciṅ gnas pa med I
I ma rig rgyu las śin tu byuṅ II thog ma dbus mtha' rnam par spaṅs I

19d skyes : skye NP
21c lam : las NP
22d dam pa'i chos NP : de ni chos V

19. That which has arisen dependently on this and that *that* has not arisen substantially (*svabhāvataḥ*). That which has not arisen substantially, how can it literally (*nāma*) be called 'arisen'?

20. A [compound thing] quieted (*śānta*) due to an extinguished cause (*kṣīṇahetu*) is understood to be extinguished (*kṣīṇa*) [but] that which is not extinguished by nature (*prakṛtyā*), how could it be spoken of as extinguished (*kṣīṇa*)?

21. So to conclude (*evam*): There is no origination (*utpāda*), there is no destruction (*nirodha*). – The path of origination and destruction (*utpādanirodhamārga*) has [however] been expounded [by the Buddhas] with a practical purpose (*kāryārtham*):

22. By understanding origination (*utpāda*), destruction (*vināśa*) is understood; by understanding destruction, impermanence (*anityam*) is understood; by understanding impermanence (*anityatā*) the true principle (*saddharma*) is also understood.

23. Those who have come to understand that dependent co-origination (*pratītyasamutpāda*) is devoid of origination (*utpāda*) and destruction (*vināśa*) have crossed the ocean of existence consisting of dogmas (*dṛṣṭibhūtabhavārṇava*).

24. Profane people (*pṛthagjana*) with their positivistic attitude (*bhāvātmaka*) are, due to the fault of being perverted about being and non-being, dominated by passions (*kleśa*); they are deceived by their own mind (*svacitta*)!

25. Those who understand facts (*bhāva*) see that things are impermanent (*anitya*), fraudulent (*moṣadharman*), vain (*tuccha*), empty (*śūnya*), selfless (*anātman*) and isolated (*vivikta*).

26. Stationless (*anāspada*), inobjective (*nirālamba*), rootless (*nirmūla*), unfixed (*asthita*), totally arisen as a result of ignorance (*avidyāhetutaḥ*), without a beginning, middle or end ...

19. Sanskrit quoted (from *Subhāṣitasaṃgraha*) in *Vimalakīrtinirdeśa*, p. 41, n. 7, q.v. Here the reading *svabhāve na yad utpannam* has been emended to *svabhāvena yan notpannam* (cf. *Madhyamakāvatāra*, p. 228) in accordance with Tib. and a quotation occuring *Advayavajrasaṃgraha* (ed. Śāstrī), p. 25, q.v.

20. Cf. above 7-8.

21. Cf. ŚS, 1. Inspired by *Laṅkāvatāra*, II, 138 (often cited with v.l.).

22. The reading **saddharma* (for the significance of which see SS, 227b, and note to CS, III, 22) is supported by a quotation of this verse in Kamalaśīla's *Madhyamakāloka*, TP, No. 5287, Sa *fol.* 230a: *dam pa'i chos*.

23. On *dṛṣṭi*, v. 14, 46-53; May, *op.cit.*, p. 277, n. 1015.

24-27. On *māyā* see ref. to CS, I, 3.

27.
| chu śiṅ bźin du sñiṅ po med || dri za'i groṅ khyer 'dra ba ste |
| rmoṅs pa'i groṅ khyer mi bzad pa'i || 'gro ba sgyu ma bźin du snaṅ |

28.
| tshaṅs sogs 'jig rten 'di la ni || bden par rab tu gaṅ snaṅ ba |
| de ni 'phags la rdzun źes gsuṅs || 'di las gźan lta ci źig lus |

29.
| 'jig rten ma rig ldoṅs gyur pa || sred pa rgyun gyi rjes 'braṅs daṅ |
| mkhas pa sred pa daṅ bral ba || dge ba rnams lta ga la mñam |

30. sarvam astīti vaktavyam ādau tattvagaveṣiṇaḥ |
paścād avagatārthasya niḥsaṅgasya viviktatā ||
| de ñid tshol la thog mar ni || thams cad yod ces brjod par bya |
| don rnams rtogs śiṅ chags med la || phyis ni rnam par dben pa 'o |

31.
| rnam par dben don mi śes la || thos pa tsam la 'jug byed ciṅ |
| gaṅ dag bsod nams mi byed pa || skyes bu tha śal de dag brlag |

32.
| las rnams 'bras bu bcas ñid daṅ || 'gro ba dag kyaṅ yaṅ dag bśad |
| de yi raṅ bźin yoṅs śes daṅ || skye ba med pa dag kyaṅ bstan |

33. mamety aham iti proktaṃ yathā kāryavaśāj jinaiḥ |
tathā kāryavaśāt proktāḥ skandhāyatanadhātavaḥ ||
| dgos pa'i dbaṅ gis rgyal ba rnams || ṅa daṅ ṅa'i źes gsuṅs pa ltar |
| phuṅ po khams daṅ skye mched rnams || de bźin dgos pa'i dbaṅ gis gsuṅs |

34. mahābhūtādi vijñāne proktaṃ samavarudhyate |
tajjñāne vigamaṃ yāti nanu mithyā vikalpitam ||
| 'byuṅ ba che la sogs bśad pa || rnam par śes su yaṅ dag 'du |
| de śes pas ni 'bral 'gyur na || log pas rnam brtags ma yin nam |

27c rmoṅs : smoṅs NP; bzad : zad NP
28b snaṅ ba NP : brjod pa C *et* V
30d phyis : 'phyis NP

27. Without a core (*asāra*) like a plantain (*kadalī*), like the city of Gandharvas (*gandharvanagara*) [thus] the dreadful world (*tīvrajagat*) – a city of confusion (*mūḍhanagara*) – appears as an illusion!

28. Brahmā etc., which appear quite true to this world, have been said to be false (*mṛṣā*) to the noble (*ārya*). What about the rest apart from that?

29. The world (*loka*) which is blinded by ignorance and follows the current of desire (*tṛṣṇānusārin*) and [on the other hand] the wise, who are free from desire, how can their view of the good (*kuśala*) be similar?

30. To begin with [a teacher] should say that everything exists to his truth-seeking [pupil]. Later when he has understood the meaning he gains isolation (*viviktatā*) without being attached.

31. Those who do not understand the meaning of isolation (*viviktārtha*) but keep on merely learning without enacting merit (*puṇya*), such base (*khala*) people are lost!

32. The [various kinds of] karma with its results (*phala*) and the places of rebirth (*gati*) have also been fully explained [by the Buddhas]. The full knowledge of its nature and its unorigination have also been taught [by them].

33. Just as the Buddhas have spoken of 'my' and 'I' for pragmatic reasons, thus they have also spoken of the aggregates, the sense-fields and the elements for pragmatic reasons.

34. Such things spoken of as the great elements (*mahābhūta*) are absorbed in consciousness. They are dissolved by understanding them. Certainly they are falsely imagined!

28. Same canonical allusion as v. 35, q.v. Cf. *Laṅkāvatāra*, III, 122.

29. Cf. MK, XVII, 28 (*Saṃyutta*, II, p. 178 sq. which is also the source of SL, 66 sq., q.v.).

30. Sanskrit cited *Subhāṣitasaṃgraha*, p. 385 (with *tattve gaveṣiṇā* in b, which I have emended acc. to Tib.) and in *Nyāyaviniścayavivaraṇa* (ed. M. K. Jain), II, p. 17-18 (with *gaveṣiṇā* in b, and *bhāvagrāho nivartate* in d). – On *sarvam asti* (i.e. *skandha, āyatana* and *dhātu*), see ref. *MCB*, V, p. 88, n. 1.

31. Cf. a similar verse *Subhāṣitasaṃgraha*, p. 46.

32. See MK, XVII; ŚS, 33-44; SL; SS; RĀ, *passim*.

33. Cited and identified by LVP, *Pañjikā*, p. 376.

34. Cited *Jñānaśrīmitranibandhāvali* (ed. Thakur), p. 545 and 405 (v.l. °*vijñāne* and *yānti*). The *āgama* is *Dīgha*, I, p. 223 (cf. RĀ, I, 94); also *Laṅkāvatāra*, III, 9. See also CPD s.v. *uparujjhati*.

35.
। mya ṅan 'das pa bden gcig pur ।। rgyal ba rnams kyis gaṅ gsuṅs pa ।
। de tshe lhag ma log min źes ।। mkhas pa su źig rtog par byed ।

36.
। ji srid yid kyi rnam gyo ba ।। de srid bdud kyi spyod yul te ।
। de lta yin na 'di la ni ।। ñes pa med par cis mi 'thad ।

37.
। 'jig rten ma rig rkyen can du ।। gaṅ phyir saṅs rgyas rnams gsuṅs pa ।
। 'di yi phyir na 'jig rten 'di ।। rnam rtog yin źes cis mi 'thad ।

38.
। ma rig 'gags par gyur pa na ।। gaṅ źig 'gog par 'gyur ba de ।
। mi śes pa las kun brtags par ।। ji lta bu na gsal mi 'gyur ।

39. hetutaḥ saṃbhavo yasya sthitir na pratyayair vinā ।
vigamaḥ pratyayābhāvāt so 'stīty avagataḥ katham ।।

। gaṅ źig rgyu daṅ bcas 'byuṅ źiṅ ।। rkyen med par ni gnas pa med ।
। rkyen med phyir yaṅ 'jig 'gyur ba ।। de ni yod ces ji ltar rtogs ।

40.
। gal te yod par smra ba rnams ।। dṅos mchog źen nas gnas pa ni ।
। lam de ñid la gnas pa ste ।। de la ṅo mtshar cuṅ zad med ।

41.
। saṅs rgyas lam la brten nas ni ।। kun la mi rtag smra ba rnams ।
। rtsod pas dṅos rnams mchog gzuṅ bas ।। gnas pa gaṅ yin de rmad do ।

42.
। 'di 'am de 'o źes gaṅ du ।। rnam par dpyad nas mi dmigs na ।
। rtsod pas 'di 'am de bden źes ।। mkhas pa su źig smra bar 'gyur ।

41c rtsod N : brtsod P; d rmad : smad NP
42c pas : pa NP; 'di 'am N : 'am P

35. Inasmuch as the Buddhas (*jina*) have stated that Nirvāṇa is true, which clever person (*paṇḍita*) will then imagine that the rest is not false?

36. As long as mind (*manaḥ*) is fickle (*cala*) it is [under] the dominion (*gocara*) of Māra. [But when it is not so] in that case how is it not reasonable that there is no fault (*adoṣa*) in the [thorough knowledge of non-origination]?

37. Since the Buddhas have stated that the world is conditioned by ignorance, how is it not reasonable that this world therefore is a [result of] discrimination (*vikalpa*)?

38. When ignorance is stopped why is it not clear that that which stops was imagined by ignorance?

39. That which originates due to a cause (*hetu*) and does not abide without [certain] conditions (*pratyaya*) but disappears when the conditions are absent, how can it be understood to 'exist'?

40. If the adherents of being (*astivādin*) who keep on clinging to being, go on in the same way, there is nothing strange (*adbhuta*) about that;

41. But it is strange indeed that the exponents of the impermanence of everything [who] rely on Buddha's method (*mārga*) keep on adhering (*parāmṛś-*) to things (*bhāva*) with strife (*vivāda*).

42. When 'this' and 'that' said about something is not perceived by being analysed (*vicāra*), which wise man (*vicakṣaṇa*) will claim with strife (*vivāda*) that 'this' or 'that' is true (*satya*)?

35. The canonical passage e.g. *Prasannapadā*, p. 41, 237: '... *etad dhi bhikṣavaḥ paramaṃ satyaṃ yad uta amoṣadharma nirvāṇam, sarvasaṃskārāś ca mṛṣā moṣadharmāṇaḥ*. *Majjhima*, III, 245 and *Akutobhayā* ad MK, XIII, 1.

36. On *Mārakarman*, SS, 190 b sq.; BS, 96 with note.

37. Cf. v. 29; ŚS, 64 (on *kalpanā/vikalpa/avidyā*); CS, III, 21. – Candrakīrti glosses *loka* with *ñe bar len pa'i phuṅ po rnams* (25b). Ref. in CPD, II, p. 490.

38. Similarly RĀ, I, 98 (cited *Prasannapadā*, p. 188; *Āloka*, p. 66).

39. Sanskrit in *Pañjikā*, p. 500. – Cf. above v. 7-8 with ref.

40 sq. Sarvāstivādins lack true analytical insight (*prajñā*). One must resort to *vicāra* (cf. *parīkṣā* in the titles of the chapters of MK) to see *śūnyatā*. Otherwise one is captivated by *viparyāsa* (MK, XXIII) giving rise to *kleśa* etc. Also ŚS, 59-62.

43.
| gaṅ dag gis ni ma brten par || bdag gam 'jig rten mṅon źen pa |
| de dag kye ma rtag mi rtag || la sogs lta bas phrogs pa yin |

44.
| gaṅ dag brten nas dṅos po rnams || de ñid du ni grub 'dod pa |
| de dag la yaṅ rtag sogs skyon || de dag ji ltar 'byuṅ mi 'gyur |

45.
| gaṅ dag brten nas dṅos po rnams || chu yi zla ba lta bur ni |
| yaṅ dag ma yin log min par || 'dod pa de dag bltas mi 'phrog |

46. rāgadveṣodbhavas tīvraduṣṭadṛṣṭiparigrahaḥ |
vivādās tatsamutthāś ca bhāvābhyupagame sati ||
| dṅos por khas len yod na ni || 'dod chags źe sdaṅ 'byuṅ ba yi |
| lta ba mi bzad ma ruṅs 'dzin || de las byuṅ ba'i rtsod par 'gyur |

47. sa hetuḥ sarvadṛṣṭīnāṃ kleśotpattir na taṃ vinā |
tasmāt tasmin parijñāte dṛṣṭikleśaparikṣayaḥ ||
| de ni lta ba kun gyi rgyu || de med ñon moṅs mi skye ste |
| de phyir de ni yoṅs śes na || lta daṅ ñon moṅs yoṅs su 'byaṅ |

48. parijñā tasya keneti pratītyotpādadarśanāt |
pratītya jātaṃ cājātam āha tattvavidāṃ varaḥ ||
| gaṅ gis de śes 'gyur sñam na || brten nas 'byuṅ ba mthoṅ ba de |
| brten nas skye ba ma skyes par || de ñid mkhyen pa mchog gis gsuṅs |

49.
| log pa'i śes pas zil gnon pa || bden pa min la bden 'dzin pa'i |
| yoṅs su 'dzin daṅ rtsod sogs kyi || rim pas chags las 'byuṅ bar 'gyur |

50.
| che ba'i bdag ñid can de dag || rnams la phyogs med rtsod pa med |
| gaṅ rnams la ni phyogs med pa || de la gźan phyogs ga la yod |

43a gaṅ dag V : de dag NP; d phrogs : 'phrogs NP
46b yi : yin NP; c bzad : zad NP; 'dzin V : 'byuṅ NP
49a pas : pa NP

43. Those who adhere (*abhiniviś-*) to a Self (*ātman*) or the world (*loka*) as unconditioned (*anupādāya*), alas they are captivated by dogmas about permanent, impermanent etc. (*nityānityadṛṣṭi*)!

44. Those who postulate that conditioned things (*bhāva*) are established (*siddha*) in reality (*tattvataḥ*), how are they not also overtaken by mistakes about permanence etc. (*nityādidoṣa*)!

45. But those who are convinced that conditioned things (*bhāva*) are like the moon in the water ((*u*)*dakacandra*), neither true nor false, they are not carried away by dogmas (*dṛṣṭi*).

46. When one affirms 'being' there is a seizing of awful and vicious dogmas which arise from desire and hatred, and from that contentions (*vivāda*) arise.

47. That is the cause of all dogmas, without it the passions (*kleśa*) do not arise. So when this is thoroughly understood, dogmas and passions disappear.

48. But how is it thoroughly known? – By seeing dependent origination! The [Buddha] best among knowers of reality (*tattva*) also said that that which is dependently born is unborn.

49. For those who suppressed by false knowledge (*mithyājñāna*) take the untrue for true (*satye satyagrah-*) a series of seizing and contention etc. (*parigrahavivādādikrama*) will arise.

50. The magnanimous (*mahātman*) have neither thesis (*pakṣa*) nor contention (*vivāda*). How can there be an opposing thesis (*parapakṣa*) to those who have no thesis (*pakṣa*)?

45. Cf. RĀ, II, 4: *na satyaṃ na mṛṣoditam*. (*Vajracchedikā*, § 5.)

46-48. Sanskrit of these oft quoted stanzas in *Āloka*, p. 343-344 (with *parijñātasya* in 48 a for *parijñā tasya*, cf. Tib.). – For 48 cd see ref. to v. 19, and cf. ŚS, 21. – For 46 in particular, *Dīgha*, II, p. 58.

49. sq. These stanzas show some affinity to *Suttanipāta*, especially *Aṭṭhakavagga*, cf. L.O. Gómez: 'Proto-Mādhyamika in the Pāli canon', *PEW*, XXVI, pp. 137-165.

50. Cf. *Suttanipāta*, 919; *ajjhattaṃ upasantassa n' atthi attā, kuto nirattaṃ vā*. – On *vivāda*, *ibid.*, 863, 877, 912, 832 etc. Also *Madhyamakāvatāra*, p. 233.

51.
| gaṅ yaṅ ruṅ ba'i gnas rñed nas || ñon moṅs sbrul gdug gyo can gyis |
| źin par gyur te gaṅ gi sems || gnas med de dag źin mi 'gyur |

52.
| gnas bcas sems daṅ ldan rnams la || ñon moṅs dug chen cis mi 'byuṅ |
| gaṅ tshe tha mal 'dug pa yaṅ || ñon moṅs sbrul gyis źin par 'gyur |

53.
| byis pa bden par 'du śes pas || gzugs brñan la ni chags pa bźin |
| de ltar 'jig rten rmoṅs pa'i phyir || yul gyi gzeb la thogs par 'gyur |

54.
| bdag ñid che rnams dṅos po dag || gzugs brñan lta bur ye śes kyi |
| mig gis mthoṅ nas yul źes ni || bya ba'i 'dam la mi thogs so |

55. bālāḥ sajjanti rūpeṣu vairāgyaṃ yānti madhyamāḥ |
svabhāvajñā vimucyante rūpasyottamabuddhayaḥ ||
| byis pa rnams ni gzugs la chags || bar ma dag ni chags bral 'gyur |
| gzugs kyi raṅ bźin śes pa yi || blo mchog ldan pa rnam par grol |

56.
| sdug sñam pa las chags par 'gyur || de las bzlog pas 'dod chags bral |
| sgyu ma'i skyes bu ltar dben par || mthoṅ nas mya ṅan 'da' bar 'gyur |

57.
| log pa'i śes pas mṅon gduṅ ba'i || ñon moṅs skyon rnams gaṅ yin te |
| dṅos daṅ dṅos med rnam rtog pa || don śes 'gyur la mi 'byuṅ ṅo |

58.
| gnas yod na ni 'dod chags daṅ || 'dod chags bral bar 'gyur źig na |
| gnas med bdag ñid chen po rnams || chags pa med ciṅ chags bral min |

53c *omm.* NP, *sed* v. V

51. By taking any standpoint whatsoever one is attacked by the twisting snakes of the passions (*kleśasarpa*). But those whose mind (*citta*) has no standpoint (*sthāna*) are not caught

52. How can those whose mind takes a stand avoid the strong poison (*mahāviṣa*) of passions? Even if they live [like] ordinary [people] they are consumed by the snakes of passions.

53. Just as a fool (*bāla*) is attached to a reflection (*pratibimba*) because he conceives it to be true (*satya*), thus the world (*loka*) gets stuck in the cage of objects (*viṣayapañjara*) because of [its] stupidity (*moha*).

54. When the great souls (*mahātman*) see that things (*bhāva*) are like a reflection (*pratibimba*) with their eye of knowledge (*jñānacakṣuḥ*) they do not get stuck in the mire of the so-called 'objects' (*viṣaya iti paṅka*).

55. Fools (*bāla*) are attached to material form (*rūpa*), the moderate attain absence of passions, but those of supreme intellect (*buddhi*) are liberated by knowing the nature of material form (*rūpa*).

56. One desires by thinking of [something] pleasant; by turning away from it one becomes free from desires, but by seeing it to be void (*vivikta*) like a phantom (*māyāpuruṣa*) one obtains Nirvāṇa.

57. The faults of passion (*kleśadoṣa*) that torment due to false knowledge (*mithyājñāna*) do not arise for those who understand the meaning of judgements concerning being and non-being (*bhāvābhāvavikalpārtha*).

58. If there were a standpoint there would be passion (*rāga*) and dispassion [or distaste] (*vairāgya*), but the great souls (*mahātman*) without standpoint have neither passion nor dispassion.

51-54. See *ibid.*

55. Sanskrit incorporated in *Cittaviśuddhiprakaraṇa,* 20 (cf. v. 5 above) with v. l. *rajyanti* in a, and it also occurs in *Śuklavidarśanā* (v. *MCB*, I, p. 395) with *matsamāḥ* in b for *madhyamāḥ,* cf. Tib.

58. Cf. *Suttanipāta,* 795: *na rāgarāgī na virāgaratto ...*

59.
| gaṅ dag rnam par dben sñam du || gyo ba'i yid kyaṅ mi gyo ba |
| ñon moṅs sbrul gyis dkrugs gyur pa || mi bzad srid pa'i rgya mtsho brgal |

60.
| dge ba 'di yis skye bo kun || bsod nams ye śes tshogs bsags te |
| bsod nams ye śes las byuṅ ba'i || dam pa gñis ni thob par śog |

59d bzad : zad NP

59. Those whose fickle mind (*calacitta*) is not moved – not even at the thought of the void (*viveka*) – have crossed the awful ocean of existence (*tīvrabhavārṇava*) which is agitated by the monsters of passions.

60. May all people by this merit (*kuśala*) gather a collection of merit and insight (*puṇyajñānasaṃbhāra*) and obtain the two goods (*sat*) which arise from merit and insight!

59. Cf. MK, XXII, 11: *śūnyam iti na vaktavyam ...*

60. Allusion to *rūpa-* and *dharmakāya,* respectively the result of *puṇya-* and *jñānasaṃbhāra,* see RĀ, III, 12-13 (cf. *Madhyamakāvatāra,* p. 62). – The verse forms a *pariṇāmanā,* RĀ, IV, 90.

VII. Catuḥstava (CS)

Though the question *which* of the numerous hymns ascribed to Nāgārjuna[143] belong to 'The *four* hymns'[144] has given rise to some controversy,[145] such hesitation is, however, unwarranted for at least three reasons.

First, the Sanskrit text of CS is available in four Mss.[146] The titles and order of the hymns given here are without exception: *Lokātītastava, Niraupamyastava, Acintyastava* & *Paramārthastava.* This coincides with the testimony given by the *Catuḥstavasamāsārtha* by a certain Amṛtākara.[147] Finally, precisely these four hymns are in

143. For the list and Buddhist hymns in general v. D. Schlingloff, *Buddhistische Stotras aus ostturkistanischen Sanskrittexten,* Berlin 1955, n. 16.

144. The earliest reference to *Catuḥstava* (Tib. *bstod pa bži pa*) as a whole known to me occurs in Vairocanarakṣita's *Bodhisattvacaryāvatārapañjikā*, TP, No. 5277, Śa *fol.* 169a 2 & 174b 8. Prajñākaramati's *Bodhicaryāvatārapañjikā* (ed. La Vallée Poussin) twice gives the form *Catustava* (pp. 420; 488). Candrakīrti speaks of the *Saṃstuti* (cf. n. 89). In most cases the individual hymns are quoted without mention of source.

145. The various options have been summarized by de Jong, 'Emptiness', *JIP*, II, pp. 11-12, q.v. Professor Hahn kindly forwarded me a copy of S. Sakai: 'On the Four Hymns ascribed to Nāgārjuna', *The Journal of the Nippon Buddhist Research Association,* XXIV, pp. 1-44, which contains a revised edition of CS, II & IV and a Japanese version of the two other hymns with notes.

146. See below. – Copies of these were courteously put at my disposal by the authorities of the Akademia Nauk (Leningrad), Dr. M. Hara (Tokyo) and Dr. V. V. Gokhale (Poona). I am particularly grateful to Dr. Gokhale who originally planned to edit the *Catuḥstava* himself (cf. *Festschrift Kirfel,* Bonn 1955, p. 102, n. 3).

147. Edited by G. Tucci, *Minor Buddhist Texts,* I, Roma 1956, pp. 235-246. Let us recall that Tucci also edited and translated CS, II and IV i.e. *Niraupamya-* and *Paramārthastava* in 'Two hymns of the Catuḥstava of Nāgārjuna', *JRAS* (1932), pp. 309-325. Cf. *MCB,* III, p. 374. – The Mss at my disposal require these emendations in Tucci's text: CS, II, 1b: read *niḥsvabhāvārthavedine;* 2d, *tattvārthadarśinī;* 3a, *boddhavyam;* 4d, *padam;* 23b. *īkṣyase;* CS, IV, 5a, *harin māñjiṣṭho;* b, *nopalabhyate;* c, *pītaḥ kṛṣṇaḥ śuklo* (cf. *IiJ*, II, p. 168, n. 12); 9a, *evam stute.* – A French version of these two hymns was published by L. Silburn, *Le bouddhisme,* Paris 1977, pp. 201-209; an Italian (including *Lokātīta-* and *Acintyastava,* from the Tibetan) by R. Gnoli, *op.cit.,* pp. 157-179.

fact those that are quoted by the commentators, not only Bhavya, Candrakīrti and Śāntarakṣita, but also several lesser-known Indian authors.[148]

Since the doctrine and, to a certain extent, the style of the hymns – especialy I & III[149] – matches well with that of MK etc., I see no reason to dispute the authenticity of CS.[150]

I shall confine myself to some remarks concerning I & III of which I subjoin an *editio princeps* of the Sanskrit text and which are also the philosophically most significant of all the hymns ascribed to Nāgārjuna, and even of all ancient Buddhist hymns at large.[151]

The content of these two hymns is too reflective and abstract to render it credible that they were composed with some ritual objec-

148. See the *conspectus testium*. Though far from exhaustive it shows that the hymns exerted a considerable influence.
149. Discussing the authenticity of *Catuḥstava* Gnoli says (*op.cit.*, p. 12): 'L'unica obiezione contro la loro autenticità, può concernere, semmai, uno solo di essi, l'*Acintyastava* o 'Laude dell' Inconcepibile', il terzo e più lungo della raccolta, che, per l'eccessiva concisione di alcune parti, per l'oscurità di altre (forse imputabile, d'altronde, alla versione tibetana), per certi bruschi passagi e certe ripetizioni, non è, in realtà, escluso che sia una compilazione posteriore. Specialmente sospette, in questo senso, le stanze 43-44 [= 45-46 in my Sanskrit edition!], nelle quali è un'evidente allusione alla scuola dei Vijñānavādin o dell'Idealismo buddhistico, considerata, per tradizione, posteriore a Nāgārjuna. Ma la data di Nāgārjuna è poi sicura?' – But these arguments do not carry much weight: The stylistic features noticed by Gnoli are, in fact, also known from ŚS and YṢ the authenticity of which cannot be impeached. The allusions to Vijñānavāda – or more precisely to the Vijñānavāda of *Laṅkāvatārasūtra* (v. n. to CS, III, 45), generally held to be posterior to Nāgārjuna – are quite consistent with the fact that Nāgārjuna also refers to this sūtra elsewhere (cf. e.g. MK, XVIII, 7 with *Laṅkāvatāra,* III, 9; XXI, 11 with X, 37; XVII, 33 with X, 279; YṢ, 3 with X, 466; SS, 222b 2-3 = X, 640, etc.). – These hymns (cf. the very titles) show Nāgārjuna's 'conception' of the Buddha consistent with MK, XXII, 15: ... *buddhaṃ prapañcātītam avyayam.* – Some of the verses in CS, II & IV were discussed by D. S. Ruegg in the paper referred to above, n. 46, pp. 454-463.
150. The main theme of CS, I and III is *pudgala-* and *dharmanairātmya.* The composition is – like YṢ – not structurally strict. Though CS, I first refutes *sattva* (2) and then the skandhas, first in general (3-4), then in particular *rūpa* (5), *vedanā* (6), *saṃjñā* (7), *saṃskāra* (8-9) and *vijñāna* (10), it is none the less on the whole a loose collection of aphorisms about *anutpāda,* like CS, III, teeming with allusions to Mahāyānasūtras.
151. Cf. however, n. 22 above.

tive in mind.[152] Nor should we attach too much importance to the motive of obtainment of *puṇya*.[153] No, these hymns are outbursts of a sincere and enthusiastic appraisal of the Buddha as the teacher who out of sheer compassion took pains to propagate his conviction of the emptiness of all phenomena. This accounts for the curious composition of the two hymns compared with the other genuine works: An abundance of quotations from or allusions to Mahāyāna sūtras are intertwined with the author's own either rationalizing or approving comments, all *in majorem Buddhae gloriam*.[154]

Sigla

T Sanskrit Ms of CS (accompanied by A) kept in the Tokyo University Library (cf. Matsunami (1965), p. 122, No. 340).[155] – 36 numbered pages. Material: paper. Size: 23,5 x 7 cm. Number of lines: 9. An occasional *secunda manus* in the upper or lower margin. Date: uncertain, but hardly more than a few centuries. Quality: on the whole very good. Reproduced as *Appendix*, q.v.

M A copy (microfilm in my possession) of the late Prof. M. Tubiansky's transcript or recension (cf. Obermiller (1960), p. 3) of a Sanskrit Ms of CS from Mongolia. – No information accessible concerning the date, condition etc. of this Ms.

G Xerox (in my possession) of a handcopy of CS prepared by Dr. V.V. Gokhale (Poona): 'In 1949 I was permitted to take a *handcopy* of the original papermanuscript [i.e. of CS and other texts]

152. Some glimpses of how and when hymns etc. were chanted we get from RĀ, V, 65; *Bhāvanākrama*, III, p. 13; *Ratnapradīpa*, 355a; J. Takakusu (tr.), *A record of the Buddhist religion as practised in India and the Malay archipelago (A.D. 671-695), by I-tsing*, London 1896, pp. 152-166, q.v.

153. As expressed in the *pariṇāmanā* at the end of each hymn. Note that MK, ŚS and VV, i.e. the purely dialectical works, do not contain any such *puṇyapariṇāmanā*.

154. Cf. the remarks on *buddhamāhātmya*, RĀ, IV, 84-87.

155. S. Matsunami, *A Catalogue of the Sanskrit Manuscripts in the Tokyo University Library*, Tokyo 1965. – I also collated the two Mss of CS, I listed here p. 149 (No. 419, III, 153 = *fol.* 292b 4-294a 5; No. 420, XI, 5 = *fol.* 10b 5-21a 4) but not to encumber the apparatus needlessly I have not given the numerous *voces nihili* found here.

by the abbot of the Kundeling monastery. It was a Ms written in the Bengal script of about the 13th or 14th century, I suppose ...' (Quoted from a letter dated 7.10.1976).

A *Akāriṭīkā* subjoined to the text of CS in T (described above). – Merely provides simply synonyms and analyses the syntax in a most elementary manner. Without the slightest philosophical import but valuable for the substantiating of the readings of its *mūla*.

W Microfiche of a Sanskrit Ms in the possession of Manavajra Vajracharya, Kathmandu. Written in Nevārī script on fairly recent Nepali paper. 6 lines to a page. Size: 8 x 20 cm. CS, I, 1-5 and 15-25 missing (at least on the microfiche edition which The Institute for Advanced Studies of World Religions kindly put at my disposal). Quality: on the whole not as good as T, M or G.

N Narthang (sNar thaṅ) edition of the Tibetan trans. of
a) CS I (i.e. *Lokātītastava*) by Kṛṣṇapaṇḍita & Tshul khrims rgyal ba. – TN, No. 12, Ka *fol.* 75b-77a.
b) CS III (i.e. *Acintyastava*) by Tilaka & Ñi ma grags. – TN, No. 19, Ka *fol.* 84b-87a.

P Peking edition of the Tibetan trans. of
a) CS I (same translator team). – TP. No. 2012, Ka *fol.* 79a-80b.
b) CS III (same translator team). – TP. No. 2019, Ka *fol.* 88b-91a.

S A *varia lectio* in the Sanskrit Ms(s), now presumably lost, but inferable from a recension of the Tibetan trans. based on N & P.

Conspectus testium

1. abbreviaturae

AĀ Haribhadra: *Abhisamayālaṃkārāloka* (ed. P. L. Vaidya)
AS Advayavajra: *Advayavajrasaṃgraha* (coll. et ed. H. P. Śāstrī)
BT Maitreyanātha (II?): *Bhavasaṃkrāntiṭīkā* (ed. N. A. Śāstrī)
BC Prajñākaramati: *Bodhi*[*sattva*]*caryāvatārapañjikā* (ed. La Vallée Poussin)

BD	Atiśa: *Bodhimārgadīpapañjikā* (TP, No. 5344)
BP	Vairocanarakṣita: *Bodhisattvacaryāvatārapañjikā* (TP, No. 5277)
BV	Vibhūticandra: *Bodhicaryāvatāratatparyapañjikā* ... (TP, No. 5282)
CG	Munidatta: *Caryāgītikośavṛtti* (ed. P. Kværne)
CP	Āryadeva (II): *Caryāmelāyanapradīpa* (TP, No. 2668)
CS	Amṛtākara: *Catuḥstavasamāsārtha* (ed. G. Tucci)
MP	Bhavya: *Madhyamakaratnapradīpa* (TP, No. 5254)
MV	Candrakīrti: *Madhyamakāvatārabhāṣya* (ed. La Vallée Poussin)
PK	Nāgārjuna (II): *Pañcakrama* (ed. La Vallée Poussin)
PP	Candrakīrti: *Prasannapadā* (ed. La Vallée Poussin)
PS	Candrakīrti: *Pañcaskandhaprakaraṇa* (ed. C. Lindtner)
PU	Āryadeva (II): *Pradīpoddyotanābhisaṃdhiprakāśikā* (TP, No. 2658)
SP	Nāgārjuna (II): *Sekacatuḥprakaraṇa* (TP, No. 2664)
SŚ	Jñānaśrīmitra: *Sākārasiddhiśāstra* (ed. A. Thakur)
SS	Anonymus: *Subhāṣitasaṃgraha* (ed. C. Bendall)
ŚV	Candrakīrti: *Śūnyatāsaptativṛtti* (TP, No. 5259)
TA	Jñānakīrti: *Tattvāvatārākhya...prakaraṇa* (TP, No. 4532)
TS	Śāntarakṣita: *Tattvasiddhi* (TP, No. 4531)
TV	Dharmendra: *Tattvasārasaṃgraha* (TP, No. 4534)
YV	Candrakīrti: *Yuktiṣaṣṭikāvṛtti* (TP, No. 5265)

2. loci

CS, I (*Lokātītastava*):

4: PP, p. 413; BC, p. 583; TV, f. 95a; BP, f. 183b
5: MV, p. 200; TV, f. 95a
8: BC, p. 476
9: BC, p. 476
11: PP, p. 64
12: AĀ, p. 299; AS, p. 28
13: BC, p. 587
18: BC, p. 533; MV, p. 97
19: BC, p. 533

20: BC, p. 533
21: PP, pp. 55 & 234
22: AĀ, pp. 348, 381, 405, 441, 482, 490 & 536; SŚ, p. 481; BC, p. 417; PS, p. 26
23: BC, pp. 359 & 415; TV, f. 98b; MV, p. 310
24: BC, p. 489; TV, f. 98b
26: ŚV, f. 315a
27: MV, p. 23

CS, II (*Niraupamyastava*):
1: CS, p. 239
7: BC, 420; AS, p. 22; BP, f. 169a
9: BC, p. 489; BP, f. 174b
13: PP, p. 215; ŚV, f. 335b
15: TS, f. 30b
18-19: PK, p. 36; CP, f. 104a; PU, f. 212a; SP, f. 33a
21: SS, p. 388; AS, p. 22; BD, f. 298b; TV, f. 92b; TA, f. 46a
24: AS, p. 22; MP, f. 361a

CS, III (*Acintyastava*):
1: CS, p. 242
4: BV, f. 310a
9: TS, f. 40a
19: BC, p. 375; BT, p. 82; MP, f. 372; TV, f. 105a; BV, f. 308b
25: BC, p. 573 (a/d)
29: BC, p. 573
36: BC, p. 573
38: TV, f. 102a
39: TV, f. 102a
40: TV, f. 102a; BC, p. 528
41: TV, f. 102a; BC, p. 528
43: AS, p. 24 (a/b); CG, p. 209 (a/b)
48: TV, f. 97a
49: TV, f. 97a
57: TS, f. 39b

CS, IV (*Paramārthastava*):
1: CS, p. 245 (a/b)
3: CS, p. 245 (a)

4: SŚ, p. 489 (d)
5: SŚ, p. 489 (a); CG, p. 190 (a/b)
8: CS, p. 245 (d)
9: CS, p. 245 (a); BD, f. 284a (c/d)
10: CS, p. 245 (a); BD, f. 284a

Lokātītastava ||

'Jig rten las 'das par bstod pa ||

1. lokātīta namas tubhyaṃ viviktajñānavedine |
   yas tvaṃ jagaddhitāyaiva khinnaḥ karuṇayā ciram ||

| dben pa'i ye śes rig gyur pa || 'jig rten 'das khyod phyag 'tshal 'dud |
| gaṅ khyod 'gro la phan pa'i phyir || yun riṅ thugs rjes ṅal bar gyur |

2. skandhamātravinirmukto na sattvo 'stīti te matam |
   sattvārthaṃ ca paraṃ khedam agamas tvaṃ mahāmune ||

| phuṅ po tsam las grol ba yi || sems can med par khyod bźed la |
| sems can don la'aṅ mchog gźol bar || thub pa chen po khyod ñid bźugs |

3. te 'pi skandhās tvayā dhīman dhīmadbhyaḥ saṃprakāśitāḥ |
   māyāmarīcigandharvanagarasvapnasaṃnibhāḥ ||

| blo ldan khyod kyis phuṅ de 'aṅ || sgyu ma smig rgyu dri za yi |
| groṅ khyer rmi lam ji bźin du || blo ldan rnams la rab tu bstan |

4. hetutaḥ saṃbhavo yeṣāṃ tadabhāvān na santi ye |
   kathaṃ nāma na te spaṣṭaṃ pratibimbasamā matāḥ ||

| gaṅ dag rgyu las byuṅ ba rnams || de med par ni yod min pas |
| gzugs brñan ñid daṅ mtshuṅs pa ru || gsal bar ci yi phyir mi 'dod |

1d karuṇayā ci – T *mutil.*; yun riṅ N : yul riṅ P
2a skandhamātravini – T *mutil.*; b na sattvo 'stīti T : sattvo nāstīti GM
3a 'pi skandhās tvayā dhī – T *mutil.*

Hymn to [the Buddha] transcending the world

1. O You who are beyond the world! Obeisance to You versed in the cognition of the void. Solely for the benefit of the world You have for long been exhausted by compassion!

2. You are convinced that apart from the mere skandhas no soul (*sattva*) exists, and yet, great sage, You have suffered great pain for the sake of the living beings (*sattva*)!

3. You who are a sage! To the sages [= bodhisattvas] You have declared that the skandhas also are comparable to an illusion, a mirage, a city of Gandharvas and dreams!

4. [As to the skandhas] whose occurrence is due to a cause and which do not exist in lack of such – how are You not quite clearly convinced that they are like reflections?

1. Cf. *Niraupamyastava, 1: niraupamya namas tubhyaṃ niḥsvabhāvārthavedine | yas tvaṃ dṛṣṭivipannasya lokasyāsya hitodyataḥ || Prajñāpāramitāstotra*, 1 for *pādas* a and c. – For *vivikta* etc. (*śūnya*), see ref. in Conze (1973), pp. 363-364; YṢ, 30-31, 56; ŚS, 38. Also BCA, VIII, 2 (*kāyacittaviveka*). – For *khinnaḥ karuṇayā ciram* cf. *Śatapañcāśatka*, 58: *tvaṃ jagatkleśamokṣārthaṃ baddhaḥ karuṇayā ciram*; RĀ, III, 26 (cited *Madhyamakāvatāra*, p. 29): *de ni sñiṅ rjes 'jig rten sdug || de ñid kyis ni yun riṅ gnas* ||); similarly *Rāhulastava*, 9: *ciraṃ kliṣṭo 'si saṃsāre kāruṇyād eva kevalam* ||; BCA, VIII, 104-105; *Praṇidhānasaptati*, 17.
2. Similar paradox (*na sattvo 'stīti ... sattvārthaṃ ca*), BS, 72; CS, II, 9. – For *skandhamātra*, see *Kośa*, III, p. 57.
3. This verse states that bodhisattvas (= *dhīmat*, cf. e.g. *Pañjikā*, p. 23, n. 2) not only accept *pudgalanairātmya* but also *dharmanairātmya*, cf. CS, III, 2; *MCB*, II p. 17; *Vimalakīrtinirdeśa*, pp. 407-408; *Traité*, pp. 1995-2151. – For the various *māyādṛṣṭāntas* see e.g. *Traité*, pp. 357-387; May (1959), pp 507-509 (ref.).
4. This stanza (of which *pāda* a may be compared with YṢ, 39) refutes the *skandhas* in general whereas the following stanzas refute them separately: *rūpa* (5), *vedanā* (6), *saṃjñā* (7), *saṃskāra* (8-9) and *vijñāna* (10).

5. bhūtāny acakṣurgrāhyāṇi tanmayaṃ cākṣuṣaṃ katham ǀ
rūpaṃ tvayaivaṃ bruvatā rūpagrāho nivāritaḥ ǁ

ǀ 'byuṅ ba mig gi gzuṅ min pas ǁ de dṅos mig gi ji ltar yin ǀ
ǀ gzugs ñid gzuṅ bar rab bkag pa ǁ gzugs ñid khyod kyis de ltar gsuṅs ǀ

6. vedanīyaṃ vinā nāsti vedanāto nirātmikā ǀ
tac ca vedyaṃ svabhāvena nāstīty abhimataṃ tava ǁ

ǀ tshor bya med par de med pas ǁ tshor ba ñid ni bdag med pas ǀ
ǀ tshor bya de yaṅ raṅ bźin gyis ǁ yod pa med par khyod ñid bźed ǀ

7. saṃjñārthayor ananyatve mukhaṃ dahyeta vahninā ǀ
anyatve 'dhigamābhāvas tvayoktaṃ bhūtavādinā ǁ

ǀ miṅ daṅ don dag tha dad min ǁ me yis kha ñid 'tshig par 'gyur ǀ
ǀ gźan na'aṅ rtogs pa med 'gyur źes ǁ bden pa gsuṅ ba khyod kyis bstan ǀ

8. kartā svatantraḥ karmāpi tvayoktaṃ vyavahārataḥ ǀ
parasparāpekṣikī tu siddhis te 'bhimatānayoḥ ǁ

ǀ byed po raṅ dbaṅ las ñid kyaṅ ǁ tha sñad du ni khyod kyis bstan ǀ
ǀ phan tshun bltos pa can ñid du ǁ grub par khyod ni bźed pa lags ǀ

9. na kartāsti na bhoktāsti puṇyāpuṇyaṃ pratītyajam ǀ
yat pratītya na taj jātaṃ proktaṃ vācaspate tvayā ǁ

ǀ byed po yod min spyod pa'aṅ med ǁ bsod nams de min rten 'brel skyes ǀ
ǀ brten nas skyes gaṅ ma skyes źes ǁ tshig gi bdag po khyod kyis gsuṅs ǀ

5a gzuṅ : gzugs NP; c – vam T *mutil.*; bruvatā TG : vādinā M
6c tshor bya : tshor ba NP; d nāstīty abhima – T *mutil.*
7b dahyeta va – T *mutil.*
8c parasparāpekṣikī tu TMGA : parasparāpremaṣikīndrā W
9c gaṅ : kyaṅ NP

5. The [four great] elements are imperceptible to the eye, so how can the 'visible' consist of them? – Speaking thus of matter (*rūpa*) You rejected the belief in matter.

6. As it does not exist without [an object of feeling] feeling therefore is without self. And You are convinced that the object of feeling does not exist by own-being either.

7. If a concept [= a name, *miṅ*] and its object were non-different one's mouth would be burned by [the word] fire. If [they both] were different there would be no comprehension [of anything]. – Thus You have spoken as a speaker of truth.

8. That an agent is self-dependent and [his] action also is, You have [only] expressed conventionally. Actually You are convinced that both are established in mutual dependence.

9. [In the ultimate sense] no agent exists and no experiencer exists. Merit and demerit are dependently born. You have declared, O Master of words, that that which is dependently born is unborn!

5. Acc. to Abhidharma *rūpa* (= *saṃsthāna* & *varṇa*, cf. ŚS, 50) is made up of *catvāri mahābhūtāni* serving as *rūpakāraṇa*, cf. MK, IV, 1ff. The notion of *rūpa* (*rūpabuddhi*) is refuted at length ŚS, 45-54; BV, 16-24. Cf. also RĀ, I, 99 (cited *Prasannapadā*, p. 413), VI, 58; YṢ, 34. The argument is: no *bhūta*, no *bhautika*. – See also *Bhavasaṃkrāntisūtra* quoted *Prasannapadā*, p. 120 (*na cakṣuḥ prekṣate rūpam* ...).
6. This *skandha* also refuted ŚS, 55.
7. A celebrated argument: *Traité*, p. 1617; *Laṅkāvatārasūtra*, p. 87; *Nyāyasūtra*, II, 1, 51. Similarly VP, 51. Cf. also *Prajñāpāramitāpiṇḍārthasaṃgraha*, 48ff.
8. *kartā svatantraḥ* = Pāṇini I, 4, 54. – It is clear from the context that *kartṛ* here signifies a *pudgala* who '*punarbhavāya saṃskārān avidyānivṛtas tridhā abhisaṃskurute* ...' (MK, XXVI, 1) and not, as usual, and as the *ṭīkā* supposes, *īśvarādi* (cf. CS, III, 33-34 and notes). – The use of √*iṣ*, √*man* etc. (*ṭīkā* glosses *abhimata* with *svīkṛta*) indicating philosophical persuasion is interesting, cf. the use of Latin *placet* (translating Greek ἀρέσκει) and Spinoza's remark: '*Voluntas et intellectus unum et idem sunt*' (*Corr. ad Ethicam*, 2, 49). – *Nyāyabhāṣya* (KSS, XXXXIII, p. 194) attempts to refute the notion of *parasparāpekṣikī siddhi* thus: ... *netaretarāpekṣā kasya cit siddhir iti, 'yasmād ekābhāve 'nyatarābhāvād ubhayābhāvaḥ': yady ekasyānyatarāpekṣā siddhir anyatarasyedānīṃ kim apekṣā? yady anyatarasyaikāpekṣā siddhir ekasyedānīṃ kim apekṣā? evam ekasyābhove anyataran na sidhyatīty ubhayābhavaḥ prasajyate.* – Cf. BV, 63; MK, XVII, YṢ, 32; ŚS, 33-44.
9. Probably – like YṢ 48 (*pratītya jātaṃ cājātam āha tattvavidāṃ varaḥ*) – an allusion to *Anavataptahradāpasaṃkramaṇasūtra* (see *Vimalakīrtinirdeśa*, p. 26 etc.). Also *Varṇārhavarṇastotra*, V, 23-28; MK, VIII, 12.

10. ajñāyamānaṃ na jñeyaṃ vijñānaṃ tad vinā na ca |
tasmāt svabhāvato na sto jñānajñeye tvam ūcivān ||

| śes pa med par śes bya min || de med rnam par śes pa'aṅ med |
| de phyir śes daṅ śes bya dag || raṅ dṅos med ces khyod kyis gsuṅs |

11. lakṣyāl lakṣaṇam anyac cet syāt tal lakṣyam alakṣaṇam |
tayor abhāvo 'nanyatve vispaṣṭaṃ kathitaṃ tvayā ||

| mtshan ñid mtshon bya gźan ñid na || mtshon bya mtshan ñid med par 'gyur |
| tha dad min na'aṅ de med par || khyod kyis gsal po ñid du bstan |

12. lakṣyalakṣaṇanirmuktaṃ vāgudāhāravarjitam |
śāntaṃ jagad idaṃ dṛṣṭaṃ bhavatā jñānacakṣuṣā ||

| mtshan ñid mtshon bya rnam bral źiṅ || tshig gis brjod pa rnam spaṅs par |
| khyod kyis ye śes spyan ñid kyis || 'gro ba 'di dag źi bar mdzad |

13. na sann utpadyate bhāvo nāpy asan sadasan na ca |
na svato nāpi parato na dvābhyāṃ jāyate katham ||

| dṅos po yod pa ñid mi skye || med pa'aṅ ma yin yod med min |
| bdag las ma yin gźan las min || gñis min skye ba ji ltar bu |

14. na sataḥ sthitiyuktasya vināśa upapadyate |
nāsato 'śvaviṣāṇena samasya śamatā katham ||

| yod pa gnas par rigs 'gyur gyi || 'jig par 'gyur ba ma yin no |
| med pa mi gnas par rigs pas || 'jig par 'gyur ba ma yin no |

10a bya : pa NP; tvam ūcivān TG : te sūcitam M
11a na : ni NP; c abhāvo TM : abhāve G
14c nāsato 'śvaviṣāṇena TG : nāsataś ca viṣāṇena M; d śamatā T : samatā GM : samata W

10. [An object of knowledge is] no object of knowledge unless it is being known. But [this is impossible since] consciousness does not exist [previously] without it! – Therefore You have said that knowledge and the object of knowledge do not exist by own-being.

11. If a mark were different from the marked then the marked would exist [as such] without the mark [– which is absurd]. You have [also] clearly stated that neither exists if [conceived of as] non-different.

12. This world which is devoid of marked and mark, and free from the utterances of words You have regarded as calm (*śānta*) with your eye of cognition (*jñānacakṣuḥ*).

13. An existent thing does not arise, nor does a non-existent nor an existent and non-existent, neither from itself, [something] else nor both. [So] how can it be born [at all]?

14. It is not reasonable that an existent [thing which must be] connected with duration should be destroyed. [And] how can a non-existent [thing being] like the horns of a horse be extinguished?

10. Refutation of *vijñānaskandha:* BV, 26-56. About *jñāna/vijñāna* etc., see ref. May (1959), p. 104, n. 252. – For Nāgārjuna *manas, vijñāna* and *citta* are (as for Vasubandhu etc.) synonyms, as are *buddhi, mati* and (*tattva-*)*jñāna*. Here *jñāna* and *jñeya* are, of course, used, *metri causa,* for *vijñāna* and *vijñeya*. – For the form *svabhāvena* cf. *Mahāyānaviṃśikā,* 1-2; YṢ, 19; CS, III, 3.

11. For other refutations of *lakṣaṇa-lakṣya* see **Dvādaśadvāraka,* VI, 1; ŚS, 27; MK, V.

12. The first *pāda* = *Laṅkāvatārasūtra,* X, 255. In b CS, II, 14 has *lakṣyalakṣaṇavarjitam,* cf. MK, V, 5. Its use is not confined to *saṃskṛtalakṣaṇa,* but to any *dharmalakṣaṇa,* and thus it alludes polemically to Abhidharma. – There are *pañca cakṣūṃṣi,* cf. *Traité,* pp. 2260 ff; 439; *Vimalakīrtinirdeśa,* p. 168, n. 57. This verse refers to the *prajñācakṣus,* cf. CS, II, 16.

13. This is, to use later terminology, the *catuṣkoṭyutpādapratiṣedhamahāhetu* (cf. Atiśa, *Bodhipathapradīpa,* 193-196) for which cf. e.g. MK, I, 1; **Dvādaśadvāraka,* II, 1; ŚS, 3; CS, III, 9; **Madhyamaka-Śālistambasūtra* (BST, XII, p. 115) quoting MK, I, 1 and *Jñānasārasamuccaya,* 28. Cf. also MK, I, 7 (with which compare *Nyāyasūtra,* IV, I, 44 and *Laṅkāvatārasūtra,* II, 22).

14. Here *sthitiyukta* = *sat.* The verse corresponds to MK, VII, 27 (cf. *ibid.,* 20). In *pāda* c and d the translators had: *nāsato 'sthitiyuktasya vināśa upapadyate* ||.

15. bhāvān nārthāntaraṃ nāśo nāpy anarthāntaraṃ matam ।
arthāntare bhaven nityo nāpy anarthāntare bhavet ॥

16. ekatve na hi bhāvasya vināśa upapadyate ।
pṛthaktve na hi bhāvasya vināśa upapadyate ॥

17. vinaṣṭāt kāraṇāt tāvat kāryotpattir na yujyate ।
na cāvinaṣṭāt svapnena tulyotpattir matā tava ॥

। re źig źig pa'i rgyu las kyaṅ ॥ 'bras bu 'byuṅ bar mi rigs la ।
। ma źig las min rmi lam daṅ ॥ 'dra ba'i skye ba khyod ñid bźed ।

18. na niruddhān nāniruddhād bījād aṅkurasaṃbhavaḥ ।
māyotpādavad utpādaḥ sarva eva tvayocyate ॥

। sa bon źig daṅ ma źig las ॥ myu gu 'byuṅ ba ma yin pas ।
। khyod kyis skye ba thams cad ni ॥ sgyu ma 'byuṅ ba bźin du gsuṅs ।

19. atas tvayā jagad idaṃ parikalpasamudbhavam ।
parijñātam asadbhūtam anutpannam na naśyati ॥

। de phyir khyod kyis 'gro 'di dag ॥ yoṅs su brtags pa las byuṅ bar ।
। kun tu śes bya 'byuṅ ba na'aṅ ॥ skye ba med ciṅ 'gag med gsuṅs ।

20. nityasya saṃsṛtir nāsti naivānityasya saṃsṛtiḥ ।
svapnavat saṃsṛtiḥ proktā tvayā tattvavidāṃ vara ॥

। rtag la 'khor ba yod ma yin ॥ mi rtag pa la'aṅ 'khor ba med ।
। de ñid rig pa'i mchog khyod kyis ॥ 'khor ba rmi lam 'dra bar gsuṅs ।

21. svayaṃkṛtaṃ parakṛtaṃ dvābhyāṃ kṛtam ahetukam ।
tārkikair iṣyate duḥkhaṃ tvayā tūktaṃ pratītyajam ॥

। sdug bsṅal raṅ gis byas pa daṅ ॥ gźan gyis byas daṅ gñis kas byas ।
। rgyu med par ni rtog ge 'dod ॥ khyod kyis brten nas 'byuṅ bar gsuṅs ।

15c nityo TG : nityam M
17c svapnena TM : svapne 'pi G
18d MV, p. 97 : źig daṅ ma źig pa dag gis ॥ rgyu las 'bras bu 'byuṅ ba dag ॥ sgyu ma 'byuṅ ba bžin du 'byuṅ ॥ kun kyaṅ de bźin khyod kyis bsruṅs ॥ NP
19c parijñeyaṃ ca saṃbhūtaṃ ? Ṣ; d na naśyati TG : anaśvaram M

15. Destruction is not different from the entity (*bhāva*), nor can it be thought of as something non-different, [for] if it were something other [that the entity, it] would be permanent, and it could not occur if it were something non-different [from the entity supposed to be destroyed].

16. Of course (*hi*) destruction is not reasonable if the thing is a unity [and] of course destruction is not reasonable if the thing is manifold.

17. First of all (*tāvat*) it is not logical that the effect should arise from a cause which is destructed nor from one which is not [yet] destructed. [Therefore] You are convinced that origination is like a dream.

18. Neither from the destructed nor the non-destructed seed can the sprout possibly arise. You have stated that all origination is like the origination of an illusion.

19. Therefore You have fully understood that this world has arisen due to imagination. It is unreal [and as] unoriginated it cannot be destroyed.

20. There is no migration of a permanent [self], there is no migration of an impermanent [self]. [Therefore] You, the best among speakers of truth, have declared migration to be like a dream.

21. Dialecticians maintain that suffering is created by itself, created by [someone] else, created by both [or] without a cause, but You have stated that it is dependently born.

15. This and the following verse (which both lack Tib. versions) should be compared with MK, VII, 30-31. – For *matam* in *pāda* c (not *mataḥ*) cf. e.g. 11, 22 etc.

17. A *kāraṇa* (= *hetu*) neither exists previously nor subsequently to a *kārya* (= *phala*), let alone simultaneously with its effect. This is demonstrated MK, XX, 7-14. Also RĀ, I, 47; ŚS, 6.

18. This verse is inspired by *Śālistambasūtra* cited *Madhyamakāvatāra*, p. 97; *Pañjikā*, p. 579.

19. For *parikalpa* see *Laṅkāvatārasūtra, passim* (Suzuki's *Index*, p. 104) and May (1959), p. 65, n. 64. – While *sadbhūta* taken *saṃvṛtitaḥ* amounts to *kriyāyukta* (cf. May, *op.cit.*, p. 144, n. 414), *paramārthataḥ*, however, it indicates *anapekṣyasiddha, sasvabhāva* etc. (cf. *Akutobhayā* ad MK, II, 24; VV 57; MK, XXIV, 38).

20. This verse corresponds to MK, XVII, q.v.

21. Again this verse is closely related to MK, XII, 1 (= **Dvādaśadvāraka*, X, 1), cf. *Saṃyutta*, II, p. 19. - *tārkikaiḥ* = *vaiṣṇavādibhiḥ*.

22. yaḥ pratītyasamutpādaḥ śūnyatā saiva te matā |
bhāvaḥ svatantro nāstīti siṃhanādas tavātulaḥ ||

| rten ciṅ 'brel par gaṅ byuṅ ba || de ñid khyod ni stoṅ par bźed |
| dṅos po raṅ dbaṅ yod min źes || mñam med khyod kyi seṅ ge'i sgra |

23. sarvasaṃkalpanāśāya śūnyatāmṛtadeśanā |
yasya tasyām api grāhas tvayāsāv avasāditaḥ ||

| kun rtog thams cad spaṅs pa'i phyir || stoṅ ñid bdud rtsi ston mdzad na |
| gaṅ źig de la źen gyur pa || de ñid khyod kyis śin tu smad |

24. nirīhā vaśikāḥ śūnyā māyāvat pratyayodbhavāḥ |
sarvadharmās tvayā nātha niḥsvabhāvāḥ prakāśitāḥ ||

| bems po gźan dbaṅ stoṅ pa ñid || sgyu ma bźin du rkyen 'byuṅ bar |
| mgon po khyod kyis chos kun gyi || dṅos med goms par mdzad pa lags |

25. na tvayotpāditaṃ kiṃ cin na ca kiṃ cin nirodhitam |
yathā pūrvaṃ tathā paścāt tathatāṃ buddhavān asi ||

| khyod kyis cuṅ źig ma bskyed ciṅ || 'ga' yaṅ bkag pa ma mchis la |
| sṅon gyi ji ltar phyis de bźin || de bźin ñid ni thugs su chud |

26. āryair nisevitām enām anāgamya hi bhāvanām |
nānimittaṃ hi vijñānaṃ bhavatīha katham cana ||

| 'phags pa rnams kyis brten pa yi || bsgoms ma źugs par mtshan med 'di |
| rnam par śes par 'gar 'gyur ram || + + + + + + + |

22d tavātulaḥ AGMQW : tavātula TS
23c yasya TMS : tasya G
24d prakāśitāḥ TGM : prabhāvitāḥ ? S
26c nānimittaṃ hi TMGA : nimittaṃ na W. NP *corrup. sed v. Q* (ŚV, f. 315a): 'phags pa brten pa'i 'di lta bu || dṅos por rtogs pa ma yin źiṅ || rgyu mtshan med pa rnam śes ni || nam yaṅ 'byuṅ bar mi 'gyur to || (*sic!*); nānimittaṃ hi TMGA : nimittaṃ na W

22. The [fact of] dependent origination is exactly what You think of as emptiness. O, Your incomparable lion's roar is that no independent thing exists!

23. The ambrosial teaching of emptiness aims at abolishing all conceptions (*saṃkalpa*). But if someone believes in that [emptiness] You [have declared that] he is lost!

24. O saviour! [Since they] are inactive, dependent, empty, dependently arisen like an illusion, You have made it clear that all phenomena (*dharma*) are without own-being.

25. You have not put anything forward and not denied anything. Now as then You are aware of Suchness.

26. Unless one resorts to the development (*bhāvanā*) practised by the noble (*ārya*) ones, consciousness will of course never become signless (*animitta*) here.

22. For this celebrated stanza cf. the ref. given by May (1959), p. 237, n. 840. It is also discussed by La Vallée Poussin, *MCB*, III, p. 380. – For *siṃhanāda* v. note to BS, 101.

23. Like MK, XIII, 8 (see *Kāśyapaparivarta*, §§63-65) and XVII, 30 this verse leaves no doubt about *śūnyatāprayojana* acc. to Nāgārjuna. Also Candrakīrti's comm. to *Catuḥśataka*, XVI, 7; *Madhyamakāvatāra*, p. 310. – For *grāha* May, *op.cit.*, p. 190, n. 618.

24. See *Pañjikā*, p. 488 for this verse which may be inspired by *Lalitavistara*, XIII, 97-98, cited, *ibid.*, p. 532.

25. Acc. to *ṭīkā kiṃ cit* = *dharmādikam*. – The phrase *yathā pūrvaṃ tathā paścāt* also occurs *Dharmadhātustava*, 31; *Ratnagotravibhāga*, I, 51; *Samādhirāja*, XXIV, 5; *Aṅguttara*, I, p. 236 etc. – For the thought ŚS, 70; CS, II, 4, and for the conception of *sarvadharmasamatā* Hōbōgirin, s.v. *byōdō*. *Siddhi*, pp. 757-761 for *tathatā* acc. to the Mādhyamikas.

26. *ānimitta* (or *animitta*) is the second *vimokṣamukha*, cf. BS, 63ff; *Mahābhārata*, XII, 190, 11; XII, 191, 7 etc.; CPD, s.v.; *Laṅkāvatārasūtra*, p. 200; BHSD, s.v. – For *bhāvanā* cf. especially *Madhyamakaratnapradīpa*, VII (*Bhāvanākramādhikāra*); *MCB*, II, pp. 102-104.

27. animittam anāgamya mokṣo nāsti tvam uktavān I
atas tvayā mahāyāne tat sākalyena deśitam II

I mtshan ma med la ma źugs par II thar pa med ces gsuṅs pa'i phyir I
I de phyir khyod kyis theg chen la II ma lus par ni de ñid bstan I

28. yad avāptaṃ mayā puṇyaṃ stutvā tvāṃ stutibhājanam I
nimittabandhanāpetaṃ bhūyāt tenākhilaṃ jagat II

I bstod pa'i snod khyod bstod pa las II bdag gis bsod nams gaṅ thob pa I
I des ni 'gro ba ma lus rnams II mtshan ma'i 'chiṅ las grol gyur cig I

II iti lokātītastavaḥ samāptaḥ II

I "jig rten las 'das pa bstod pa
slob dpon 'phags pa klu sgrub kyis mdzad pa rdzogs so I

27c ła : rnams NP
28b gis : gi NP

27. You have said that there is no liberation unless one resorts to the signless. Therefore You have demonstrated it in all details in Mahāyāna.

28. May the entire world by the merit which I have obtained by praising You, a fit vessel of praise, become free from the bondage of signs (*nimitta*)!

27. *Pañjikā*, p. 154 glosses *sākalyena* with *vistarataḥ*.

28. This verse forms a *puṇyapariṇāmanā* as do the final verses in the other hymns. – Cf. also the verse ascribed to Nāgārjuna by Jñānaśrīmitra (*Sākārasiddhiśāstra*, p. 405): *bādhe* (for *bandhe?*) *nāmanimittānām ākārasya ca na kṣatiḥ* ...

Acintyastava ||
bSam gyis mi khyab par bstod pa ||

1. pratītyajānāṃ bhāvānāṃ naiḥsvābhāvyaṃ jagāda yaḥ |
   taṃ namāmy asamajñānam acintyam anidarśanam ||

| gaṅ źig dṅos po rten 'byuṅ rnams || ṅo bo med pa ñid du gsuṅs |
| ye śes mñam med bsam mi khyab || dpe med de la phyag 'tshal lo |

2. yathā tvayā mahāyāne dharmanairātmyam ātmanā |
   viditaṃ deśitaṃ tadvad dhīmadbhyaḥ karuṇāvaśāt ||

| ji ltar khyod kyis theg chen la || ñid kyis chos la bdag med rtogs |
| de bźin blo daṅ ldan rnams la || thugs rje'i dbaṅ gis bstan pa mdzad |

3. pratyayebhyaḥ samutpannam anutpannaṃ tvayoditam |
   svabhāvena na taj jātam iti śūnyaṃ prakāśitam ||

| rkyen rnams las ni 'brel 'byuṅ ba || ma skyes lags par khyod kyis gsuṅs |
| ṅo bo ñid kyis de ma skyes || de phyir stoṅ par rab tu bstan |

4. yadvac chabdaṃ pratītyeha pratiśabdasamudbhavaḥ |
   māyāmarīcivac cāpi tathā bhavasamudbhavaḥ ||

| ji ltar 'di na sgra brten nas || brag ca kun tu 'byuṅ ba ltar |
| sgyu ma smig rgyu bźin du daṅ || de bźin srid pa kun tu 'byuṅ |

5. māyāmarīcigandharvanagarapratibimbakāḥ |
   yady ajātāḥ saha svapnair na syāt taddarśanādikam ||

| sgyu ma daṅ ni smig rgyu daṅ || dri za'i groṅ khyer gzugs brñan daṅ |
| rmi lam gal te ma skyes na || mthoṅ ba la sogs dpe med 'gyur |

1b naiḥsvābhāvyaṃ AGMQ : naiḥsvabhāvyaṃ T
2c deśitaṃ TG : karuṇāvaśāt M; d karuṇāvaśāt TG : deśitam M
4b pratītyeha AGMQT : pratītyajam W; brag ca N : brag cha P

Hymn to the Inconceivable [Buddha]

1. I bow down to the inconceivable, incomparable [Buddha] whose cognition (*jñāna*) is unequalled [for] he has preached that [all] dependently born things lack own-being.

2. Just as You in Mahāyāna personally understood the selflessness of phenomena, accordingly You have, under the sway of compassion, demonstrated it to the wise [bodhisattvas].

3. You have stated that [all that] has arisen from conditions is unoriginated. You have declared that it is not born through own-being (*svabhāva*), and thus it is empty.

4. Just as an echo here [in this world] arises dependently upon a sound thus also the [entire] origination of existence is like an illusion and a mirage.

5. If illusions, mirages, cities of Gandharvas and reflections are unborn along with dreams, there can be no [real] vision etc. of them.

1. For the form *naiḥsvābhāvya*, v. VV, 17 with ed. note. – The epithet *acintya* is confined to five things, cf. *Traité*, pp. 1639, 1983. Note that *pāda* d also occurs infra, 59; *Śatapañcāśatka*, 151 (= 59).
2. Buddha's motive for delivering his *dharmadeśanā* (= *pudgaladharmanairātmya*) to bodhisattvas (*dhīmat*) is sheer *karuṇā*, v. CS, I, 1-3 and notes and the initial stanza of *Mahāyānaviṃśikā: avācyo vācakair dharmaḥ kṛpayā yena deśitaḥ* | *namo 'cintyaprabhavāya buddhāyāsaṅgabuddhaye* ||.
3. Perhaps the same canonical allusion as CS,I, 9, q.v.; cf. YṢ, 18-19; *Stutyatītastava*, 5: *gaṅ źig rkyen las de ma mchis* || *dṅos rnams rkyen las ji ltar skye* || *de skad mkhas pa khyod gsuṅs pas* || *spros pa rnams ni bcad pa lags* ||.
4. Here, as often, *bhava* refers to *pañca skandha*, v. MK, XXVI, 8. – For the various ˬxamples see ref. CS, I, 3.
5. The comm. takes *tad°* (in *pāda* d) as referring to *māyādi*, but surely the context requires that it refers to *skandha* etc., cf. BV, 24.

6. hetupratyayasaṃbhūtā yathaite kṛtakāḥ smṛtāḥ |
tadvat pratyayajaṃ viśvaṃ tvayoktaṃ nātha sāṃvṛtam ||
| ji ltar rgyu rkyen las byuṅ ba || de dag byas pa can du bźed |
| de bźin rkyen las byuṅ ba kun || mgon po khyod kyis kun rdzob gsuṅs |

7. asty etat kṛtakaṃ sarvaṃ yat kiṃcid bālalāpanam |
riktamuṣṭipratīkāśam ayathārthaprakāśitam ||
| byis pa gaṅ dag ci brjod pa || bgyis pa źes 'brid de mchis te |
| chaṅ pa stoṅ pa 'dra ba lags || don bźin ma lags rab tu bstan |

8. kṛtakaṃ vastu no jātaṃ tadā kiṃ vārtamānikam |
kasya nāśād atītaṃ syād utpitsuḥ kim apekṣate ||
| gaṅ tshe byas pa'i dṅos ma skyes || de tshe da ltar byuṅ ba ci |
| gaṅ źig pas na 'das par 'gyur || ma 'oṅs pa yaṅ ji ltar bltos |

9. svasmān na jāyate bhāvaḥ parasmān nobhayād api |
na san nāsan na sadasan kutaḥ kasyodayas tadā ||
| raṅ las dṅos po skye ba med || gźan daṅ gñis ka las ma yin |
| yod min med min yod med min || de tshe gaṅ las gaṅ źig 'byuṅ |

10. ajāte na svabhāvo 'sti kutaḥ svasmāt samudbhavaḥ |
svabhāvābhāvasiddhyaiva parasmād apy asaṃbhavaḥ ||
| ma skyes pa la raṅ bźin med || ci phyir raṅ las kun tu 'byuṅ |
| raṅ bźin dṅos po med grub pas || gźan las kyaṅ ni 'byuṅ ba med |

6b smṛtāḥ TG : matāḥ M; d sāṃvṛtam TG : saṃvṛtam M; kun rdzob : de ltar NP
7a asty etat AGTW : asti tat MTW; b bālalāpanam T : bālalāpitam GM; 'brid : bgyid NP; d ayathārthaprakāśitam TG : yathārtham aprakāśitam M
8b ci : yi NP
9d kutaḥ TGS : kṛtaḥ M; gaṅ źig : gźan źig NP
10b svasmāt TMS : kasmāt G; ci phyir : de phyir NP

6. Just as [things] arising from causes and conditions are handed down as composite (*kṛtaka*), thus You have, O saviour, said that the entire conditionally born [world exists only] by convention.

7. It is a meaningless [statement] enticing fools [that] something created (*kṛtaka*) exists as a whole (*sarva*)! It is a false statement, [delusive] like an empty fist.

8. If a composite thing (*vastu*) is not born, how then can it be present? From the destruction of what could it be past? How can it be related (*apekṣate*) when about to arise [as future]?

9. A thing is not born from itself, [something] else or both, whether it be existent, non-existent, or existent and non-existent. How then can anything arise?

10. The unborn has no own-being [for] how could it arise from itself? Nor can it arise from [something] else since it is definitely established that there is no own-being.

6. For *kṛtaka*, MK, XV, 1-2. – *sāṃvṛta* May (1959), p. 226, n. 777.
7. *sarvam* (like *viśvam* supra) refers to *sarve dharmāḥ*, i.e. *skandha*, *āyatana*, *dhātu*, see YṢ, 30; BV, 66; *Traité*, p. 1748; *Tattvasaṃgrahapañjikā*, p. 14; May, *op.cit.*, p. 206, n. 689 (ref.); Schayer, *Contributions* ... p. 41, n. – Nāgārjuna's point is that one cannot say '*asti*' about something which is *pratītyasamutpanna*, cf. YṢ, 37; ŚS, 71. – For *yat kiṃcit*, May, *op.cit.*, p. 62, n. 51 (ref.). – The form *bālalāpana* is probably a metrical substitute for the common *bālollāpana* (cf. ref. *Traité*, p. 1195, n. 2) but *bālapralāpa* (*Prasannapadā*, p. 12), *bālopalāpana* (*Ālokamālā*, 177), *bālālāpana* (*Daśabhūmika*, p. 43) also occur. For *riktamuṣṭi*, *Traité*, *ibid.*; *Upālipariprcchā*, p. 131, n. 12; *Suvikrāntavikrāmipariprcchā*, p. 110 etc. – Most recently CPD, II, p. 476, s.v. *upalāpanā*. – *bālalāpana* also *Majjhima*, II, p. 261 (not in PED).
8. Other refutations of *kālatraya* in MK, XIX; ŚS, 29; BV, 31; *Traité*, pp. 1691-1996. – *utpitsu* = *anāgata* (as e.g. *Madhyamakahṛdayakārikā*, III, 161 etc.).
9. In other words: nothing whatsoever (cf. the *catuṣkoṭyutpādapratiṣedhamahāhetu*, referred to supra, CS, I, 13) arises from anything whatsoever (the *vajrakaṇa-mahāhetu, ibid.*, and *Pañjikā* to *Bodhipathapradīpa*, 197-200). For *pāda* c see also note to CS, I, 13 and MHK, III, 241-242.
10. The commentary reads *ajātena* (... *kena? ajātena, anutpannena* ...) which is most unlikely, cf. Tib. and the verse quoted by Haribhadra (*Āloka*, p. 39): *ajātasya svabhāvena śāśvatocchedatā kutaḥ* ... – *svabhāvābhāvasiddhyaiva* ... corresponds to *kutaḥ svabhāvasyābhāve* ... MK, XV, 3, q.v.

11. svatve sati paratvaṃ syāt paratve svatvam iṣyate |
    āpekṣikī tayoḥ siddhiḥ pārāvāram ivoditā ||

| raṅ ñid yod na gźan yod 'gyur || gźan ñid yod na raṅ ñid yod |
| de dag bltos pa can du grub || pha rol tshu rol bźin du gsuṅs |

12. yadā nāpekṣate kiṃ cit kutaḥ kiṃ cit tadā bhavet |
    yadā nāpekṣate dīrghaṃ kuto hrasvādikaṃ tadā ||

| gaṅ tshe ci la'aṅ mi bltos pa || de tshe gaṅ la gaṅ źig 'byuṅ |
| gaṅ tshe riṅ la mi bltos pa || de tshe thuṅ sogs ga la mchis |

13. astitve sati nāstitvaṃ dīrghe hrasvaṃ tathā sati |
    nāstitve sati cāstitvaṃ yat tasmād ubhayaṃ na sat ||

14. ekatvaṃ ca tathānekam atītānāgatādi ca |
    saṃkleśo vyavadānaṃ ca samyaṅmithyā svataḥ kutaḥ ||

| ji ltar gcig du ma mchis pa || 'das daṅ ma 'oṅs la sogs pa |
| ñon moṅs rnam byaṅ de bźin te || yaṅ dag log pa'aṅ raṅ las ci |

15. svata eva hi yo nāsti bhāvaḥ sarvo 'sti kas tadā |
    para ity ucyate yo 'yaṃ na vinā svasvabhāvataḥ ||

| dṅos gaṅ raṅ las ma mchis na || de tshe thams cad ci źig mchis |
| gźan źes brjod pa gaṅ lags te || raṅ gi raṅ bźin med na min |

16. na svabhāvo 'sti bhāvānāṃ parabhāvo 'sti no yadā |
    bhāvagrahagrahāveśaḥ paratantro 'sti kas tadā ||

| gaṅ tshe gźan gyi dṅos med pa || de tshe dṅos rnams raṅ bźin med |
| de tshe gźan dbaṅ dṅos 'dzin pa || gdon gyi theg pa ci źig mchis |

11d pārāvāram TM : pārāvāra G
13b tathā AGMQT : yathā W
14a ekatvaṃ ca AGMQT : ekatvādi W; du : sogs NP; c rnam byaṅ : rnams kyaṅ NP
15c yo 'yaṃ M : yo yaṃ TG; d svasvabhāvataḥ : GMS : sa svabhāvataḥ T
16b 'sti no yadā AGMQT : yadāsti na W; c bhāvagrāha° M (*cf.* n.); dbaṅ : dṅos NP; d gdon : don NP

11. If there were own-being there would be other-being. In case of other-being own-being [could be] maintained: Establishment of those two has been stated [by You] to be correlative like the further and nearer shore.

12. When it is not related to anything how, then, can that thing exist? When it is not related to [something] long how can [something] short etc. exist?

13. When there is existence there is non-existence, as there is short when there is long. And since (*yat*) there is existence when there is non-existence therefore each of the two (*ubhaya*) do not exist.

14. Unity and multiplicity, past and future etc., defilement and purification, true and false – how [can they exist] by themselves?

15. Of course, when a thing (*bhāva*) does not exist quite by itself how, then, can it exist as a whole? That [thing] which is called 'other' does not exist without its own-being.

16. When there is no other-being things have no own-being. What [kind of] seizure (*grahāveśa*) of materialism (*bhāvagraha*) is then [the concept of an independent] dependent [nature]!

11. *pārāvāra* in this sense, e.g. *Prasannapadā*, pp. 101, 264, 458; *Mahāyānaviṃśikā*, 2: *pārāvāram ivotpannāḥ svabhāvena pratītyajāḥ* ... (against Tucci's reading ... *na cotpannāḥ* ...). – *svatva* in *pāda* a and b ~ *raṅ gi bdag ñid* (ŚS, 53).

12. For this and the following verse see RĀ, I, 48-49 (cf. *Prasannapadā*, p. 10, n. 4; *Madhyamakāvatāra*, p. 227). – This standpoint is related *Viśeṣāvaśyakabhāṣya*, p. 337-338: ... *bhavato 'bhiprāyo yathā na svataḥ, na parataḥ, nobhayataḥ, na cānyataḥ siddhiḥ sambhāvyate bhāvānām, hrasvadīrghādivyapadeśavat; iha na hrasvaṃ svataḥ sidhyati dīrghāpekṣatvāt; na parataḥ, parasiddhyabhāvāt; nobhayataḥ, tabudhayābhāvat; na cānyato 'napekṣatvāt* ...

14. *eka-aneka* etc. are *pratītyasamutpanna*, cf. ŚS, 7. – *saṃkleśa-vyavadāna*, v. *Siddhi*, pp. 214-220.

15. See MK, XV, 3 for the interpretation: *svabhāvaḥ parabhāvasya parabhāvo hi kathyate* |.

16. The compound *bhāvagrahagrahāveśa* also occurs in a verse quoted in *Subhāṣitasaṃgraha* (ed. Bendall), p. 388. The form *bhāvagrāha*° would be more correct (cf. May, *op.cit.*, p. 190, n. 618) but it is poorly supported textually. But cf. *Gauḍapādīyakārikā*, II, 29; III, 32, 38; IV, 82, 84 (*graha* for *grāha*). Here *paratantra*, like *sarva* in 15 b, signifies a relative entity, something dependent conceived as a whole.

17. ādāv eva samaṃ jātāḥ svabhāvena ca nirvṛtāḥ |
anutpannāś ca tattvena tasmād dharmās tvayoditāḥ ||
| gdod ma ñid nas mñam gyur pa || raṅ bźin gyis kyaṅ mya ṅan 'das |
| yaṅ dag par ni ma skyes lags|| de slad chos rnams khyod kyis gsuṅs |

18. niḥsvabhāvās tvayā dhīman rūpādyāḥ saṃprakāśitāḥ |
phenabudbudamāyābhramarīcikadalīsamāḥ ||
| blo ldan khyod kyis gzugs la sogs || ṅo bo ñid med par bstan pa |
| dbu ba chu bur sgyu la sogs || smig rgyu chu śiṅ 'dra ba lags |

19. indriyair upalabdhaṃ yat tat tattvena bhaved yadi |
jātās tattvavido bālās tattvajñānena kiṃ tadā |
| dbaṅ po rnams kyis gaṅ dmigs de || gal te yaṅ dag mchis gyur na |
| byis pas yaṅ dag rig par 'gyur || de tshe yaṅ dag śes pas ci |

20. jaḍatvam apramāṇatvam athāvyākṛtatām api |
viparītaparijñānam indriyāṇāṃ tvam ūcivān ||
| dbaṅ po rnams ni bems po daṅ || tshad ma ñid kyaṅ ma yin daṅ |
| luṅ ma bstan pa ñid daṅ ni || log par yoṅs śes khyod kyis gsuṅs |

21. ajñānenāvṛto yena yathāvan na prapadyate |
lokas tena yathābhūtam iti matvā tvayoditam ||
| gaṅ gis ci źig ma rtogs pa || yaṅ dag ji bźin thugs chud nas |
| des na 'jig rten mi śes pas || bsgribs pa źes kyaṅ khyod kyis gsuṅs |

22. astīti śāśvatī dṛṣṭir nāstīty ucchedadarśanam |
tenāntadvayanirmukto dharmo 'yaṃ deśitas tvayā ||
| yod ces pa ni rtag par lta || med ces pa ni chad par lta |
| des na mtha' gñis bral ba yi || chos de khyod kyis bstan pa mdzad |

17a de tshe : gaṅ tshe NP
20d ūcivān TG : uktavān M (*cf.* CS, I, 10)
21b prapadyate TG : pratipannaḥ M
22a śāśvatī TG : śāśvata° M; rtag N : ltag P

17. [Since] they are originally born equal and extinguished by own-being, therefore You have said that phenomena (*dharma*) are in reality unborn.

18. You have, O sage, shown that form and [the remaining aggregates] lack own-being [and that they are] like foam, bubbles, illusions, clouds, mirages, and plantains.

19. If that which is perceived with the senses were [connected] with [any] reality, fools would be born with knowledge of reality. What then would knowledge of reality be worth?

20. You have stated that the senses are dull, unreliable, unprecise and [sources of] wrong understanding.

21. Having thought of it You have stated that it is because the world is shrouded in ignorance that it does not obtain the truth correctly.

22. 'Exists' is the dogma of Eternalism. 'Exists not' is the dogma of Annihilation. [In order to avoid the two extremes] You have therefore shown this principle (*dharma*) [of dependent co-origination] which is free from the two extremes.

17. Allusion to an often cited verse from the *Ratnameghasūtra*, v. *Prasannapadā*, p. 225; May, *op.cit.*, p. 177, n. 572. Cf. also *Mahāyānaviṃśikā*, 1: *svabhāvena na cotpannā nirvṛtāś ca na tattvataḥ* | *yathākāśaṃ tathā buddhāḥ sattvāś caivaikalakṣaṇāḥ* ||.
18. Cf. CS, I, 3; ŚS, 6; *Catuḥśataka*, XIII, 25. The author above all has *Saṃyutta*, III, p. 142 in mind, see *Traité*, p. 358; BV, 12-13.
19. This is an echo of *Laṅkāvatāra*, III, 36; X, 136, q.v. Cf. also YṢ, 3.
20. I have not traced the source of this important verse. For *jaḍa*, SS, 231b.
21. Perhaps the same canonical allusion as MK, XVII, 28: *avidyānivṛto jantus tṛṣṇāsaṃyojanaś ca saḥ* ... It is quoted *in extenso* in *Jñānaprasthāna*, I, 5, 9, q.v.
22. Similarly MK, XV, 10; YṢ, 1 etc. – *dharmo 'yam*, or *saddharmo 'yam* refers to Buddha's *dharmadeśanā*, i.e. *pratītyasamutpāda* or *śūnyatā*, see RĀ, I, 25 ff; II, 16-18; MK, XXIV, 12; XXV, 24; XXVI, 30 etc.

23. catuṣkoṭivinirmuktās tena dharmās tvayoditāḥ I
vijñānasyāpy avijñeyā vācāṃ kim uta gocarāḥ II

I des na chos rnams mu bźi daṅ II bral bar khyod kyis bka' stsal lags I
I rnam śes bya ba'am ma lags la II + + + + + + + I

24. svapnendrajālikodbhūtaṃ dvicandrodvīkṣaṇaṃ yathā I
bhūtaṃ tadvastu no bhūtaṃ tathā dṛṣṭaṃ jagat tvayā II

I rmi lam mig 'phrul las byuṅ daṅ II zla ba gñis la sogs mthoṅ bźin I
I 'gro ba 'byuṅ ba de dṅos su II ma byuṅ de bźin khyod kyis gzigs I

25. utpannaś ca sthito naṣṭaḥ svapne yadvat sutas tathā I
na cotpannaḥ sthito naṣṭa ukto loko 'rthatas tvayā II

26. kāraṇāt saṃbhavo dṛṣṭo yathā svapne tathetaraḥ I
saṃbhavaḥ sarvabhāvānāṃ vibhavo 'pi matas tathā II

I ji ltar rgyu las rmi lam na II 'byuṅ ba mthoṅ ba de bźin du I
I dṅos po thams cad 'byuṅ ba bźin II 'jig pa'aṅ de bźin bźed pa lags I

27. rāgādijaṃ yathā duḥkhaṃ saṃkleśasaṃsṛtī tathā I
saṃbhārapūraṇān muktiḥ svapnavad bhāṣitā tvayā II

I de bźin chags sogs sdug bsṅal daṅ II 'khor ba sdug bsṅal kun ñon moṅs I
I tshogs rdzogs pa daṅ thar pa yaṅ II rmi lam 'dra bar khyod kyis gsuṅs I

28. jātaṃ tathaiva no jātam āgataṃ gatam ity api I
baddho muktas tathā jñānī dvayam icchen na tattvavit II

I de bźin skyes daṅ ma skyes daṅ II 'oṅs pa daṅ ni soṅ ba yaṅ I
I de bźin bciṅs grol ye śes la II gñis 'dod yaṅ dag rig ma lags I

23d vācāṃ TG : vācaḥ M : vātā W; d NP †

24b dvicandrodvīkṣaṇaṃ AGMQT : divicandrādikṣaṇa W; c tadvastu no bhūtam TM (nodbhūtam G) : tadvastunābhūtam ? S

25b sutas TM : svatas G

26d matas tathā TG : tathā mataḥ MW

27a rāgādijaṃ AGMQT : rāgādikaṃ WS; yathā TGM : tathā WS; b saṃkleśasaṃsṛtī (°saṃsṛtir M) tathā TM : tathā ... saṃsṛtī G; c °pūraṇān TGM : °pūraṇaṃ ? S

28c baddho muktas AGMQT : mukto baddhas W; d icchen TG : icchan M : icche W

23. Therefore You have said that phenomena (*dharma*) are beyond the four categories (*koṭi*). They are not knowable to consciousness, much less within the sphere of words.

24. As is the appearance of a magician [in a] dream [or] the sight of a double-moon, thus You have seen the world as a creation not created as a substance (*vastu*).

25. Just as a son who is born, established and deceased in a dream, thus the world, You have said, is not really born, enduring or destroyed.

26. Just as origination in a dream is experienced due to causality, thus You are convinced that the common origination and dissolution of all things is the same.

27. You have announced that suffering born from desire etc., as well as defilement, migration and liberation [resulting] from the fulfilment [of both] collections are like a dream.

28. When [someone] cognizes [something] as born or unborn, present or gone, bound or liberated [then] he maintains duality [and consequently] does not know the truth (*tattva*).

23. Cf. *Prasannapadā*, p. 374: ... *paramārthasatyaṃ katamat? yatra jñānasyāpy apracāraḥ kaḥ punar vādo 'kṣarāṇām* ... Quoted *Prajñāpradīpa* (234 a 7) from *Akṣayamatinirdeśasūtra;* also *Prajñāpradīpaṭīkā,* Za 101a 4 and *Satyadvayavibhaṅgavṛtti,* Ṣa 5a. – The notion of *catuṣkoṭi* (or *catuṣprakāra,* cf. RĀ, II, 15) has been the subject of much discussion, see recently e.g. D. Seyfort Ruegg: 'The Uses of the Four Positions of the Catuṣkoṭi and the Problem of the Description of Reality in Mahāyāna Buddhism', *JIP,* V, pp. 1-71.

24. Cf. ref. CS, I, 3.

25. This verse, which does not occur in Tib. is quoted *Pañjikā*, p. 573 (*pādas* c and d). It is inspired by *Samādhirāja,* IX 17 cited e.g. *Prasannapadā,* p. 178; *Caryāgīti,* p. 217; *Tattvasārasaṃgraha,* 89b 7 etc.

26. MK, XX is devoted to a critique of *saṃbhava-vibhava.* See in particular v. 11: *dṛśyate saṃbhavaś caiva mohād vibhava eva ca* obviously moulded from *Laṅkāvatāra,* X, 37: *saṃbhavaṃ vibhavaṃ caiva mohāt paśyanti bāliśāḥ | na saṃbhavaṃ na vibhavaṃ prajñāyukto vipaśyati ||.*

27. This and the following verse would seem to allude to some such passage as *Aṣṭasāhasrikā,* cited *Prasannapadā,* pp. 449-450. – On *advaya* in Mahāyāna in general, *Vimalakīrtinirdeśa,* pp. 301-318.

29. utpattir yasya naivāsti tasya kā nirvṛtir bhavet |
māyāgajaprakāśatvād ādiśāntatvam arthataḥ ||
| gaṅ la skyes pa yod ma lags || de la mya ṅan 'das gaṅ yod |
| sgyu ma'i glaṅ po 'dra bas na || don du gzod nas źi ba ñid |

30. utpanno 'pi na cotpanno yadvan māyāgajo mataḥ |
utpannaṃ ca tathā viśvam anutpannaṃ ca tattvataḥ ||
| skyes pa ñid na'aṅ ma skyes pa || sgyu ma'i glaṅ po ji bźin bźed |
| de bźin thams cad skyes pa 'am || yaṅ dag par ni ma skyes lags |

31. ameyair aprameyānāṃ pratyekaṃ nirvṛtiḥ kṛtā |
lokanāthair hi sattvānāṃ na kaś cin mocitaś ca taiḥ ||
| 'jig rten mgon po dpag med kyis || sems can dpag tu ma mchis pa |
| so sor mya ṅan 'das mdzad kyaṅ || de dag gis kyaṅ gaṅ ma bkrol |

32. te ca sattvāś ca no jātā ye nirvānti na te sphuṭam |
na kaś cin mocitaḥ kaiś cid iti proktaṃ mahāmune ||
| thub chen gaṅ phyir sems can rnams || raṅ las ma skyes de yi phyir |
| gaṅ yaṅ gaṅ gis ma bkrol źes || de skad khyod kyis gsal bar gsuṅs |

33. māyākārakṛtaṃ yadvad vastuśūnyaṃ tathetarat |
vastuśūnyaṃ jagat sarvaṃ tvayoktaṃ kārakas tathā ||
| ji ltar sgyu ma mkhan gyis byas || dṅos po stoṅ pa de bźin du |
| byas pa thams cad dṅos stoṅ gźan || khyod gsuṅs de bźin byed pa po |

34. kārako 'pi kṛto 'nyena kṛtatvaṃ nātivartate |
atha vā tatkriyākartṛ kārakasya prasajyate ||
| byed pa po yaṅ gźan gyis bgyis || byas pa can du 'gyur ba lags |
| yaṅ na de yi bya ba byed || byed pa por ni thal bar 'gyur |

29a yasya naivāsti T : naiva yasyāsti GM; la : las NP; d gzod : bzod NP
32b raṅ las *pro* myaṅ 'das ? NP; sphuṭam TMS : 'sphuṭam G
33a sgyu N : sgyur P; d gsuṅs : gsuṅ NP
34b kṛtatvaṃ TGMS : kartṛtvaṃ AW; c °kartṛ T (= S ?) : °kartrā ? G: °kartrī (!) M : °kartā W

29. That which does not arise, how can that be extinguished? Since it is like an illusory elephant it is in reality originally at peace.

30. Just as [we] are convinced that an illusory elephant, though [apparently] born, is however not born, thus the whole [world is apparently] born but in reality unborn.

31. Immeasurable World-saviours have [apparently] liberated innumerable beings one by one, but [in reality] not one [being] has been liberated by them!

32. Is it not a clear statement of Yours, O great sage, that when those beings who are extinguished are [in fact] not born [at all, then] no one is liberated by anyone!

33. Just as the work of a magician is empty of substance, all the rest of the world has been said by You to be empty of substance – including a creator:

34. If the creator is created by another [creator], he cannot avoid being created [and, consequently, is not permanent]. Alternatively (*atha vā*) [if he is created by himself] it implies that the creator is the agent of the activity affecting himself (*tatkriyā*) [– which is absurd, *svātmani kriyāvirodhāt*].

29. For the *māyāgaja,* RĀ, II, 10-13; VS, '2': *MCB,* II, p. 48.

31. For this v. *Traité,* pp. 1260-1261 and *Vajracchedikā,* § 3: ... *na kaś cit sattvaḥ parinirvāpito bhavati. tat kasya hetoḥ? sacet ... bodhisattvasya sattvasaṃjñā pravarteta, na sa bodhisattva iti vaktavyaḥ* ... Cf. CS, II, 9 etc.

33. The *māyākāra, Saṃdhinirmocana,* p. 170; *Mahāyānaviṃśikā,* 17-18.

34. Refutation of *kāraka:* BV, 6-9; **Dvādaśadvāraka,* X; *WZKSO,* XII-XIII, pp. 85-100; MK, VIII; *Bhāvanākrama,* I, pp. 200-201.

35. nāmamātraṃ jagat sarvam ity uccair bhāṣitaṃ tvayā |
abhidhānāt pṛthagbhūtam abhidheyaṃ na vidyate ||

| 'di dag thams cad miṅ tsam źes || khyod kyis gsuṅ ni bstod de gsuṅs |
| brjod pa las ni gźan gyur pa || brjod par bgyi ba yod ma mchis |

36. kalpanāmātram ity asmāt sarvadharmāḥ prakāśitāḥ |
kalpanāpy asatī proktā yayā śūnyaṃ vikalpyate ||

| de phyir chos rnams thams cad ni || rtog pa tsam źes khyod kyis gsuṅs |
| gaṅ gis stoṅ par rnam rtog pa'i || rtog pa yaṅ ni med ces gsuṅs |

37. bhāvābhāvadvayātītam anatītaṃ ca kutra cit |
na ca jñānaṃ na ca jñeyaṃ na cāsti na ca nāsti yat ||

| dṅos daṅ dṅos med gñis 'das pa || la lar ma 'das pa yaṅ lags |
| śes pa med ciṅ śes bya'aṅ med || med min yod min gaṅ lags daṅ |

38. yan na caikaṃ na cānekaṃ nobhayaṃ na ca nobhayam |
anālayam athāvyaktam acintyam anidarśanam ||

| gaṅ yaṅ gcig min du ma'aṅ min || gñis ka ma yin gcig kyaṅ med |
| gźi med pa daṅ mi gsal daṅ || bsam mi khyab daṅ dpe med daṅ |

39. yan nodeti na ca vyeti nocchedi na ca śāśvatam |
tad ākāśapratīkāśaṃ nākṣarajñānagocaram ||

| gaṅ yaṅ mi skye mi 'gag daṅ || chad pa med ciṅ rtag med pa |
| de ni nam mkha' 'dra ba lags || yi ge ye śes spyod yul min |

40. yaḥ pratītyasamutpādaḥ śūnyatā saiva te matā |
tathāvidhaś ca saddharmas tatsamaś ca tathāgataḥ ||

| de ni rten ciṅ 'brel par 'byuṅ || de ni stoṅ par khyod bźed lags |
| dam pa'i chos kyaṅ de lta bu || de bźin gśegs pa'aṅ de daṅ mtshuṅs |

35b gsuṅ P : bsuṅ N
36d yayā TMS : yathā G
37c jñātaṃ T (= S?) : jñānaṃ GM
38c gźi : bźi NP
40a °samutpādaḥ TGQS : °samudbhavaḥ M

35. You have loudly announced that the entire world is merely a name. Nothing expressible (*abhidheya*) is to be found isolated from the expression (*abhidhāna*).

36. Therefore You have declared that all phenomena are merely abstractions (*kalpanā*). Yes, even the abstraction through which emptiness is conceived is said to be untrue.

37-39. [That which] has transcended the duality of being and non-being without, however, having transcended anything at all; that which is not knowledge or knowable, not existent nor non-existent, not one nor many, not both nor neither; [that which is] without foundation, unmanifest, inconceivable, incomparable; that which arises not, disappears not, is not to be annihilated and is not permanent, *that* is [Reality] which is like space [and] not within the range of words [or] knowledge (*akṣarajñāna*).

40. The fact of dependent co-origination is exactly what You maintain to be emptiness. Of that kind is the true principle (*saddharma*) and the Tathāgata is like that.

35. This and the following allude to *Bhavasaṃkrāntisūtra* (ed. N.A. Śāstri) p. 5-6, q.v. Also *Āloka,* pp. 44, 685. For *pādas* cd cf. *Laṅkāvatāra*, III, 78: *abhidhānavinirmuktam abhidheyaṃ na lakṣyate* ||.

36. *Laṅkāvatāra*, X, 10: *asārakā ime dharmā manyanāyāḥ samutthitāḥ* |*sāpy atra manyanā śūnyā yayā śūnyeti manyate* ||. Cf. MK, XXII, 11; *Stutyatītastava*, 9: *lta ba thams cad spaṅ ba'i phyir* || *mgon po khyod kyis stoṅ pa gsuṅs* || *de yaṅ yoṅs su brtags pa ste* || *dṅos su mgon po khyod mi bźed* ||.

37. This and the following verses treat *paramārtha* (*tattva*) and its *paryāyas: advaya, anālaya, avyakta* etc.

38. *pāda* d also supra, v. 1. – For *anālaya,* YṢ, 1; CS, IV, 1.

39. *ākāśa:* BV, 46. – CS, IV, 1: *vākpathātītagocaram.* See also v, 23.

40. See CS, I, 22. – *saddharma,* supra 22. – *tathāgata:* MK, XXII, 16: *tathāgato niḥsvabhāvo* ...

41. tat tattvaṃ paramārtho 'pi tathatā dravyam iṣyate |
bhūtaṃ tad avisaṃvādi tadbodhād buddha ucyate ||

| de ni de ñid don dam ni || de bźin ñid daṅ rdzas su bźed |
| de ni yaṅ dag mi bslu ba || de rdzogs pas na saṅs rgyas brjod |

42. buddhānāṃ sattvadhātoś ca tenābhinnatvam arthataḥ |
ātmanaś ca pareṣāṃ ca samatā tena te matā ||

| saṅs rgyas rnams daṅ chos dbyiṅs daṅ || des na don du tha mi dad |
| bdag ñid daṅ ni gźan rnams daṅ || des na mñam par khyod bźed lags |

43. bhāvebhyaḥ śūnyatā nānyā na ca bhāvo 'sti tāṃ vinā |
tasmāt pratītyajā bhāvās tvayā śūnyāḥ prakāśitāḥ ||

| dṅos po rnams las stoṅ gźan min || de med par yaṅ dṅos po med |
| de phyir rten ciṅ 'byuṅ ba'i chos || stoṅ pa lags par khyod kyis bstan |

44. hetupratyayasaṃbhūtā paratantrā ca saṃvṛtiḥ |
paratantra iti proktaḥ paramārthas tv akṛtrimaḥ ||

| rgyu daṅ rkyen las byuṅ ba'aṅ lags || gźan gyi dbaṅ las kun rdzob ste
| gźan gyi dbaṅ źes rab tu gsuṅs || dam pa'i don ni bcos ma yin |

45. svabhāvaḥ prakṛtis tattvaṃ dravyaṃ vastu sad ity api |
nāsti vai kalpito bhāvo paratantras tu vidyate ||

| ṅo bo ñid daṅ raṅ bźin daṅ || yaṅ dag rdzas dṅos yod pa'aṅ lags |
| brtags pa'i dṅos po med pa ñid || gźan gyi dbaṅ ni yod ma lags |

46. astīti kalpite bhāve samāropas tvayoditaḥ |
nāstīti kṛtakocchedād ucchedaś ca prakāśitaḥ ||

| brtags pa'i dṅos po yod ces pa || sgro 'dogs lags par khyod kyis gsuṅs |
| byas pa chad nas med ces pa || chad pa lags par khyod kyis gsuṅs |

41a dam : daṅ NP
42a sattvadhātos TGMQ : dharmadhātoś S
44c paratantra iti proktaḥ AGMQT : paratantram iti proktaṃ W
45b dravyaṃ vastu TM : dravyavastu G (= S?); b vai kalpito MG (= S?): vaikalpito TA; d tu vidyate TG : na vidyate S (cf. n.) : vidyetāpi (!) M
46a brtags : btags NP; c kṛtakocchedād TMS : kṛtakoccheda G

41. It is also accepted as the truth (*tattva*), the ultimate meaning, suchness and the real (*dravya*). It is the indisputable (*avisaṃvādi*) fact. By understanding it [one] is called Buddha.

42. Therefore there is really no difference between the world of living beings and Buddhas. Hence You are convinced of the identity of yourself and others.

43. Emptiness is not different from things and there is no thing without it. Therefore You have declared that dependently born things are empty.

44. Convention (*saṃvṛti*) arises from causes and conditions and is relative (*paratantra*). Thus the relative has been spoken of [by You]. – The ultimate meaning, however, is absolute (*akṛtrima*);

45. It is also termed (*iti*) own-being, nature, truth, substance, the real [and the] true. – [Conventionally] an imagined thing does not exist but a relative is found [to exist].

46. You have stated that [affirmative] attribution (*samāropa*) is to state about a constructed entity that it exists. [You] have also declared that cutting off [i.e. negation] is to state that a compound [entity] does not exist because it is annihilated.

41. On *tattva* etc. e.g. Ramanan (1966), pp. 251-275; *Traité,* pp. 2181-2201. – *pāda* d also occurs *Madhyamakahṛdayakārikā*, III, 267; *Sākārasiddhiśāstra*, p. 433, q.v. – The distinction between *prajñaptisat* and *dravyasat* already occurs *Laṅkāvatāra,* III, 27. Cf. also May, *op.cit.*, p. 159, n. 489.

42. On the relationship between *dharma-* and *sattvadhātu* see e.g. D. Seyfort Ruegg (1971), pp. 459-461 with ref. Also MK, XXII, 16. – *samatā, Vimalakīrtinirdeśa,* p. 474 (ref.).

43. On *sarvadharmaśūnyatā, Traité,* pp. 2015 ff; BV, 57-58, etc.

44. This and the following three verses show the relationship between *svabhāvatraya* (as expounded in the *Laṅkāvatāra,* v. *Index,* s.s.v.) and *satyadvaya* acc. to Nāgārjuna. *Paramārthataḥ* they are *śūnya* (v. BV, 28) but *saṃvṛtitaḥ paramārtha* (i.e. *parinispannasvabhāva* = *prakṛti, tattva* etc.) is *akṛtrima* etc. (cf. MK, XV, 2) and *paratantra,* i.e. *saṃvṛti* exists, whereas *parikalpita* does not.

45. Cf. supra, 37-42, and *Laṅkāvatāra,* II, 189: *nāsti vai kalpito bhāvaḥ paratantraś ca vidyate* ... The interpretation of this verse was to become the starting-point of a long controversy between Mādhyamikas who held that *paratantrasvabhāva* only exists *saṃvṛtitaḥ,* not *paramārthataḥ,* and Yogācāras who held that *paratantra,* as *Laṅkāvatāra* itself states, exists. See *Prajñāpradīpa,* 305b 1; Dharmapāla, Taishō, 1571, 247b; *Pañcaskandhaprakaraṇa,* p. 22; *Śūnyatāsaptativṛtti,* 320b 4; also Avalokitavrata, Jñānagarbha, Śāntarakṣita, Kamalaśīla.

46. Here *uccheda* in *pāda* d corresponds to *apavāda,* see *Laṅkāvatāra, loc.cit., pāda* c. Negation is understood similarly *saṃvṛtitaḥ,* RĀ, I, 72: *vināśāt pratipakṣād vā syād astitvasya nāstitā* ...

47. tattvajñānena nocchedo na ca śāśvatatā matā |
vastuśūnyaṃ jagat sarvaṃ marīcipratimaṃ matam ||

| yaṅ dag śes pas chad pa med || rtag pa ñid kyaṅ med par bźed |
| 'gro ba dṅos pos stoṅ pa lags || de slad smig rgyu 'dra bar bźed |

48. mṛgatṛṣṇājalaṃ yadvan nocchedi na ca śāśvatam |
tadvat sarvaṃ jagat proktaṃ nocchedi na ca śāśvatam ||

| ji ltar ri dvags skom chu ni || chad med rtag pa yod ma yin |
| de bźin 'gro ba thams cad kyaṅ || chad med rtag pa med par gsuṅs |

49. dravyam utpadyate yasya tasyocchedādikaṃ bhavet |
antavān nāntavāṃś cāpi lokas tasya prasajyate ||

| gaṅ la rdzas śig ste 'gyur ba || de la chad sogs 'jigs pa 'byuṅ |
| de la 'jig rten mtha' yod daṅ || mtha' med par yaṅ 'gyur ba lags |

50. jñāne sati yathā jñeyaṃ jñeye jñānaṃ tathā sati |
yatrobhayam anutpannam iti buddhaṃ tadāsti kim ||

| śes pa yod pas śes bya bźin || śes bya yod pas de śes bźin |
| gaṅ tshe gñis ka ma skyes par || rtogs pa de tshe ci źig yod |

51. iti māyādidṛṣṭāntaiḥ sphuṭam uktvā bhiṣagvaraḥ |
deśayām āsa saddharmaṃ sarvadṛṣṭicikitsakam ||

| de ltar sgyu ma la sogs dpe || sman pa'i mchog gis gsal bstan nas |
| lta ba thams cad 'gog byed pa'i || dam pa'i chos ni bstan pa lags |

52. etat tat paramaṃ tattvaṃ niḥsvabhāvārthadeśanā |
bhāvagrahagṛhītānāṃ cikitseyam anuttarā ||

| ṅo bo med pa ñid bstan pa || de ni yaṅ dag dam pa lags |
| dṅos po'i gdon gyis zin rnams kyi || gso ba de ni bla na med |

47a °jñānena no° TGS : °jñāne na co° M; bźed : bśad NP
48c sarvam TG (= S?) : sarva° M
50c yatrobhayam TG : yadobhayam MSW; d buddham GM (= S?) : buddha T
52a etat tat P : etad eva (!) G : etat tu M; tattvaṃ TMS : satyaṃ G

47. According to cognition of truth [however] You maintain that there is no annihilation or permanence. [You are] convinced that the entire world is empty of substance, like a mirage.

48. As a mirage is neither annihilated nor permanent, thus the entire world is said to be neither annihilated nor permanent.

49. One to whom a substance presents itself, upon him [the dogmas of] annihilation and [permanence] incur; and he implicitly accepts (*tasya...prasajyate*) that the world is finite or infinite [etc.].

50. Just as there is cognisable when there is cognition, there is cognition when there is cognisable. Where both of them are unborn what then is [there to be] understood?

51. By thus expressing himself clearly through analogies such as illusions etc. the Supreme Physician has shown the Good Law which cures [its adherents] from all dogmas.

52. The ultimate truth (*tattva*) is the teaching that things (*artha*) are without own-being. This is the unsurpassed medicine for those obsessed by the fever of positivism (*bhāvagraha*).

47. This is *paramārthataḥ*, cf. e.g. MK, XV, 10; XVII, 11 etc. – For *marīci*, RĀ, I, 52-56; *Traité*, p. 363.

48. The *mṛgatṛṣṇā* is very common in *Laṅkāvatāra*, e.g. III, 151, q.v. for an explanation.

49. I.e. the acceptance (*abhyupagama, abhiniveśa*) of *dravya*, i.e. *bhāva* (cf. ŚS, 21; YṢ, 46-47; MK, XXI, 14 etc.) invariably entails *śāśvatocchedagrāha* (ref. May, *op.cit.*, p. 213, n. 720) which again ramifies itself in various *ātmalokadṛṣṭi* (v. *ibid.* p. 276, n. 1015). Also supra, v. 22.

50. V. BV. 39; 45; 45; YṢ, 1; RĀ, I, 93-97; supra v. 37ff.

51. Cf. CS, I, 23 and supra v. 22.

52. For *bhāvagraha*- supra, vv. 16, 49 etc. – This verse does not leave any doubt about Nāgārjuna's conception of *tattva* and the purpose of teaching it, cf. ŚS, 68-69, 73; VV, 22; YṢ, 1; BV, 48-49, etc.

53. dharmayājñika tenaiva dharmayajño niruttaraḥ |
abhīkṣṇam iṣṭas trailokye niṣkapāṭo nirargalaḥ ||

| des na chos kyi mchod sbyin pa || mchod sbyin rim pas rtag rgyun du |
| 'jig rten gsum po sbyin sreg mdzad | + + + + + + + |

54. vastugrāhabhayocchedī kutīrthyamṛgabhīkaraḥ |
nairātmyasiṃhanādo 'yam adbhuto naditas tvayā |

| dṅos 'dzin 'jigs pa gcod bgyid ciṅ || mu stegs ri dvags 'jigs bgyid pa |
| bdag med seṅ ge'i ṅa ro'i sgra || rmad byuṅ de ni khyod kyis gsuṅs |

55. śūnyatādharmagambhīrā dharmabherī parāhatā |
naiḥsvābhāvyamahānādo dharmaśaṅkhaḥ prapūritaḥ ||

| stoṅ pa ñid daṅ chos zab pa'i || chos kyi rṅa chen brduṅ ba lags |
| ṅo bo ñid med sgra bo che'i || chos kyi duṅ ni bus pa lags |

56. dharmayautukam ākhyātaṃ buddhānāṃ śāsanāmṛtam |
nītārtham iti nirdiṣṭaṃ dharmāṇāṃ śūnyataiva hi ||

| saṅs rgyas bstan pa bdud rtsi yi || chos kyi rdzas ni gsuṅs pa lags |
| chos rnams kyi ni ṅo bo ñid || ṅes pa'i don do źes kyaṅ bstan |

57. yā tūtpādanirodhādisattvajīvādideśanā |
neyārthā ca tvayā nātha bhāṣitā saṃvṛtiś ca sā ||

| gaṅ yaṅ skye daṅ 'gag la sogs || sems can srog la sogs bstan pa |
| de ni bkri don kun rdzob tu || mgon po khyod kyis bstan pa lags |

58. prajñāpāramitāmbhodher yo 'tyantam pāram āgataḥ |
sa puṇyaguṇaratnāḍhyas tvadguṇārṇavapāragaḥ ||

| śes rab pha rol phyin mtsho yi || pha rol gaṅ gis gtan phyin te |
| bsod nams yon tan rin chen phyug || mgon khyod yon tan phal rol phyin |

53a tenaiva TG (= S?) : tvayaiva M; c iṣṭas PG (= S?) : hutas M; d *omm.* NP; d nirargalah AGMQT : niramtalam W

55a °gambhīrā TG (= S?) : °gambhīra° M; daṅ *pro* kyi NP; c °nādo PG (= S?) : °nada° (!) M; sgra N : dgra P

56a °yautukam TG : °yautakam M

57c ca T : sā MQW : yā G; d sā AGMQT : tu W

58b pāram AGM : param T : svayam? S (raṅ NP), *aut* gtan ('tyantam?); d tvadgu° TG : tvaṃ gu° M (= S?)

53. Precisely therefore, O Sacrifice-priest of the Dharma, You have repeatedly performed an unsurpassed dharma-sacrifice in the three worlds which is unhindered and unimpeded.

54. You have uttered this wonderful lion's roar of not-self which removes the fear [due to] belief in things [and which] terrifies the deer, viz. the mean heretics!

55. [You] have beaten the dharma-drum which is deep [with its] principle of emptiness. [You] have blown the dharma-conch with its high pitch of selflessness.

56. The gift of dharma has been proclaimed [by You, viz.] the nectar of the Buddha's teaching. The final meaning has been indicated, that is, of course (*hi*), that phenomena are empty.

57. But the teaching about origination, cessation etc., beings, souls etc., [only] has a provisional meaning (*neyārtha*). You have also, O Saviour, called it convention.

58. One who has finally reached the further shore of the ocean of perfect wisdom (*prajñāpāramitā*), abounds in the jewels of the virtues of merit [and] is fully conversant with the ocean of Your virtues.

53. For *dharmayajña*, *Vimalakīrti*, pp. 212-216. – *niṣkapāṭa:* BHSD, p. 167 (s.v. *kapāṭa*); BCA, VI, 101 (Tib. *sgo 'phar*). – For *nirargala* (or *nirargaḍa*) – often said about *yajña*, Tib. is usually *sruṅs ma med pa'i mchod sbyin* – see BHSD, p. 299; CPD, s.v. *aggaḷa*.

54. For the terrifying *siṃhanāda*, ref. CS, I, 22; BS, 101; BV, 52.

55. For *dharmabherī* and *śaṅkha*, also clichés, e.g. *Suvarṇabhāsottamasūtra*, V, 22-23; *Saddharmapuṇḍarīka*, VII, 42; *Aṣṭasāhasrikā*, p. 327.

56. See RĀ, I, 62 for *dharmayautuka* (or *-yautaka?*), cf. *Prasannapadā*, p. 275 (read *khud pa* in n. 7 for *khyud pa*, cf. *Madhyamakāvatāra*, p. 184). – *pāda* b also occurs, RĀ, I, 62; II, 9; MK, XVIII, 11. – For *nītārtha*, *Prasannapadā*, pp. 43-44, cf. *ibid.*, p. 276.

57. This verse also seems to refer to *Samādhirāja* and *Akṣayamatinirdeśa*, v. 56. See also *Madhyamakāvatāra*, p. 200; Wayman (1978), pp. 178-180; May, *op.cit.*, p. 298, n. 1089 (ref.).

58. Allusion to the usual 'etymology' of *pāramitā* (*pāram ita*), cf. *Traité*, p. 1058 (ref.); final verse of *Mahāyānaviṃśikā*; Har Dayal, op.cit., p. 165. – Like MK etc. the main *abhidheya* of this hymn has been *prajñā*, the foremost *pāramitā*, cf. BS, 5-7.

59. iti stutvā jagannātham acintyam anidarśanam |
yad avāptaṃ mayā puṇyaṃ tenāstu tvatsamaṃ jagat ||
| de ltar dpe med bsam mi khyab || 'gro ba'i mgon po bstod pa yis |
| bdag gis bsod nams gaṅ thob des || 'gro ba khyod daṅ mtshuṅs par śog |

|| ity acintyastavaḥ samāptaḥ ||

| bsam gyis mi khyab par bstod pa
slob dpon chen po klu sgrub kyi źal sṅa nas mdzad pa rdzogs so |

59. May the world by virtue of the merit I have obtained by thus praising [You], the inconceivable [and] incomparable Leader of the world, become like You!

59. *puṇyapariṇāmanā*.

VIII. Ratnāvalī (RĀ)

This verse text composed in 500 *anuṣṭubh* with an extra verse added at the end, is not only ascribed to Nāgārjuna in the colophons of its Tibetan and Chinese versions but also by authorities like Bhavya,[156] Candrakīrti,[157] Śāntarakṣita[158] and many other later authors.

RĀ is only partially extant in Sanskrit.[159] An Indian commentary composed by a certain Ajitamitra (TP, No. 5659) is only available in a Tibetan translation. It is particularly useful for the first two chapters but on the whole far too brief to be of much use for the study of the remaining three *paricchedas*.

The philosophical tenets of RĀ do not differ from those advanced in MK, ŚS, YṢ, etc., but it supplements these dialectical texts by affording a code of Mahāyāna Buddhist principles – practical as

156. *Tarkajvālā*, TP, No. 5256, Dza *fol.* 145a (= RĀ, V, 35-39).

157. Cf. n. 89. Also *Madhyamakāvatāra*, pp. 7, 8, 20, 21, 22, 23, 29, 184, 224; *Prasannapadā*, pp. 135-188, 275, 245, 346, 347, 359, 360, 413, 458, 460 (= RĀ, II, 48-49), 496, 549. Cf. de Jong *IIJ*, XX, p. 137.

158. *Madhyamakālaṃkāravṛtti*, 75a (= RĀ, I, 60), 83a (= RĀ, IV, 79).

159. I, 1-77 edited and translated by G. Tucci, *JRAS* (1934), pp. 307-324 (reprinted in *Opera Minora*, II, Roma 1971, pp. 321-366). – II, 1-46 and IV, 1-100 in *JRAS* (1936), pp. 237-252, 423-435. Tucci's edition was reprinted by P. L. Vaidya, *Madhyamakaśāstra of Nāgārjuna*, Darbhanga 1960, pp. 296-310 and H. Chatterjee Sastri, *The philosophy of Nāgārjuna as contained in the Ratnāvalī*, Calcutta 1977, pp. 83-100 without significant changes. Partial versions by E. Frauwallner, *Die Philosophie des Buddhismus*, Berlin 1969, pp. 204-217; K. S. Murty, *Nāgārjuna*, New Delhi 1978, pp. 87-103. Complete versions by J. Hopkins *et al.*, *The Precious Garland and The Song of the Four Mindfulnesses*, London 1975, and myself in *Nāgārjuna: Juvelkæden og andre skrifter*, København 1980. Cf. also de Jong in *IIJ*, XX, pp. 136-140; Nakamura (1977), p. 83, n. 44 for Japanese works. Some of my emendations to the Sanskrit text will appear in the forthcoming edition of *Ratnāvalī* (Sanskrit-Tibetan) by M. Hahn.

The first chapter contains several allusions to the ancient sūtras: For 5 cf. *Saṃyutta*, I, p. 214; 10 v. *Majjhima*, III, 22; 14-19 v. *Majjhima*, III, p. 203 ff.; 26 v. *Majjhima*, I, p. 40; 31 v. *Saṃyutta*, III, p. 105; 34 v. *Saṃyutta*, III, p. 132 ff.; 52-56 cf. *Saṃyutta*, III, p. 141; 80 cf. *Majjhima*, III, p. 31; 93-96 v. *Dīgha*, I, p. 223. (Many of these are of course repeated elsewhere in the canon to which Nāgārjuna might as well be referring.)

well as theoretical – with particular regard to a *gṛhastha,* more specifically to a king (see I, 2; 78 etc.). It thus places Nāgārjuna's philosophy within a wider framework. Taken as a whole we notice that, as in the case of MK, ŚS, SL, CS and BS, no strict structural principle is adhered to. But if no unity of composition is conspicuous there is certainly, as we shall see, a unity of thought in the light of which RĀ may be said to be a homogeneous work.

Since RĀ is already available in modern translations I shall confine myself to offer an analysis of the main themes of its five chapters.[160]

The first *pariccheda* is entitled **Abhyudayanaiḥśreyasopadeśa* (Tib.: *mṅon par mtho ba daṅ ṅes par legs par bstan pa;* Chin. is free but good: *ān lè jiě tuō*). After a brief introduction about *abhyudaya* (= *sukha*) and *naiḥśreyasa* (= *mokṣa*) (cf. *Vaiśeṣikasūtra,* I, 1, 2; RĀ, III, 30) respectively presupposing *śraddhā* and *prajñā,* the author encourages his reader to have faith in the *dharma* which, to put it briefly, has two aspects: *nivṛttir aśubhāt kṛtsnāt pravṛttis tu śubhe sadā* (22). One should, in other words, not act under the influence of the *kleśas* but only, as we shall see, motivated by *karuṇā.* Now that Nāgārjuna has spoken (1-24) of the means of true *sukha* here in *saṃsāra* he deals with the second and the foremost *mokṣasādhana,* namely *prajñā.* This consists in realizing the *pudgaladharmanairātmya* specific to Mahāyāna. It amounts to *nirvāṇa* which is simply *bhāvābhāvaparāmarśakṣaya* (42) or freedom from rebirth in *saṃsāra.* Having elaborated his doctrine about transcending being and non-being (46-75) the author finally lays down a method according to *āgama* of how one can argue that there is neither a *pudgala* nor any *dharma,* such as the *skandhas, mahābhūtas, dhātus* etc., and thus personally realize the *nairātmyadvaya* of Mahāyāna, or *mokṣa* (76-100).

The second chapter, **Miśraka* (Tib.: *spel ma;* Chin.: *zá*), amplifies the two *mokṣasādhana* discussed previously. First (1-24) some remarks concerning *māyāvāda,* the 'ontological' foundation of Nāgārjuna's soteriology. However, *yāvad avijñāto dharmo 'haṃkāraśātanaḥ,* one must as shown above (I, 1-24) devote oneself to the practice of the *dharma.* In case of a king he must be devoted to the *pāramitās,* viz. *dāna, śīla*

160. Note that TP, No. 5428: *Ratnāvalyudbhavasaptāṅgavidhigāthāviṃśaka* and TP, No. 5928: *Rājaparikathānāmodbhavapraṇidhānagāthāviṃśaka* – both ascribed to Nāgārjuna – are extracts from RĀ, V, 66-85.

and *kṣānti* and other virtues prescribed in Mahāyāna. Thus the other *pāramitās* will also gradually prosper (cf. RĀ, IV, 80-83). Now some warnings against vices liable to afflict a monarch. Devices for abandoning the *kleśas* are given (41-74). By following the *dharma* the king will succeed in obtaining the 32 *lakṣaṇas* and the 80 *anuvyañjanas* specific to a *mahāpuruṣa* (76-100).

The third chapter, **Bodhisaṃbhāra* (Tib.: *byaṅ chub kyi tshogs bsdus pa;* Chin.: *pú tí zī liáng*) resumes (1-10) the traditional doctrine of the *mahāpuruṣalakṣaṇa*. Now (12-13) a couple of significant verses succinctly summarize the entire purpose of Mahāyāna in theory and practice, viz. the attainment of Buddhahood. It has two aspects, a *rūpakāya* which is the outcome of an immense mass of merit (*puṇyasaṃbhāra*), and a *dharmakāya,* the result of an unlimited *jñānasaṃbhāra*. After this culmination the remaining 86 verses depict some of the endless forms a *bodhisattvacaryā* (cf. MK, XXIV, 32) intent upon *puṇyasaṃbhāra* may take motivated by *karuṇā*. It is a life of mental and physical happiness (*sukha,* cf. I, 4). In another cardinal stanza (30) the notion of *saṃbhāra* is linked to that of *abhyudaya* and *naiḥśreyasa* (cf. I, 3-4). With a wealth of casuistic details, often of great cultural interest, the king is advised to benefit himself as well as others by developing the *pāramitās*. – Note that while the theme of this chapter is the same as that of **Bodhisaṃbhāra* (translated below) the treatment of this 'endless subject' (cf. BS, 2-4) differs so much that the author hardly ever has to repeat himself.

Again, as he has done before, in the fourth chapter, *Rājavṛttopadeśa* (Tib.: *rgyal po'i tshul bstan pa;* Chin.: *zhèng jiāo wáng*), Nāgārjuna takes up where he left off in the previous *pariccheda*. After a *captatio benevolentiae* (1-6) the king is admonished to practise *dānapāramitā* in various ways (7-17) and adhere to the principles of justice (*dharma*) in matters of state and law. Punishment should only be inflicted out of compassion. These instructions, which so to speak form an *arthaśāstra* according to Mahāyāna, do, of course, fall under the heading of *puṇyasaṃbhāra*. In order to enhance the king's *jñānasaṃbhāra* the author then (46-65) argues that *vedanā* (and, naturally, the other *skandhas* etc. as well) lack *svabhāva* since they are *pratītyasamutpanna*. Indeed, it can only be ascribed to ignorance that certain individuals (i.e. Śrāvakas) mock at Mahāyāna which is characterized by altruistic and lofty ideals of various kinds. Actually the teachings of Mahāyāna are exceedingly profound, hence easily misunderstood, and therefore the Buddha has prudently adapted his teachings to the *vineyāśaya* (cf. MK, XVIII, 8 etc.).

So to sum up, as a *gṛhastha* the king should above all practise *dāna, śīla, kṣānti* and *satya*. However, *lokasya vaidharmya* may enforce him to become a *pravrajita*.

Accordingly the final chapter is entitled **Bodhisattvacaryopadeśa* (Tib.: *byaṅ chub sems dpa'i spyod pa bstan pa;* Chin. possibly better: *chū jiā zhèng xíng, *Pravrajitacaryā*). As we saw the *dharma* has a *nivṛtti-* and a *pravṛtti*-aspect (I, 22). It was thus shown how a *gṛhastha* should abstain from the ten *akuśalakarmapatha* and instead collect *puṇya* by engaging himself in the perfection of *dāna, śīla, kṣānti* etc. – Now the author focuses on the duties of a *pravrajita*. Disciplining himself in the (three) *śikṣās* (cf. SL, 105), the code of *prātimokṣa* and studying the sūtras etc. he should abandon the 57 *doṣas*. Here (3-33) we encounter an interesting list of *upakleśas, pañcamithyājīvas* etc. Though each of these 57 items also occurs in other Abhidharma texts (*Vibhaṅga, Mahāvibhāṣā*, etc. etc.), the list as a whole, if I am not mistaken, occurs in no other manual of Abhidharma. Thus I am inclined to agree with my learned friend the Ven. Thrangu Rinpoche (oral communication, Nov. 1980) according to whom Nāgārjuna himself is responsible for the number and order of these *doṣas*. (I subjoin a reconstruction of the Sanskrit based on the Tibetan version – Peking and Narthang editions – occasionally compared with the Chinese version. A few emendations have tacitly been made, all obvious.) Along with the 119 *kuśaladharma* registered in the *svavṛtti* to VV, 7 (see *IHQ*, XIV, pp. 314-323 for a detailed discussion of these) and BS, 147, this *catalogus vitiorum* proves a valuable contribution to the question of the relationship between early Madhyamaka and traditional Abhidharma.

Having thus abandoned these and other *doṣas*, a bodhisattva performs the six *pāramitās* in a spirit of *karuṇā* (35-39). Doing so he will gradually advance through the ten *bodhisattvabhūmis* (here Nāgārjuna follows *Daśabhūmikasūtra*) and accomplish his task by finally becoming a buddha (40-64). While still a bodhisattva he must not forget to perform the *saptavidhānuttarapūjā* (cf. BS, 48ff.) regularly (65-87). – A final exhortation to practise Buddhism so as to attain *bodhi* for the benefit of all living beings (88-101).

The above analysis has brought us in a position to summarize the content of RĀ. As suggested by its very title 'A String of Pearls' a common theme combines the individual verses into a unity. This is *puṇyajñānasaṃbhāra.* While there is hardly a single verse which is not more or less directly related to that topic, many of them may to some extent be read as *'ratnas'* in their own right. Still their context should not be overlooked. Thus I find that the title of our text is well-chosen to suggest that here a variety of instructions are unified by one basic theme, *bodhisaṃbhāra.*

The *saptapañcāśaddoṣāḥ* of RĀ, V, 3-33: Tibetan and Sanskrit

1. khro ba, *krodha*
2. khon du 'dzin pa, *upanāha*
3. 'chab pa, *mrakṣa*
4. 'tshig pa, *pradāśa*
5. gyo, *śāṭhya* (= 6., but m.c. 5.)
6. sgyu, *māyā* (= 5., but m.c. 6.)
7. phrag dog, *īrṣyā*
8. ser sna, *mātsarya*
9. ṅo tsha med pa, *ahrīkatā* (for *āhrīkya*)
10. khrel med pa, *anapatrāpya*
11. kheṅs pa, *stambha*
12. ñes rtsom, *saṃrambha*
13. rgyas pa, *mada*
14. bag med pa, *pramāda*
15. (1) ṅa rgyal, *māna*
    (2) ṅa rgyal las kyaṅ ṅa rgyal, *mānātimāna*
    (4) ṅa'o sñam pa'i ṅa rgyal, *asmimāna*
    (5) mṅon pa'i ṅa rgyal, *abhimāna* (m.c.: *abhimānitā*)
    (6) log pa'i ṅa rgyal, *mithyāmāna*
    (7) dman pa'i ṅa rgyal, *adhamamāna* (for *ūnamāna*)
16. tshul 'chos pa, *kuhanā*
17. kha gsag, *lapanā*
18. gźogs sloṅ, *naimittikatva*
19. thob kyis 'jal ba, *naiṣpeṣikatva*
20. rñed pas rñed pa rnams 'dod pa, *lābhena lipsā lābhānām* (m.c.)
21. skyon zlos, *śiṅga*? (cf. Pāli *siṅga*, BHS *śṛṅgī*)
22. spuṅs med pa, *staimitya* (cf. Pāli *tintiṇa*)
23. tha dad pa'i 'du śes, *nānātvasaṃjñā*
24. yid la mi byed pa, *amanaskāra*

25. bcom ldan tshul min, *abhagavadvṛtti* (*abhāga*°? cf. Pāli *asabhāgavutti*)
26. źen pa, *gardha* (cf. Pāli *gedha*, BHS *godha*)
27. yoṅs su źen pa, *parigardha* (cf. Pāli *paligedha*, BHS *paligodha*)
28. chags pa, *lobha*
29. mi rigs par chags pa, *viṣamalobha*
30. chos ma yin pa la 'dod pa (read thus for chags pa ma yin ... cf. Chinese *fēi fǎ yù*), *adharmarāga*
31. sdig 'dod pa, *pāpecchatā*
32. 'dod chags chen po, *mahecchatā*
33. thob par 'dod pa, *icchepsutā* (for *icchasvitā*?, thus *Abhidharmadīpa*, p. 310!)
34. mi bzod pa, *akṣānti*
35. ma gus pa, *anādara* (*anācāra* is not definiendum in spite of Tib., cf. Chinese *bù guì* and e.g. *Abhidharmadīpa*, p. 311 etc.)
36. bka' blo bde ba ma yin, *daurvacasya* (cf. Chinese *nàn yǔ*)
37. ñe du daṅ 'brel ba'i rnam par rtog pa, *jñātisaṃbandhavitarka*
38. yul du sred du, *janapadātṛ̈ṣ*? (m.c. for *janapadavitarka*, cf. Chinese *tǔ jué* and e.g. *Abhidharmadīpa*, p. 310 etc.)
39. mi 'chi ba'i rnam par rtog pa, *amaravitarka*
40. rjes rnam rigs daṅ ldan rtog, *anavajñaptisaṃyukto vitarka* (Tib. is a correct rendering of *anuvijñapti*° (thus Sanskrit Ms), but this must be an early corruption of *anavajñapti*°, cf. Chinese *shùn jué jué* and Pāli *anavaññati*° (CPD, I, p. 159))
41. gźan rjes su chags pa daṅ ldan pa yi rnam par rtog pa, *parānudayatāpratisaṃyukto vitarka* (Hahn suggests *parānunayatā*° against Ms, but cf. Pāli *parānuddayatāpaṭisaṃyutto vitakko* (see CPD ref. I, p. 190, add *Vibhaṅga*, p. 346.))
42. chags (reg pa), *sneha* (*-saṃsparśa*) (for *kāmavitarka*!)
43. gnod sems reg pa, *vyāpādasaṃsparśa* (for *vyāpādavitarka*, cf. 42 and e.g. *Abhidharmadīpa*, p. 311 etc.)
44. mi dga' ba, *arati* (for this and the following v. *Vibhaṅga*, p. 352)
45. phrad 'dod (Hahn for phrag dog), *samutkaṇ̈ṭhā*
46. sñoms pa, *tandrī*
47. sgyid lug pa, *ālasya* (*Note:* V, 28 has *four* definienda)
48. 'gyur ba, *vijṛmbhikā* (cf. Chinese *pín*)
49. za ma 'dod pa (read thus for zad mi 'dod pa), *bhaktasaṃmada* (Hahn: *bhaktāsaṃmada*, but cf. Pāli *bhattasammada* and Chinese *shí zuí*. Possibly also *bhaktāsamatā*, e.g. *Abhidharmadīpa*, p. 311)

50. sems źum yin pa ñid, *cetolīnatva*
51. 'dod dun, *kāmacchanda*
52. gnod sems, *vyāpāda*
53. rmi ba, *styāna* (cf. Chinese *ruò*)
54. gñid, *middha*
55. rgod pa, *auddhatya*
56. 'gyod pa, *kaukṛtya*
57. the tshom, *vicikitsā*

(*Additional note:* Originally I had worked out a list of the fifty-seven *doṣas* giving the Tibetan with references to Chinese and suggested Sanskrit originals. Then, quite recently, the Sanskrit text of RĀ, V, 1-55 and 79-100 was published by S. Dietz in *Journal of the Nepal Research Centre,* IV, pp. 189-220, and just a few days ago (2.3.1981) I received a paper: 'On a Numerical Problem in Nāgārjuna's Ratnāvalī' from Prof. Michael Hahn (Bonn). The work of Dr. Dietz and the courtesy of Prof. Hahn have enabled me to correct a number of the Sanskrit terms originally proposed by me. Though I do not quite agree with all Prof. Hahn's views concerning numbers and readings I am sincerely grateful for having had the opportunity to consult his very valuable critical notes. I am also very glad to learn that he is now preparing a critical edition of RĀ, I-V (Tibetan and the extant portions of the Sanskrit) (letter dated 28.1.1981).)

IX. Pratītyasamutpādahṛdayakārikā (PK)

As I have had occasion to note elsewhere PK 2-'6' is quoted and ascribed to 'ācārya' i.e. Nāgārjuna by Bhavya. Other quotations also occur.[161] Apparently a piece of counter-evidence is provided by the fact that one of the Chinese versions (Taishō, No. 1651) attributes PK and its *Vyākhyāna* to a certain bodhisattva called *jìng yì*, 'Clear Mind'. But if we take this as a somewhat interpretative rendering of Sanskrit *Sumati or the like (on the basis of Tib. *blo gros bzaṅ po,* which, on the authority of Śāntarakṣita and Kamalaśīla is known to have been another name of Nāgārjuna, or perhaps merely an epithet as *sudhī, dhīmat* etc. are stock terms for bodhisattvas) we may conclude that PK is ascribed to this author by all sources known to us.[162]

Internal evidence is provided first of all by a closely related passage BV, 59-63 q.v., RĀ, I, 29ff.; ŚS, 34, 37; MK, XVII, 27; XVIII, 5; XXIII, 1; VS, '6' are to the same effect. Moreover the *āgama* which inspired PK is the same as the one behind e.g. RĀ, V, 41-60, viz. *Daśabhūmikasūtra* (also quoted SS, 249 b 7).

Though Nāgārjuna does not show any originality in PK the theory expounded here is of vital importance to him inasmuch as it

161. I have edited PK and discussed its authenticity in my 'Adversaria Buddhica', *WZKS,* XXVI (1982). – For further bibliographical details v. C. Dragonetti, 'The Pratītyasamutpādahṛdayakārikā and the Pratītyasamutpādahṛdayavyākhyāna of Śuddhamati', *WZKS,* XXII, pp. 87-93; Nakamura (1977), p. 83, n. 40; V.V. Gokhale in collaboration with M.G. Dhadphale, *Encore:* The Pratītyasamutpādahṛdayakārikā of Nāgārjuna , in M.G. Dhadphale (ed.), *Principal V.S. Apte Commemoration Volume,* Poona 1978, pp. 62-68 (with a plate).

162. To be sure, Chinese *jìng* (usually *viśuddha, śuddha,* also *svaccha, nirañjana, śubha* etc.) cannot be taken as an *exact* rendering of the Sanskrit corresponding to Tibetan *bzaṅ po* (usually *bhadra, su-,* but also *śubha, praṇīta* etc., e.g. Lokesh Chandra, *Tibetan-Sanskrit Dictionary,* New Delhi 1961, p. 2094). However, recalling, on the one hand, how free Bodhiruci's renderings often are, and on the other, that Indo-Tibetan and Chinese tradition otherwise ascribe PK (and its commentary) to Nāgārjuna (or *Sumati) I do not hesitate to deem the external evidence unanimous.

marks an exegetical attempt to reconcile the traditional *dvādaśāṅgaḥ pratītyasamutpāda* with the *śūnyatā*-doctrine.[163]

On the other hand we have the twelve sectors *avidyādi*, and the purpose of this formula is clearly to explain the genesis of *duḥkha* no matter how obscure it may seem in details. In Abhidharma *avidyā* and *saṃskāra* are generally assigned to the past, *vijñānādi* to the present and *jātyādi* to the future and this is also the interpretation tacitly endorsed by MK, XXVI, q.v.

However, the formula should also be understood in another sense so as to accord with Nāgārjuna's opinion that strictly speaking, i.e. *paramārthataḥ*, it is not rational to admit of *pūrvāparasahakrama* (see MK, XI, 2). In order to do so the twelve sectors are first reduced to three groups. Thus *avidyā, tṛṣṇā* and *upādāna* constitute *kleśavartman*, *saṃskāra* and *bhava* make up *karmavartman.* The remaining seven are *duḥkhavartman* (in other sources, e.g. RĀ, I, 35, called *janman*).

By adopting this scheme from *Daśabhūmikasūtra* and various works of Abhidharma Nāgārjuna has paved the way for introducing his notion of *bhavacakra* (or *saṃsāramaṇḍala;* RĀ, I, 36). It has three phases preceding and succeeding one another from time without beginning: *vikalpa* (or *ahaṃkāra,* or simply *kleśa;* ŚS, 34, 37), *karma* (RĀ, I, 35) and finally *janman* (*ibid.*).[164]

Moreover these three aspects may be reduced to two, *hetu* and *phala* (RĀ, I, 38; VS, '6'), i.e. – and here we have to resort to other sources for a helping hand (see ref. to BV, 59-63) – *avidyā, saṃskāra, tṛṣṇā* and *upādāna,* in short *kleśa* and *karma* are *hetu,* whereas the remaining *aṅgas* are *phala.* Now the author has achieved his initial purpose: being *hetu-phala* the 'entire world' (i.e. the five *skandhas,* cf. note to BV, 66) are *pratītyasamutpanna,* i.e. *śūnya,* like illusions etc.

Thus the '*hṛdaya*' of *pratītyasamutpāda* amounts to the *nairātmyavāda* specific to Mahāyāna: not only is there no *sattva* (= *pudgala*) but the *skandhas* are also empty being neither one nor many (cf. MK, II, 21).

We shall find occasion to revert to a full discussion of this important topic .

163. See above all May's annotated version of MK, XXVI, *op.cit.*, pp. 251-276, with ref. La Vallée Poussin in *MCB*, II, pp. 7-26.

164. For *trivartman* in Abhidharma see e.g. J. van den Broeck (tr.), *La saveur de l'immortel (A-p'i-t'an Kan Lu Wei Lun)*, Louvain-la-Neuve 1977, p. 131, n. 2; *Kośa,* III, p. 68; *Traité,* p. 349; *Bodhicaryāvatārapañjikā,* p. 351 (based on *Daśabhūmikasūtra*); *Triṃśikābhāṣya* (ed. S. Lévi), p. 28.

X. Sūtrasamuccaya (SS)

This compilation or anthology of sūtras – mainly Mahāyānasūtras – is ascribed to Nāgārjuna by Candrakīrti[165] and Śāntadeva.[166] Some quotations are given in Kamalaśīla's *Bhāvanākrama*.[167] Otherwise it is only available in Tibetan and Chinese translations.[168]

Like BS and SL etc. SS is an exposition of Mahāyāna as a *duṣkara-caryā* strictly *yathāgamam*. It is addressed to bodhisattvas, *pravrajitas* as well as *gṛhasthas* (similarly RĀ, BS, BV).

That Nāgārjuna should have felt the need to present an authoritative selection of Mahāyāna texts is only what one would expect, not only because he himself is one of the earliest and certainly the foremost exponent of that school, but also, as we gather from RĀ, IV, 67-98, because in his days Mahāyāna still met with severe criticism from various quarters, above all, it seems, from the 'orthodox' Śrāvakas.

On the whole SS is a most significant document for at least two reasons. First of all the abundance of quotations from Mahāyāna scriptures at such an early date lends it a historical value that future translators and editors of these sūtras are bound to take into account. Secondly the outspoken religious convictions found in SS

165. Cf. n. 89; *Madhyamakāvatāra*, p. 402.

166. *Bodhi[sattva]caryāvatāra*, V. 106. Discussion and references in A. Pezzali, *op. cit.*, pp. 80-97. – I prefer Śānt*a*deva to Śānt*i*deva as the former is invariably the transcription given in our earliest source, Atiśa's *Bodhimārgadīpapañjikā* (TP, No. 5344, Ki *fol.* 288b 5, 288b 7, 299b 7, 329a 2, 329a 7). TD *item.*

167. In G. Tucci (ed.), *Minor Buddhist Texts*, III, Roma 1971, pp. 22, 25, 27, q.v. (Having collated the Leningrad Ms of *Bhāvanākrama*, III, I found these misreadings in Tucci's text: p. 2,6 read *nirūpayed;* p. 2,16, °*paryantādhi*°; p. 7, 19, *śūnyāni* (clear!); p. 11, 19, *kālaṃ vā;* p. 27, 12, °*ratnacūḍe* (not °*kūṭe*!).)

168. TP, No. 5330; Taishō, No. 1653. Sanskrit fragments are available not only from sūtras still extant in Sanskrit and quoted by Nāgārjuna (see the list Nos. 7, 17, 22, 24, 26, 36, 45, 46, 47, 50, 63) but also in later compilations etc. quoting from SS, e.g. *Śikṣāsamuccaya*. (I regret that M. Ichishima: 'Sūtrasamuccaya [Kyōshū] no bonbun danpen', in *Tendai gakuhō*, XIV, pp. 165-169 was not available to me.) – Ref. to an English version of SS in *IIJ*, XXIII, p. 326.

contribute considerably to our understanding of the author himself. As SS is intended to expound Mahāyāna in the words of *āgama* we must not expect to discover much of a more philosophical interest. Still § 11 on *saddharmaparigraha* has particular bearing on *prajñā* for here we find some of the *āgamas* which most certainly inspired Nāgārjuna to his concept of *śūnyatā* and induced him to provide arguments (*yukti*) to that effect.

In its extent SS only falls a bit short of that of the remaining authentic writings. Thus I must abstain from translating or paraphrasing the entire text, the more so since a version of SS is expected from the hand of Amalia Pezzali.

Still, for our purpose this need not be deemed a serious drawback inasmuch as the compiler himself has arranged his selections from no less than 68 (collections of) sūtras under 13 main headings summarizing the topics dealt with in the sūtras cited.

I shall therefore confine myself to extract these 'headings' from the body of the text. Finally I subjoin a list of the titles of sūtras from which Nāgārjuna has drawn his selections.[169] I have reconstructed the Sanskrit titles in close agreement with the Tibetan version. Though the reconstructions offered in a few cases do not correspond exactly to the title under which the sūtra is generally known (i.e. from other quotations, colophons etc.) they may, I believe, with a few exceptions, easily be located in the Chinese or Tibetan Tripiṭaka (most conveniently by consulting Hōbōgirin. Fascicule annexe: Répertoire du Canon bouddhique sino-japonais d'après l'édition Taishō Daizōkyō. Tōkyō 1978, and e.g. the index volume to the *Tibetan Tripiṭaka, Peking edition*. Tōkyō 1962).

§ 1. *Buddhotpāda* is *atidurlabha*
(172b3: *saṅs rgyas' byuṅ ba śin tu rñed par dka' ste*)

§ 2. To be born as a human being is *atidurlabha*
(173b6: *mi 'gyur ba śin tu rñed par dka' ste*)

§ 3. The [eight kinds of] *kṣaṇasaṃpad* are *durlabha*
(174a7: *dal ba 'byor ba rñed par dka' ste*)

§ 4. *Tathāgatadeśanāśraddhā* is *durlabha*
(175b3: *de bźin gśegs pa'i bstan pa la dad pa rñed par dka' ste*)

169. This list is a critical revision of A. Banerjee, 'The Sūtrasamuccaya', in *IHQ*, XVII, pp. 121-126.

§ 5. Living beings who produce *bodhicitta* are *durlabha*

(178a3: *gaṅ dag byaṅ chub tu sems bskyed pa'i sems can de dag rñed par dka' ste*)

§ 6. *Mahākaruṇā* towards living beings is *durlabha*

(182b8: *sems can rnams la sñiṅ rje che ba ni rñed par dka' ste*)

§ 7. Those *sattvas* who renounce *āntarāyikadharmas* such as *karmāvaraṇa* wounding a *bodhisattva*, *mārakarman*, a contemptuous attitude (*avamānacitta*) and *saddharmaprahāṇa* are even more *durlabha*

(184b8: *gaṅ dag byaṅ chub sems dpa' la rma 'byin pa'i las kyi sgrib pa daṅ | bdud kyi las daṅ | brñas pa'i sems daṅ | dam pa'i chos spoṅ ba la sogs pa bar du gcod pa'i chos rnams yoṅs su spoṅ ba'i sems can dag ni ches rñed par dka' ste*)

§ 8. Those *sattvas* who live as householders but still are able to accomplish the *dharmas* with earnestness are even more *durlabha*

(193a2: *gaṅ dag khyim par gyur kyaṅ chos rnams la nan tan gyis sgrub pa'i sems can rnams ni ches rñed par dka' ste*)

Note: This is a lengthy and very interesting paragraph treating the ethical aspects of the *bodhisattvacaryā* of a *gṛhastha*. It would certainly deserve to be carefully compared with the corresponding passages in RĀ, SL and BS.

§ 9. Those *sattvas* who are truly devoted to the *parinirvāṇa* of the Tathāgata are *atidurlabha*

(217b2: *gaṅ dag de bźin gśegs pa rnams kyi yoṅs su mya ṅan las 'das pa yaṅ dag pa ji lta ba bźin du mos pa'i sems can de dag ni śin tu rñed par dka'o*)

§ 10. Those *sattvas* who are devoted to *ekayāna* are *atidurlabha*

(222b3: *theg pa gcig la mos pa'i sems can de dag ni śin tu rñed par dka' ste*)

§ 11. A bodhisattva should constantly embrace the *saddharma*

(225b1: *byaṅ chub sems dpa' dam pa'i chos rtag tu yoṅs su bzuṅ bar bya'o*)

Note: From the philosophical point of view this is essentially the most interesting paragraph in SS. Here we find various scriptural sources dealing with the fundamental notions of Nāgārjuna's philosophy as seen in MK etc.: *śūnyatā*, *vimokṣamukha*, *anutpāda*, *prajñāpāramitā* etc. – Again, like § 8, this long paragraph deserves a separate treatment.

§ 12. A bodhisattva must not apply himself to the *gambhīradharmatā* without *upāyakauśalya*

(243b7: *byaṅ chub sems dpa' thabs la mkhas pa daṅ bral bar chos ñid zab mo la sbyor bar mi bya ste*)

Note: The main source is here *Vimalakīrtinirdeśa,* IV, 17, 20; XII, 17 (in Lamotte's translation).

§ 13. *Sattvas* who enter (*praveśa*) the lofty grandeur (*māhātmya*) of the buddhas and bodhisattvas are *atidurlabha*

(246a3: *gaṅ saṅs rgyas daṅ byaṅ chub sems dpa'i che ba ñid rgya chen po la 'jug pa'i sems can de dag ni śin tu rñed par dka'o*)

Note: See *Vimalakīrtinirdeśa,* V, 20.

Fontes

---

1. *Adhyāśayasaṃcodanasūtra,* 210 a 7, 210 b 2, 211 b 8.
   lhag pa'i bsam pa bskul ba'i mdo
2. *Ajātaśatruparivarta,* 180 a 7, 210 a 3, 211 a 4, 230 b 1, 243 b 5.
   ma skyes dgra'i le'u
3. *Ākāśagarbhasūtra,* 205 a 7.
   nam mkha'i sñiṅ po'i le'u
4. *Akṣayamatinirdeśasūtra,* 182 a 2, 245 a 6.
   blo gros mi zad pas bstan pa'i mdo
5. *Anavataptasūtra,* 212 b 2.
   ma dros pa'i mdo
6. *Anupūrvasamudgatasūtra,* 216 b 7.
   mthar gyis yaṅ dag par 'phags pa'i mdo
7. *Arthaviniścayasūtra,* 200 b 3.
   don rnam par ṅes pa'i mdo
8. *Avadāna(!),* 173 a 1.
   rtogs pa brjod pa
9. *Avaivartikacakrasūtra,* 224 a 6.
   phyir mi ldog pa'i 'khor lo'i mdo
10. *Bhadrakalpikasūtra,* 173 b 2, 182 a 6.
    bskal pa bzaṅ po'i mdo
11. *Bhadramāyākārasūtra,* 233 b 2.
    sgyu ma mkhan bzaṅ po'i mdo
12. *Bodhisattvapiṭaka,* 173 a 7, 176 b 8, 183 a 3, 183 a 6, 215 a 6, 215 a 8, 226 a 3, 228 a 6.
    byaṅ chub sems dpa'i sde snod(kyi mdo)
13. *Brahmaparipṛcchā,* 211 b 6, 221 a 1, 227 b 7, 242 a 4.
    tshaṅs pas źus pa('i mdo)
14. *Buddhāvataṃsakasūtra,* 233 b 4, 251 a 4, 252 b 6.
    saṅs rgyas phal po che'i mdo

15. *Candragarbhaparivarta*, 173 b 1, 175 a 8, 175 b 1, 177 a 8, 183 a 1, 206 a 7, 228 a 3.
zla ba'i sñiṅ po'i le'u
16. *Candraprabhaparivarta*, 209 b 3.
zla 'od gyi le'u
17. *Candrapradīpa*, 186 b 4, 195 a 7, 211 a 8, 241 b 2.
zla ba sgron ma'i mdo
18. *Daśabhūmikasūtra*, 249 b 7.
sa bcu'i mdo
19. *Dhāraṇīśvararājaparipṛcchā*, 184 a 1, 223 b 4.
gzuṅs kyi dbaṅ phyug gi rgyal pos źus pa('i mdo)
20. *Dharmasaṃgītisūtra*, 181 b 4, 227 b 5.
chos yaṅ dag par sdud pa'i mdo
21. *Ekottarikāgama*, 174 a 6.
gcig las 'phros pa'i luṅ
22. *Gaṇḍavyūhasūtra*, 173 b 1, 178 a 4, 212 b 4 (!), 224 b 7, 246 b 3, 248 a 4.
sdoṅ po bkod pa'i mdo
23. *Jñānavaipulyasūtra*, 173 a 7, 221 a 5.
ye śes śin tu rgyas pa'i mdo
24. *Kāśyapaparivarta*, 181 a 1.
'od sruṅs kyi le'u
25. *Kṣitigarbhasūtra*, 207 a 3, 208 a 5, 209 a 2.
sa'i sñiṅ po'i mdo
26. *Laṅkāvatārasūtra*, 222 b 2, 224 b 3, 240 a 7, 241 b 1.
laṅ kar gśegs pa'i mdo
27. *Lokottaraparivarta*, 221 a 1.
'jig rten las 'das pa'i le'u
28. *Mahākaruṇāsūtra*, 214 a 5, 220 b 7.
sñiṅ rje chen po'i mdo
29. *Mahāsaṃnipātaparivarta*, 223 b 3.
'dus pa chen po'i le'u
30. *Maitreyasiṃhanādasūtra*, 186 a 7, 217 a 4.
byams pa'i seṅ ge'i sgra'i mdo
31. *Mañjuśrīvikrīḍitasūtra*, 186 b 3.
'jam dpal rnam par rol pa'i mdo
32. *Mañjuśrīvikurvitaparivarta(!)*, 190 b 6, 191 b 4, 234 b 6.
'jam dpal rnam par 'phrul ba'i le'u
33. *Māradamanaparivarta*, 243 a 4, 244 b 6.

bdud 'dul ba'i le'u(mdo)

34. *Niyatāniyatāvatāramudrāsūtra,* 186 b 7, 188 a 5.
ṅes pa daṅ ma ṅes pa la 'jug pa'i phyag rgya'i mdo

35. *Pitāputrasamāgamasūtra,* 181 a 4, 222 a 2, 229 b 3.
yab sras mjal ba'i mdo

36. *Prajñāpāramitā (!),* 182 b 6, 190 a 2, 217 a 7, 220 b 3, 223 a 8, 237 b 2, 238 a 5, 239 b 1, 242 a 6.
śes rab kyi pha rol tu phyin pa

37. *Pravrajyāntarāyasūtra,* 193 a 8.
rab tu 'byuṅ ba'i bar du gcod pa'i mdo

38. *Praśāntaviniścayaprātihāryasūtra,* 180 a 4, 226 b 7, 227 a 1.
rab tu źi ba rnam par ṅes pa'i cho 'phrul gyi mdo

39. *Prasenajitparipṛcchā,* 179 b 4, 196 b 7.
gsal rgyal gyis źus pa

40. *Puṣpakūṭasūtra,* 214 a 3.
me tog brtegs pa'i mdo

41. **Ratnadārikādattasūtra,* 241 b 5.
khye'u rin po ches byin pa'i mdo

42. *Ratnameghasūtra,* 183 b 3, 209 b 8, 226 b 2.
dkon mchog sprin gyi mdo

43. *Ratnarāśisūtra,* 180 b 4, 182 b 4, 211 a 1, 213 b 6, 216 a 2, 216 a 4.
rin po che'i phuṅ po'i mdo

44. **Ratnasamuccayadeśanāsūtra,* 235 b 3, 235 b 7, 236 b 4.
rin po che bsags pa bstan pa'i mdo

45. *Saddharmapuṇḍarīkasūtra,* 172 b 4, 220 b 4 (*bis*), 222 b 4.
dam pa'i chos padma dkar po'i mdo

46. *Saddharmasmṛtyupasthānasūtra,* 195 b 4.
dam pa'i chos dran pa ñe bar gźag pa'i mdo

47. *Saptaśatikā,* 234 b 1.
bdun brgya pa

48. *Sāgaramatiparipṛcchāsūtra,* 192 b 2, 193 a 1, 217 a 2, 225 b 7.
blo gros rgya mtshos źus pa'i mdo

49. *Sāgaranāgarājaparipṛcchā,* 177 b 1, 215 a 2.
klu'i rgyal po rgya mtshos źus pa

50. *Saṃyuktāgama,* 173 b 6, 212 a 5, 221 a 3.
yaṅ dag par ldan pa'i luṅ

51. *Satyakaparivarta,* 203 a 6, 223 a 1.
bden pa po'i le'u

52. *Śraddhābalādhānāvatāramudrāsūtra*, 176 a 8, 176 b 4, 185 a 1, 187 a 4, 225 b 2.
dad pa'i stobs bskyed pa la 'jug pa'i phyag rgya'i mdo
53. *Śrīmālāsiṃhanādasūtra*, 224 b 2, 227 b 3.
dpal gyi phreṅ ba seṅ ge'i sgra'i mdo
54. *Sūryagarbhaparivarta*, 204 a 4.
ñi ma'i sñiṅ po'i 'e'u
55. *Tathāgatabimbaparivarta*, 215 b 2.
de bźin gśegs pa'i gzugs kyi le'u
56. *Tathāgataguhyasūtra*, 175 b 3, 175 b 8, 181 b 1, 181 b 2, 227 b 1.
de bźin gśegs pa'i gsaṅ ba'i mdo
57. *Tathāgataguṇajñānācintyaviṣayāvatāranirdeśasūtra*, 177 b 3, 250 a 8.
de bźin gśegs pa'i yon tan daṅ ye śes bsam gyis mi khyab pa'i yul la 'jug pa bstan pa'i mdo
58. *Tathāgatakoṣa(garbha)sūtra*, 242 b 2.
de bźin gśegs pa'i mdzod kyi mdo
59. *Tathāgatotpattisaṃbhavasūtra*, 217 b 4.
de bźin gśegs pa skye ba srid pa'i mdo
60. *Udayanavatsarājaparipṛcchā*, 194 a 7.
bat sa la'i rgyal po śar pas źus pa'i mdo
61. *Ugraparipṛcchāsūtra*, 193 a 3.
drag śul can gyis źus pa'i mdo
62. *Upāyakauśalyasūtra*, 192 a 4.
thabs la mkhas pa'i mdo
63. *Vajracchedikā*, 240 a 3 (!), 241 b 7.
rdo rje gcod pa (*sive* sum brgya pa)
64. **Vimatisamudghātasūtra*, 174 a 1, 204 a 1.
yid gñis yaṅ dag (legs) par 'joms pa'i mdo
65. *Vimalakīrtinirdeśa*, 201 b 7, 237 a 4, 237 a 7, 243 b 8, 244 a 7, 245 a 2, 246 a 4.
66. **Viniścayarāja* [*-sūtra*], 172 b 6.
rnam par gtan la dbab pa'i rgyal po['i mdo]
67. *Vīradattagṛhapatiparipṛcchā*, 183 a 6, 201 a 6, 201 b 3.
khyim bdag dpas byin gyis źus pa
68. *Viśeṣacintibrahmaparipṛcchā*, 234 a 5.
tshaṅs pa khyad par sems kyis źus pa'i mdo

XI. Bodhicittavivaraṇa (BV)

This regrettably neglected text comprises 112 stanzas (*anuṣṭubh*) introduced by a brief prooemium in prose. It has sometimes been grouped as a tantric work[170] but a glance at the contents of BV shows how unwarranted such a classification is.

BV is never mentioned or cited by Buddhapālita or Candrakīrti. On the other hand it forms one of the basic authorities for Bhavya in his most mature work, the *Ratnapradīpa*.[171] It is never quoted in his earlier works, *Tarkajvālā, Prajñāpradīpa* and [**Kara-*]*talaratna*. Among 'good authors' citing BV are especially Asvabhāva and Śāntarakṣita.[172] I have also come across scores of quotations by other commentators; fortunately several of these are in Sanskrit.[173] It is my general impression that YṢ, CS and BV are the most frequently quoted among all works ascribed to Nāgārjuna in later Indian literature.

The style of BV is similar to that of YṢ, RĀ and CS. From a historical point of view the most significant feature of this text is its extensive critique of Vijñānavāda, i.e. Buddhist idealism as testified in the *Laṅkāvatārasūtra*.[174] Having seen how vehemently Nāgārjuna attacks any kind of acceptance of *svabhāva* one would also expect him to have criticized those who might have thought themselves justified in maintaining the absolute existence of *vijñāna* (*citta*). But in the texts dealt with hitherto this has only happened incidentally.[175] Here BV provides us with the missing link.

170. Cf. Bu-ston, II, p. 126; J. Naudou, *op.cit.*, p. 187. (Note that two verses allegedly from RĀ are quoted by Bu-ston, I, p. 133, though in fact from BV, 91-92). BV is seldom referred to by modern authors though P. Patel identified some quotations from it in *IHQ*, VIII, pp. 790-793. See also my paper WZKS, XXVI (1982).
171. *Ibid.*
172. Both quote the celebrated verse 20, see *ibid.*
173. V. 12, 13a, 20, 25, 27, 45, 46, 52ab, 57, 98, 99.
174. Cf. n. 149 above for evidence of Nāgārjuna's acquaintance with *Laṅkāvatāra-sūtra*.
175. CS, I, 10; III, 50; ŚS, 56-57.

None of Nāgārjuna's other works exhibit such a well-balanced and coherent structure as BV. This is to some extent a natural consequence of the fact that the theme is at once simple and comprehensive: *bodhicitta.* It has a relative aspect consisting in the desire (*prārthanā*) for the *bodhi* of all living beings,[176] and an absolute consisting in the unlimited cognition of *śūnyatā,* or *bodhi.*[177] BV thus provides us with a compendium of the practice and theory of Mahāyāna addressed to bodhisattvas, *gṛhasthas* as well as *pravrajitas.* It may indeed be said to be nothing but a *vivaraṇa* of the celebrated formula RĀ, IV, 96: *śūnyatākaruṇāgarbham ekeṣāṃ bodhisādhanam.*

Sanskrit fragments apart, only two Tibetan versions of BV are at our disposal:[178]

Sigla

A *Bodhicittavivaraṇa,* trans. by Rab źi chos kyi bśes gñen *et al.*[179] TP, No. 5470, Gi *fol.* 221a-226b; TN, No. 3461, Gi *fol.* 210b-215b.

B *Bodhicittavivaraṇa,* trans. by Guṇākara & Rab źi [chos kyi] bśes gñen, revised by Kanakavarman & Ñi ma grags.

176. B has *smon pa* (*praṇidhi,* or *prārthanā*), A has *smon lam* (*praṇidhāna*). For *bodhicitta* in general, see EOB, III, pp. 184-189; Har Dayal. *op.cit.,* pp. 58-64; RĀ, III, 86.

177. See 71 for this equivalence: *tathatā* = *bhūtakoṭi* = *ānimitta* = *paramārtha paramabodhicitta* = *śūnyatā.* Cf. ŚS, 69; CS, I, 27; III, 41, 45. – *Siddhi,* pp. 757-761.

178. To be sure TP, No. 2666, Gi *fol.* 48a-50b (TN, No. 665), i.e. *Bodhicittavivaraṇa* ascribed to Nāgārjuna, is a brief prose commentary on the verse *sarvabhāvavigatam ...* from the *Guhyasamājatantra,* which it quotes (*loc.cit.,* 49b 6), cf. note, p. 183 to the poem of BV. It does not seem unlikely that the author of this tract is identical with the one of *Guhyasamājatantraṭīkā* referred to above (n. 12 & 47).

Taishō, No. 1661, i.e. *Pú tí xīn lí xiàng,* also ascribed to Nāgārjuna is in fact nothing but a Chinese prose paraphrase of BV. Dr. Eric Grinstead who carefully compared it with my version of BV succeeded in identifying all 112 verses (in some cases only slight traces) including the proem. Consequently the Chinese title should be taken as rendering Sanskrit *Bodhicittavivaraṇa,* not **Bodhicittanimittarahita* (?) as Robinson, *op.cit.,* p. 27 has, or **Lakṣaṇavimukta-bodhihṛdayaśāstra,* as Ramanan, *op. cit.,* p. 35 suggests. – For strictly philological purposes it has proved to be of no avail.

179. For the full list and a few other details v. EOB, III, p. 190.

TP, No. 2665, Gi *fol.* 42b-48a; TN, No. 664, Gi *fol.* 41b-46b.
C *Bodhicittavivaraṇaṭīkā,* trans. by Smṛtijñānakīrti (= author).
TP, No. 2694, Gi *fol.* 454b-484b; TN, No. 693, Gi *fol.* 449b-476b

---

B is, as we would expect from the names of the revisors, an excellent piece of work, and it forms the basis of my edition. Throughout I have carefully compared A and C. In a few cases A has proved invaluable, e.g. for v. 16 left out in B due to haplography (homoearcton). C is a commentary of high standard. It quotes *pratīkas* from all the 112 stanzas and explains all moot points exhaustively. In a few cases, like A, it permits us to emend corruptions in B. I have, however, only registered variants in A and C when they affect the sense in such a way that it may possibly be more authentic than the one transmitted by B.[180]

Synopsis

I. *Prooemium:*	The theme of this treatise is *bodhicitta; saṃvṛtitaḥ* it is a yearning for the *bodhi* of all living beings, *paramārthataḥ* it is the realization of *śūnyatā,* i.e. *bodhi.* *
II. a. 1-3:	The significance of developing *bodhicitta.*
b. 4-9:	Refutation of the belief in an *ātman,* a permanent soul and a creator, as held by Tīrthikas.
c. 10-25:	Refutation of the existence of the skandhas as held by the Śrāvakas.

180. I have refrained from editing A as it would take up too much space without contributing the least to a better understanding of the sense intended by the author of BV. On the other hand a comparison of A and B would (especially if carried out as meticulously as done e.g. in N. Simonsson, *Indo-tibetische Studien,* Uppsala 1957) shed some light into the workshop of the translators and revisors.

Note that in the *apparatus criticus* A, B and C indicate the *consensus* of the P and N editions. My collation of these two editions of B has revealed remarkably few variants: 5d *brten* P : *rten* N; 19c *ni* N : *na*; 74e *bzo* P : *bza* N.

d. 26-56:	Refutation of the fundamentals of Vijñānavāda, viz. *trisvabhāva, svasaṃvedanā, āśrayaparivṛtti* and *ālayavijñāna.* – In reality *vijñāna* is dependent, momentary, illusory and empty (39-56).
e. 57-72:	All internal and external dharmas are *pratītyasamutpanna,* or *śūnya.* To understand this is to realize the absolute *bodhicitta,* or *mokṣa* from the bonds of karma due to *kleśa.*
III. a. 73-104:	A bodhisattva who has thus become a buddha is motivated by *karuṇā* (i.e. by the power of his previous *praṇidhānas*) to apply all possible means (= *upāyakauśalya*) in order to rescue all *sattvas* from *saṃsāra.*
b. 105-111:	Conclusion. The reader is encouraged to produce *bodhicitta.*
c. 112:	A final *puṇyapariṇāmanā.*

---

* This introduction calls for some remarks. – The initial stanza is, as C 455 b 4 notes, from the *Guhyasamāja* (v. ed. Bhattacharya, p. 12, where it is printed as if prose!): *sarvabhāvavigataṃ skandhadhātvāyatanagrāhyagrāhakavarjitam* | *dharmanairātmyasamatayā svacittam ādyanutpannaṃ śūnyatābhāvam* ||. It also occurs in *Bodhicittavivaraṇa* (TP, No. 2666, Gi *fol.* 48a 4) also ascribed to Nāgārjuna (corresponds to Taishō, XXXII, 1661). The corresponding Sanskrit text is reproduced in P. Python, *Vinaya-viniścaya-Upāli-paripṛcchā,* 'Hors-texte', *fol.* 10 a 3 (not 10 b as the editor assumes, cf. de Jong, *IIJ,* XIX, p. 131) with the variant in d *śūnyatāsvabhāvam.* – How we are to account for the fact that a verse from a tantric text occurs in BV I am not to say. Since, however, BV otherwise has nothing tantric about it (cf. v. 1) – nor has this verse taken in itself – it should not, I think, induce us to regard the author of BV as being identical, e.g. with the author of *Pañcakrama.* Moreover, it is also also found in *Bodhicittotpādavidhi,* pure Mahāyāna, cf. n. 17, p. 12.

There are two aspects of *bodhicitta* (not the same as those of *Bodhicaryāvatāra,* I, 15, q.v.). The relative is merely desire, or quest (*prārthanā*) for *bodhi.* It is expressed in a *praṇidhāna,* here alluding to *Aṣṭasāhasrikā,* p. 215 (cf. Har Dayal (1932), p. 65; see also *Śatapañcāśatka,* p. 40, which like BV presupposes the reading *atīrṇān* etc. for *tīrṇāḥ* etc.). The absolute is simply *bodhi,* see BV, 45 sq. – This passage is also quoted in F. D. Lessing and A. Wayman (1968), p. 334, q.v.; Guenther (1959), p. 131. – I have corrected B's *sñiṅ po byaṅ chub* (a simple transposition) to *byaṅ chub sñiṅ po* (thus A and C, **bodhimaṇḍa,* cf. BHSD, p. 402).

C 460b 4 explains *sṅags* (not *gsaṅ sṅags* as A and B): *de la sṅags ni śes skyob ste* | *rnam par mi rtog pa'i ye śes daṅ sñiṅ rje'i raṅ bźin saṅs rgyas nas bzlas pa'i phyir ro* ||. I thus take **mantramukha* as equivalent of *dhāraṇīmukha,* see BV, 100 and *Traité,* p. 1854 sq. for a full explanation.

Bodhicittavivaraṇa ||

Byaṅ chub sems kyi 'grel pa ||

dṅos po thams cad daṅ bral ba		phuṅ po khams daṅ skye mched kyi
gzuṅ daṅ 'dzin pa rnam spaṅs pa		chos bdag med pas mñam ñid pas
raṅ sems gdod nas ma skyes pa || stoṅ pa ñid kyi raṅ bźin no || źes bya ba 'byuṅ ṅo	

saṅs rgyas bcom ldan 'das rnams daṅ | byaṅ chub sems dpa' chen po de rnams kyis ji ltar byaṅ chub chen por thugs bskyed pa de bźin du | bdag gis kyaṅ sems can ma bsgral ba rnams bsgral ba daṅ | ma grol ba rnams grol ba daṅ | dbugs ma byuṅ ba rnams dbugs dbyuṅ ba daṅ | yoṅs su mya ṅan las ma 'das pa rnams yoṅs su mya ṅan las bzla ba'i phyir dus 'di nas bzuṅ nas byaṅ chub sñiṅ po la mchis kyi bar du byaṅ chub chen por sems bskyed par bgyi'o ||

byaṅ chub sems dpa' gsaṅ sṅags kyi sgor spyad pa spyod pa rnams kyis de ltar kun rdzob kyi rnam pas byaṅ chub kyi sems smon pa'i raṅ bzin can bskyed nas | don dam pa'i byaṅ chub kyi sems bsgom pa'i stobs kyis bskyed par bya ba yin pas de'i phyir de'i raṅ bźin bśad par bya'o ||

*

1.
| byaṅ chub sems kyi bdag ñid dṅos || dpal ldan rdo rje rnams btud de |
| byaṅ chub sems kyi bsgom pa ni || srid pa 'jig de bdag gis bśad |

1a dṅos B : sku AC; b rnams B : 'chaṅ A

Exposition of bodhicitta

It has been stated: 'Due to the sameness [or] selflessness of [all] phenomena (*dharma*) one's own mind (*svacitta*) being devoid of all entities (*sarvabhāvavigata*), exempt from the aggregates, elements, sense-fields, object and subject (*skandhadhātvāyatanagrāhyagrāhakavarjita*), is originally unborn (*ādyanutpanna*) [and] essentially empty (*śūnyatābhāva*).'

Just as the Buddhas, our Lords (*bhagavat*), and the great bodhisattvas have produced the thought of Great Enlightenment (*mahābodhicitta*), thus I shall also, from now on until [I dwell] in the heart of enlightenment (*bodhimaṇḍa*), produce the thought of Great Enlightenment (*mahābodhicitta*) in order that [we] may save living beings unsaved, liberate those not liberated, console those not consoled and extinguish those not extinguished (*atīrṇān tārayemāmuktān mocayemāśvastān āśvāsayemāparinirvṛtān parinirvāpayema iti*).

When a bodhisattva having practised a course by way of mantras has thus produced the *bodhicitta* which in its relative aspect (*saṃvṛtyākāreṇa*) has the nature of aspiration (*prārthanā*), he must, by means of meditational development (*bhāvanābalāt*) produce the absolute (*paramārtha*) *bodhicitta*. Therefore I will expose its nature (*svabhāva*).

*

1. Bowing to the glorious (*śrīmat*) Vajrasattvas embodying the mind of enlightenment (*bodhicittātmabhāva*), I shall expound the development (*bhāvanā*) of the *bodhicitta* which abolishes [the three kinds of] existence (*bhava*) [in *saṃsāra*].

1. I take *bdag ñid dṅos* (or *bdag ñid sku* with A and C) as translating *ātmabhāva*, for which cf. May, *op.cit.*, p. 278, n. 1017. – In b A reads *śrī-Vajradhara* (*dpal ldan rdo rje 'chaṅ*), whereas C speaks of *rdo rje sems dpa'i sku* (which it identifies with *mahāmudrā*, hence the epithet *śrī*, which may also be explained *lha'i rigs phun sum tshogs pa daṅ ldan pa'i phyir* ... etc. *more tantrico*, see 461a 5-8) without showing any sign of the plural. If B transmits the authentic reading I take this

2.

| saṅs rgyas rnams kyi byaṅ chub sems || bdag daṅ phuṅ sogs rnam rig gi |
| rtog pa rnams kyis ma bsgribs pa || rtag tu stoṅ ñid mtshan ñid bźed |

3.

| sñiṅ rjes brlan pa'i sems kyis ni || 'bad pas bsgom par bya ba yin |
| thugs rje'i bdag ñid saṅs rgyas kyis || byaṅ chub sems 'di rtag tu bsgoms |

4.

| mu stegs can gyis gaṅ brtags pa || bdag de rigs pas rnam dpyad na |
| phuṅ rnams kun gyi naṅ rnams na || gaṅ źig gnas kyaṅ rñed ma yin |

5.

| phuṅ rnams yod kyi de rtag min || de yaṅ bdag gi ṅo bo min |
| gaṅ yaṅ rtag daṅ mi rtag gñis || rten daṅ brten pa'i dṅos po med |

6.

| bdag ces bya ste yod min na || byed po źes bya ga la rtag |
| chos can yod na chos rnams la || 'jig rten na ni spyod pa 'jug |

7.

| gaṅ phyir rtag pas don byed pa || rim daṅ cig car gyis min pa |
| de phyir phyi rol naṅ du ni || rtag pa'i dṅos de med pa ñid |

6d spyod BC : dpyod A (*cf.* TD, No. 3868, Ya *fol.* 344a 4 : dpyad)

2. The Buddhas maintain that *bodhicitta* is not enveloped (*nivṛta*) in notions (*kalpanā*) conscious of a self, aggregates etc. (*ātmaskandhādi*) [but that it] is always characterized by being empty (*śūnyatālakṣaṇa*) [of any such notions].

3. [Those] with minds (*citta*) [only] tinged by compassion (*karuṇā*) must develop [the *bodhicitta*] with particular effort (*prayatnena*). This *bodhicitta* is constantly (*sadā*) developed by the compassionate (*kṛpātmaka*) Buddhas.

4. When the self (*ātman*) which is conceived (*kalpita*) by the sectarians (*tīrthika*) is analysed (*vicāryamāṇa*) logically (*yuktyā*) it cannot obtain a place inside any of the [five] aggregates (*skandha*).

5. Being [identical with] the aggregates (*skandha*) [the self] would not be permanent (*nitya*), but the self (*ātman*) has no such nature. A container-content relationship (*ādhārādheyabhāva*) is not [possible] between a permanent [self] and impermanent [aggregates].

6. When there is no so-called self (*ātman*) how can the so-called creator (*kāraka*) be permanent (*nitya*)? If there were a subject (*dharmin*) one may begin investigating its attributes (*dharma*) in the world (*loke*).

7. Since a permanent [creator] cannot create things (*arthakriyā*) whether it be gradually (*krameṇa*) or all at once (*yugapat*), therefore there are no permanent things whether it be exterior (*bāhya*) or interior (*antaḥ*).

to indicate bodhisattvas such as Samantabhadra etc. mentioned BV, 90, 111. – For *bhava* see C 461b 2: *de la srid pa ni ñe bar len gyi phuṅ po lṅa'i raṅ bźin 'dod pa daṅ | gzugs daṅ gzugs med pa'i srid pa ste | 'byuṅ źiṅ 'gyur ba'i phyir ro* ||. Cf. MK, XXVI, 8.

2. The genitive *kyi* (which C 462a 2 also has) should be retained and construed with *bźed*. It reflects **buddhānām ... mata* or *iṣṭa*.

3. C 462a 3 sq. lists the eight *arthākāra* of *mahākaruṇā*, explained *Traité*, p. 1707, q.v.

4-5. One cannot conceive *ātman* – *skandhas* as *eka* or *anya*; MK, XVIII; Schayer (1931), p. 90, n. 60.

6. A *kāraka* who is *nitya* is impossible, not only because there is no *ātman* (see above) but also because he, as a *dharmin* related to *dharmas* would have to be *anitya* like them, see 7-9. See also CS, III, 34 with ref.

7-8. A creation all at once is against experience, a gradual one is incompatible with the notion of a creator's omnipotence (*śakti/sāmarthya*), cf. e.g. *Siddhi*, p. 30; *Pramāṇavārttika,* I, 9 sq. This is possibly the earliest occurrence of this celebrated argument.

8.
| gal te nus na ci de ltos || de ni cig car dṅos 'byin 'gyur |
| gaṅ źig dṅos gźan la ltos la || de ni rtag daṅ nus ldan min |

9.
| gal te dṅos na rtag min te || dṅos rnams rtag tu skad cig phyir |
| gaṅ phyir mi rtag dṅos po la || byed pa po ñid bkag pa med |

10.
| bdag sogs bral ba'i 'jig rten 'di || phuṅ po khams daṅ skye mched daṅ |
| gzuṅ daṅ 'dzin pa ñid dag gi || blo yis rnam par 'joms par 'gyur |

11.
| phan par bźed pa rnams kyis ni || gzugs daṅ tshor ba 'du śes daṅ |
| 'du byed rnam śes phuṅ po lṅa || de ltar ñan thos rnams la gsuṅs |

12. phenapiṇḍopamaṃ rūpaṃ vedanā budbudopamā |
marīcisadṛśī saṃjñā saṃskārāḥ kadalīnibhāḥ ||
| rkaṅ gñis mchog gis rtag tu yaṅ || gzugs ni dbu ba rdos daṅ 'dra |
| tshor ba chu yi chu bur 'dra || 'du śes smig rgyu daṅ mtshuṅs śiṅ |

13. māyopamaṃ ca vijñānaṃ
...
| 'du byed chu śiṅ daṅ 'dra la || rnam śes sgyu ma lta bu źes |
| phuṅ po bstan pa 'di lta bu || byaṅ chub sems dpa' rnams la gsuṅs |

14.
| 'byuṅ chen bźi yi raṅ bźin can || gzugs kyi phuṅ por rab tu bśad |
| lhag ma gzugs med ñid du ni || med na mi 'byuṅ phyir na 'grub |

8a ci de B : ci phyir A
10a 'di B : ni A; cd A *pro* : gzuṅ 'dzin blo yis 'joms par 'gyur B
12b daṅ 'dra A : 'dra snaṅ B
14b bśad BA : gsal C; d med na mi 'byuṅ ... B : the tshom med par ... A

8. If [a creator] were efficient (*śakta*) why [would he be] dependent (*apekṣate*)? He would of course (*hi*) emit things (*bhāva*) all at once (*yugapat*). That [creator] who depends upon something else (*bhāvāntara*) is neither eternal (*śāśvata*) nor efficient (*śakta*).

9. If [he] were an entity (*bhāva*) he [would] not be permanent (*śāśvata*), for things (*bhāva*) are perpetually momentaneous (*kṣaṇika*), since it is not denied (*niṣiddha*) [by you] that impermanent things have a creator (*kārakatva*).

10. This [empirical] world (*loko 'yam*) which is free from a self etc. (*ātmādi*) is vanquished by the [Disciples'] notion (*buddhi*) about [the reality of] the aggregates, elements, sense-fields, object and subject (*skandhadhātvāyatanagrāhyagrāhaka*).

11. Thus the solicitous (*hitaiṣin*) [Buddhas] have spoken of the five aggregates (*pañcaskandha*) to the Disciples (*śrāvaka*) [viz.], form (*rūpa*), feeling (*vedanā*), apprehension (*saṃjñā*), karma-formations (*saṃskāra*) and consciousness (*vijñāna*).

12-13. But to the bodhisattvas [the Buddha], the best among bipeds (*dvipādānām agrya*), has always taught this doctrine (*deśanā*) about the aggregates (*skandha*): 'Form (*rūpa*) is like a mass of foam (*phenapiṇḍa*), feeling (*vedanā*) is like bubbles (*budbuda*), apprehension (*saṃjñā*) is like a mirage (*marīci*), karma-formations (*saṃskāra*) are like the plantain (*kadalī*) and consciousness (*vijñāna*) is like an illusion (*māyā*).'

14. The form-aggregate (*rūpaskandha*) is declared to have the four great elements (*mahābhūta*) as its nature. The remaining [four aggregates] are inseparably established (*avinābhāvāt siddha*) as immaterial (*arūpin*).

9. Being included among all things a creator (C 463b 7: *dbaṅ phyug la sogs pa*) must also be *anitya*.

10. This refers to the Śrāvakas (BS, 25-26 etc.). As in its canonical usage the term *loko 'yam* or *ayaṃ loka* occasionally has a somewhat pejorative tone.

11-13. The Śrāvakas only endorse *pudgalanairātmya* but by quoting a celebrated passage from their *āgama* (*Saṃyutta*, III, p. 142; Sanskrit: *Prasannapadā*, p. 41; cf. also *Traité*, p. 370) Nāgārjuna shows that even here we find evidence of the Buddha's teaching of *dharmanairātmya* (cf. CS, I, 3 with ref.). – See p. 260.

14. Following (14-24) is a refutation of *rūpa* (i.e. *upādāyarūpa*, cf. *Traité*, p. 782, or *bhautika*) for which cf. ÇS, I, 5 with ref.

15.
| de dag rnams kyi mig gzugs sogs || khams rnams bśad pa de dag ñid |
| skye mched dag ni gzuṅ ba daṅ || 'dzin par yaṅ ni śes par bya |

16.
| gzugs rdul med gźan dbaṅ po med || byed po'i dbaṅ po śin tu med |
| skyod pa po daṅ skyed pa dag || yaṅ dag bskyed par rigs ma yin |

17.
| gzugs rdul dbaṅ śes skyed min te || de ni dbaṅ po las 'das yin |
| 'dus pas de rnams skyed byed na || tshogs pa de yaṅ mi 'dod do |

18.
| phyogs kyi dbye bas phye ba yis || rdul phran la yaṅ dbye ba mthoṅ |
| gaṅ la cha śas kyis brtags pa || der ni rdul phran ji ltar 'thad |

19.
| phyi rol don ni rnam gcig la || tha dad śes pa 'jug par 'gyur |
| yid 'oṅ gzugs ni gaṅ yin pa || de ñid gźan la gźan du 'gyur |

20. parivrāṭkāmukaśunām ekasyāṃ pramadātanau |
kuṇapaḥ kāminī bhakṣya iti tisro vikalpanāḥ ||

| bud med gzugs ni gcig pu la || ro daṅ 'dod bya bza' ba la |
| kun rgyu chags can khyi rnams bźin || rnam par rtog pa gsum yin no |

21.
| don mtshuṅs pa yis don byed pa || rmi lam gnod pa bźin min nam |
| rmi lam sad pa'i gnas skabs la || don byed pa la khyad par med |

16 AC, *sed om.* B
17d tshogs pa de yaṅ B : 'dus par yaṅ ni A
19a ni rnam gcig la B : rnams gcig la yaṅ A : ... rnam pa gcig daṅ | yaṅ C
21b gnod pa bźin min nam B : na ni rmis pa bźin A: gnod sbyin don byed pa C (*cf. Viṃśatikā*, 4)

15. Among these eye, form etc. (*cakṣūrūpādi*) are classified as [the eighteen] elements (*dhātu*). These again are, as object-subject (*grāhyagrāhaka*), to be known as the [twelve] sense-fields (*āyatana*).

16. Form (*rūpa*) is not the atom (*aṇu*). Again, it is not the [organ] of sense (*indriya*) [and] it is absolutely not the active sense (*kārakendriya?*) [of consciousness]. [Therefore] an instigator (*skyod pa po*) and a creator (*janaka*) are not fitted for producing [form].

17. The form-atom (*rūpaparamāṇu*) does not produce sense-consciousness (*indriyavijñāna*) [because] it transcends the senses (*indriyātīta*). If these [empirical forms are supposed to] be created by an assemblage (*saṃghāta*) [of atoms] this accumulation (*samūha*), however, is unacceptable (*aniṣṭa*).

18. If you analyse by spatial division (*digbheda*) even the atom (*paramāṇu*) is seen to possess parts (*bheda*). That which is analysed into parts (*aṃśa*), how can that logically be an atom?

19. Concerning one single exterior object (*bāhyārtha*) divergent judgements may prevail. That form (*rūpa*) which is pleasant (*manohara*) [to one person], precisely that may appear different to others.

20. In respect to the same female body, an ascetic, a lover and a dog entertain three different notions: 'A corpse', 'A mistress', 'A titbit'.

21. It is [merely] due to [their] *similarity* to objects (*arthasama*) that 'things' are efficient (*arthakriyā*). It is like an offence while dreaming [i.e. emissio seminis] (*svapnopaghāta*), is it not? In the state of being awakened from the dream there is no difference (*viśeṣa*) as far as the efficiency of things is concerned.

15. Cf. e.g. MK, III-V.

16-18. Refutation of *anu/paramāṇu*, *Traité*, p. 725; *Bhāvanākrama*, I, pp. 20-22; May (1959), p. 54, n. 15(ref.). This is *sūkṣmarūpa*.

19-20. Refutation of *sthūlarūpa*. Cf. *Traité*, p. 733 which also cites the Sanskrit verse from *Sarvadarśanasaṃgraha*. For further ref. see Mimaki (1976), p. 309, n. 432. Similarly ŚS, 60; *Catuḥśataka*, VIII, 2; *Saundarananda*, XIII, 52.

21. Though things are capable of efficiency they are nevertheless *śūnya*, cf. *svavṛtti* ad VV, 22. – For *svapnopaghāta*, see *Viṃśatikā*, 4.

22.
I gzuṅ daṅ 'dzin pa'i ṅo bo yis II rnam śes snaṅ ba gaṅ yin pa I
I rnam śes las ni tha dad par II phyi rol don ni 'ga' yaṅ med I

23.
I de phyir dṅos po'i ṅo bor ni II phyi don rnam pa kun tu med I
I rnam śes so sor snaṅ ba 'di II gzugs kyi rnam par snaṅ bar 'gyur I

24.
I ji ltar skye bo sems rmoṅs pas II sgyu ma smig rgyu dri za yi I
I groṅ khyer la sogs mthoṅ ba ltar II de bźin gzugs sogs snaṅ ba yin I

25. ātmagrahanivṛttyarthaṃ skandhadhātvādideśanā I
sāpi dhvastā mahābhāgaiś cittamātravyavasthayā II

I bdag tu 'dzin pa bzlog pa'i phyir II phuṅ po khams sogs bstan pa yin I
I sems tsam po la gnas nas ni II skal chen rnams kyis de yaṅ spaṅs I

26.
I rnams par śes par smra ba la II sna tshogs 'di ni sems su grub I
I rnam śes raṅ bźin gaṅ źe na II da ni de ñid bśad bya ste I

27. cittamātram idaṃ sarvam iti yā deśanā muneḥ I
uttrāsaparihārārthaṃ bālānāṃ sā na tattvataḥ II

I 'di dag thams cad sems tsam źes II thub pas bstan pa gaṅ mdzad de I
I byis pa rnams kyi skrag pa ni II spaṅ ba'i phyir yin de ñid min I

23c snaṅ ba 'di B : snaṅ ba ni A : snaṅ ba'i C
25b khams sogs BS : la sogs A
26c da B : 'dir A

22. As to the appearance of consciousness (*vijñāna*) under the form of object and subject (*grāhyagrāhakākāra*) [one must realize] that there exists no external object (*bāhyārtha*) apart from consciousness (*vijñāna*).

23. Therefore there is in no way at all an exterior thing in the mode of an entity (*vasturūpa*). This particular appearance of consciousness appears under the aspect of form (*rūpākāra*).

24. Just as people (*jana*) due to mental delusions (*cittamohana*) see illusions, mirages, cities of Gandharvas etc. (*māyāmarīcigandharvanagarādi*), the manifestation of form (*rūpadarśana*) is just like that.

25. The [Buddha's] instruction about the aggregates, elements etc. [merely] aims at dispelling the belief in a self (*ātmagraha*). By establishing [themselves] in pure consciousness (*cittamātra*) the greatly blessed [bodhisattvas] also abandon that [instruction].

26. According to the Idealists (*vijñānavādin*) this manifold (*citra*) [world] is established to be mere consciousness (*citta*). What the nature (*svabhāva*) of this consciousness might be [however], we shall analyse at once (*adya*).

27. The Anchorite's (*muni*) doctrine that 'The entire [world] is mere mind' is [in fact] intended to remove the fear of fools. It is not a [doctrine] concerning reality.

22. Following concludes that there is no *bāhyārtha*, cf. *Mahāyānaviṃśikā*, 19: *utpādo hi vikalpo 'yam artho bāhyo na vidyate* ||. Cf. *Laṅkāvatāra*, X, 154-155. – But, as we shall see, the author takes great pains to show that the *cittamātratā* of the *Laṅkāvatāra* (see Suzuki's *Index*, p. 69) should be taken *neyārtha*, i.e. *nairātmyāvatārataḥ*. For 24 note that 'dans les textes des Śrāvakas, on ne recontre jamais l'exemple de la ville de Gandharva' (*Traité*, p. 370); cf. also CS, III, 5; RĀ, II, 12-13 (*cittamohana*).

25. Sanskrit *Jñānaśrīmitranibandhāvalī*, p. 488 (v.l. *citra*°).

26. Following is a refutation of those Buddhists who interprete *cittamātratā*, especially in the *Laṅkāvatāra*, *nītārtha* (26-45).

27. Sanskrit *Subhāṣitasaṃgraha* (ed. Bendall), p. 20; Jñānaśrīmitra, *loc.cit.* (with *tattrāsa*° for *uttrāsa*°). Cf. *Śikṣāsamuccaya*, p. 263; *Prasannapadā*, p. 264, n. 2.

28.
| kun brtags daṅ ni gźan dbaṅ daṅ || yoṅs su grub pa 'di ñid ni |
| stoṅ ñid bdag ñid gcig pu yi || ṅo bo sems la brtags pa yin |

29.
| theg chen dga' ba'i bdag ñid la || chos la bdag med mñam pa ñid |
| sems ni gdod nas ma skyes te || saṅs rgyas kyis ni mdor bsdus gsuṅs |

30.
| rnal 'byor spyod pa pa rnams kyis || raṅ gi sems kyi dbaṅ byas te |
| gnas yoṅs gyur nas dag pa'i sems || so sor raṅ gi spyod yul brjod |

31.
| 'das pa gaṅ yin de ni med || ma 'oṅs pa ni thob pa min |
| gnas phyir gnas ni yoṅs gyur pa || da lta ba la ga la yod |

32.
| de ji ltar de ltar snaṅ min || ji ltar snaṅ de de ltar min |
| rnam śes bdag med ṅo bo ste || rten gźan rnam par śes pa med |

33.
| ji ltar khab len daṅ ñe bas || lcags ni myur du yoṅs su 'khor |
| de la sems ni yod min te || sems daṅ ldan bźin snaṅ bar 'gyur |

28c gcig pu yi B : tshul gcig gi A
29c sems ni B : raṅ sems AC (*recte?*)
32b min AC : yin B
33d bźin AC : źiṅ B

28. [The three natures, viz.] the imagined (*parikalpita*), the dependent (*paratantra*) and the absolute (*parinişpanna*) have only one nature of their own: emptiness. They are the imaginations (*kalpanā*) of mind (*citta*).

29. To [bodhisattvas] enthusiastic about Mahāyāna the preaching of the Buddhas is in brief: the selflessness (*nairātmya*) and equality (*samatā*) of [all] phenomena (*dharma*) [and the doctrine] that mind is originally unborn (*ādyanutpanna*).

30. The Idealists (*yogācārin*) have allotted predominance to mind in itself (*svacitta*). [They] claim that mind purified by shifting position (*āśrayaparivṛtti*) [becomes] the object of its own specific [knowledge] (*svapratyātma*[*gati*]*gocara*).

31. [But to this we object that mind] which is past (*atīta*) does not exist [and] that which is future (*anāgata*) is not discovered (*aprāpta*). How can [finally] the present [mind] shift over from place [to] place?

32. [The store-consciousness (*ālayavijñāna*)] does not appear the way it is. As it appears, it is not like that. [Therefore] consciousness (*vijñāna*) essentially lacks substance (*nairātmyarūpa*). [Hence] consciousness (*vijñāna*) has no other basis [than insubstantiality].

33. Just as iron (*ayaḥ*) moves swiftly around (*paribhram-*) when approached by a loadstone (*ayaskānta*) [though] it possesses no mind (*citta*) [but] appears as if it possessed mind (*cittavad iva dṛśyate*) ...

28. C 467b 7: *de la kun brtags ni gzuṅ 'dzin te | phyi naṅ brtags pa tsam ni yin la raṅ bźin med pa'i phyir ro || gźan dbaṅ ni rtog pa'i raṅ bźin te | rgyu rkyen gźan dbaṅ byas pa'i phyir ro || yoṅs su grub pa ni gzuṅ 'dzin gyi rnam par rtogs pa med pas so || mi 'gyur bar yoṅs su gnas pa'i phyir ro* ||. – *Laṅkāvatāra,* pp. 127-133; CS, III, 44; *Siddhi,* pp. 514-561, for *svabhāvatraya.* Nāgārjuna's position is that of *Laṅkāvatāra,* II, 198, q.v.

29. Seems to allude to the verse quoted above from '*Guhyasamāja*', but now it is a question of bodhisattvas devoted to Mahāyāna! – On the *samatā* of all *dharmas* e.g. *Prasannapadā,* p. 374.

30. For *āśrayaparāvṛtti* (as here in *Laṅkāvatārasūtra*), or *āśrayaparivṛtti* v. the study by L. Schmithausen (1969), pp. 90-104. For the term *svapratyātmagatigocara,* see Suzuki's *Index,* p. 193.

31. Thus the author refutes this notion *ekaprahāreṇa!*

32. C 468b 7: *tshogs drug gi rnam par śes pa daṅ | ñon moṅs pa can gyi yid ji ltar rnam pa daṅ dmigs pa daṅ snaṅ ba de ltar kun gźi ma yin te phyi rol gyi spyod yul la yoṅs su spyod mi nus pa'i phyir ro || des na ṅo bo ñid bdag med rnam śes te don dam par raṅ bźin med pa'i phyir ro* ||.

33. For this comparison *Laṅkāvatāra,* X, 14.

34.
| de bźin kun gźi rnam śes ni || bden min bden pa bźin du ni |
| gaṅ tshe 'gro 'oṅ gyo bar 'gyur || de tshe srid pa 'dzin par byed |

35.
| ji ltar rgya mtsho daṅ ni śiṅ || sems ni med kyaṅ gyo bar 'gyur |
| de bźin kun gźi rnam śes ni || lus brten nas ni gyo ba yin |

36.
| lus med na ni rnam par śes || yod pa min źes yoṅs rtog na |
| de yi so so raṅ rig ñid || ci 'dra źes kyaṅ brjod par gyis |

37.
| so so raṅ rig ñid brjod pas || de ni dṅos po ñid du brjod |
| 'di de yin źes brjod pa ni || nus min źes kyaṅ brjod pa yin |

38.
| raṅ la de bźin gźan dag la || ṅes pa bskyed par bya ba'i phyir |
| rtag tu 'khrul pa med par ni || mkhas rnams rab tu 'jug pa yin |

39.
| śes pas śes bya rtogs pa ste || śes bya med par śes pa med |
| de ltar na ni rig bya daṅ || rig byed med ces cis mi 'dod |

40.
| sems ni miṅ tsam yin pa ste || miṅ las gźan du 'ga' yaṅ med |
| miṅ tsam du ni rnam rig blta || miṅ yaṅ raṅ bźin med pa yin |

41.
| naṅ ṅam de bźin phyi rol lam || yaṅ na gñis ka'i bar dag tu |
| rgyal ba rnams kyis sems ma rñed || de phyir sgyu ma'i raṅ bźin sems |

34c 'gro AC : sgra B
35 A *valde differt*
38a de bźin B : ṅes bźin A
40b 'ga' A : dga' B
41c kyis A : kyi B

34. Thus the store-consciousness (*ālayavijñāna*) appears to be real though it is false [and] when it moves to and fro [as *ādānavijñāna*] it [seems to] retain the [three] existences (*bhavatraya*).

35. Just as the ocean and trees are moved though they have no mind (*citta*) likewise the store-consciousness (*ālayavijñāna*) is [only] active dependent upon a body (*kāyāśritya*).

36. So considering the fact that without a body there is no consciousness, you must also state what kind of specific knowledge of itself (*svapratyātmagati*) this [consciousness] possesses!

37. By saying that a specific knowledge of itself (*svapratyātmagati*) [exists] one [*eo ipso*] says that it is an entity (*bhāva*). But one also says that it is not possible to say that 'this is it'!

38. In order to convince oneself as well as others clever people [should] always proceed without error!

39. The cognisable (*jñeya*) is known by a cognisant (*jñātṛ*). Without cognisable no cognition (*jñāna*) [is possible]. So why not accept that object (*vedya*) and subject (*vedaka*) do not exist [*per se*]?

40. Mind is but a name (*nāmamātra*). It is nothing apart from [its] name. Consciousness must be regarded as but a name. The name too has no own-being (*svabhāva*).

41. The Jinas have never found mind (*citta*) to exist either inside, outside or between both. Therefore mind has an illusory nature (*māyāsvabhāva*).

35. *Ibid.*, X, 57-59.
37. One should not speak of that which cannot be spoken of. But here the author is not quite fair, cf. MK, XXII, 11.
38. Recalls *Dhammapada*, XII, 2.
39. Cf. CS, III, 50, q.v. – Though B and A have *rig bya/rig byed* this surely refers to *vedanāskandha* (as 40 refers to *saṃjñāskandha*). C 469b 7 correctly has *tshor bya/tshor ba*. – Cf. CS, I, 6; ŚS, 55.
40. *Ibid.*, I, 7; III, 35 (with ref.).
41. Cf. ŚS, 51.

42.
| kha dog dbyibs kyi dbye ba 'am || gzuṅ ba daṅ ni 'dzin pa 'am |
| skyes pa bud med ma niṅ sogs || ṅo bo sems ni gnas pa min |

43.
| mdor na saṅs rgyas rnams kyis ni || gzigs par ma gyur gzigs mi 'gyur |
| raṅ bźin med pa'i raṅ bźin can || ji lta bur na gzigs par 'gyur |

44.
| dṅos po źes bya rnam rtog yin || rnam rtog med pa stoṅ pa yin |
| gaṅ du rnam rtog snaṅ gyur pa || der ni stoṅ ñid ga la yod |

45. na bodhyabodhakākāraṃ cittaṃ dṛṣṭaṃ tathāgataiḥ |
yatra boddhā ca bodhyaṃ ca tatra bodhir na vidyate ||

| rtogs bya rtogs byed rnam pa'i sems || de bźin gśegs rnams kyis ma gzigs |
| gaṅ na rtogs bya rtogs byed yod || der ni byaṅ chub yod ma yin |

46. alakṣaṇam anutpādam asaṃsthitam avāṅmayam |
ākāśaṃ bodhicittaṃ ca bodhir advayalakṣaṇā ||

| mtshan ñid med ciṅ skye ba med || yod gyur ma yin ṅag lam bral |
| mkha' daṅ byaṅ chub sems daṅ ni || byaṅ chub gñis med mtshan ñid can |

47.
| byaṅ chub sñiṅ po la bźugs pa'i || bdag ñid chen po'i saṅs rgyas daṅ |
| brtse ldan kun gyis dus kun tu || stoṅ pa mkha' daṅ mtshuṅs par mkhyen |

48.
| de phyir chos rnams kun gyi gźi || źi źiṅ sgyu ma daṅ mtshuṅs par |
| gźi med srid par 'jig byed pa'i || stoṅ po ñid 'di rtag tu bsgom |

42a kyi A : kyis B
46b yod gyur ma yin B : gnas pa med ciṅ ACS

42. Mind has no fixed forms such as various colours and shapes (*varṇasaṃsthānabheda*), object and subject (*grāhyagrāhaka*) or male, female and neuter (*strīpuruṣanapuṃsaka*).

43. In brief: Buddhas do not see [what cannot] be seen (*adṛṣṭa*) [for] how could they see that which has lack of own-being as its own-being (*naiḥsvābhāvyasvabhāva*)!

44. A 'thing' (*bhāva*) is construction (*vikalpa*). Emptiness is absence of construction (*nirvikalpa*). Where constructions have appeared how can there be emptiness (*śūnyatā*)?

45. The Tathāgatas do not regard mind under the form of cognisable (*bodhya*) and cognisant (*bodhaka*). Where cognisant and cognisable [prevail] there is no enlightenment (*bodhi*).

46. Space (*ākāśa*), *bodhicitta* and enlightenment (*bodhi*) are without marks, without generation. They have no structure, they are beyond the path of words. Their mark [so to speak] is non-duality (*advaya*).

47. The magnanimous (*mahātman*) Buddhas who reside in the heart of enlightenment (*bodhimaṇḍa*) and all the compassionate [bodhisattvas] always know emptiness (*śūnyatā*) to be like space (*ākāśavat*)

48. Therefore [bodhisattvas] perpetually develop this emptiness (*śūnyatā*) which is the basis (*āśraya*) of all phenomena (*dharma*), calm (*śānta*), illusory (*māyāvat*), baseless (*anālaya*) [and] the destroyer of existence (*bhavavināśaka*).

42. *citta* (= *manas* = *vijñāna*) is – *saṃvṛtitaḥ* – *arūpin*. Thus it cannot be established by means of *rūpa*.

43. For the *buddhacakṣus* see CS, II, 2: *na ca nāma tvayā kiṃ cid dṛṣṭaṃ bauddhena cakṣuṣā* |.

44. Cf. e.g. MK, V, 7; XV, 4; May, *op.cit.*, p. 92, n. 204. (*śūnyatā* = *niḥsvabhāvatā* = *tattva* = *nirvikalpa* etc.)

45. Sanskrit *Pañjikā*, p. 406. – Cf. CS, II, 2: *na boddhā na ca boddhavyam astīha paramārthataḥ* |.

46. Sanskrit, *ibid.*, p. 421 with *asaṃskṛtam* in b (thus also C 471a 8) which I have corrected to *asaṃsthitam* with A (*gnas pa med*) and B (*yod gyur ma yin*). In b Sanskrit may have read *avākpatham* (cf. CS, IV, 1 etc.).

48. I.e. *śūnyatā* destroys those *dṛṣṭis* which give rise to *kleśa*, *karma* and *punarbhava*, cf. MK, XVIII, 5; YṢ, 46-48; CS, I, 23 etc.

49.
| skye med daṅ ni stoṅ ñid daṅ || bdag med ces byar stoṅ pa ñid |
| bdag ñid dman pa gaṅ sgom pa || de de sgom par byed pa min |

50.
| dge daṅ mi dge'i rnam rtog ni || rgyun chad pa yi mtshan ñid can |
| stoṅ ñid saṅs rgyas kyis gsuṅs gźan || de dag stoṅ pa ñid mi bźed |

51.
| sems la dmigs pa med pa ni || gnas pa nam mkha'i mtshan ñid yin |
| de dag stoṅ ñid sgom pa ni || nam mkha' sgom par bźed pa yin |

52. śūnyatāsiṃhanādena trasitāḥ sarvavādinaḥ |
...
| stoṅ ñid seṅ ge'i sgra yis ni || smra ba thams cad skrag par mdzad |
| gaṅ daṅ gaṅ du de dag bźugs || de daṅ der ni stoṅ ñid 'gyur |

53.
| gaṅ gi rnam śes skad cig ma || de yi de ni rtag ma yin |
| sems ni mi rtag ñid yin na || stoṅ pa ñid du ji ltar 'gal |

54.
| mdor na saṅs rgyas rnams kyis ni || sems ni mi rtag ñid bźed na |
| de dag sems ni stoṅ ñid du || ci'i phyir na bźed mi 'gyur |

55.
| thog ma ñid nas sems kyi ni || raṅ bźin rtag tu med par 'gyur |
| dṅos po raṅ bźin gyis grub pa || raṅ bźin med ñid brjod pa min |

56.
| de skad brjod na sems kyi ni || bdag gi gnas pa spaṅs pa yin |
| raṅ gi raṅ bźin las 'das pa || de ni chos rnams chos ma yin |

50a ni AC : gi B
51a dmigs pa BA : mtshan bya C; ni C(A) : yi B; c ni B : 'di A
52b smra ba BC: rgol ba A

49. Emptiness expresses non-origination (*anutpāda*), voidness (*virahitatā?*) and lack of self (*nairātmya*). What inferior (*hīna*) [persons] develop is not to be developed by [bodhisattvas].

50. Notions about positive and negative (*śubhāśubhavikalpa*) [karma] are characterized by being disintegrated (*vyavaccheda*). [While] the Buddhas have spoken [of their] emptiness, the others do not accept [their] emptiness.

51. The abode of a mind (*citta*) which has no support (*anālambana*) has the character of [empty] space. These [bodhisattvas] maintain that development of emptiness (*śūnyatābhāvanā*) is development of space.

52. All dogmatists have been terrified by the lion's roar of emptiness (*śūnyatāsiṃhanāda*). Wherever they may reside emptiness lies in wait!

53. An [Idealist] to whom consciousness (*vijñāna*) is momentary (*kṣaṇika*) cannot accept it to be permanent (*nitya*). How could it be inconsistent (*viruddha*) with emptiness that mind (*citta*) is actually impermanent (*anitya*)?

54. When the Buddhas, in brief, are convinced that mind (*citta*) is impermanent, why should they not be convinced that mind is [*eo ipso*] empty?

55. From the very beginning mind has never had any own-being (*svabhāva*). Things proved to be substantial (*svabhāvena siddha*) [we] are not to declare insubstantial (*naiḥsvābhāvya*).

56. The effect of this statement is that mind lacks substantial foundation (*ātmasthāna*). It is not the nature of things to transcend [their] particular own-being (*svasvabhāva*)!

49. C 472a 3 ref. to MK, XIII, 8, q.v. – For *bdag ñid dman pa*, cf. *alpabuddhi* (MK, V, 8), *mandamedhas* (MK, XXIV, 11); *avipaścit* (RĀ, II, 19). Contrariwise the *bdag ñid chen po*, YṢ, 50, 54.

50. All *vikalpas* are *kṣaṇika*, i.e. *śūnya;* cf. v. 53. (This is of course only *saṃvṛtitaḥ*, cf. RĀ, I, 66-70.)

52. Sanskrit *Caryāgīti* (ed. Kværne), p. 246 with °*śatravaḥ* which I have emended acc. to A's *rgol ba*, B's *smra ba* and C's (*dños por*) *smra ba* (472b 5). – For *śūnyatāsiṃhanāda*, CS, I, 22; BS, 101.

56. Cf. e.g. MK, XV, 7-8 for this axiom.

57. guḍe madhuratā cāgner uṣṇatvaṃ prakṛtir yathā |
śūnyatā sarvadharmāṇāṃ tathā prakṛtir iṣyate ||
| ji ltar bu ram mṅar ba daṅ || me yi raṅ bźin tsha ba bźin |
| de bźin chos rnams thams cad kyi || raṅ bźin stoṅ pa ñid du 'dod |

58.
| stoṅ ñid raṅ bźin du brjod pas || gaṅ źig chad par smra ba min |
| des ni rtag pa ñid du yaṅ || 'ga' źig smras pa ma yin no |

59.
| ma rig nas brtsams rga ba yi || mthar thug yan lag bcu gñis kyi |
| brten nas byuṅ ba'i bya ba ni || kho bo rmi lam sgyu 'drar 'dod |

60.
| yan lag bcu gñis 'khor lo 'di || srid pa'i lam du 'khor ba ste |
| de las gźan du sems can gaṅ || las 'bras spyod par 'dod pa med |

61.
| ji ltar me loṅ la brten nas || bźin gyi dkyil 'khor snaṅ gyur pa |
| de ni der 'pho ma yin źiṅ || de med par yaṅ de yod min |

62.
| de bźin phuṅ po ñiṅ mtshams sbyor || srid pa gźan du skye ba daṅ |
| 'pho ba med par mkhas rnams kyis || rtag tu ṅes par bya ba yin |

63.
| mdor na stoṅ pa'i chos rnams las || chos rnams stoṅ pa skye bar 'gyur |
| byed po las 'bras loṅs spyod pa || kun rdzob tu ni rgyal bas bstan |

57a bu ram A : bur ram B
59a rga ba yi : rga śi'i (mtha') A : dga' ba yin B
63a las A : la B

57. Just as sweetness is the nature of sugar and hotness that of fire, thus the nature of all things is maintained [by us] to be emptiness.

58. When one speaks of emptiness as the nature [of all phenomena] one in no sense advocates Nihilism (*ucchedavāda*). Nor does one advocate Eternalism (*śāśvata*).

59. The twelve members of relativity starting with ignorance (*avidyā*) and ending with decay (*jarā*), which are subject to dependent co-origination (*pratītyasamutpāda*) [we] maintain to be like a dream and an illusion (*svapnamāyāvat*).

60. This wheel (*cakra*) with twelve spokes (*aṅga*) rolls along the road of life (*bhavavartman*). It is unacceptable (*aniṣṭa*) that there should exist a living entity (*sattva*) exempt from this partaking of the fruits of its deeds (*karmaphala*).

61. Just as dependent on a mirror (*ādarśa*) the outline of a face (*mukhamaṇḍala*) appears though it has not moved into it (*saṃkrānta*) but on the other hand (*api*) does not exist without it ...

62. Thus the wise must always be convinced that the aggregates (*skandha*) appear in a new existence (*bhava*) [due to] recomposition (*pratisaṃdhi*), but they do not migrate [as identical or different].

63. To sum up: Empty things (*bhāva*) are born from empty things. The Jina has taught that agent (*kāraka*), deed (*karma*), result (*phala*), and enjoyer (*bhoktṛ*) are [only] conventional (*saṃvṛtitaḥ*).

57. Sanskrit *Advayavajrasaṃgraha* (ed. Śāstri), p. 42.

58. The *madhyamā pratipad* avoids the extremes of *uccheda* and *śāśvata*, MK, XV, 10; XVII, 21; CS, III, 49.

59-63. As I have shown *WZKS*, XXVI (1982), these verses are closely related to PK, q.v. – See also *Daśabhūmika* (ed. Rahder), p. 50 which reduces *avidyā*, *tṛṣṇā* and *upādāna* to *kleśavartman*, *saṃskāra* and *bhava* to *karmavartman*, and the remaining seven *aṅgas* to *duḥkhavartman*. As C observes 473b 7 *avidyā*, *saṃskāra*, *tṛṣṇā*, *upādāna* and *bhava* may also be regarded as *hetu* whereas the remaining *aṅgas* are *phala*. Similarly in the small treatise *Dharmadhātugarbhavivaraṇa* ascribed to Nāgārjuna (see *IHQ*, XXXIII, pp. 246-249); cf. PK, 4. See also *Traité*, pp. 349-351. – For the final *pādas* of 63 see CS, I, 8; *Saṃyutta*, II, pp. 75-76; *Daśabhūmika*, p. 49.

64.
| ji ltar rṅa yi sgra daṅ ni || de bźin myu gu tshogs pas bskyed |
| phyi yi rten ciṅ 'brel 'byuṅ ba || rmi lam sgyu ma daṅ mtshuṅs 'dod |

65.
| chos rnams rgyu las skyes pa ni || nam yaṅ 'gal bar mi 'gyur te |
| rgyu ni rgyu ñid kyis stoṅ pas || de ni skye ba med par rtogs |

66.
| chos rnams kyi ni skye ba med || stoṅ ñid yin par rab tu bśad |
| mdor na phuṅ po lṅa rnams ni || chos kun źes ni bśad pa yin |

67.
| de ñid ji bźin bśad pas na || kun rdzob rgyun ni 'chad mi 'gyur |
| kun rdzob las ni tha dad par || de ñid dmigs pa ma yin te |

68.
| kun rdzob stoṅ pa ñid du bśad || stoṅ pa kho na kun rdzob yin |
| med na mi 'byuṅ ṅes pa'i phyir || byas daṅ mi rtag ji bźin no |

69.
| kun rdzob ñon moṅs las las byuṅ || las ni sems las byuṅ ba yin |
| sems ni bag chags rnams kyis bsags || bag chags bral na bde ba ste |

68d byas : byas pa B

64. As for instance the sound of a drum (*bheriśabda*) and a sprout (*aṅkura*) are created by [their] totality (*sāmagrī*) [of causes and conditions, thus we] maintain that exterior dependent co-origination (*bāhyapratītyasamutpāda*) is like a dream and an illusion (*svapnamāyāvat*).

65. It is not at all (*jātu*) inconsistent (*viruddha*) that phenomena (*dharma*) are born from causes (*hetuja*). Since a cause is empty of cause (*hetuśūnya*) [we] understand it to be unoriginated (*anutpanna*).

66. That phenomena (*dharma*) [are said] not to arise (*anutpāda*) indicates that they are empty. Briefly the five aggregates (*skandha*) are denoted by 'all phenomena'.

67. When truth is [accepted] as explained convention (*saṃvṛti*) is not obstructed. By neglecting convention (*saṃvṛti*) one will not get hold of the truth (*tattva*).

68. Convention is explained as emptiness, convention is simply emptiness for [these two] do not occur without one another just as created (*kṛta*) and impermanent (*anitya*) [invariably concur].

69. Convention (*saṃvṛti*) is born from karma [due to the various] passions (*kleśa*), and *karma* is created by mind (*caitasika*). Mind (*citta*) is accumulated by the residues (*vāsanā*). Happiness (*sukha*) consists in being free from the residues (*vāsanā*).

64. As the previous verses treated *ādhyātmikapratītyasamutpāda* – *saṃvṛtitaḥ* of course – this verse refers to *bāhyapratītyasamutpāda*, presumably as treated in the *Śālistambasūtra* (quoted *Pañjikā*, pp. 577-579) though the *bheriśabda* (cf. *Prasannapadā*, p. 72) does not figure here.

65. In the *saṃsāramaṇḍala* any '*hetu*' is also '*phala*' and vice versa. Thus it is *hetusvabhāvaśūnya*. Cf. RĀ, I, 36, 47.

66. Cf. RĀ, IV, 86: *anutpādo mahāyāne pareṣāṃ śūnyatā kṣayaḥ* |. – For *sarve dharmāḥ* (= *sarvam*), ref. May, *op.cit.*, p. 206, n. 689; YṢ, 30.

67. Cf. MK, XXIV, 8-10.

68. Here I understand *saṃvṛti* as *sarve dharmāḥ* (cf. *Madhyamakahṛdayakārikā*, III, 13. Also CS, III, 44, with which cf. *Laṅkāvatāra*, II, 187). I take *śūnyatā* = *pratītyasamutpāda* (cf. MK, XXIV, 18), i.e. *pratītyasamutpanna* (CS, III, 44).

69. For the interpretation of this see MK, XVII, 26: *karma kleśātmakam*, and *ibid.*, XVIII, 5: *karmakleśā vikalpataḥ*. – For *citta* (= *vikalpa*) cf. *Laṅkāvatāra*, III, 38: *cittena cīyate karma*. – Again, *citta* itself is the outcome of previous karma (*vāsanā*) due to *kleśa* born from *vikalpa* (*citta*) etc. from time without beginning.

70.
| bde ba'i sems ni źi ba ñid || sems źi ba ni rmoṅs mi 'gyur |
| rmoṅs med de ñid rtogs pa ste || de ñid rtogs pas grol thob 'gyur |

71.
| de bźin ñid daṅ yaṅ dag mtha' || mtshan ma med daṅ don dam ñid |
| byaṅ chub sems mchog de ñid dan || stoṅ ñid du yaṅ bśad pa yin |

72.
| gaṅ dag stoṅ ñid mi śes pa || de dag thar pa'i rten ma yin |
| 'gro drug srid pa'i btson rar ni || rmoṅs pa de dag 'khor bar 'gyur |

73.
| de ltar stoṅ pa ñid 'di ni || rnal 'byor pa yis bsgom byas na |
| gźan gyi don la chags pa'i blo || 'byuṅ bar 'gyur ba the tshom med |

74.
| gaṅ dag pha daṅ ma daṅ ni || gñen bśes gyur pas bdag la sṅon |
| phan pa byas par gyur pa yi || sems can de dag rnams la ni ||
| byas pa bzo bar gyur par bya |

75.
| srid pa'i btson rar sems can ni || ñon moṅs me yis gduṅs rnams la |
| bdag gis sdug bsṅal byin pa ltar || de bźin bde ba sbyin bar rigs |

76.
| 'jig rten bde 'gro ṅan 'gro yis || 'dod daṅ mi 'dod 'bras bu de |
| sems can rnams la phan pa daṅ || gnod pa las ni 'byuṅ bar 'gyur |

77.
| sems can brten pas saṅs rgyas kyis || go 'phaṅ bla med ñid 'gyur na |
| lha daṅ mi yi loṅs spyod gaṅ || tshaṅs daṅ dbaṅ po drag po daṅ |

78.
| 'jig rten skyoṅ bas brten de dag || sems can phan pa tsam źig gis |
| ma draṅs pa ni 'gro gsum 'dir || 'ga' yaṅ med la mtshar ci yod |

70d rtogs pas : rtogs pa **B** : rig pas **A**
74c yi : yis **B**; (**A** *quattuor* pāda)
77a brten **A** : bsten **B**

70. A happy mind is tranquil (*śānta*). A tranquil mind is not confused (*mūḍha*). To be unperplexed (*amūḍha*) is to understand the truth (*tattva*). By understanding truth one obtains liberation (*mokṣa*).

71. It is also defined as reality (*tattva*), real limit (*bhūtakoṭi*), signless (*animitta*), ultimate meaning (*paramārtha*), the highest *bodhicitta* and emptiness.

72. Those who do not know (*jñā-*) emptiness will have no share in liberation (*mokṣa*). Such fools migrate in the prison of existence [in] one of the six destinies (*ṣaḍgatibhavacāraka*).

73. So when ascetics (*yogācārin*) have thus developed this emptiness their mind (*buddhi*) will, no doubt (*na saṃśaya*) be devoted to the weal of others (*parahita*):

74. 'I should be grateful to those beings (*sattva*) who previously bestowed benefits (*hitaṃkara*) upon me, by being my parents or friends (*bandhu*).'

75. 'As I have given suffering (*duḥkha*) to the living beings (*sattva*) in the prison of existence (*bhavacāraka*) who are being scorched by the fire of passions (*kleśāgni*), it is also befitting that I [now] afford them happiness.'

76. The sweet or bitter fruit (*iṣṭāniṣṭaphala*) the world [gets] in the form of a good or bad rebirth (*sagutidurgati*) is the outcome of whether they hurt or benefit living beings (*sattva*).

77-78. If the Buddhas arise to the unsurpassed stage (*anuttarapada*) by [rendering] living beings support (*sattvāśraya*), what is so strange if [those] who are not guided by the slightest altruism (*sattvahita*) do not have any of those pleasures (*bhoga*) which the guardians of the world (*lokapāla*) Brahmā, Indra and Rudra are supported by in the three worlds (*trailokye*)?

70. By thus destroying *vikalpa* (= *citta, avidyā* etc.) by means of *śūnyatā* the result is: *karmakleśakṣayān mokṣaḥ* (MK, XVIII, 5).

71. For other synonyms of the absolute, CS, I, 27; III, 37-41, 52; MK, XVIII, 9; XXV, 3; ŚS, 24.

72. Cf. YṢ, 31.

73. What follows is mainly devoted to an exposition of the *tathyasaṃvṛtibodhicitta* (C 476a 8) and only calls for a few notes (74-104). In general we here find the same ideal of *karuṇā* as in RĀ; BS; SS, *passim*.

77. On these gods, RĀ, I, 24; SL, 69; *Traité*, 137 sq.

79.
| sems dmyal dud 'gro yi dags su || sdug bsṅal rnam pa du ma'i dṅos |
| sems can rnams kyis myoṅ ba gaṅ || de ni sems can gnod las byuṅ |

80.
| bkres skom phan tshun bdeg pa daṅ || gzir ba yi ni sdug bsṅal ñid |
| bzlog par dka' źiṅ zad med de || sems can gnod pa'i 'bras bu yin |

81.
| saṅs rgyas byaṅ chub sems ñid daṅ || bde 'gro daṅ ni ṅan 'gro gaṅ |
| sems can gaṅ gi rnam smin kyaṅ || ṅo bo gñis su śes par bya |

82.
| dṅos po kun gyis rten bya źiṅ || raṅ gi lus bźin bsruṅ bar bya |
| sems can rnams la chags bral ba || dug bźin 'bad pas spaṅ bar bya |

83.
| ñan thos rnams ni chags bral bas || byaṅ chub dman pa thob min nam |
| sems can yoṅs su ma dor bas || rdzogs saṅs rgyas kyi byaṅ chub thob |

84.
| de ltar phan daṅ mi phan pa'i || 'bras bu 'byuṅ bar dpyad pa na |
| de dag skad cig gcig kyaṅ ni || raṅ don gnas źiṅ ji ltar gnas |

85.
| sñiṅ rjes brtan pa'i rtsa ba can || byaṅ sems myu gu las byuṅ ba |
| gźan don gcig 'bras byaṅ chub ni || rgyal ba'i sras rnams sgom par byed |

86.
| gaṅ źig bsgom pas brtan pa ni || gźan gyi sdug bsṅal gyis bred nas |
| bsam gtan bde ba dor nas kyaṅ || mnar med pa yaṅ 'jug par byed |

80c zad med B : mi bzod AC
81a sems ñid B : sems dpa' A
83d kyi : kyis B : pa'i A
86a gaṅ źig BA : gaṅ gis C

79. The different kinds of suffering (*duḥkha*) which beings (*sattva*) experience as creatures in hell (*niraya*), as beasts (*paśu*) and as ghosts (*preta*) are a result of hurting beings.

80. The inevitable and unceasing suffering (*duḥkha*) of hunger (*kṣudh*), thirst (*pipāsā*), mutual slaughter and torments are the results of molesting beings.

81. One must know that beings (*sattva*) are subject to two kinds of maturation (*vipāka*): [that of] Buddhas [and] bodhisattvas and that of good and bad rebirth (*sugatidurgati*).

82. One should support [living beings] with one's whole nature (*sarvabhāvena*) and protect them like one's own body. Indifference (*vairāgya*) towards the beings must be avoided like poison!

83. Perhaps the Disciples (*śrāvaka*) obtain an inferior enlightenment (*hīnabodhi*) thanks to indifference (*vairāgyāt*) but the *bodhi* of the Perfect Buddhas (*saṃbuddha*) is obtained by not abandoning living beings (*sattva*).

84. How can those who consider how the fruit of good and offensive deeds comes about persist in their selfishness (*svārtha*) even for a single moment?

85. The bodhisattvas (*jinaputra*) are active in developing enlightenment (*bodhi*) which has compassion as its solid roots and which grows from the sprout of *bodhicitta* and has the sole fruit of altruism (*parārtha*).

86. Those who are strengthened by meditational development (*bhāvanā*) are frightened by the sufferings of others. [In order to support them] they even forsake the pleasures of trance (*dhyānasukha*) and even go to the Avīci hell (*avīci*)!

81. C 477b 8: *saṅs rgyas daṅ byaṅ chub sems dpa' zag pa med pa'i dge ba'i rtsa ba'i las kyi rnam par smin pa'i sems can no* ||. The *vipāka* specific to Buddhas and bodhisattvas is the *kāyadvaya,* cf. BS, 3 with ref.

83. The *pratisaṃkhyānirodha* of the Śrāvakas is inferior to the *anuttarā samyaksaṃbodhi* of the Buddhas, cf. *Vimalakīrtinirdeśa,* p. 422.

86. Cf. BS, 164 with ref.

87.
| 'di ni ṅo mtshar 'di bsṅags 'os || 'di ni dam pa'i tshul lugs mchog |
| de dag rnams kyi raṅ lus daṅ || nor rnams byin pa ṅo mtshar min |

88.
| chos rnams stoṅ pa 'di śes nas || las daṅ 'bras bu sten pa gaṅ |
| de ni ṅo mtshar bas ṅo mtshar || rmad du 'byuṅ bas rmad du 'byuṅ |

89.
| sems can bskyab pa'i bsam pa can || de dag srid pa'i 'dam skyes kyaṅ |
| de byuṅ ñid pas ma gos pa || chu yi padma'i 'dab ma bźin |

90.
| kun bźaṅ la sogs rgyal ba'i sras || stoṅ ñid ye śes me yis ni |
| ñon moṅs bud śiṅ bsregs mod kyi || de lta'aṅ sñiṅ rjes brlan 'gyur ciṅ |

91.
| sñiṅ rje'i dbaṅ du gyur pa rnams || gśegs daṅ bltam daṅ rol pa daṅ |
| khab nas 'byuṅ daṅ dka' ba spyod || byaṅ chub che daṅ bdud sde 'joms |

92.
| chos kyi 'khor lo skor ba daṅ || lha rnams kun gyis źus pa daṅ |
| de bźin du ni mya ṅan las || 'das pa ston par mdzad pa yin |

93.
| tshaṅs daṅ dbaṅ po khyab 'jug daṅ || drag sogs gzugs su sprul mdzad nas |
| 'gro ba 'dul ba'i sbyor ba yis || thugs rje'i raṅ bźin can gar mdzad |

94.
| srid pa'i lam la skyo rnams la || ṅal so'i don du theg pa che |
| 'byuṅ ba'i ye śes gñis po yaṅ || gsuṅs pa yin te don dam min |

89c de byuṅ ñid pas B : srid pa'i skyon gyis A(d)
90b A, *sed om.* B
94c ye śes (**jñāna-*) B : theg pa (**yāna-*) A(a)C

87. They are wonderful, they are admirable, they are most extraordinarily excellent! Nothing is [more] amazing than those who sacrifice their person and property!

88. Those who understand this emptiness of phenomena (*dharma*) [but also] believe in [the law of] karma and its results, they are more wonderful than wonderful, more astonishing than astonishing!

89. Wishing to protect the living beings (*sattva*) they are even born in the mud of existence (*bhavapaṅka*). Unsullied (*alipta*) by its events they are like a lotus in mire.

90. Even though bodhisattvas (*jinaputra*) such as Samantabhadra etc. have burnt the fuel of passions (*kleśendhana*) by the cognitive fire of emptiness (*śūnyatājñānāgni*) they are still moistened by compassion!

91-92. And under the influence of compassion they display [their] descent [from *Tuṣita*], birth, merriments, renunciation, penances, great enlightenment, victory over the hosts of Māra, turning of the *dharmacakra*, the request of all the Gods as well as Nirvāṇa.

93. Having emanated such forms as Brahmā, Indra, Viṣṇu and Rudra the compassionate natures make a performance agreeing with the world which must be guided (*vaineyajana*).

94. Though it has been said, in order to comfort those who are disgusted with the way of life, that there are two [kinds] of knowledge (*jñāna*) arising [from] Mahāyāna [this, however] is not the ultimate meaning (*paramārtha*).

91. For *pāda* cf. CS, I, 1 with note. – On the twelve deeds cf. e.g. CS, II, 23; *Dvādaśakāranayastotra* (TP, No. 2026); Bu-ston, I, p. 133 (the verse cited here from '*Ratnāvalī*' is actually BV, 91-92!).

95.
| ji srid saṅs rgyas kyis ma bskul || de srid ye śes lus dṅos can |
| tiṅ 'dzin myos pas rgyal 'gyur ba || ñan thos de dag gnas par 'gyur |

96.
| bskul na sna tshogs gzugs kyis ni || sems can don la chags gyur ciṅ |
| bsod nams ye śes tshogs bsags nas || saṅs rgyas byaṅ chub thob par 'gyur |

97.
| gñis kyi bag chags yod pa'i phyir || bag chags sa bon brjod pa yin |
| sa bon de dṅos tshogs pa ni || srid pa'i myu gu skyed par byed |

98. deśanā lokanāthānāṃ sattvāśayavaśānugāḥ |
bhidyante bahudhā loka upāyair bahubhiḥ punaḥ ||
| 'jig rten mgon rnams kyi bstan pa || sems can bsam dbaṅ rjes 'gro ba |
| 'jig rten du ni thabs maṅ po || rnam pa maṅ po tha dad 'gyur |

99. gambhīrottānabhedena kva cid vobhayalakṣaṇā |
bhinnāpi deśanābhinnā śūnyatādvayalakṣaṇā ||
| zab ciṅ rgya che'i dbye ba daṅ || la lar gñis ka'i mtshan ñid can |
| tha dad bstan pa yin yaṅ ni || stoṅ daṅ gñis med tha dad min |

100.
| gzuṅs rnams daṅ ni sa rnams daṅ || saṅs rgyas pha rol phyin gaṅ dag |
| de dag byaṅ chub sems kyi char || kun mkhyen rnams kyis gsuṅs pa yin |

101.
| lus ṅag yid kyis rtag par ni || de ltar sems can don byed pa |
| stoṅ ñid rtsod par smra rnams la || chad pa'i rtsod pa ñid yod min |

97c de dṅos tshogs pa ni B : rjes mthar tshogs pa yis A(C)
98a kyi S : kyis B
101a rtag par : brtags par B : rtag tu A(b)C

95. As long as they have not been admonished by the Buddhas, the Disciples (*śrāvaka*) [who are] in a bodily state of cognition (*jñāna-kāyabhāva*) remain in a swoon intoxicated by concentration (*samādhi*).

96. But when [they have been] admonished they are devoted to living beings (*sattva*) in various ways. Collecting moral and intellectual provisions (*puṇyajñānasaṃbhāra*) they [finally] obtain the enlightenment of Buddhas.

97. Since it is the potentiality (*vāsanā*) of both [collections (*saṃbhāra*)], the residues (*vāsanā*) are said to be the seed (*bīja*) [of *bodhi*]. That seed [that is] the accumulation of things (*bhāvasamūha*) produces the sprout of life (*bhavāṅkura*).

98. The instructions of the saviours of the world (*lokanātha*) follows the sway of the resolutions of living beings. They also differ variously among men due to the different devices (*upāya*) [employed by the Buddhas].

99. [The instruction may differ] due to difference in profundity and superficiality [and] occasionally it is characterized by being both. Though it sometimes may differ it is indifferently characterized by emptiness and non-duality.

100. Whatever may be the spells (*dhāraṇī*), stages (*bhūmi*) and perfections (*pāramitā*) of the Buddhas, the omniscient (*sarvajña*) [Buddhas] have stated that they form a part (*aṃśa*) of the *bodhicitta*.

101. Those who thus always benefit living beings (*sattva*) by body, words and mind, advocate the claims of emptiness, not the contentions of annihilation (*ucchedavāda*).

96. On *puṇyajñānasaṃbhāra*, RĀ, III; BS, *passim*.

97. Cf. above v. 81.

98-99. Sanskrit quoted *Sarvadarśanasaṃgraha* (ed. Abhyankar), p. 45 with *cobha°* in 99b and *bhinnā hi* in 99c. Also in *Bhāmatī* (ed. Sastri), p. 414 with *kila* in 98d. – For the idea, MK, XVIII, 8; RĀ, II, 35.

100. For *dhāraṇī*, *Traité*, p. 1854 sq. – I have not traced the *sūtra*.

101. Cf. above, v. 58.

102.
| 'khor ba mya ṅan 'das pa la || bdag ñid che de mi gnas pa |
| de phyir saṅs rgyas rnams kyis ni || mi gnas mya ṅan 'das 'dir bśad |

103.
| sñiṅ rje ro gcig bsod nams gyur || stoṅ ñid ro ni mchog gyur pa |
| bdag daṅ gźan don sgrub don du || gaṅ 'thuṅ de dag rgyal sras yin |

104.
| dṅos po kun gyis de la 'dud || srid pa gsum na rtag mchod 'os |
| saṅs rgyas gduṅ ni 'tshob don du || 'jig rten 'dren pa de dag bźugs |

105.
| byaṅ chub sems 'di theg chen po || mchog ni yin par bśad pa ste |
| mñam par gźag pa'i 'bad pa yis || byaṅ chub sems ni bskyed par gyis |

106.
| raṅ daṅ gźan don bsgrub don du || srid na thabs gźan yod ma yin |
| byaṅ chub sems ni ma gtogs pas || saṅs rgyas kyis sṅar thabs ma gzigs |

107.
| byaṅ chub sems bskyed tsam gyis ni || bsod nams phuṅ po gaṅ thob pa |
| gal te gzugs can yin na ni || nam mkha' gaṅ ba las ni lhag |

108.
| skyes bu gaṅ źig skad cig tsam || byaṅ chub sems ni sgom byed pa |
| de yi bsod nams phuṅ po ni || rgyal ba yis kyaṅ bgraṅ mi spyod |

109.
| ñon moṅs med pa'i rin chen sems || 'di ni nor mchog gcig pu ste |
| ñon moṅs bdud sogs chom rkun gyis || gnod min phrogs par bya ba min |

102b de (cf. *Tattvasārasaṃgraha*, 97a) : ste B : *om.* A

102. The magnanimous (*mahātman*) [bodhisattvas] do not abide in Nirvāṇa or Saṃsāra. Therefore the Buddhas have spoken of this as 'the dynamic extinction' (*apratiṣṭhitanirvāṇa*).

103. The unique elixir (*ekarasa*) of compassion functions as merit (*puṇyabhūta*) [but] the elixir of emptiness functions as the highest. Those who drink it for the sake of themselves and of others, they are sons of the Hero (*jinaputra*).

104. Salute these [bodhisattvas] with your entire being (*sarva-bhāva*)! They are always worthy of honour in the three worlds (*trailokya*) [for] these guides of the world are trying to represent the lineage (*vaṃśa*) of the Buddhas.

105. [In] Mahāyāna this *bodhicitta* is said to be the highest. [Therefore] you must produce the *bodhicitta* with determined efforts!

106. [In this] existence (*bhava*) there is no other means (*upāya*) for the realisation of one's own and others' interests (*svaparārthasiddhi*). The Buddhas [at least] have to date seen no means apart from the *bodhicitta!*

107. Simply by generating the *bodhicitta* a mass of merit (*puṇyarāśi*) is collected. If it happened to take form it would fill more than the expanse of space!

108. If a person, only for a moment, developed *bodhicitta,* the mass of his merit (*puṇyarāśi*) not even the Jinas could calculate!

109. The most unique jewel is a precious mind (*ratnacitta*) without passions (*kleśa*). It cannot be damaged or stolen by such robbers as passions (*kleśa*) and Māra.

102. Cf. BS, 75 with ref. and G.M. Nagao in L.S. Kawamura (ed.), *The Bodhisattva Doctrine in Buddhism,* Waterloo, Ontario 1981, pp. 61-79.

105-109. For similar *bodhicittānuśaṃsā,* BS, 57 and *Bodhicaryāvatāra,* I.

110.
| ji ltar 'khor bar saṅs rgyas daṅ || byaṅ chub sems dpa'i smon lam ni |
| mi gyo de ltar blo ñid ni || byaṅ chub sems ǵzol rnams kyis bya |

111.
| ṅo mtshar gyis kyaṅ khyed cag gis || ji ltar bśad pa la 'bad kyis |
| de rjes kun bzaṅ spyod pa ni || raṅ ñid kyis ni rtogs par 'gyur |

112.
| rgyal mchog rnams kyis bstod pa'i byaṅ chub sems ni bstod byas pa'i |
| bsod nams mtshuṅs med deṅ du bdag gis thob pa gaṅ yin pa |
| de yis srid pa'i rgya mtsho dba' kloṅ naṅ du nub pa yi |
| sems can rkaṅ gñis dbaṅ pos bsten pa'i lam du 'gro bar śog |

110b 'khor bar (*saṃsāra-) B : sdom pa (*saṃvara-) AC

110. Just as the high aspirations (*praṇidhāna*) of Buddhas and bodhisattvas in *saṃsāra* are unswerving (*acala*) thus those who tackle the *bodhicitta* must make [their] intellect (*buddhi*) [firm].

111. No matter how strange [all this seems] you must make efforts as explained. Thereafter you will personally (*svayam*) understand the course (*caryā*) of Samantabhadra!

112. May the living beings (*sattva*) submerged in the waves of life's ocean (*bhavārṇava*) perforce of the incomparable merit I have now (*adya*) collected while praising the excellent *bodhicitta* praised by the excellent Jinas, gain a foothold on the road followed by the Leader of bipeds (*dvipādendra*)!

110. In *pāda* a A and C apparently read **saṃvaro* (sdom pa) against B's **saṃsāre* ('khor bar).

111. This refers to Samantabhadra's celebrated *praṇidhānas*. For *Bhadracaryāpraṇidhāna* (or *Bhadracarīpraṇidhānarāja*) v. EOB, II, pp. 632-638. – I do not think that the commentary ascribed to Nāgārjuna (TP, No. 5512) is authentic. – For a modern edition of the verses see e.g. J. P. Asmussen, *The Khotanese Bhadracaryādeśanā: Text, translation, and glossary, together with the Buddhist Sanskrit original*, København 1961. – Cf. also SS, 247 b.

112. The final verse forms a *parināmanā*, cf. YṢ, 60; CS, III, 59; BS, 165 etc.

XII. Suhṛllekha (SL)

While not a single Sanskrit fragment seems to have survived of the 123 *āryāgītis* in which *Suhṛllekha* was originally composed, it is, however, available in no less than three Chinese translations (Taishō, XXXII, Nos. 1672-1674), a Tibetan (TP, No. 5409, cf. No. 5682 which is a duplicate with a few important variants) and a very good commentary (TP, No. 5690) corresponding to its name *Vyaktapadā Suhṛllekhaṭīkā* by a certain Mahāmati.[181]

I have only come across one quotation in Indian *śāstras* from SL. It occurs in Candrakīrti's *Catuḥśatakaṭīkā* (TP̄, No. 5266), Ya *fol.* 113b) without indication of source. It is v. 43. That SL is so seldom cited is perhaps not surprising when one looks at its content. It is mainly concerned with an exposition of the ethics of a layman and was, incidentally, addressed to a certain king called bDe spyod (cf. *ṭīkā, loc. cit.*, 325a) perhaps to be identified with Gautamīputra Śatakarṇī of the Śātavāhana dynasty.[182]

There can be no doubt that the author is a devotee of Mahāyāna – he speaks of *sugatapratimā* (2), the six *pāramitā* (8), Avalokiteśvara (120) and Amitābha (121). On the other hand the theory of *śūnyatā* is hardly mentioned (but see 40, 49) and the dialectics of *prajñā* known from MK etc. do not occur. But this is only what we would expect from an author who adheres to the Mahāyāna ideal of *upāya-kauśalya* (see BS, 6, 17 etc.; BV, 98-99). Thus it shows great similarity to BS, SS and certain parts of RĀ, without, however, actually

181. Apart from several partial versions three complete English ones are known to me: L. Kawamura, *Golden Zephyr: Instructions from a Spiritual Friend*, Emeryville 1975, and Ven. Lozang Jamspal *et.al.*, *Nāgārjuna's Letter to King Gautamīputra*, Delhi 1978. They supersede the pioneer version of H. Wenzel: 'Friendly Epistle', *JPTS* (1886), pp. 1-32. Further bibliographical information Kawamura, *loc.cit.*, pp. 114-117. (Dr. S. Dietz is now preparing a critical edition of Tib.) For a Danish version (from Tibetan) see *Indiske Studier* I.

182. For the identity of this king, Kawamura, *loc.cit.*, p. 4 (ref.); de Jong, *IIJ*, XX, p. 137. Also n. 71 above. Recently S. Dietz, *Die buddhistische Briefliteratur Indiens*, Bonn 1980, I, pp. 36-39.

repeating the *dharmadeśanā* given in those texts.

SL is written in a straightforward and pleasing style.[183] Though Tibetan commentators have taken great pains to detect some subtle principle of composition, there is, in my opinion, none such to be found.[184] As is often the case with Nāgārjuna a progressive composition is not to be expected. But surely there is a unity of thought: all human endeavours are subsumed under one heading, viz. the desire for release from the round of rebirth (cf. 104). This, as we have seen in RĀ, is achieved by fulfilling *puṇyajñānasaṃbhāra.* And, to put it briefly, SL is concerned with the *puṇyasaṃbhāra* of a *gṛhapati* according to the teachings of the ancient *āgamas.*

There being several modern versions of SL I shall merely attempt to point out some parallels in Nāgārjuna's other works and identify some of the canonical sources upon which SL proves to be dependent (cf. 2: '*... ṅag 'di ṅan yaṅ dam chos brjod la brten ...*') for its very rich technical inventory.[185]

1-3 form an exhortation to study the Dharma so as to aspire for *puṇya.* The Dharma comprises –

4: six *anusmṛti,* viz. *buddha,*° *dharma,*° *saṃgha,*° *tyāga,*° *śīla*° and *devatānusmṛti,* see ref. BHSD, p. 36; CPD, s.v. *anussati* etc.

5: ten *kuśalakarmapatha,* viz. abstention from *prāṇātipāta, adattādāna, kāmamithyācāra; mṛṣāvāda, paiśunyavāda, pāruṣyavāda, saṃbinnapralāpa; abhidhyā, vyāpāda* and *mithyādṛṣṭi,* cf. RĀ, I, 7-9; MK, XVII, 11; *Vimalakīrtinirdeśa,* p. 118, n. 73 for canonical ref. – To these ten are also added *amadyapāna* and *svājīva* in RĀ, I, 8; cf. *Traité,* p. 771; 816.

6: cf. RA, *ibid.: dānam ādarāt,* and on the nature, *kṣetra* and effect

183. Or, to quote the celebrated words of his Chinese translator, I-tsing (tr. Takakusu, *op.cit.,* pp. 159-160): 'The beauty of the writing is striking, and his exhortations as to the right way are earnest. His kindness excels that of kinship, and the purport of the epistle is indeed manifold ...'

184. See Mi pham's and Sa skya paṇḍita's scholastic and elaborate 'tables of content' in Kawamura, *loc.cit.,* pp. 96-113.

185. Only very few allusions or quotations were traced to their canonical sources by Wenzel. As a rule the Tibetan commentators were either ignorant of Nāgārjuna's sources (most of them never having been translated into Tibetan), or (being devout Buddhists) simply not inclined to assess their sacred texts from a historical point of view. To a very wide extent this is also the case with Indian commentators of the Madhyamaka lineage. These circumstances tend to obscure how 'traditional' Nāgārjuna really was when composing SL, BS etc.

of *dānapāramitā* in general *Traité*, pp. 650-769; *Dānaparikathā*, TP, No. 5661.

7: this verse (quoted Guenther (1959), p. 164) describes *śīlapāramitā* in general (cf. *Traité*, pp. 770-864) whereas 5 specified it. Also *Praṇidhānasaptati*, 24; *Madhyamakāvatāra*, pp. 32-45.

8: the six *pāramitās*, viz. *dāna*,° *śīla*,° *kṣānti*,° *vīrya*,° *dhyāna*° and *prajñāpāramitā*, see RĀ, I, 12; II, 25; IV, 80-82; BS, *passim*; *Traité*, pp. 650-1113; Har Dayal (1932), pp. 165-269; Guenther (1959), pp. 148-231.

9: a ref. to the *sabrahmakāni kulāni* of *Aṅguttara*, I, p. 132 etc.

10-11: for the *aṣṭāṅgapoṣadha*, *Traité*, p. 825 sq.; *Aṅguttara*, IV, p. 248 sq. (rep. *Traité*, p. 828); BHSD, s.v. *upoṣadha*; CPD, s.v. *aṭṭhaṅguposatha*. – *kāmāvacaradeva*, *Dharmasaṃgraha*, § 127.

12: the eight dharmas (*ṭīkā*, 333b) are *mātsarya*, *śāṭhya*, *māyā*, *saṅga?* (*chags pa*), *tandrī?* (*sñoms las*), *kauśīdya* (or *ālasya*, *le lo*), *rāga*, *dveṣa*, cf. similar lists of faults RĀ, V, 3 sq.; BS, 147etc. – The five kinds of *mada*, viz. *kula*,° *rūpa*,° *śruta*,° *yauvana*° and *mahābhāgamada?* (*dbaṅ thaṅ che ba*), are known from e.g. *Abhidharmadīpa*, p. 307; 27 kinds *Vibhaṅga*, p. 350; cf. PED, s.v. *mada*.

13-14: the celebrated verse on *apramāda* (*pramāda* listed as an *upakleśa*, cf. p. 167) is quoted *in extenso* by the *ṭīkā* (326b) with *sadā* (for *yathā*) in *pāda* d: *Udānavarga*, IV, 1 etc. etc. – For Nanda etc. v. PPN s.s.v.

15: ref. to *Dhammapada*, XIV, 6 (cf. *Bodhicaryāvatāra*, VI, 2). Also PED, s.v. *khanti* and *Traité*, pp. 865-926 on *kṣāntipāramitā*. *Śūraṃgamasamādhi*, p. 157 on *avaivartikatva*, i.e. the eighth *bhūmi*, *viz*. *Acalā*, characterized by *anutpattikadharmakṣāntipratilābha*. Also BS, 21, 23 etc. – *ṭīkā* quotes a sūtra, q.v. (335b), not traced.

16: *Udānavarga*, XIV, 9 etc. (this is *sattvakṣānti*, cf. *Traité*, p. 865).

17: this verse (which all transl. seem to have misunderstood not seeing that *sems* = *sems can*!) refers to *Aṅguttara*, I, p. 283: *pāsāṇalekhūpamo puggalo*, *paṭhavilekhūpamo puggalo*, *udakalekhūpamo puggalo*.

18: these three persons – *gūthabhāṇī*, *pupphabhāṇī* and *madhubhāṇī* – are described *Aṅguttara*, I, p. 128, q.v. (Kern's emendation to *kūṭa*° for *gūtha*° cf. PED, p. 253, is not supported by Tib. *mi gtsaṅ*).

19: again a ref. to *Aṅguttara*, II, p. 85. Āryadeva also alludes to this in *Catuḥśataka*, VII, 16, q.v.

20: the four *ambūpamā puggalā* occur *Aṅguttara*, II, p. 107.

21: the *ṭīkā* first ref. to a sūtra: *btsun pa bud med la ji ltar bsgrub par bgyi źes gsol ba daṅ | kun dga' bo mi ltas so* ..., cf. *Dīgha*, II, p. 141, and then quotes another sūtra (not identified) instructing householders how to look upon women (337a); cf. RĀ, II, 48, sq.

22: the *ṭīkā* ref. to: *sems dul bas ni bde ba 'thob,* cf. *Dhammapada,* III, 35 etc., and PED, p. 267. – On the dangers of *kāmasukha* see e.g. *Lalitavistara* cited *Śikṣāsamuccaya,* p. 204.

23: possibly inspired by the *Saddharmasmṛtyupasthānasūtra,* see Kawamura's transl. p. 25. The form *kimpaka* (not, as here, *kimpa*) is found in *Prajñādaṇḍa,* 204.

24: cf. e.g. *Dhammapada,* VIII, 4.

25: see *Aṅguttara,* IV, p. 386; *Traité,* p. 1154.

26: for the leper (*kuṣṭhin*) see *Majjhima,* I, p. 506. Also in *Catuḥśataka,* III, 14, q.v.

27: important verse suggesting that only *paramārthadarśana* (i.e. *śūnyatādarśana*) can destroy the *kleśas* and thus *karma* and *janma,* cf. MK, XVIII, 5; XXVI, 11 etc.

28: on *śīla* and *jñāna* (= *tattvajñāna*) cf. BS, 157; *Catuḥśataka,* XII, 11; *Dhammapada,* XVI, 9 (here *dassana* = *ñāṇa*).

29: the eight *lokadharma,* BS, 20 (with ref.); 117.

30: similar warning against 'nepotism' (*saṃvibhāga*) e.g. in *Catuḥśataka,* IV, 24; *Narakoddharastava,* 4.

31: on karma cf. Guenther (1959), p. 74 sq.

32: the seven *dhana,* viz. *śraddhā* (cf. RĀ, I, 5), *śīla* (above, 5 and 7), *hrī, apatrāpya, śruta, tyāga* and *prajñā,* see CPD, s.v. *ariyadhana.*

33: these are the *cha bhogānaṃ apāyamukhāni* of *Dīgha,* III, p. 182, q.v.

34: seems to allude to *Dhammapada,* XV, 8 etc.: *saṃtuṭṭhi paramaṃ dhanaṃ.*

35: the source of this legend about the *nāgarāja* has not been traced.

36: the three kinds of wives to be avoided, *Aṅguttara,* IV, p. 92.

37: the four kinds of wives to be revered, *ibid.,* p. 92.

38: this passage on a *bhikkhu bhojane mattaññū* seems to be inspired by *Aṅguttara,* I, p. 114, q.v.

39: one should be awake in five of the six watches of the day and night, see *Aṅguttara,* I, p. 114, on a *bhikkhu jāgariyam anuyutto.* Cf. *Dhammapada,* XII, 1.

40: on the four *apramāṇa,* viz. *maitrī, karuṇā, muditā* and *upekṣā,* also called the four *brahmavihāra,* see RĀ, I, 24; *Traité,* pp. 1239-1273.

41: on the four *dhyāna,* RĀ, *ibid.; Traité,* pp. 1233-1238.

42: when karma is based on *rtag pa, mṅon par źen pa, gñen po med pa* and two *gźi*, viz. *yon tan dan ldan pa* and *phan 'dogs pa* it brings a great result, *kuśala* or *akuśala* (see *ṭīkā*, 345b).

43: see *Aṅguttara*, I, p. 250 for this simile.

44: on the five *nivaraṇa*, viz. *kāmacchanda*, *vyāpāda*, *styānamiddha*, *auddhatyakaukṛtya* and *vicikitsā*, RĀ, V, 30-33; BHSD, p. 311; *Dharmadhātustava*, 18-19; *Traité*, p. 1013.

45: the five *bala* or *indriya*, viz. *śraddhā*, *vīrya*, *smṛti*, *samādhi* and *prajñā*, see BS, 97; *Traité*, pp. 1125-1127. The *ṭīkā*, perhaps by way of anachronism, relates these five to the four degrees of the *prayogamārga*, viz. *ūṣman*, *mūrdhan*, *kṣānti* and *laukikāgradharma*.

46: here *rgyags* (*mada*, see *Aṅguttara*, III, pp. 71-75, its source) is nearly a synonym of *ahaṃkāra*, cf. *Catuḥśataka*, IV *passim*.

47: good karma leads to *svarga* but *śūnyatā* is conducive to *mokṣa*, see RĀ, I, 43-45.

48: the four *smṛtyupasthāna*, viz. *kāya*°, *vedanā*°, *citta*°, and *dharmasmṛtyupasthāna* serve to destroy the four *viparyāsa*, viz. *śuci*°, *sukha*°, *nitya*° and *ātmaviparyāsa*, see *Traité*, pp. 1150 sq. with ref.

49: a canonical allusion (e.g. *Saṃyutta*, III, p. 44) for the Sanskrit of which see *Prasannapadā*, p. 355.

50: the skandhas are created by *avidyā* etc. (see MK, XVII, 28; XXVI), not by any other cause such as Īśvara etc. (see the introduction to *Akutobhayā*, TP, No. 5229, 34a: ... *dbaṅ phyug daṅ | skyes bu daṅ | gñi ga daṅ | dus daṅ | raṅ bźin daṅ | ṅes pa daṅ | 'gyur ba daṅ | rdul phran gyi rgyus* ...; cf. *Śvetāśvataropaniṣad*, I, 2: '*kālaḥ svabhāvo niyatir yadṛcchā bhūtāni yoniḥ puruṣa iti* ...'.

51: the three *saṃyojana*, viz. *satkāyadṛṣṭi*, *vicikitsā* and *śīlavrataparāmarśa*, see ref. PED, p. 656.

52: the four *satya* must be cultivated with *śruta*, *śīla* and *dhyāna*, i.e., I assume, with *śīla*, *samādhi* and *prajñā* (viz. *śrutamayī*, *cintāmayī* and *bhāvanāmayī*, cf. *Dharmasaṃgraha*, § 110).

53: the three *śikṣā* (*adhiśīla*, *adhicitta* and *adhiprajñā*, cf. BHSD, p. 527) comprise all the rules of *prātimokṣa*, '*diyaḍḍhasikkhāpadasata*', v. *Aṅguttara*, I, p. 230.

54: on the four *smṛtyupasthāna*, *Traité*, pp. 1121-1123; 1150 sq.

55: allusion to *anitye nityam iti viparyāsa*, cf. v. 48 above; *Traité*, pp. 925, 1076; MK, XXIII; *Catuḥśataka*, I.

56: also ref. to *aśucau śucir iti viparyāsa*, cf. *ibid*.

57: this ref. to *Aṅguttara*, IV, pp. 100-103, q.v.

58: *saṃsāra* without *sāra*, e.g. *Dharmadhātustava*, 15. – For the *kadalīskandha*, RĀ, II, 1; YṢ, 27; PED, p. 185.

59: for the *mahārṇavayugacchidrakūrmagrīvārpaṇopamā*, *Majjhima*, III, 169; *Therīgāthā*, 500; also *Pañjikā*, p. 9; *Śatapañcāśatka*, 5; *Saddharma-puṇḍarīka*, p. 463, etc.

60: the simile of the **suvarṇapātra* also occurs in *Catuḥśataka*, II, 21, q.v. See also *Traité*, p. 1674.

61: this refers to the four *cakra*, see *Aṅguttara*, II, p. 32.

62: seems to refer to *Saṃyutta*, I, pp. 87-89, q.v. Cf. BS, 141.

63-64: the eight *akṣaṇa*, *Vimalakīrtinirdeśa*, p. 118, n. 71 (ref.); RĀ, III, 87.

65: acc. to the commentary (356a) *saṃsāradoṣa* is sevenfold: *ṅes pa med pa* (see 66), *ṅoms mi śes pa* (see 67), *lus yaṅ daṅ yaṅ du 'dor na* (68), *yaṅ daṅ yaṅ du ñiṅ mtshams sbyor ba* (68), *yaṅ daṅ yaṅ du mtho dman gyi ṅo bor gyur pa* (69 sq.), *grogs med pa ñid* (76), and *'gro ba drug pa* (77 sq.).

66: see, in general, *Saṃyutta*, II, p. 178 sq.

67: this simile occurs *Saṃyutta*, II, p. 180.

68: *ibid.*, p. 185 and p. 179.

69-103: following is a description – *yathāgamam* – of the repeated ascent and descent through *ṣaḍgati* (69-75) and an account of the sufferings of the various hells. *Traité*, pp. 951-968 (with ref.) forms a detailed commentary to this. See also Guenther (1959), pp. 55-73.

104: a reminiscence of *Aṅguttara*, IV, p. 320, q.v. See also BS, 21 with note.

105: *śīla*, *samādhi* and *prajñā* sum up the *aṣṭāṅgikamārga* (cf. above v. 52). For the description of *nirvāṇa* see *Udāna*, pp. 80-81.

106: the seven *bodhyaṅga*, *Traité*, p. 1128.

107: here *dhyāna* and *prajñā* apparently correspond to *śamatha* and *vipaśyanā*, cf. *Aṅguttara*, II, p. 157. – The simile *gopade udaka* is also canonical, e.g. *Aṅguttara*, III, p. 188. – *Dhammapada*, XXV, 13.

108: on *caturdaśāvyākṛtavastu*, MK, XXII, 12 (*Prasannapadā*, p. 446); *Traité*, p. 154; May (1959), p. 278, n. 1015; CPD, s.v.

109-111: here the author merely propounds the canonical version of the *dvādaśāṅga* (e.g. PED, p. 394 for ref.), but in MK, XXVI and PK he offers two current interpretations.

112: allusion to *Śālistambasūtra* (ed. Sastri), p. 1 (cf. *Majjhima*, I, p. 190). See also *svavṛtti* ad VV, 54; MK, XXIV, 40.

113-115: the four *āryasatya*, see e.g. May (1959), pp. 206-250 with ref.

116: for the interpretation of this verse see MK, XVIII, 12; CS,

II, 15. I have not traced the similes.

117: like RĀ, IV, 73 this refers to *Dhammapada,* I, 1 etc.

118-123: a final exhortation to practise the Dharma not only as prescribed in the *āgamas* but also along the lines of Mahāyāna as is obvious from the ref. to *puṇyānumodanā* (cf. BS, 51-52; RĀ, V, 67), Avalokiteśvara (cf. EOB, II, pp. 407-415), Amitābha (cf. RĀ, III, 99), the *pāramitās* and *pariṇāmanā* (cf. BS, 53; RĀ, IV, 90). – The canonical passage for *nirvāṇa* as *saṃjñāmātra* (cf. *ṭīkā,* 376a) occurs e.g. *Prasannapadā,* p. 389; *Ṣaḍdarśanasamuccaya* (ed. Suali), p. 46; *Pañcaskandhaprakaraṇa* (my ed.), p. 22.

[Additional note: SL, 55 and 104 are quoted in Bodhibhadra's *Samādhisaṃbhāraparivarta,* TD, No. 3924, Ki *fol.* 85b.]

XIII. *Bodhisaṃbhāra[ka] (BS)

The *Pú tí zī liáng lùn*, **Bodhisaṃbhāraśāstra*, or simply *Bodhisaṃbhāra*[*ka*], belongs to that group of texts ascribed to Nāgārjuna which is only extant in a Chinese version. It is accompanied by a commentary composed by a certain Bǐ qiū zì zài, *Bhikṣu Īśvara, or more likely, Īśvarabhikṣu. Both texts (Taishō, XXXII, No. 1660, 517b-541b) were translated by Dharmagupta between 605 and 616 A.D. Neither the Sanskrit original nor a Tibetan version is extant, at least in the Tanjur. Howevei, the fact that the scope of BS was known to Bu-ston ('... *rab byuṅ gi spyod pa gtso bor ston pa Byaṅ chub kyi tshogs* ...') renders it probable that a Tibetan version may have existed – and perhaps still does.[186]

The external evidence is provided by two quotations from Nāgārjuna's 'Byaṅ chub kyi tshogs', **Bodhisaṃbhāra* (44) in Candrakīrti's *Catuḥśatakaṭīkā* (TP, No. 5266, Ya *fol.* 103a).[187] I have also come across a quotation from BS (26) in Asvabhāva's *Mahāyānasaṃgrahopanibandhana* (TP, No. 5552, Li *fol.* 329b).[188]

Moreover an early date of BS is ensured by the fact that BS is quoted in the *Daśabhūmikavibhaṣā* of which a Chinese version from ca. 408 still exists, whereas an earlier one (by Dharmarakṣa) from ca. 265 is lost. In both cases Nāgārjuna was held to be the author.[189]

The subject matter of BS is the same as that of the third *pariccheda* of RĀ, i.e. *bodhisaṃbhāra* but the manner in which the author of BS handles his 'endless' topic (3) differs. Clearly these expositions are intended to be complementary to one another. – Though a Chinese

186. Otherwise Bu-ston may have based his description on Indian oral tradition. Anyhow, one or two quotations would not warrant any such generally correct classification of BS. –There is a Japanese translation of BS, v. Nakamura (1977), p. 83, n. 39 (not seen). In the West BS has virtually remained unnoticed.
187. For the other quotation see v. 64 (with note).
188. See p. 231.
189. Cf. Ramanan, *op.cit.*, p. 340, n. 61; *Vimalakīrtinirdeśa*, p. 76.

version of a lost Sanskrit original is by no means an ideal starting-point for a description of the author's style, one cannot, however, fail to notice that BS bears great resemblance not only to RĀ but also to SL: The author desires to expose his subject strictly *yathāga-mam* – and so he does. Without in any way disavowing abstruse points such as *śūnyatā* etc. he takes pains not to deter *ādikarmikas* by indulging too much in such matters. Again the style is not encumbered with philosophical arguments or abstract accounts. Here, as in SL – not to mention SS – the author shows a predilection for numerical lists of various wholesome or unwholesome *dharmas*. Finally one may observe the many *dṛṣṭāntas* adduced by the author. Most, if not all of them are taken out of the canonical scriptures: in the case of SL mainly from the *āgamas* (*Dīrgha* etc.), in the case of BS mainly from various Mahāyānasūtras but certainly also from the ancient *āgamas*.

In the sequel I have ventured to offer a translation of the Chinese version of BS. Without dilating upon the difficulties and uncertainties inherent in such a task in general I shall only emphasize that my main objective has been to come as close as possible to the original Sanskrit underlying the idiosyncrasies of the Chinese. Though Eric Grinstead has rendered precious support *in rebus sinicis* I expect – and hope – that other scholars will some day be able to improve my work in various ways.[190]

The following abstract is intended to facilitate the understanding of BS as a whole:

The text is addressed to bodhisattvas, i.e. to *pravrajitas* and *gṛha-sthas* devoted to Mahāyāna (165). The subject matter is, as indicated by the very title, the equipments, or collections for enlightenment (*bodhisaṃbhāra*) (1), as they have been proclaimed in various *sūtras* of the Mahāyāna. Though *bodhisaṃbhāra* is *ananta* it may conveniently be placed under two main headings (see RĀ, III, 12-13), *puṇya-* and *jñāna-saṃbhāra* respectively resulting in the attainment of a *rūpa-* and a *dharmakāya* i.e. in a *buddhakāya*. Though *prajñā* (constituting *jñānasaṃ-bhāra*) is the most important *saṃbhāra* (5-7) it does in fact only play a subordinate role within the body of BS (see especially 19, 28-29,

190. A particular debt of gratitude is due to Prof. de Jong who went carefully through the version which I myself and Dr. Grinstead had already revised thoroughly at least four times. (Finally Prof. S. Egerod, Copenhagen, also offered some remarks.)

40, 63ff., 96, 149, 153). It is reasonable to suppose that a *bhājana* would have to refer to MK, also called *Prajñā,* though, to be sure, BS never refers to any other of the author's works. The great majority of verses are devoted to an exposition of the other five *pāramitās,* viz. *dāna, śīla* (*parārtham,* acc. to RĀ, IV, 81), *kṣānti, vīrya* (*svārtham, ibid.*) and *dhyāna* (which acc. to RĀ, *ibid.,* together with *prajñā* is *mokṣārtham*). A bodhisattva's fundamental attitude towards all other living beings (*sattva*) is one of *karuṇā* and *upāyakauśalya.* Thus all virtues (*guṇa*) apart from *dhyāna* and *prajñā* may be classified as various kinds of *puṇyasaṃbhāra.* Obviously there is really no end to the multifarious forms a *bodhisattvacaryā* devoted to these ideals may take. Suffice it to mention that the main topics treated under this broad heading in BS are *saṃgrahavastu, daśabhūmi* (above all the sixth, *Abhimukhī,* and the eighth, *Acalā*; cf. RĀ, V, 41-61 for the full list), *bodhicittotpādavidhi, mahāpuruṣalakṣaṇa* (extensively treated RĀ, II, 74-100, q.v.), *sattvaparipācana, pūjā, dharmadeśanā, śrāvakapratyekabhūmiprahāṇa,* etc. etc.

For further details I must refer to the notes and BS itself.

The [two] collections for enlightenment (Bodhisaṃbhāra)

1. Now in the presence of the Buddhas I fold my hands (*añjali*) and bow my head. I intend to explain – according to tradition (*yathāgamam*) – a Buddha's collections for enlightenment (*bodhisaṃbhāra*). (517b 10)

2. How is it possible to explain without omission the collections for enlightenment (*bodhi*), [for] the Buddhas are the only ones who individually obtain infinite (*ananta*) enlightenment (*bodhi*)! (517c 14)

3. The body (*kāya*) of a Buddha has infinite qualities (*anantaguṇa*). The [two] collections for enlightenment constitute the basis (*mūla*). Therefore the collections for enlightenment do not have any final limit either. (517c 24)

4. I can only explain a small part of these [two collections]. – I praise (*vand-*) the Buddhas and the bodhisattvas. All the bodhisattvas etc. I revere (*pūj-*) successively to the Buddhas. (518a 11)

5. Since [perfection of wisdom] is the mother of bodhisattvas it is also the mother of Buddhas. Perfection of wisdom (*prajñāpāramitā*) is the foremost (*prathama*) collection for enlightenment. (518c 3)

6. Perfection of wisdom is the mother of bodhisattvas. Skill in means (*upāyakauśalya*) is their father, and compassion (*karuṇā*) is their daughter. (519a 24)

1. With 'according to tradition' Nāgārjuna here, as in RĀ, SS etc., not only has Mahāyānasūtras in mind but also the ancient sūtra-collections. – Note that RĀ, III has the title **Bodhisaṃbhāra* and that it treats the same subject though it hardly ever overlaps the account given in the present work.
3. For *buddhakāya* see *Vimalakīrtinirdeśa*, p. 138-140; *Samādhirājasūtra*, XXII. – Strictly speaking Nāgārjuna acknowledges a *rūpakāya* due to *anantapuṇyasaṃbhāra*, and a *dharmakāya* due to *anantajñānasaṃbhāra*, see RĀ III, 9-13; YṢ, 60.
4. *Vandanā* and *pūjanā* form a part of the *anuttarapūjā*, cf. note to BS, 48.
5. *Prajñāparamitā* is often called 'mother of Buddhas', cf. Murti, *op. cit.*, p. 277; *Prajñāpāramitāstotra*. – In RĀ I, 5 *prajñā* is *pradhāna* compared to *śraddhā*, a theme elaborated SS, 175b 3-178a 3 according to the *Tathāgataguhya-*, **Vimatisamudghāta-*, *Śraddhābalādhānāvatāramudrāsūtra*, *Bodhisattvapiṭaka*, *Candragarbhaparivarta*, *Sāgaranāgarājaparipṛcchā* and *Tathāgataguṇajñānācintyaviṣayāvatāranirdeśasūtra*. *Śraddhā* in *buddhadeśanā* is realized in *pāramitācaryā*, etc.
6. For a definition of *upāyakauśalya*, see v. 17; also Har Dayal (1932) pp. 248 ff; *Vimalakīrtinirdeśa*, p. 116; SS, 243b 7-246a 3. – Correct *rén* in *pāda* b to *zíng*.

7. Charity (*dāna*), morality (*śīla*), patience (*kṣānti*), energy (*vīrya*), trance (*dhyāna*) and the rest (*śeṣa*) beyond these five [perfections] are all due to wisdom (*prajñā*) and comprised by [this] *pāramitā*. (519b 21)

8. Great compassion (*mahākaruṇā*) penetrates into the marrow of the bone (*asthimajjan*). It is the support of all living beings (*sarvasattvāśrayabhūta*). Like [the love of a] father for his only son (*ekaputra*) the tenderness [of a Buddha] pervades everything. (525c 24)

9. If one thinks of the Buddha's virtues (*guṇa*) and listens to the miracles (*ṛddhi*) of the Buddha [this creates] love, joy, a feeling [of happiness] and purity. This is called great joy (*mahāmuditā*). (526a 13)

10. As far as living beings are concerned a bodhisattva must not desert or abandon them. He should, to the best of his ability, at all times take care (*saṃgrah-*) of them. (526b 11)

11. From the very beginning [of his career] a bodhisattva ought – in accordance with available strength – to be skilled in the means of converting people so that they may enter Mahāyāna. (526b 17)

12. One may convert beings [as numerous as] the grains of sand in the Ganges (*gaṅgavālukā*) so that they obtain sainthood (*arhatphala*), but to convert one [single person] to Mahāyāna – *that* creates greater merit (*puṇya*)! (526b 24)

13. Some [persons] are instructed according to Śrāvakayāna and Pratyekabuddhayāna. Because of their weak powers (*mandabala*) they are not fit for conversion [to Mahāyāna]. (526c 6)

14. Those who are not fit for conversion either to Śrāvakayāna, Pratyekabuddhayāna, or to Mahāyāna must be assigned to meritorious tasks (*puṇyakriyāvastu*). (526c 12)

7. For *pāramitā* see also RĀ, IV, 80-82; V, 35-39; *Traité*, pp. 650-1111.
8. For *mahākaruṇā* see *Traité*, III, pp. 1705-1717. For the common image of *asthimajjan*, see *ibid.*, p. 2230, n. 1; Har Dayal (1932), p. 24.
9. The *buddhaguṇa* are *daśabala*, the four *vaiśāradya*, the four *pratisaṃvid* and the eighteen *āveṇikadharma*, exhaustively treated in *Traité*, pp. 1505-1707. On *ṛddhi*, *ibid.*, pp. 329-330; 381-385. *Muditā* is the third *apramāṇa*, *ibid.*, pp. 1239-1273; *mahāmuditā*, *ibid.*, p. 1709, n. See also *ibid.*, pp. 1340-1361 on *buddhānusmṛti*.
14. There are three *puṇyakriyāvastu* (*dāna*, *śīla*, *bhāvanā*), *Traité*, pp. 2245-2260.

15. If people are [utterly] unfit to receive conversion [conducive to] heaven (*svarga*) and liberation (*mokṣa*), then by advantages in this world (*dṛṣṭalokahita*) [a bodhisattva] must attract them in accordance with this power. (526c 20)

16. Towards people who cannot possibly be induced to conversion a bodhisattva should generate great compassion (*mahākaruṇā*). He must not discard them! (526c 28)

17. Attracting with gifts (*dānasaṃgraha*), teaching the Dharma (*dharmadeśanā*), also listening to the teaching of the Dharma, and also practising acts of benefit to others (*parahita*) – these are skilful means (*upāyakauśalya*) of attracting [others]. (527a 5)

18. While he benefits living beings without being tired and without carelessness (*apramāda*) [a bodhisattva] expresses his aspiration for enlightenment (*bodhipraṇidhāna*): To benefit others is to benefit oneself! (527a 14)

19. By entering the profound foundation of phenomena (*gambhīradharmadhātu*), exempt and separate from conceptual constructions (*vikalpa*), entirely without effort (*yatna*), all matters are spontaneously (*svayam*) abandoned. (527a 22)

20. Profit (*lābha*), reputation (*yaśas*), honours (*praśaṃsā*) and pleasure etc. (*sukhādi*) are four things one should not be attached to. In the opposite ones [viz. *alābha* etc.] one should not become embroiled (*apratigha*): this is called [worldly] renunciation (*tyāga*). (527b 5)

21. As long as he has not obtained the Irreversible [stage] (*avaivartika*) a bodhisattva should, for the sake of enlightenment (*bodhi*) perform these actions as zealously (*prayatnataḥ*) as if his headdress (*śirobhūṣaṇa*) was on fire. (527b 12)

15. I.e. these people neither perform good karma which results in rebirth in *svarga*, nor do they attain that *jñāna* which amounts to *mokṣa;* cf. RĀ, I, 43.

19. The word *gambhīradharma* (i.e. *pratītyasamutpāda*) is explained *Traité*, pp. 337-338; 396 (– the verse quoted here 107a 11-12 is surely MK, XXIV, 18). Otherwise only a few stanzas in BS refer directly to *śūnyatā,* see especially 28-29 and 64.

20. Here the author refers to *lokadharmatyāga,* cf. *Vimalakīrtinirdeśa*, p. 108, n. 50. For other kinds of *tyāga*, *Traité*, pp. 1413-1419.

21. The image *śirobhūṣaṇa* (or *śiraścaila*) is canonical, cf. *Upāliparipṛcchā*, p. 114, n. 1; SL, 104; *Śūraṃgamasamādhi*, p. 212, n. 217; BHSD, s.v. *ādīptaśiraścailopama*. – The eighth *bodhisattvabhūmi* (i.e. *Acalā*) is also called *avaivartika* (or *avivartya*), see RĀ, V, 55; *Śūraṃgamasamādhi*, p. 120, n. 5; pp. 208-210; *Traité*, pp. 243-245; 1502, n. 3; 1804.

22. Thus all the bodhisattvas while seeking enlightenment (*bodhi*) have energy (*vīrya*), without rest, for they shoulder a heavy burden (*bhāra*). (527b 27)

23. When he has not yet produced great compassion (*mahākaruṇā*) and patience (*kṣānti*) although he may have acquired the Irreversible (*avaivartika*) a bodhisattva would become like a mortal by being careless (*pramatta*). (527c 4)

24. If he enters the Śrāvaka- and Pratyekabuddhabhūmis then he becomes a mortal. It is because the roots of the knowledge of deliverance (*mokṣajñānamūla*) of the bodhisattvas are cut off. (527c 11)

25. Even if he fell into hell (*niraya*) a bodhisattva would not becomes a mortal. It is because the roots of the knowledge of deliverance (*mokṣajñānamūla*) of the bodhisattva are cut off. (527c 21)

26. While falling into hell (*niraya*) does not afford an absolute hindrance (*atyantavighna*) to *bodhi*, it is in fact an absolute hindrance to fall into the lands of the Śrāvakas and Pratyekabuddhas. (527c 25)

27. Just as it is said that people who love life (*āyuḥ*) are afraid to have their head cut off (*śīrṣaccheda*) [thus] the lands (*bhūmi*) of the Śrāvakas and Pratyekabuddhas ought to evoke similar fear. (528a 4)

28. [The *anutpādakṣānti* consists in seeing everything as] unborn (*anutpanna*), undestructed (*aniruddha*), neither unborn nor undestructed, neither both nor neither, neither empty (*śūnya*) nor non-empty (*aśūnya*). (528a 11)

29. When one does not swerve from the Middle View (*madhyamadarśana*) with regard to any phenomenon (*dharma*) whatsoever, there is acceptance [of the fact that things are] unborn (*anutpādakṣānti*), because all ideas (*vikalpa*) are eliminated. (528a 22)

26. This verse is quoted (without indication of source) in Asvabhāva's *Mahāyānasaṃgrahopanibandhana*, 329b 1-2: *dmyal bar 'gro ba byaṅ chub la* || *gtan du bgegs byed ma yin gyi* || *raṅ saṅs rgyas kyi sa daṅ ni* || *ñan thos sa dag bgegs byed do* ||.

27. Sūtra-quotation not traced (*Saddharmasmṛtyupasthāna?*).

28. For *anutpāda* etc. see above all *Vimalakīṛtinirdeśa*, pp. 41-43. Apparently this verse is quoted (but not identified) in *Traité*, p. 327 (97b 27-29. The lines *ibid.*, 12-14 are, of course, the *maṅgalaślokau* of MK, cf. *Traité*, p. 326). What remains of *pāda* d apparently occurs 97c 1 as *kōng fei kōng!*

29. All this is only suggested here: one must turn to MK, ŚS etc. for details.

30. As soon as you have obtained this conviction (*kṣānti*) at that very moment you receive the prediction (*vyākaraṇa*). You certainly will become a Buddha once you have obtained the Irreversible. (528b 2)

31. Until (*yāvat*) a bodhisattva attains the stage of Presence (*abhimukhī*) he should strengthen his *samādhi* and ought not to become careless (*pramatta*). (528c 13)

32. The [sixth *bhūmi*], the *abhimukhī*-stage of a [future] Buddha is steadfast concentration. This is the father of a bodhisattva [and] great compassion (*mahākaruṇā*) is his mother. (529a 1)

33. Perfection of wisdom (*prajñāpāramitā*) is his mother and [skill in] means (*upāya*) is his father. Because they [respectively] generate and sustain, the term 'bodhisattva's parents' is employed. (529a 10)

34. A small-scale quantity of merit (*puṇyarāśi*) cannot bring about enlightenment (*bodhi*). By collecting a quantity of merit the size of a hundred Sumerus one brings it about. (529a 17)

35. Even though [a bodhisattva] performs slight merit (*puṇya*) it [must] on the other hand be expedient (*sopāya*). He must produce a support (*ālamba*) for all living beings [thinking,] (529b 6)

36. All the actions I perform shall always be for the benefit of the living beings (*sattva*)! – Who can measure the merit of an intention like this? (529b 17)

37. Not to cherish one's own family, or one's body, life (*jīva*) or riches (*dhana*), not to covet pleasures (*sukha*) and power (*aiśvarya*), or the world (*loka*) of Brahmā and the other gods (*deva*), (529b 26)

38. Not to covet *nirvāṇa*, but to act for the sake of living beings – this is precisely (*eva*) to care for the living beings. – Who can measure this merit? (529c 2)

39. To save and protect a world lacking support and protection from suffering and pain – who can measure the merit (*puṇya*) of entertaining such intentions? (529c 12)

40. To possess the perfection of wisdom (*prajñāpāramitā*) for one month or for several months as [intensively as] when milking a cow for a short time – who can measure the merit? (529c 19)

30. For *vyākaraṇa* see the commentary translated in a valuable note in *Śūraṃgamasamādhi*, p. 203.

31. For the sixth *bhūmi* (*Abhimukhī*), RĀ, IV, 51 (– follows *Daśabhūmika*, q.v.); *Traité*, pp. 2418-2420; Har Dayal, *op.cit.*, p. 289.

33. Cf. BS, 6.

41. To recite for oneself and to teach others the profound scriptures praised by the Buddha, and to explain the various meanings (*artha*) – this is called a mass of merit (*puṇyarāśi*). (529c 26)

42. By causing innumerable beings (*sattva*) to turn their minds to enlightenment (*bodhi*) the store of merit (*puṇyakośa*) will excel even more so that one will obtain the Immovable stage (*acalā bhūmi*). (530a 6)

43. To follow [the Buddha] and to turn the victorious *dharmacakra* turned by the Buddha, and to calm and quench bad impulses – this is a bodhisattva's store of merit (*puṇyagarbha*). (530a 17)

44. By bearing the great suffering of hell – not to mention a little extra suffering – so as to benefit and please living beings – *bodhi* will be in the right hand. (530b 3)

45. To initiate action not for oneself but only to benefit and please living beings (*sattvahitasukhāya*) motivated by compassion – *bodhi* is in the right hand. (530b 9)

46. Wisdom (*jñāna*) without conceptualization (*prapañca*), zeal (*vīrya*) without sloth (*kausīdya*), generosity (*dāna*) without stinginess (*mātsarya*) – *bodhi* is in the right hand. (530b 15)

47. Being independent, without thoughts obsessed, having perfectly complete and unsullied morals (*śīla*), accepting [that things] are unborn (*anutpādakṣānti*) – *bodhi* is in the right hand. (530b 23)

48. In front of the fully enlightened Buddhas who are present (*pratyutpanna*) in the ten regions I entirely confess my sins (*pāpa*). (530c 4)

49. If the Buddhas who have attained *bodhi* in the universe of ten directions (*daśadigdhātu*) are reluctant to expound their teaching (*dharmadeśanā*) I entreat them to turn the *dharmacakra*! (530c 12)

44. Quoted in Candrakīrti's *Catuḥśatakaṭīkā*, 103a 2 (from »Nāgārjuna's *Byaṅ chub kyi tshogs*«): *sdug bsṅal gźan lta yar 'dug cig* || *gaṅ źig sems can phan bde'i phyir* || *dmyal ba'i sdug bsṅal che bzod pa* || *de'i lag gyas na byaṅ chub po* ||.

48. This is *pāpadeśanā*, followed by *adhyeṣaṇā* (49), *yācanā* (50), *puṇyānumodanā* (51-52) and *pariṇāmanā* (53). Cf. RĀ, V, 65-87 (*śaraṇagamana*, *pūjanā*, *pāpadeśaṇa*, *adhyeṣaṇā*, *yācanā*, *bodhicittotpāda* and *parināmanā*); *Bodhicittotpādavidhi* (*vandanā*, *pāpadeśanā*, *puṇyānumodanā*, *śaraṇagamana*, *ātmatyāga*, *bodhicittotpāda* and *pariṇāmanā*); *Upālipariprcchā*, p. 107, n. 4 with ref.; *Dharmasaṃgraha*, XIV.

50. If the *samyaksambuddhas* present in the universe of ten directions desire to give up their life (*jīvitasaṃskāra*) [in *saṃsāra*], I bow my head and request them to remain. (530c 18)

51. The merit of liberality and good morals (*dānaśīlapuṇya*), and [good] thoughts and actions produced by living beings by means of body, mouth and mind – (530c 24)

52. We all rejoice in the merit (*puṇya*) accumulated by holy men (*ārya*) and common people (*pṛthagjana*) of the past, present and future. (530c 26)

53. If only I could make all the merit I have into a lump (*piṇḍī-kṛ-*) and pass it on to the living beings so that they may obtain *saṃbodhi!* (531a 5)

54. In this way I repent, exhort [the Buddha to preach], request [the Buddha to remain], and turn [my merit] over to *bodhi*. One must know [that thus I will be] like the Buddhas. (531a 13)

55. One [ought to] express remorse for one's unwholesome sins, request the Buddhas [to abide in *saṃsāra*], rejoice in merit and transfer it to *bodhi* as the Jinas have stated. (531a 21)

56. One must do so every third hour, day and night, joining palms (*kṛtāñjali*), with the right knee-cap touching the ground, and the upper garment arranged on one shoulder. (531a 27)

57. If the merit (*puṇya*) created [in this way] in one hour had outward form [then realms amounting to] many thousand [times the] number of grains of sand in the Ganges still could not contain it. (531b 5)

58. Once [a bodhisattva] first has produced the thought [of enlightenment, *bodhicitta*] he ought to show respect and kindness towards all minor bodhisattvas as if they were his teacher or parents. (531b 17)

53. This recalls *Aṣṭasāhasrikā*, p. 70, q.v.

56. Acc. to RĀ, V, 65 this rite is to be performed three times daily (*ñin gcig bźin yaṅ dus gsum ...*). – The posture is familiar, cf. e.g. *Suvikrāntavikrāmiparipṛcchā*, p. 3: ... *ekāṃsam uttarāsaṅgaṃ kṛtvā dakṣiṇaṃ jānumaṇḍalaṃ pṛthivyāṃ pratiṣṭhāpya ...*

57. The *bodhicittotpādapuṇya* is described similarly in RĀ, V, 86. It was probably inspired by a well known verse from *Vīradattaparipṛcchā*, see *Bodhipathapradīpa*, pp. 110-111.

59. Even if a bodhisattva has committed a sin he should not talk about it, even less (*kā kathā*) tell an untruth. One should only speak the truth. (531b 28)

60. If a man expresses the vow (*praṇidhāna*) to become a Buddha, one must wish that he does not fall back, show [him the merit of the Buddha], fire his zeal, and produce joy. (531c 11)

61. If he has not yet unravelled the very profound (*atigambhīra*) sūtras he must not say that they are not Buddha's words. If he makes such statements he will get great suffering in return. (531c 21)

62. If all sins as the five *ānantarya* etc., are added together in a sum and compared with the above two sins they do not amount to a fraction [of those two]. (531c 28)

63. One should carefully develop (*su-bhāvay-*) the three doors to release (*vimokṣamukha*), first emptiness (*śūnyatā*), next the markless (*ānimitta*), and third the wishless (*apraṇihita*). (532a 12)

64. Since *dharmas* lack own-being (*niḥsvabhāva*) they are empty (*śūnya*), being empty how can they have marks (*nimitta*)? All marks being extinct (*śānta*) and abolished (*niruddha*) how can wise men make wishes [for anything]? (532a 19)

65. While [the bodhisattva] is cultivating and contemplating these [three doors to release, and] traversing the path to *nirvāṇa* he must not think that the *buddhakāya* does not exist. Do not relax efforts on this score! (532a 27)

66. As far as *nirvāṇa* is concerned he will not realize it at once (*sākṣātkaroti*), but he must produce this thought (*citta*): We must ripen the perfection of wisdom (*prajñāpāramitā*). (532b 3)

62. By committing one of the five *ānantarya* (cf. e.g. *Vimalakīrtinirdeśa*, p. 156, n. 33) one *samanantaraṃ narakeṣūpapadyate*. However, this is not »*byaṅ chub la gtan du bgegs*«, cf. BS, 26, as are the two sins mentioned in 60-61.

63. The three *vimokṣamukha* are discussed *Traité*, pp. 321-325 (note that the verse quoted here p. 323 = 96 c 13-14 must be identified as MK, XVIII, 7); *ibid.*, pp. 1213-1232; *Vimalakīrtinirdeśa*, p. 148, n. 16.

64. This is cited by Tsoṅ kha pa, *Lam rim*, 414 b 1-2 (from »*Byaṅ chub kyi tshogs*«): *raṅ bźin med pas stoṅ la stoṅ pa ni* || *yin daṅ mtshan mas ci źig byed par 'gyur* || *mtshan ma thams cad log par 'gyur ba'i phyir* || *mkhas pas ci ste smon lam 'debs par 'gyur* ||. His source is *Catuḥśatakaṭīkā*, 215b 2, identified by Uryūzu Ryūshin in *IBK*, XVII, p. 518, to which Prof. de Jong has kindly called my attention. – Cf. also Wayman (1978), p. 252.

66. Cf. *Catuḥśataka*, VIII, 22.

67. For instance, a master archer (*iṣvastrācārya*) releases his arrows so that each of them are aimed one at the other and, mutually supported, do not fall – the great bodhisattva is also like that. (523b 10)

68. Carefully he aims the arrow of mind (*citta* = *prajñā*) at the *vimokṣamukha* [called] 'empty' (*śūnya*); the arrows of [skill in] means (*upāya*) concomitantly support it so that [his *prajñā*] is not allowed to fall into *nirvāṇa*. (532b 14)

69. Let us not desert the living beings (*sattva*)! In order to benefit the living beings first generate this attitude (*manas*) and then be in possession of the (*vimokṣamukha-*)practice. (532b 21)

70. There are living beings who have attachments during a long time (*dīrgharātram*) and cultivate (*samudācarati*) misconceptions (*viparyāsa*) and [wrong] notions (*nimitta*). All this is due to delusion (*moha*). (532c 3)

71. Those who are addicted to [wrong] notions (*nimitta*) [and] misconceptions (*viparyāsa*) can get rid of them by proclaiming the Dharma (*dharmadeśanā*). First one focuses mind (*citta*) on reality (*tathatā*?) and then comes into possession of the (*vimokṣamukha-*)practice. (532c 9)

72. Bodhisattvas benefit living beings (*sattva*) but do not see any living beings! This is indeed a very difficult point, exquisite, one cannot grasp it. (532c 16)

73. Even if [a bodhisattva] is predestined (*nityatipatita*) he must practise the *vimokṣamukha*. Since the original vow (*praṇidhāna*) is not yet fulfilled [a bodhisattva] does not realize *nirvāṇa*. (532c 22)

74. If he has not yet attained his predestination (*samyaktvaniyama*) being [only] concerned with skilful means (*upāyakauśalya*) the original vow is not yet fulfilled. So, again, he does not realize *nirvāṇa*. (533a 1)

67. A celebrated image, cf. *Traité*, p. 1140, n.1.

69. The correct attitude is, of course, *bodhicitta;* the term *yoga* refers to the three *vimokṣamukha* as the commentator notes and as shown by 73.

70. The first part of this verse alludes to *Udānavarga*, I, 19 etc. (cited *Traité*, p. 2296, n.1.).

72. Cf. *Niraupamyastava*, 9: *sattvasaṃjñā ca te nātha sarvathā na pravartate* | *duḥkhārteṣu ca sattveṣu tvam atīva kṛpātmakaḥ* ||. *Śūraṃgamasamādhi*, p. 148.

73. Cf. RĀ, I, 24; SL, 40.

75. [A bodhisattva has] extreme distaste for *saṃsāra* but still turns towards *saṃsāra*. He should have faith and joy in *nirvāṇa*, yet also turn his back on *nirvāṇa*. (533a 6)

76. One should fear the passions (*kleśa*) but one should not exhaust the passions (*kleśa*); one must accumulate good karma in order to suppress the suppressing passions. (533a 15)

77. A bodhisattva has a passionate nature, he does not yet have a *nirvāṇa*-nature. [So only when] the passions are not [yet] burned away [can a bodhisattva] produce the seed of enlightenment (*bodhibīja* = *bodhicitta*). (533a 23)

78. A bodhisattva predicts [the destiny of] other beings; this prediction has as necessary condition a Tathāgata's merit and skill enabling them to reach the further shore (*pāram* = *nirvāṇa*). (533b 4)

79. A [bodhisattva should] propagate and establish all the śāstras, techniques, sciences and arts (*śilpasthānavidyākalā*) for the use and benefit of mankind. (533c 8)

80. According to the stages of transmigration (*gati*) and caste (*jāti*) in the world of potential converts (*vaineyasattvadhātu*) a bodhisattva proceeds there as he wishes; by virtue of his vows (*praṇidhānabalāt*) he accepts rebirth. (533c 20)

81. When faced with various evil matters and flattering (*śāṭhya*) or deception (*māyā*) of people one must put on stout armour (*saṃnāha*) without being disgusted [by *saṃsāra*], and without being afraid [of seeking *bodhi*]. (534a 2)

82. [Bodhisattvas with] a completely pure (*pariṣamāptaviśuddha*) mind do not flatter or deceive. They reveal all [their] sins and evils, but conceal and store [their good deeds [without boasting]. (534a 13)

75. For *apratiṣṭhitanirvāṇa* etc., see *Vimalakīrtinirdeśa*, pp. 144.

79. The various *śāstras* are, acc. to the commentator: mathematics, metallurgy, medicine, exorcism, botany, mineralogy, astronomy, oneiromancy and anatomy. – For *śilpakarmasthāna*, *vidyā* and *kalā* cf. *Traité*, p. 1856; *Śūraṃgamasamādhi*, p. 145; BS, 103; *Mahāvyutpatti*, §§ 217-218; 76; Bu-ston, I p. 44 with notes.

81. *śāṭhya* and *māyā* often occur together, cf. e.g. *Vimalakīrtinirdeśa*, p. 114, n. 61. – For *saṃnāha*, cf. *Traité*, p. 1841, n. 2; *Śūraṃgamasamādhi*, p. 179, n. 154.

83. Being pure [in regard to] the karma of body and speech, and also [in regard to] the karma of mind [a bodhisattva] cultivates all the moral rules (*śikṣāpada*) not allowing any shortcoming or diminution. (534a 25)

84. [A bodhisattva must] peacefully dwell in mindfulness (*smṛti*). He selects an object (*ālambana*) and contemplates in solitude employing mindfulness (*smṛti*) to safeguard himself [so that his] mind becomes a mind without attachment (*asaṅga*). (534b 7)

85. If discursive thoughts (*vikalpa*) should arise he must determine whether they are wholesome (*kuśala*) or unwholesome (*akuśala*). He should abandon all the unwholesome ones and increase (*bahulīkṛ-*) the wholesome thoughts. (534b 16)

86. If his mind is disturbed by objects (*viṣaya*) he should concentrate his mindfulness (*smṛti*), lead his mind back to the object and in case it is fickle, cause it to remain still. (534b 21)

87. Do not relax or fall into clinging (*abhiniveśa*) but cultivate strenuousness (*vīrya*). In case [a bodhisattva] cannot uphold his concentration (*samādhi*) he must therefore constantly strive. (534b 28)

88. If [you are about to] ascend the Śrāvakayāna or the Pratyekabuddhayāna merely acting for [your, or its] own benefit (*svahita*) do not abandon firm energy (*vīrya*)! (534c 5)

89. Not to speak of the great bodhisattva (*mahāpuruṣa*)! – Being his own saviour and also the saviour of other people should he not put forth ten thousand million (*koṭisahasra*) times the zeal (*vīrya*)! (534c 9)

90. For half an hour one may practise various [meditations] and for one hour follow a different procedure, but to practise concentration (*samādhi*) is not feasible in this way! – One must let [one's mind] be fixed on *one* object (*viṣaya*)! (534c 14)

91. There should be no affection for the body, and no regret for one's life (*āyuḥ*). Even if one wants to protect this body, still it will in the end be of a rotten and miserable nature. (534c 19)

83. Allusion to *daśakuśalakarmapatha*, see *Vimalakīrtinirdeśa*, p. 118, n. 73, and ibid., n. 72 for *śikṣāpada*.

84. These verses (84-87) on *dhyānapāramitā* may be compared with *Traité*, pp. 984-1057; *Arthaviniścayasūtra*, §§ 12-14 (the four *samādhibhāvanā*, *smṛtyupasthāna* and *samyakprahāṇa*).

92. Onc should altogether (*ekānta*) not be attached to gains (*lābha*), honours (*satkāra*) and fame (*yaśas*). As if one's head [or] clothes were on fire one should act vigorously to fulfil one's vow (*praṇidhāna*) [to liberate oneself and others]. (534c 27)

93. Determined, then, to produce the *summum bonum* (*uttamahita*) [a bodhisattva] cannot wait till tomorrow. Tomorrow is far away. How can one preserve a transient existence (*āyuḥ*)? (535a 2)

94. [A bodhisattva must] peacefully dwell in mindfulness (*smṛti*) [as indifferently] as if he [had] to eat the flesh of his favourite son. While eating it he is neither attracted nor repelled. (535a 8)

95. What the purpose (*kimartham*) is of becoming a mendicant (*pravrajita*), [and how] one must consider whether what we have done or have not yet done must be done or not – this is explained in the *Daśadharmakasūtra.* (535a 15)

96. See that compound things (*saṃskṛta*) are impermanent (*anitya*) [and that] there is no I (*aham*) or mine (*mama*). One must be aware of all the deeds of Māra and abandon them. (535b 2)

97. Produce zeal and cultivate the [five] *indriya,* the [five] *bala,* the [seven] *bodhyaṅga,* the [four] *ṛddhipāda,* the [four] *prahāṇa,* the [eight-fold] *mārga,* and the four *smṛtyupasthāna.* (535b 12)

98. A mind can continually be a place of birth for good things (*hita*), happiness (*sukha*) and merit (*kuśala*), but it can also be a root of evil. One must consider this carefully. (535b 23)

99. As far as positive phenomena (*dharma*) are concerned, I must daily watch closely how they increase and how they diminish. (535c 3)

92. Cf. note on 21. – The three concepts *lābhasatkārayaśas* are well known as Pāli *lābhasakkārasiloka,* see ref. in PED, s.v.

93. The *summum bonum (pradhāna-* or *viśiṣṭahita?)* refers to *naiḥśreyasa,* or *mokṣa,* cf. RĀ, I, 4; III, 30; SL, 104. Also SL, 55.

94. The image is canonical, see PED, s.v. *puttamaṃsa* (especially *Saṃyutta,* II, p. 98). – Adopt the variant *niàn* in *pāda* a.

95. *Daśadharmakasūtra:* Taishō, No. 314. (Quoted thrice in *Śikṣāsamuccaya.*)

96. For *Mārakarma* see YṢ, 36; SS, 190 b 1 ff.; *Traité,* pp. 339-346. – For *nirmamo nirahaṃkāraḥ,* MK, XVIII, 2-3.

97. The 37 *bodhipākṣika* are treated at length *Traité,* pp. 1119-1207. Also mentioned SL, 106 (*bodhyaṅga*), 113 (*mārga*), 45 (*bala, indriya*), 48 (*smṛtyupasthāna*). BS, 121 for *ṛddhipāda.*

98. Cf. SL, 42.

100. If one sees others achieve increase of profit (*hitapuṣṭi*), support (*poṣa*), respect (*gaurava*) and fame (*nāma*) one's mind should not react even with the slightest envy (*mātsarya*) or jealousy (*īrṣyā*). (535c 8)

101. Without desiring the objects [of the senses] (*viṣaya, gocara*) one should live as if dullwitted, blind, dumb and deaf. At the right moment the lion's roar (*siṃhanāda*) frightens the heretical deer (*tīrthyamṛga*)! (535c 15)

102. Welcoming and farewelling, one must honour those to be respected. In all matters of *dharma* [one must be] kind and helpful. (535c 23)

103. By saving and releasing those who suffer annihilation one's own self prospers and is not destroyed. [By] cultivating the sciences (*vidyā*) and crafts (*śilpakarman*) well one trains oneself and instructs others. (535c 28)

104. As far as particularly good phenomena (*dharma*) are concerned one must strenuously keep to them. Practise the four foundations of propitiation (*saṃgrahavastu*), and donate clothing, beverages and food. (536a 8)

105. Do not rebuff those who beg for alms. Reconcile all your kindred. Do not turn against your followers (*parivāra*). Donate dwellings and property. (536a 16)

106. One's parents, relatives and friends should be duly treated. The extent to which they should be treated is that of the supreme (*anuttara*) Lord (*īśvara*). (536a 25)

107. Even if it be a slave, one should speak kindly to him and take care of him. One should show him great respect, distribute medicine and heal all diseases. (536b 2)

100. Cf. BS, 20, 92.

101. For *siṃhanāda*, *Vimalakīrtinirdeśa,* p. 98, n. 4; BV, 52; CS, III, 54.

103. Cf. BS, 79.

104. The four *saṃgrahavastu* (*dāna, priyavāditā, arthacaryā* and *samānārtha*), see *Vimalakīrtinirdeśa,* p. 116, n. 67; RĀ, II, 72; *Akṣayamatinirdeśa,* Bu *fol.* 149a-150a.

105. This, acc. to the commentator, produces the *suvarṇavarṇamahāpuruṣalakṣaṇa,* cf. RĀ, II, 86.

108. [Those whose] head is [adorned with an *uṣṇīṣa* due to] the good karma of previous actions, [whose] voice is fine, smooth, beautiful and wonderful, [whose] voice [i.e. *brahmasvara,* is due to] good karma and a correct mentality [they will] – in the future (*paścāt*) as in the past (*pūrvam*) – [never] fail to be respected. (536b 7)

109. Do not harm the followers of others. Look at living beings with a compassionate eye. Also [look at all beings] without a jealous spirit, as if they were [your own] relatives and friends. (536b 23)

110. One must unfailingly do as one has promised. If one acts according to one's words others will have confidence in one. (536c 1)

111. One should support Buddhism (*dharma*) and be aware of those who are idle (*pramatta*). – Also make golden precious nets and cast them over the shrines (*caitya*). (536c 5)

112. If one wants to seek out a fair maid [then] one should give her ornaments (*alaṃkāra*). But one must also discourse on the virtues of the Buddha (*buddhaguṇa*) as well as give her various jewels. (536c 10)

113. One should cast statues of Buddha sitting upright on exquisite lotus-blooms. – As far as the six principles (*dharma*) are concerned one should practise [them with] joy and pleasure. (536c 19)

114. Those who are honourable (*pūjya*) are not to be dishonoured. Even in order to [save your] life do not criticise the *dharma* spoken by the Buddha or those people who discourse on the *dharma*. (536c 26)

115. [Make] distributions of gold (*kanaka*) and jewels (*ratna*) to the teachers (*ācārya*) and to the *caityas* of the teachers. – If one forgets what one learns, concentrate [upon it] so as not to be confused. (537a 3)

116. When one has not yet fully thought out one's actions one must neither panic nor just imitate [the actions] of others. – Do not believe in any of the gods (*deva*), serpents (*nāga*) or ghosts (*yakṣa*) of the heretics (*tīrthika*). (537a 11)

108. For *brahmasvara* (also a *mahāpuruṣalakṣaṇa*), see e.g. RĀ, II, 91. – For a complete list of all the *lakṣaṇa* and their causes, *Traité,* pp. 271-281; RĀ, II, 74-100; *Arthaviniścayasūtranibandhana,* §26. –*yathā pūrvaṃ tathā paścāt,* also CS, I, 25.

113. This refers to the six *sārāṇīyā dhammā* known from *Dīgha,* III, p. 245. Perhaps they are also referred to RĀ, III, 35. – *Traité,* p. 1739, n. 4.

117. One's mind should be like a thunderbolt (*vajra*): capable of penetrating all *dharmas*. One's mind should be like a mountain: imperturbable in all situations. (537a 18)

118. Enjoy expressions transcending the world (*lokottara*). Take no pleasure based upon transactions of the world (*lokavyavahāra*). In oneself one must keep all the virtues and help others to keep them too. (537a 23)

119. Develop the five spheres of liberation (*vimokṣa*). Contemplate the ten notions of impurity (*aśubha*). Also reflect upon the eight thoughts of a *mahāpuruṣa*. (537b 3)

120. One must clearly develop the five superknowledges (*abhijñā*), viz. *divyacakṣuḥ, divyaśrotra, ṛddhi, paracitta*[*jñāna*] and *pūrvanivāsānusmṛti*. (537b 20)

121. The four bases of power (*ṛddhipāda*) form the root, viz. will (*chanda*), mind (*citta*), energy (*vīrya*) and deliberation (*mīmāṃsā*). The four infinite foundations (*vihāra*) are love (*maitrī*), compassion (*karuṇā*), joy (*muditā*) and equanimity (*upekṣā*). (537c 5)

122. The four elements (*dhātu*) as a poisonous snake, the six bases (*āyatana*) as an empty village, the five aggregates (*skandha*?) as a murderer – thus one must look upon these! (537c 25)

123. Revere the Dharma and the teachers of the Dharma. Also put aside any animosity towards the Dharma. The teacher must not clench his hand. The audience must not be annoyed. (538a 8)

124. One should preach the Dharma to people without rudeness and without expectations – only with a compassionate heart, a devoted and respectful mind. (538a 14)

117. »In all situations«, i.e. in regard to the eight *lokadharma* (Comm.).

119. The *pañca vimuttāyatanāni* are known from *Dīgha*, III, p. 241, q.v. – The ten *aśubhasaṃjñā*, *Traité*, p. 1312 ff. Eight *mahāpuruṣavitarka*, *Dīgha*, III, p. 287 (= *aṭṭha dhammā uppādetabbā*).

120. For the five *abhijñā*, *Traité*, pp. 328-333. The six are listed RĀ, III, 92-97. Also *Traité*, pp. 1809 ff.

121. *Traité*, p. 1124 for *ṛddhipāda*. – For the four *brahmavihāra*, or *apramāṇa*, *ibid.*, pp. 1239-1273; RĀ, I, 24; SL, 40.

122. These comparisons (*āśīviṣa, śūnyagrāma* and *vadhaka*) are well known, see *Vimalakīrtinirdeśa*, p. 136, n. 28. **kāya/parṣad* in *pāda* c, and comm. **vedanākāya*, is not plausible.)

125. Be insatiable (*atṛpta*) for learning and commit to memory what you have learned. Do not be deceitful to respected holy personalities (*puṇyakṣetra*) but give pleasure to the teacher (*ācārya*). (538a 21)

126. Do not let your thoughts, [when] looking at other sects, cherish any respect. Do not, on account of the difficulty of the [Buddhist] treatises, study or recite worldly texts. (538a 26)

127. Do not, on account of anger, slander any of the bodhisattvas. When one has not yet grasped and learned the Dharma one must not cause calumny. (538b 2)

128. Get rid of pride and abide by the four noble principles (*ārya-vaṃśa*). Do not despise other people; do not be self-important either. (538b 5)

129. Whether an offence is real or fictitious do not inform others about it. Do not take any notice of the faults of others. Just be aware of your own faults. (538b 11)

130. Buddha and the doctrine (*dharma*) of the Buddha should not be objects of speculation (*kalpanā*) or doubt (*saṃśaya*). Although the Dharma is very difficult to believe in one must have faith in it. (538b 15)

131. Even if [a bodhisattva] dies by stating the truth or is deprived of [his status as] cakravartin king, or Indra, he must state the truth and nothing else. (538b 21)

132. [Even if you are] hit, insulted, threatened, flogged or tied up [by someone] do not bear any resentment towards him! Future and present [evils] are all due to one's own bad karma! (538b 25)

132. The following stanzas (132-145) are inspired by the author's study of *Kāśyapaparivarta* (Ref. are to §§ in the ed. of von Staël-Holstein). – See *loc.cit.*, §1. – For the *ācāryamuṣṭi*, *Vimalakīrtinirdeśa*, p. 267, n. 19; CPD, II, p. 33.

124. *Kāśyapaparivarta*, §2.

125. *Ibid.* §2. – For *puṇyakṣetra*, see PED, s.v. *puññakkhetta; Śūraṃgamasamādhi*, pp. 231-235.

126. This and the following to be compared with §§ 3-5.

128. This and the follwing two verses are moulded upon *Kāśyapaparivarta*, §6. – For *āryavaṃśa*, ref. in *Traité*, p. 1739, n. 4.

131. *Ibid.*, §8. – A bodhisattva who is *ṛjuka* never tells a lie.

132. *Ibid.*, §8.

133. One should respect, love and support one's parents very much. One should also serve one's instructor (*upādhyāya*) and revere the teacher (*ācārya*). (538c 2)

134. To preach the very profound (*atigambhīra*) Dharma [i.e. Mahāyāna] to those who believe in the Śrāvakayāna and in the Pratyekabuddhayāna – this is an error for the bodhisattva. (538c 8)

135. If there are people who believe in the profound Mahāyāna and one still advocates the Śrāvaka- and Pratyekabuddhayāna – this is also an error for a bodhisattva. (538c 13)

136. Many people (*mahājana*) come [to the monastery] out of interest for the Dharma. If they are careless (*śaithilika*) one should not preach to them. One should, however, take care of evildoers and establish unbelievers [in Mahāyāna]. (538c 17)

137. [A bodhisattva] must abandon the [four] errors mentioned. The virtues of a purified man (*dhūtaguṇa*) should be recited and learnt. They must also be practised and cultivated. (538c 23)

138. [The four kinds of *bodhisattvamārga* are:] Equanimity (*samacitta*), balanced discourse [on the Dharma], to be well-established in impartiality (*samatāsupratiṣṭhita*) and also to be quite the same (*samasaṃyukta*) towards all living beings (*sattva*) without difference. (538c 29)

139. [The four kinds of genuine bodhisattvas] act for the sake of the Dharma, not for the sake of profit (*hitārtham*), for the sake of merit, not for the sake of reputation (*ślokārtham*). [They only] wish to save living beings from suffering (*duḥkha*) without wanting pleasure for themselves. (539a 6)

140. [If a bodhisattva] sincerely intends to seek the maturing of his actions (*karmavipāka*) he must make the [three] *puṇyakriyāvastu* arise. He must also mature living beings (*sattvaparipācana*) and reject his own affairs. (539a 11)

133. Cf. *ibid.*, §10.

134. This and the three following verses give the four *bodhisattvaskhalita, ibid.*, §11; *Śikṣāsamuccaya*, p. 54 (cf. *Traité*, p. 1846).

137. For the twelve ascetic practices (*dhūtaguṇa*), *Dharmasaṃgraha*, §63; BHSD, p. 286; *Vimalakīrtinirdeśa*, p. 150, n.

138. The Sanskrit has *sarvasattveṣu samacittatā* ... *buddhajñānasamādāpanatā* ... *samyakprayogatā*, cf. *Kāśyapaparivarta*, §12.

139. See *ibid.*, §§15-16.

140. *Ibid.*, §16. – For *puṇyakriyāvastu*, see BS, 14 and note.

141. [A bodhisattva should] approach [these four kinds of] good friends (*kalyāṇamitra*): namely, the teacher (*dharmācārya*), the Buddha, those who encourage ascetics (*pravrajita*) and [finally] monks (*bhikṣu*). (539a 16)

142. Those who rely on worldly sciences (*lokaśāstra*), those who are especially eager for worldly goods (*āmiṣa*), [those who] believe in the Pratyekabuddhayāna and [finally those who believe in] the Śrāvakayāna – (539a 24)

143. A bodhisattva must be aware of these four [kinds] of bad friends (*kumitra*)! – What must be sought after are the so-called four great treasuries (*mahānidhāna*): (539b 1)

144. The super-worldly (*lokottara*) Buddha, study of the [six] perfections (*pāramitā*), a mind looking upon the teacher (*ācārya*) without impediments (*apratihata*), [and finally] being happy to dwell in empty places. (539b 5)

145. Like earth (*pṛthivī*), water (*ap*), fire (*tejaḥ*), wind (*vāyu*) and space (*ākāśa*), entirely and everywhere, the [bodhisattvas] are equally beneficial to the living beings (*sattva*). (539b 11)

146. One should consider the very meaning (*arthamātra*) [of Buddha's words] and unremittingly produce the *dhāraṇīs*. Do not be of any hindrance whatsoever to those who are studying the Dharma. (539b 19)

147. Those who are to be disciplined in the [nine] bases of quarrelling (*āghātavastu*) [must] put aside the [twenty] minor matters without exception. The eight kinds of sloth (*kausīdya*) must also be extinguished. (539b 26)

141. *Kāśyapaparivarta,* §14. Other kinds of *kalyāṇamitra* are mentioned SS, 212 b 3, q.v.

142. The four *kumitra* mentioned here and in 143 occur *op.cit.,* §13.

144. *Ibid.,* § 17. – For *apratihatacitta* also *Traité* p. 393-394.

145. This verse sums up *Kāśyapaparivarta,* §§29-32.

147. The nine *āghātavastu* are canonical, see ref. in *Vimalakīrtinirdeśa,* p. 289, n. 18. – The twenty »minor matters« (i.e. *upakleśa*) are, acc. to the commentary: *āśraddhya, āhrīkya, śāṭhya, auddhatya, vikṣepa, pramāda, vihiṃsā, anapatrāpya, kausīdya, kaukṛtya, styāna, middha, upanāha, mrakṣa, īrṣyā, mātsarya, unnati* (or *mada?*), *krodha, vipratisāra* (or *ālekhya* etc.?) and *mūchā* (?); cf. *Dharmasaṃgraha,* § 69; VṾ, 7 (*svavṛtti*); RĀ, V, 3-33 *passim*; various treatises on Abhidharma under the headings *paryavasthāna, upakleśa* and *nivaraṇa.* – The eight *kusītavatthūni,* e.g. *Dīgha,* III, p. 255.

148. Do not have any improper affection (*rāga*), [for] unreasonable desire is not in accord with one's [true] wishes. Those who are disunited should all be united without asking whether they are friends or not (*mitrāmitra*). (539c 16)

149. A sage (*prājña*) does not base his actions on emptiness by apprehending emptiness (*śūnyatopalabdhi*). If one [absolutely] must apprehend (*upalambheta*) emptiness that error would amount to the fault (*doṣa*) of belief in a personal substance (*satkāyadṛṣṭi*). (539c 23)

150. Sweep the dust, smear [cowdung], make decorations and perform worship (*pūjā*) of the shrines (*caitya*) with many kinds of drum-music and offerings such as incense (*gandha*), hair dressed in a knot etc. (539c 29)

151. Make various lamp-wheels (*pradīpacakra*). Worship the shrines (*caitya*) and donate parasols (*chattra*), leather sandals, riding horses, carriages, chariots, etc. (540a 6)

152. [A bodhisattva] should take special delight in the Dharma and enjoy an intellectual belief (*avetyaprasāda*) in the Buddha's attainments (*prāpti*). He should gladlv supply and serve the Sangha and take pleasure in listening to the true Dharma (*saddharma*). (540a 11)

153. Unborn (*anutpanna*) in the past, not remaining (*anavasthita*)in the present and not arrived (*aprāpta*) in the future – thus one should look upon all phenomena (*dharma*)! (540a 18)

154. Be gracious to the living beings (*sattva*) without seeking a reward from them. One should bear [their] troubles alone without grasping for pleasure for oneself. (540a 24)

155. Even if one is worthy of [rebirth in heaven which is] the result of great merit (*mahāpuṇyavipāka*) one's heart should not be uplifted or elated. Even if one is in need like a hungry ghost (*preta*) one should not be downcast or sad. (540b 1)

148. Cf. *Kāśyapaparivarta,* §23.

149. The commentary to this verse is translated *Traité,* p. 1228, q.v. – See also *Kāśyapaparivarta,* §§63-65, quoted *Prasannapadā,* p. 248.

150. On *vandanā* and *pūjā* see *Śikṣāsamuccaya,* XVII.

152. For *avetyaprasāda, Vimalakīrtinirdeśa,* p. 99, n. 8; May (1959), p. 219, n. 744. – Correct *qù* in *pāda* a to *fā*.

153. This amounts to *anupalambhaśūnyatā,* cf. *Traité,* p. 2035.

156. If there are some who are fully disciplined (*śikṣita*) they must be paid full respect. Those who are not yet disciplined should enter the discipline (*śikṣā*) and must not be objects of contempt. (540b 6)

157. Those whose good conduct (*śīla*) is perfect should be respected. If [they] violate good conduct (*śīla*) they should return to [the practice of] *śīla*. Those whose wisdom (*jñāna*) is perfect [should be] approached as friends. Those who are dull should be established in wisdom (*jñāna*). (540b 10)

158. The suffering (*duḥkha*) of *saṃsāra* is manifold: Birth (*jāti*), old age (*jarā*), death (*maraṇa*) and bad rebirth (*durgati*). But do not fear such perils (*bhaya*)! Conquer Māra and bad understanding (*dauṣprajñā*). (540b 17)

159. Gather all the virtues (*guṇa*) in all the Buddha-fields (*kṣetra*). In order that all attain them one must make lofty vows (*praṇidhāna*) and efforts (*vīrya*). (540b 22)

160. Always with regard to things (*dharma*) one should not appropriate them but give them up – this is to accept the burden and take over responsibility for the sake of all living beings. (540b 28)

161. One who correctly examines (*samyakparīkṣā*) all phenomena (*dharma*) [sees] that there is no ego (*aham*) and no mine (*mama*). Still he does not abandon great compassion (*mahākaruṇā*) and great kindness (*mahāmaitrī*). (540c 6)

162. One must surpass all worship (*pūjā*) in order to worship the Buddha Bhagavat. Of what nature is this (*pūjā*)? It is the so-called *dharmapūjā* – (540c 15)

163. If one grasps the *bodhisattvapiṭaka* and obtains the various *dhāraṇī* while penetrating the profound (*gambhīra*) foundation of [all] dharmas – *that* is the *dharmapūjā*! (540c 23)

157. Apparently inspired by the *Ratnamegha*, cited SS, 183b 6-7, q.v.

159. For *buddhakṣetra*, cf. the ref. in *Vimalakīrtinirdeśa*, p. 461.

160. This is neatly summarized RĀ, IV, 96: *śūnyatākaruṇāgarbham ekeṣāṃ bodhisādhanam* (cf. *Prasannapadā*, p. 360, v.l.).

162. For *dharmapūjā*, *Vimalakīrtinirdeśa*, pp. 377-382.

163. This verse echoes *Vimalakīrtinirdeśa*, p. 378. – See, *ibid.*, n. 18 for the meaning of *bodhisattvapiṭaka*.

164. One should hold to the main thing (*artha*) and not just prefer various articulations (*vyañjana*). One must enter the profound path of the dharma with joy and not show any heedlessness (*pramāda*). (541a 10)

165. When ascetics (*pravrajita*) and householders (*gṛhastha*) have collected these collections (*saṃbhāra*) for great aeons (*mahākalpa*) numerous as the sands of Ganges they shall attain perfect enlightenment (*samyaksaṃbodhi*)! (541a 22)

164. Here *wèi* renders *vyañjana* (one of the four *pratisaraṇa*), cf. de Jong's remarks in *The Eastern Buddhist*, XIII, p. 157.

The unity of Nāgārjuna's thought

The purpose of the following pages is to present a synthesis of the tenets of Nāgārjuna's philosophy and its presuppositions. Any such attempt must be preceded by a brief sketch of the historical background if the proper perspective is not to be distorted. Without, of course, wishing to appear disparaging of previous efforts to present a survey of Madhyamaka I do, however, think that the two circumstances warrant a novel exposition of the Madhyamaka system forged by Nāgārjuna.[191] First, previous accounts of his thinking have only been based on the testimony provided by a few of Nāgārjuna's works. Secondly, and to some extent an outcome of the first, these discussions tend to present his philosophy as a series of more or less coherent and sensible ideas concerning various epistemological, logical or ontological issues. Nevertheless, in my view, an attentive perusal of Nāgārjuna's authentic writings will show that his extraordinary genius succeeded in blending a great mass of inherited moral, religious and philosophical ideas into a harmonious whole. If we had to condense his system in all its aspects to one single term we should choose *bodhisādhana* (not e.g. *śūnyatā* or *pratītyasamutpāda*).

By recognizing this (i.e. *bodhisādhana* = *puṇyajñānasaṃbhāra*) to be the heading under which all his various theories and injunctions are unified we shall, moreover, have brought ourselves in a better position to appraise each of his writings in relation to others and within its own confines.[192]

191. For previous expositions see the works referred to above n. 1, and La Vallée Poussin: 'Réflexions sur le Madhyamaka', *MCB*, II, pp. 1-59; P. Tuxen, *Indledende bemærkninger til buddhistisk relativisme,* København 1936.

192. Some remarks on this p. 265. Here much remains for 'higher criticism'.

I. Background

a) *Non-Buddhist*

While Nāgārjuna was, of course, aware of the existence of various 'heretical' *darśanas* such as Sāṃkhya, Vaiśeṣika, Jaina,[193] Nyāya,[194] Lokāyata,[195] *Īśvaravāda[196] and probably also many other sectarians, their influence upon the development of his thought virtually comes to nought. Doubtless his study of Nyāya, and, I suppose, Vaiśeṣika, provoked his endeavour to match the former's notion of *apavarga* to the Buddhist *nirvāṇa* and the latter's *abhyudaya/naiḥśreyasa* to his own *sukha/mokṣa.*[197] A similar attitude is observable in his attempt to absorb the deities of popular religion, Brahmā, Indra, Viṣṇu, Rudra etc. by interpreting them as emanations of the Buddha.[198] We never find any trace of positive influence from these sources in Nāgārjuna's authentic writings.

On the other hand it must be conceded that he could not escape the impact which orthodox Brahmin dialectics (*vāda*), natural philosophy, arts, crafts and sciences indirectly exerted upon the Buddhist milieu. Allusions to *cikitsā, śilpa, vidyā, kalā* and various worldly śāstras (BS, 79) indicate the wide scope of his erudition, and here on the level of 'empirical sciences' he obviously did not hesitate to make the best of traditional Hindu lore as means conducive to temporal happiness (*abhyudaya*).[199]

Let us finally not be oblivious of a circumstance so obvious that it may easily be overlooked. From his birth to his death Nāgārjuna

193. See RĀ, I, 61. – For an extensive critique of these schools one has to turn to the writings of Āryadeva.
194. In VP (ed. Kajiyama), p. 148 Nāgārjuna refers to the spokesmen of this school as the *rigs pa phra ba'i phyogs su lhuṅ ba.* I think that they are identical with the *Naya-sauma known from Chinese sources, v. Tucci (1929), p. xxviii; Ui (1917), p. 55, n. 3. (Surely Chinese *xiū mó* ~ Tib. *phra ba,* probably Sanskrit *sūkṣma.*).
195. RĀ, III, 68 refers to Lokāyata (or Lokāyatika, Tib. *'jig rten rgyaṅ pan*). They are frequently criticized in the *Laṅkāvatārasūtra,* see Suzuki's *Index,* p. 150. Their identity is not very clear.
196. Cf. CS, III, 34 with ref. (also Suzuki's *Index,* p. 45).
197. See VP (ed. Kajiyama), p. 155; RĀ, I, 3-4; III, 30.
198. BV, 77-78; YṢ, 28.
199. Endorsing traditional Hindu learning at the level of *saṃvṛtisatya* Nāgārjuna is in fact merely following an ideal generally advocated in Mahāyāna scriptures, cf. *Buddhāvataṃsakasūtra* cited SS, 251b and BS, 79 with ref.

must as a member of the community have received an incessant flow of impressions and convictions, prejudices and superstitions from the Hindu society surrounding him. This forms a part of his background which was never recorded and for an assessment of which no sources are available to us.

b) *Buddhist: Tripiṭaka*

Nāgārjuna's writings give ample evidence of his acquaintance not only with the sūtras of Mahāyāna but also with the Sūtras, Vinaya and Abhidharma of Hīnayāna, or as he invariably puts it conscious of the variances between the three vehicles: Bodhisattvayāna versus Śrāvaka- and Pratyekabuddhayāna.

Before considering the features which distinguish Mahāyāna from Hīnayāna it may be useful to recall the fundamentals of the Dharma propounded in the ancient sūtras.[200]

The historical Buddha himself, once enlightened (*buddha*), had no other wish than to impart to others a method (*mārga*) conducive to the attainment of deliverance (*mokṣa*) from the cycle of birth and death (*saṃsāra*), i.e. from *duḥkha.* The conviction that our life in a *gati* in *saṃsāra* without beginning in time solely depends upon our previous volitional actions (*karma*) he shared with numerous contemporary śramaṇas. The conviction that adherence to such a life was the source of nothing but *duḥkha,* and the idea that nothing could be deemed more desirable for living beings than to obtain extinction (*nirvāṇa*) from the life-process he also shared with many other contemporaries. It was in regard to the method (*mārga*) devised for escape and, surely – if we read between the lines – by virtue of his impressive personality as a teacher of 'gods and men' that the Buddha stood out among contemporary preachers with fundamentally the same presuppositions in such a way as to appeal mainly to the upper strata of society. His was a *mārga* for *āryas*, not a popular religion for *pṛthagjanas*, the *profanum vulgus*.

As said, his entire social life was devoted to teaching the *mārga* to monks and laymen. He never tired of re-formulating it from new

200. This survey is an attempt to give the gist of the Tripiṭaka, and is above all based on the testimony of the sūtras. In the majority of cases I refer to the Pāli canon as it is the most convenient to consult (Nāgārjuna, of course, used a Sanskrit recension).

and different angles according to the demands of circumstances and invariably with a keen perception of the capacities and inclinations of his proselytes. Though he surely enhanced his pedagogical experience the theory behind his teachings remained unchanged throughout his life. It is *kleśas* that motivate living beings to that karma which keeps the wheel of life turning, above all *rāga, dveṣa* and *moha*.

As the Dharma gradually gained ground and, with it, the Saṃgha, rules for the regulation of the daily life of the monks came into demand. Hence the origin of the Vinaya, the collection of monastic rules. From a doctrinal point of view they add nothing to the Dharma propounded in the collections of Sūtras. It is hardly surprising to find that the rules codified in the Vinaya of the various schools may vary in a number of instances due to geographical and other circumstances. The one referred to by Nāgārjuna seems to have been that of the Mūlasarvāstivādins.

The origins of the third *piṭaka* is to be sought in the sūtras themselves, or rather, in my opinion, with the Buddha himself. Abhidharma originally marked an attempt to group all the positive, negative and neutral dharmas familiar from the discourses of the Master systematically so as to permit the monks studying in seclusion to gain a survey of these. Through the exercise and gradual development of his intellectual faculty (*prajñā*)[201] the monk was thus enabled in a most rationalized manner to become thoroughly conversant with those dharmas to be developed and those to be abandoned. So, while the ingenious device laid down in Abhidharma on one hand had the advantage of forming, so to speak, a highway to *mokṣa,* its abstract and systematic spirit did, on the other, inevitably embody a tendency to dogmatism, an attitude which, in the end, was to render it unfaithful to the original intention of its founder. In the course of time some of the best Buddhist minds contributed to the vigorous development of Abhidharma, a development which reached its peak about the time of Nāgārjuna with the compilation of the magnificent thesaurus of Buddhist lore, the *Mahāvibhāṣā* of Sarvāstivāda. It was, as we shall see, a profound resentment against the prevailing and somewhat complacent tendency to dogmatism, or

201. For the *trividhā prajñā*, v. *Dīgha*, III, p. 219. *Vibhaṅga*, p. 324; *Dharmasaṃgraha*, §110. See also PED, s.v. *paññā* ('intellect as conversant with general truths').

'clinging', among Ābhidhārmikas that induced Nāgārjuna to adopt the non-dogmatic spirit breathing in the Prajñāpāramitāsūtras and regenerate it, as it were, among the renegades.

The fact that, as the Buddha himself phrased it, *ayaṃ dhammavinayo ekaraso vimuttiraso*[202] also accounts for his characteristic and outspoken opposition to speculative and dogmatic theories not lending themselves to personal experience and ratification. The Buddha's deliberate ἐποχή towards current 'metaphysical' *antadvayadṛṣṭi* had a decisive impact upon Nāgārjuna, and I will conclude this survey by collecting some of these and other passages from the ancient sūtras which were to be formative of his philosophical thinking.

i) It was in his celebrated sermon at Benares that the Buddha first preached the Four Noble Truths: The life of the individual (= the five *upādānaskandha*) is sheer *duḥkha*. Its origin (*samudaya*) is *tṛṣṇā*, the will to life. (Note that strictly speaking this only gives a simplified 'exoteric' account of *duḥkhasamudaya*. The real cause is *avidyā*). The purpose of human life is its *nirodha*, i.e. Nirvāṇa. The Buddha shows a path (a method) to *nirodha*, i.e. the eightfold, further reducible to *śīla*, *samādhi* and *prajñā*. – This provides us with the motive, the cause, the purpose and the method of Buddhism *in nuce*.

Here I quote the recension Nāgārjuna is most likely to have known, that of the Mūlasarvāstivādins.[203] His own paraphrase occurs SL, 113-115:[204]

1. ... *catvārīmāni bhikṣava āryasatyāni; katamāni catvāri? duḥkham āryasatyam, duḥkhasamudayo duḥkhanirodho duḥkhanirodhagāminī pratipad āryasatyam. duḥkham āryasatyam katamat? jātir duḥkham, jarā duḥkham, vyādhir duḥkham, maraṇaṃ duḥkham, priyaviprayogo duḥkham, apriyasaṃprayogo duḥkham, yad apicchan paryeṣamāṇo na labhate tad api duḥkham; saṃkṣepataḥ pañca ime upādānaskandhā duḥkham; tasya parijñāyai āryāṣṭāṅgo mārgo bhāvayitavyaḥ. duḥkhasamudayam āryasatyaṃ katamat? tṛṣṇā paunarbhavikī nandīrāgasahagatā tatra tatrābhinandinī; tasyāḥ prahāṇāya āryāṣṭāṅgo mārgo bhāvayitavyaḥ. duḥkhanirodham āryasatyaṃ katamat? yad asyā eva tṛṣṇāyāḥ*

202. *Aṅguttara*, IV, p. 203; *Udāna*, p. 56; *Vinaya*, II, p. 239.
203. Cited from R. Gnoli, *The Gilgit Manuscript of the Saṅghabhedavastu*, Roma 1977, pp. 137-138. (This ed. is in need of numerous corrections.)
204. TP, No. 5682, 289a-289b (also TP, No. 5409 with minor variants).

paunarbhavikyā nandīrāgasahagatāyās tatra tatrābhinandinyā aśeṣaprahāṇaṃ pratinisargo vāntībhāvaḥ kṣayo virāgo nirodho vyupaśamaḥ astaṃgamaḥ; tasya sākṣātkriyāyai āryāṣṭāṅgo mārgo bhāvayitavyaḥ. duḥkhanirodhagāminī pratipad āryasatyaṃ katamat? āryāṣṭāṅgo mārgaḥ – tadyathā, samyagdṛṣṭiḥ, samyaksaṃkalpaḥ, samyagvāk, samyakkarmāntaḥ, samyagājīvaḥ, samyagvyāyāmaḥ, samyaksmṛtiḥ, samyaksamādhiḥ; so 'pi bhāvayitavyaḥ ...

2. SL, 113-115.

| yaṅ dag lta daṅ 'tsho daṅ rtsol ba daṅ |
| dran daṅ tiṅ 'dzin ṅag daṅ las mtha' daṅ |
| yaṅ dag rtog ñid lam gyi yan lag brgyad |
| 'di ni źi bar bgyi slad bsgom par bgyi |

| skye 'di sdug bsṅal sred pa źes bgyi ba |
| de ni 'di yi kun 'byuṅ rgya chen te |
| 'di 'gog pa ni thar pa lags te lam |
| de thob 'phags lam yan lag de brgyad lags |

| de ltar 'phags pa'i bden pa bźi po dag |
| mthoṅ bar bgyi slad rtag tu brtson par bgyi |
| paṅ na dpal gnas khyim pa rnams kyis kyaṅ |
| śes pas ñon moṅs chu bo las brgal bgyi |

ii) No less celebrated but far more intricate is the Buddha's teaching of the *dvādaśāṅgapratīyasamutpāda*. The purpose of this formula is to explain the genesis (*samudaya*) of *duḥkha*. The author himself spoke of it as the *dharmo gambhīro gambhīrāvabhāso durdṛśo duravabodho 'tarkyo 'tarkyāvacaraḥ sūkṣmo nipuṇapaṇḍitavijñavedanīyaḥ* ... – It is, so to speak, the 'esoteric' account of *duḥkhasamudaya*.[205]

Ancient and modern attempts to interpret this enigmatic formula are not lacking. [206] That it was a matter of deep concern to

205. Gnoli, *op.cit.*, p. 128; cf. *Traité*, p. 35, n. 2. – The two different canonical accounts of *duḥkhasamudaya* are, in my view, not to be regarded as more or less inconsistent or incompatible. The former, or 'exoteric', is usually given to an audience unacquainted with the Buddha's Dharma, the latter, or 'esoteric' to monks well versed in the Dharma. Thus they are simply expressions of the Buddha's '*upāyakauśalya*'.

206. See ref. in May, *op. cit.*, p. 251, n. 1, and the late F. Bernhard: 'Zur Inter-

Nāgārjuna is seen most clearly in PK and ŚS. The significance of the principle of *pratītyasamutpāda* in its extended general sense is evident from all his writings. MK, XXVI and SL, 109-112 reproduce the traditional list of the twelve *nidānas* beginning with *avidyā*, ending with *duḥkha*.

1.

...idam evaṃ dvādaśāṅgaṃ pratītyasamutpādam anulomapratilomaṃ vyavalokayan, yaduta asmin satīdaṃ bhavati, asyotpādād idam utpadyate – yadutāvidyāpratyayāḥ saṃskārāḥ, saṃskārapratyayaṃ vijñānam, vijñānapratyayaṃ nāmarūpam, nāmarūpapratyayaṃ ṣaḍāyatanaṃ, ṣaḍāyatanapratyayaḥ sparśaḥ, sparśapratyayā vedanā, vedanāpratyayā tṛṣṇā, tṛṣṇāpratyayam upādānam, upādānapratyayo bhavaḥ, bhavapratyayā jātiḥ, jātipratyayā jarāmaraṇaśokaparidevaduḥkhadaurmanasyopāyāsā amī bhavanti; evam asya kevalasya mahato duḥkhaskandhasya samudayo bhavati; yaduta asminn asatīdaṃ na bhavati, asya nirodhād idaṃ nirudhyate – yaduta avidyānirodhāt saṃskāranirodhaḥ ...[207]

2. SL, 109-111.

| ma rig pa las las te de las ni |
| rnam śes de las miṅ daṅ gzugs rab 'byuṅ |
| de las skye mched drug ste de dag las |
| reg pa kun tu 'byuṅ bar thub pas gsuṅs |

| reg pa las ni tshor ba kun 'byuṅ ste |
| tshor ba'i gźi las sred pa 'byuṅ bar 'gyur |
| sred pas len pa bskyed par 'gyur ba ste |
| de las srid pa srid las skye ba lags |

| skye ba yod na mya ṅan na rga daṅ |
| 'dod pas 'phoṅs daṅ 'chi bas 'jigs sogs kyi |
| sdug bsṅal phuṅ po śin tu che byuṅ ste |
| skye ba 'gag pas 'di kun 'gag par 'gyur |

pretation der Pratītyasamutpāda-Formel', *WZKSO*, XII-XIII, pp. 53-63.

207. Gnoli, *op.cit.*, p. 127. – SL, 109-111 cited from TP, No. 5682, 289a (also TP, No. 5409 with insignificant variants).

iii) Nirvāṇa was really nothing but *duḥkhanirodha*, either with skandhas (= *duḥkha*) remaining (*sopadhiśeṣanirvāṇa*) or without any skandhas remaining (*nirpadhiśeṣanirvāṇa*), i.e. deliverance from future birth. This state of psycho-somatic peace may, however, be considered from various conventional angles:[208]

Psychologically it is *kleśakṣaya* barely different from the Stoic ideal of ἀπάθεια. Thus SS, 221a cites *Saṃyuktāgama: ... dge sloṅ dag khyed la mya ṅan las 'das pa daṅ | mya ṅan las 'da' bar 'gro ba'i lam bśad par bya'o || de la mya naṅ las 'das pa gaṅ źe na | 'di lta ste | 'dod chags zad pa daṅ | źe sdaṅ zad pa daṅ | gti mug zad pa'o || ...* cf. *Saṃyutta*, IV, p. 371: *... nibbānañ ca vo bhikkhave desissāmi nibbānagāmiñ ca maggaṃ ... rāgakkhayo dosakkhayo mohakkhayo ...*

Ontologically it is a world beyond *saṃsāra*. SL, 105 alludes to the well-known passage from *Udāna*, p. 80: ... *atthi, bhikkhave, tad āyatanaṃ yattha neva paṭhavī na āpo na tejo na vāyo na ākāsānañcāyatanaṃ na viññāṇañcāyatanaṃ na akiñcaññāyatanaṃ na nevasaññānāsaññāyatanaṃ nāyaṃ loko na paraloko na ubho candimasuriyā. tatrāpāhaṃ, bhikkhave, neva āgatiṃ vadāmi na gatiṃ na ṭhitiṃ na cutiṃ na upapattiṃ; appatiṭṭhaṃ appavattaṃ anārammaṇaṃ evetaṃ – esevanto dukkhassā ti.*

SL, 105.
| tshul khrims dag daṅ śes rab bsam gtan gyis |
| mya ṅan 'das źi dul ba dri med pa'i |
| go 'phaṅ mi rga mi 'chi zad mi 'tshal |
| sa chu me rluṅ ñi zla bral thob mdzod |

Epistemologically (sometimes barely distinguished from the abovementioned points of view) one may say that *paramaṃ ariyasaccaṃ yadidaṃ amosadhammaṃ nibbānaṃ* (*Majjhima*, III, p. 245, cf. YṢ, 35). Nevertheless it cannot be an object of the senses or of consciousness. Nāgārjuna alludes to *Dīgha*, I, p. 223 in YṢ, 34 (q.v.) and RĀ, I, 93-95.[209]

208. Cf. recently R. E. A. Johansson, *The Psychology of Nirvana*, New York 1970; G. R. Welbon, *The Buddhist Nirvāṇa and its Western Interpreters*, Chicago 1968; J. W. Boyd: 'The Theravāda View of Samsara', in *Buddhist Studies in honour of Walpola Rahula*, London 1980, pp. 29-43. – SL, 105 cited from TP, No. 5682, 288b-289a (also TP, No. 5409 with slight variants).

209. TP, No. 5658, 133a-133b. – Note that Pāli *sabbatopaha* (v. PED, p. 448 and *Majjhima*, I, p. 329) is rendered by Tib *kun tu bdag po*. But *-paha* is

viññāṇaṃ anidassanaṃ anantaṃ sabbatopahaṃ
ettha āpo ca paṭhavī tejo vāyo na gādhati
ettha dīghañ ca rassañ ca anuṃ thūlaṃ subhāsubhaṃ
ettha nāmañ ca rūpañ ca asesaṃ uparujjhati
viññāṇassa nirodhena etth'etaṃ uparujjhati

| sa daṅ chu daṅ me daṅ rluṅ || riṅ thuṅ phra daṅ sbom ñid daṅ |
| dge sogs ñid ni rnam śes su || 'gag par 'gyur źes thub pas gsuṅs |

| rnam śes bstan med mtha' yas pa || kun tu bdag po de la ni |
| sa daṅ chu daṅ me daṅ ni || rluṅ gi gnas thos 'gyur ma yin |

| 'dir ni riṅ daṅ thuṅ ba daṅ || phra sbom dge daṅ mi dge daṅ |
| 'dir ni miṅ daṅ gzugs dag kyaṅ || ma lus par ni 'gag par 'gyur |

iv) The initial *nidāna* of *duḥkha* (= *skandha*) is, as we saw, *avidyā*, which is not merely lack or absence of knowledge but positively, *amitravat*, more or less a synonym of *abhiniveśa, dṛṣṭi, kalpanā* or *grāha*, (cf. e.g. *Dhammasaṅgaṇi*, p. 213 which Nāgārjuna may have had in mind *ad* ŚS, 64, q.v.). It may have various objects (v. *Dhammasaṅgaṇi*, p. 190), and according to the *Pratītyasamutpādasūtra* (quoted *Prasannapadā*, p. 452, ad MK, XXIII, 1, q.v.) it also has a cause: ... *avidyāpi bhikṣavaḥ sahetukā sapratyayā sanidānā. kaś ca bhikṣavaḥ avidyāyā hetuḥ? ayoniśo bhikṣavo manaskāro 'vidyāyā hetuḥ. āvilo mohajo manaskāro bhikṣavo 'vidyāyā hetuḥ. (ity ato 'vidyā saṃkalpaprabhavā bhavati*).

More specifically *avidyā* is due to the four *viparyāsas* (ŚS, 10, q.v.). The canonical passages are scarce, e.g. *Aṅguttara*, II, p. 52: ... *anicce bhikkhave niccan ti saññāvipallāso cittavipallāso diṭṭhivipallāso, adukkhe bhikkhave dukkhan ti saññāvipallāso cittavipallāso diṭṭhivipallāso, anattani bhikkhave attā ti saññāvipallāso cittavipallāso diṭṭhivipallāso, asubhe bhikkhave subhan ti saññāvipallāso cittavipallāso diṭṭhivipallāso* ... (cf. *Vibhaṅga*, p. 376; SL, 48; MK, XXIII, *passim; Kośa*, V, p. 21 (ref.)).

I venture to think that we here have a clue to one of the most puzzling apophthegms in the ancient canonical texts, viz. '*Kātyāyanāvavāda*' referred to MK, XV, 7 q.v. This sūtra proposes to define *samyagdṛṣṭi*, cf. *Saṃyutta*, II, p. 17: ... *dvayanissito khvāyaṃ Kaccāyana loko yebhuyyena atthitañ ceva natthitañ ca. lokasamudayaṃ kho Kaccāyana yathābhūtaṃ sammappaññāya passato yā loke natthitā sā na hoti; lokanirodhaṃ kho*

surely *-prabha* as often in BHS. (Cf. also de Jong, *Buddhist Studies*, Berkeley 1979, p. 49.)

Kaccāyana yathābhūtaṃ sammappaññāya passato yā loke atthitā sā na hoti ... sabbam atthīti kho Kaccāyana ayam eko anto, sabbaṃ natthīti ayaṃ dutiyo anto ...[210]

These canonical extracts provided Nāgārjuna with his fundamental philosophical outlook: *duḥkha* (= *skandha*) is due to *avidyā*, which again is a result of the activity of the *viparyāsas*. These four are, in the final analysis, founded upon the assumption of *asti* and *nāsti*. This dichotomy is, as it were, the πρῶτον ψεῦδος of the cycle of life (*saṃsāra*).[211]

Nāgārjuna arrived at this position from a desire to achieve a consistent exegetical result of his study of the Buddha's doctrine recorded in the scriptures.[212] In the eyes of Nāgārjuna the Buddha was not merely a forerunner but the very founder of the Madhyamaka system. It would be a rewarding task but also extend the limits of the present inquiry to consider to what extent his opinion was historically justified.

v) Among the four *viparyāsas* the third: *anātmani ātmā iti* is the gravest and most basic. It consists in a *vikalpa* which imposes a self (*ahaṃkāra,* Tib. bdag tu 'dzin pa) upon the five skandhas taken collectively or separately. It is also called *satkāyadṛṣṭi* and may as such take twenty different forms (cf. SL, 49 and ref. *Traité*, p. 737, n. 3). RĀ, I, 31-35 has its counterpart *Saṃyutta*, III, p. 105:[213]

1.
... seyyathāpi āvuso Ānanda itthi vā puriso vā daharo yuvā maṇḍanakajātiko ādāse vā parisuddhe pariyodāte acche vā udakapatte sakaṃ mukhanimittaṃ paccavekkhamāno upādāya passeya no anupādāya, evaṃ eva kho āvuso Ānanda rūpaṃ upādāya asmīti hoti no anupādāya ... vedanaṃ ... saññaṃ ... saṃkhāre ... viññāṇaṃ upādāya asmīti hoti no anupādāya ...

210. For further references and a discussion of this passage see Hōbōgirin, s.v. *Chūdō,* especially p. 459. Also *Dhammasaṅgaṇi*, p. 16.

211. Cf. YS, 1; MK, XV, 10; RĀ, I, 38 etc. – See also the discussion about the fourteen *avyākṛtavastūni* in Murti, *op. cit.*, pp. 36-54. Also May, *op. cit.*, p. 277, n. 1015. – In the final analysis they are based on the assumption of *asti* or *nāsti*.

212. This is quite decisive. Nāgārjuna is not a 'free-thinker' but primarily a Buddhist patriarch with uncompromising faith in the Dharma, cf. BS, 61-62; 123-127.

213. Cf. BV, 61-62; PK, 5.

2.

yathādarśam upādāya svamukhapratibimbakam |
dṛśyate nāma tac caiva na kiṃ cid api tattvataḥ ||
ahaṃkāras tathā skandhān upādāyopalabhyate |
na ca kiṃ cit sa tattvena svamukhapratibimbakam ||
evaṃvidhārthaśravaṇād dharmacakṣur avāptavān |
āryānandaḥ svayaṃ caiva bhikṣubhyo 'bhikṣṇam uktavān ||
(skandhagrāho yāvad asti tāvad evāham ity api |
ahaṃkāre sati punaḥ karma janma tataḥ punaḥ ||*)*

3.

... rūpaṃ nātmā rūpavān nāpi cātmā rūpe nātmā nātmani rūpam ... evaṃ yāvad vijñānaṃ nātmā vijñānavān nātmā vijñāne nātmā nātmani vijñānam iti ... tathā anātmānaḥ sarvadharmā iti ...[214]

4.

SL, 48-49.
| mi ni yaṅ dag ñid du mi bde źiṅ |
| mi rtag bdag med mi gtsaṅ rig par bgyi |
| dran pa ñe bar ma gźag rnams kyis ni |
| phyin ci log bźir lta ba 'phuṅ bkrol ba |

| gzugs ni bdag ma yin źes gsuṅ ste bdag |
| gzugs daṅ ldan min gzugs la bdag gnas min |
| bdag la gzugs mi gnas te de bźin du |
| phuṅ po lhag ma bźi yaṅ stoṅ rtogs bgyi |

vi) Ancient Buddhism – and Hīnayāna – denied the existence of a permanent *ātman.* Instead it acknowledged the five skandhas which, like all other phenomena (*dharma*) are characterized by three *lakṣaṇas,* viz. *anitya, duḥkha* and *anātman.* Mahāyāna went further: In the final analysis the skandhas are no less illusory than the notion of an *ātman.* Though this was scarcely in accordance with the stage of

214. Sanskrit *Prasannapadā,* p. 355; *Subhāṣitasaṃgraha* (ed. Bendall), p. 394; *Dhammasaṅgaṇi,* p. 220; *Mahāvyutpatti,* § CCIX. – The following verses SL, 48-49 quoted from TP, No. 5682, 285b (also TP, No. 5409 without significant variants).

development reached in the ancient sūtras they nevertheless adumbrated the advent of Mahāyāna, above all in the pregnant stanzas of *Saṃyuktāgama* on which BV, 12-13 (q.v.) are based.[215]

phenapiṇḍopamaṃ rūpaṃ vedanā budbudopamā |
marīcisadṛśī saṃjñā saṃskārāḥ kadalīnibhāḥ |
māyopamaṃ ca vijñānam uktam ādityabandhunā ||
evaṃ dharmān vīkṣamāṇo bhikṣur ārabdhavīryavān |
divā vā yadi vā rātrau saṃprajānan pratismṛtaḥ |
pratividhyet padaṃ śāntaṃ saṃskāropaśamaṃ śivam ||

c) *Buddhist: Mahāyāna*

Despite an increasing number of modern contributions to the study of Mahāyāna sūtras our knowledge of the historical origins of this developed form of Buddhism still remains meagre and fragmentary and will, for all one can say, do so for decades to come.[216] Fortunately this circumstance barely has any decisive effect upon our understanding of Nāgārjuna as an exponent of Mahāyāna.[217] On the contrary, the fact that he is the first individual known to have collected the sūtras of the new school and systematized their teachings provides us not only with a *terminus ante quem* for more than three scores of sūtras but also with valuable textual and exegetical materials. As we have seen Nāgārjuna's SS is a collection of extracts culled largely from sūtras belonging to Mahāyāna. In addition CS and BS contain numerous allusions to, or even quotations from, these texts.[218]

In general, one may conclude that Nāgārjuna was thoroughly conversant with the ancient Tripiṭaka as well as the more recent

215. Frequently cited, here from *Prasannapadā*, p. 41. On *śūnyatā* in the ancient sūtras v. *Traité*, pp. 1079-1081; 2140-2144 (with ref.). Pāli, *Saṃyutta*, III, p. 142. – Cf.above all *Akṣayamatinirdeśa*, Bu *fol.* 125 a 6–126 a 6.

216. Very useful is H. Nakamura: 'A Survey of Mahāyāna Buddhism with bibliographical Notes. Part I: Mahāyāna Sūtras', in *The Journal of Intercultural Studies*, III, pp. 60-145. Speaking of Har Dayal, *The Bodhisattva doctrine in Buddhist Sanskrit literature*, Nakamura says: 'Probably the best critical study of the textual evidence dealing with the career of the Bodhisattva.' I agree.

217. It would, of course, be interesting to pose the question: Is Nāgārjuna a faithful exponent of Mahāyāna? But it is impossible to answer it at present.

218. I have done my best to locate these but much remains to be done.

developed sūtras of Mahāyāna. Without ever breaking radically with the ancient tradition these scriptures launched new ideas about the nature of the world (*śūnyatā*) and the foundation of ethical behaviour (*karuṇā*), and in Nāgārjuna they found a staunch supporter.

The main source of inspiration for his *magnum opus,* MK, with the subtitle *Prajñā,* is that group of Mahāyāna scriptures commonly known as *Prajñāpāramitāsūtras.*[219] As Yasunori Ejima puts it: 'The *Madhyamaka-kārikā* starts with and aims at nothing other than *prajñāpārāramitā* or perfect wisdom.'[220] Nāgārjuna's *ipsissima verba* prove that of these texts he knew at least *Aṣṭasāhasrikā, Saptaśatikā* and *Vajracchedikā.*[221]

If one were to condense the tenets of the Prajñāpāramitā literature into a few sentences it would perhaps amount to this: Their *view of the world* is that fundamentally all phenomena (*dharma*) are void of substance, i.e. illusory or empty. Their *view of the individual* is that as a bodhisattva gradually recognizing this fact one should, accordingly, live in the equanimity of universal emptiness, and, at the same time, through compassion, devote oneself to the task of liberating all other beings without scorning any means for the achievement of that ideal (*upāyakauśalya*).[222]

Naturally, in the course of time, the deepened conception of the world led to novel developments within the field of ontology and epistemology. The widened view of the human situation likewise inspired a flourishing movement in the field of religion and ethics. All this gave room for the work of independent thinkers, and for

219. In this field we are indebted to the work of the late Edward Conze, v. his useful bibliography in *The Prajñāpāramitā Literature,* Tokyo 1978. See also L. Lancaster (ed.), *Prajñāpāramitā and related systems. Studies in honor of Edward Conze,* Berkeley 1977.

220. Y. Ejima, *Chūgan-shisō no tenkai, Bhāvaviveka kenkyū,* Tokyo 1980, p. 495.

221. He quotes from these in SS, v. the list nos. 36, 47 and 63.

222. Cf. Conze's summary, *loc. cit.,* p. 15: 'The thousands of lines of the *Prajñāpāramitā* can be summed up in the following two sentences: 1) One should become a Bodhisattva (or Buddha-to-be), i.e. one who is content with nothing less than all-knowledge attained through the perfection of wisdom for the sake of all living beings. 2) There is no such thing as a Bodhisattva, or as all-knowledge, or as a 'being', or as the perfection of wisdom, or as an attainment. To accept both these contradictory facts is to be perfect.' Cf. *ibid.* for 'new ideas' in these *sūtras* (*tathatā, upāyakauśalya* and *puṇyapariṇāmanā*).

this reason it often proves advantageous to centre the study of Mahāyāna around its individual representatives.

Here, however, we must confine our investigation to Nāgārjuna himself. Several passages in RĀ show that he was well aware of the features distinguishing the large *yāna* from the less comprehensive one, and moreover, of the sustained opposition aroused by the prevalence of such divergences.[223]

i) First of all Mahāyāna and Hīnayāna differ in their outlook of the world. They both endorse *śūnyatā* as a fundamental feature of existence (one of the three *lakṣaṇas*) preached by the Buddha. But according to Mahāyāna this term indicates 'non-origination' i.e. the fact that all phenomena lack *svabhāva,* whereas Hīnayāna simply takes it as a synonym of impermanence (similarly MK, XIII, 3-4ab, q.v.):

IV, 86ab.
anutpādo mahāyāne pareṣāṃ śūnyatā kṣayaḥ |

ii) The ancient scriptures do not mention concepts specific to Mahāyāna such as the vows for enlightenment (*praṇidhāna*), the bodhisattva's practice (*caryā*) of the *pāramitās,* his dedication of the merit thus achieved (*puṇyapariṇāmanā*) and his extraordinary powers (*adhiṣṭhāna,* cf. BHSD, s.v.). Therefore they do not provide sufficient guidance for the achievement of *bodhi:*

IV, 90-91ab.
na bodhisattvapraṇidhir na caryāpariṇāmanā |
uktāḥ śrāvakayāne 'smād bodhisattvaḥ kutas tataḥ ||
adhiṣṭhānāni noktāni bodhisattvasya bodhaye |

Nor do the ancient texts speak of a bodhisattva's perseverance (*pratiṣṭhā* = *prasthāna,* cf. *Bodhicaryāvatāra,* I, 15) in his *bodhicaryā:*

IV, 93.
bodhicaryāpratiṣṭhārthaṃ na sūtre bhāṣitaṃ vacaḥ |
bhāṣitaṃ ca mahāyāne grāhyam asmād vicakṣaṇaiḥ ||

223. See below and BS, 24-27. Cf. Har Dayal, *op.cit.,* pp. 1-29.

Moreover, the notion of *puṇya-* and *jñānasaṃbhāra* characteristic of Mahāyāna is still an object of critique or neglect on the part of the adherents of Hīnayāna:

IV,67.
bodhisattvasya saṃbhāro mahāyāne tathāgataiḥ |
nirdiṣṭaḥ sa tu sammūḍhaiḥ pradviṣṭaiś caiva nindyate ||

IV, 83.
puṇyajñānamayo yatra buddhair bodher mahāpathaḥ |
deśitas tan mahāyānam ajñānād vai na dṛśyate ||

Due to his sense of 'human responsibility' (*kāruṇya*) a bodhisattva abstains from entering *nirvāṇa* in order to help other living beings to obtain *bodhi* (cf. RĀ, IV, 66). This is the very core of Mahāyāna ethics and to abuse it can only be considered a sign of mental depravity:

IV, 78-79.
karuṇāpūrvakāḥ sarve niṣyandā jñānanirmalāḥ |
uktā yatra mahāyāne kas tan nindet sacetanaḥ ||

atyaudāryātigāmbhīryād viṣaṇṇair akṛtātmabhiḥ |
nindyate 'dya mahāyānaṃ mohāt svaparavairibhiḥ ||

The eight stages of spiritual progress in Śrāvakayāna do not reach as far as the ten *bhūmis* in Mahāyāna.[224] The former lead to *arhattva*, the latter to *buddhatva*.

V, 40.
yathā śrāvakayāne 'ṣṭāv uktāḥ śrāvakabhūmayaḥ |
mahāyāne daśa tathā bodhisattvasya bhūmayaḥ ||

iii) Despite such divergencies one should not simply discard Śrāvakayāna as useless or unorthodox. On the contrary, this *yāna* should be regarded as preliminary to the great *yāna*. It addresses itself to

224. The eight Śrāvakabhūmis refer to the eight *āryapudgalas*, v. *Saṃyutta*, V. p. 202. For these stages and their relationship to the *bhūmis* of Mahāyāna v. *Śūraṃgamasamādhisūtra*, pp. 246-251.

those Buddhists whose moral and intellectual faculties are still at an inferior stage of development.

IV, 94-96.

yathaiva vaiyākaraṇo mātṛkām api pāṭhayet |
buddho 'vadat tathā dharmaṃ vineyānāṃ yathākṣamam ||

keṣāṃ cid avadad dharmaṃ pāpebhyo vinivṛttaye |
keṣāṃ cit puṇyasiddhyarthaṃ keṣāṃ cid dvayaniśritam ||

dvayāniśritam ekeṣāṃ gambhīraṃ bhīrubhīṣaṇam |
śūnyatākaruṇāgarbhaṃ keṣāṃ cid bodhisādhanam ||

This accounts for the fact that the Buddha often varied his teachings according to his audience and circumstances (cf. BV, 98-99; MK XVIII, 6 & 8; YṢ, 33). But this is merely a pedagogical device. Therefore, in reality, there is only one single *yāna* as Śrāvaka- and Pratyekabuddhayāna are comprised in Mahāyāna (cf. SS, § 10).[225]

IV, 88.

tathāgatābhisandhyoktāny asukhaṃ jñātum ity ataḥ |
ekayānatriyānoktād ātmā rakṣya upekṣayā ||

II. Nāgārjuna's philosophical system

The variety of Nāgārjuna's authentic writings in regard to style, themes and philosophical profundity is certainly undeniable. To be sure, one cannot quite rule out the possibility that such diversities are to some extent to be accounted for by assuming personal motives, such as shift of interests or development of thinking. However, apart from the fact that ŚS and VV certainly were written later than MK, no means of establishing a relative chronology in his authorship are at our disposal. In my view the decisive reasons for the said

225. On *ekayāna*, see *Siddhi*, p. 673 and p. 724 (the verses translated here are from Candrakīrti's *Triśaraṇasaptati*, 45-47!). Ref. in *Mahāyānasaṃgraha*, p. 63*; *Vimalakīrtinirdeśa*, p. 214, n. 144. Also F. Kōtatsu: 'One vehicle or three', *JIP*, III, pp. 79-166. – On *upekṣā*, see *Akṣayamatinirdeśa*, Bu *fol.* 140 b 1–141 b 6.

variety of Nāgārjuna's writings is to be sought in the author's desire, as a Buddhist, to address himself to various audiences, at various levels and from various angles. This motive would of course be quite consistent with the Mahāyāna ideal of *upāyakauśalya* (cf. BS, 17). Thus MK, ŚS and VV were intended to be studied by philosophically minded monks. VP was written as a challenge to Naiyāyikas. YṢ, VS and PK are contributions to Buddhist exegesis. CS is a document confessing its author's personal faith in the Buddha's *deśanā*, while SS, BV, BS, SL and RĀ on the whole addressed themselves to a wider Buddhist audience, monks as well as laymen.

I will thus take it for granted that Nāgārjuna never changed his fundamental outlook essentially, and, accordingly, look upon his writings as expressions of an underlying unity of thought conceived before he made his début in writing.

SL is the most 'elementary' of Nāgārjuna's writings. It was composed in order to arouse the reader's interest in the values of Buddhism in general (1). With the exception of a few stray allusions there is nothing here that an adherent of Śrāvakayāna would be inclined to disavow. It mainly consists of injunctions enjoined on laymen (cf. 118). Nāgārjuna's remaining works were written from the higher level of Mahāyāna and we must probably take it for granted that he assumed his readers to be well versed in the fundamentals of the Tripiṭaka.[226]

The career of a bodhisattva, i.e. a *gṛhastha* or a *pravrajita* devoted to the ideals of Mahāyāna is inaugurated the moment he forms the *bodhicitta* setting his mind on enlightenment. Now he does not merely seek his own *nirvāṇa* (= *kleśaskandhanirodha*) but yearns for the *bodhi* of himself as well as all other beings. Thus he exhibits a sense of human responsibility, or compassion (*karuṇā*) virtually foreign to Hīnayāna. Intellectually he will remain satisfied with nothing less than the omniscience of a Buddha.[227]

The first manifest expression of a bodhisattva's new attitude is his

226. Thus MK and ŚS cannot be read without a basic knowledge of Abhidharma. Verses such as RĀ, III, 35; BS, 62, 97, 119, 147; SL, 27 and 53 etc. presuppose the reader's acquaintance with some of the sūtras. RĀ, V, 34 and SL, 53 refer to Vinaya rules.

227. On *bodhicitta*, Har Dayal, *op.cit.*, pp. 50-79; BV, *passim;* RĀ, II, 74-75; *Siddhi*, p. 727; A. Bareau in *Die Religionen Indiens*, Stuttgart 1964, p. 147 (with ref. p. 146, n. 3).

regular performance of the so-called *anuttarā pūjā*, or the *bodhicittotpādavidhi*. RĀ, V, 65-87 thus enjoins a bodhisattva to declare his *śaraṇagamana*, *pūjanā*, *pādadeśanā*, *adhyeṣaṇā*, *yācanā*, *bodhicittotpāda* and *puṇyapariṇāmanā* three times a day in front of a *buddhapratimā*, a stūpa or any other sacred object.[228]

The purpose of this rite is to remind the bodhisattva of the lofty ideals to which he has obligated himself. Thus a bodhisattva embarks on Mahāyāna by declaring his lofty aspirations (*praṇidhāna*) thereby, as it were, swearing his allegiance to its principles.

But pious promises and solemn vows will not do. In order to become a buddha a bodhisattva must personally collect the moral and intellectual outfit (*saṃbhāra*) conducive for *bodhi*. In due course an *anantapuṇyasaṃbhāra* will endow him with a Buddha's physical body (*rūpakāya*) adorned with the remarkable thirty-two *mahāpuruṣalakṣaṇas* and the eighty *anuvyañjanas*, whereas an *anantajñānasaṃbhāra* will bring him in possession of the inconceivable *dharmakāya*. These two bodies constitute buddhahood.[229]

But before the bodhisattva finally becomes a buddha he must, as said, fulfil the two *saṃbhāras* for *bodhi*. This is done by practising the six *pāramitās* in a spirit of *karuṇā*, viz. *dāna*, *śīla*, *kṣānti*, *vīrya*, *dhyāna* and *prajñā* (cf. SL, 8).[230]

In RĀ, V, 36-38 Nāgārjuna briefly defines the 'perfections' and states their respective effects: 'Liberality (*dāna*) is to surrender one's own goods (*svārtha*), good morals (*śīla*) are actions beneficial to others (*parahita*), patience (*kṣānti*) is to renounce anger (*krodha*), energy (*vīrya*) is to strive for merit (*śubhaparigraha*); trance (*dhyāna*) is to

228. RĀ, V, 65. See also note to BS, 48. Recently B. C. Beresford has translated the *Triskandhakasūtra* (cf. *Upāliparipṛcchā*, p. 107, n. 4) in his *Mahāyāna Purification: The Confession Sūtra and the practice of Vajrasattva*, Dharamsala 1978. This book includes excerpts from *Bodhyāpattideśanāvṛtti* (TP, No. 5506) ascribed to Nāgārjuna. Even if the authorship of this very interesting commentary remains questionable, there can be no doubt that it originated in the 'circle' of early Madhyamaka. It is closely related to Mātṛceṭa's *Sugatapañcatriṃśatstotra* and other early texts on *bodhisattvavidhi*, e.g. *Bodhyākarapranidhāna* (TP, No. 5930) also ascribed to Nāgārjuna. (It would certainly prove a rewarding task to deal with all these early ritual texts collectively.)

229. RĀ, III, 12-13. – On the *mahāpuruṣalakṣaṇa* v. RĀ, II, 76-96; *Traité*, pp. 271281 (with ref.). For the *anuvyañjanas*, see the list in *Mahāyānasaṃgraha*, pp. 56*-58* and the ref. *ibid.*, p. 54*; Konow (1941), pp. 57-81.

230. On the *pāramitās*, Har Dayal, *op.cit.*, pp. 165-269; *Traité*, pp. 650-1113; *Siddhi*, pp. 620-638.

be concentrated without passions, insight (*prajñā*) is to ascertain the true meaning (*satyārthaniścaya*), compassion (*kṛpā*) is an attitude (*mati*) which is the same (*ekarasa*) toward all living beings (*sattva*), namely love (*karuṇā*). From *dāna* comes enjoyment (*bhoga*), from *śīla* happiness (*sukha*), from *kṣānti* grace (*kānti*), from *vīrya* brilliance, from *dhyāna* peace (*śānti*), from *mati* (= *prajñā*) liberation (*mukti*), and from *kṛpā* success in all matters (*sarvārtha*).'[231] – According to RĀ, IV, 81-82, *mahāyānārtha* is this: *dāna* and *śīla* are performed *parārtha*, *kṣānti* and *vīrya* are *svārtha*, *dhyāna* and *prajñā* are *mokṣārtha*.

The practice of these perfections is tantamount to *bodhisaṃbhāra*. According to a later source *dāna*, *śīla* and *kṣānti* are thus equivalent to *puṇyasaṃbhāra*, while *dhyāna* and *prajñā* amount to *jñānasaṃbhāra* whereas *vīrya* is 'a mutual friend' (*gñis ka'i grogs*).[232]

It would indeed be possible to read BS, SL and RĀ as expositions of these *pāramitās* and understand virtually any verse as an instance of one or more of these. This, however, I will leave for the reader himself to undertake.

The gradual process of development which a bodhisattva undergoes practising the *pāramitās* and a large number of other moral and intellectual virtues is minutely depicted in a number of Mahāyāna texts. According to the scheme of *Daśabhūmikasūtra* which is the authority followed by Nāgārjuna (and later Mādhyamikas) in this respect, a bodhisattva must ascend through ten spiritual stages (*bhūmi*) before he finally achieves *buddhatva*.[233] An abstract of the ten *bodhisattvabhūmis* is given RĀ, V, 41-61: 'The first is *Pramuditā* [so called] since the bodhisattva rejoices as he abandons the three *saṃyojanas* and is born in the *Tathāgatagotra*. By ripening this his *dānapāramitā* becomes eminent. He shakes one hundred *lokadhātus* and becomes an emperor of Jambudvīpa. The second is called *Vimalā* because the ten kinds of physical, vocal and mental karma are stainless since he naturally abides by them. By ripening this *śīlapāramitā* becomes

231. TP, No. 5658, 149a-149b; cf. the quotation in *Tarkajvālā* referred to above n. 156.

232. Commentary to BV, 96 (TP, No. 2694, 480b).

233. On the ten *bhūmis* see, above all, Har Dayal, *op.cit.*, pp. 270-291; *Siddhi*, pp. 721-742; *Traité*, pp. 2372-2445; *Śūraṃgamasamādhisūtra*, pp. 155-158.

eminent. He becomes an altruistic *cakravartin*, a glorious master of the seven *ratnas*. He is an expert in making living beings avoid bad morals. The third *bhūmi* is [called] *Prabhākarī* because the peaceful light of *jñāna* arises as *dhyāna* and *abhijñā* arise and *rāga* and *dveṣa* are completely extinguished. By ripening this he controls [the *pāramitās* of] *kṣānti* and *vīrya*. Being a clever *mahendradevānām* he resists *kāmarāga*. The fourth is called *Arciṣmatī* because the light of *samyagjñāna* arises as he cultivates all the *bodhipakṣyas* eminently. By ripening this he becomes a *devarāja* of [the gods of] Suyāma. He is a master in subduing the attacks of *satkāyadṛṣṭi*. The fifth [is called] *Sudurjayā* because it is very difficult for any of the Māras to gain power as he becomes skilled in understanding the profound meaning of the *āryasatyas* etc. By ripening this he becomes a king of the gods residing in Tuṣita. He repudiates the foundations of *kleśa* [and] *dṛṣṭi* of all the *tīrthakaras*. The sixth is called *Abhimukhī* because he faces the *buddhadharmas* as by cultivating *śamatha* and *vipaśyanā* he advances to obtain *nirodha*. By ripening this he becomes a king of the gods [of] Sunirmāṇa. Being invincible by Śrāvakas he pacifies those who have *adhimāna*. The seventh [*bhūmi* is called] *Dūraṃgamā* because it has passed far beyond calculation since moment by moment he there enters *nirodhasamāpatti*. By ripening this he becomes a master of the Vaśavartin gods. Having realized the *āryasatyas* be becomes an *ācāryamahānṛpa*. Likewise the eighth [also called] Kumārabhūmi, is *Acalā* because it is fathomless. It is also [called] *Acalā* because the *gocara* of body, speech and mind is *acintya*. By ripening this he becomes Brahmā, a master of a thousand [worlds]. He cannot be matched in *arthaniścaya* by Arhats and Pratyekabuddhas etc. The ninth *bhūmi* is called *Sādhumatī*. Here, like a crown-prince, he has a fine intellect by obtaining the *pratisaṃvids*. By ripening this he becomes Brahmā, a master of two thousand [worlds]. He cannot be surpassed by Arhats etc. in questions concerning the attitudes of living beings. The tenth is *Dharmamegha* because the rain of *saddharma* falls as the bodhisattva is consecrated with the light by the Buddha. By ripening this he becomes a master of the Śuddhavāsa gods. A lord of infinite *jñāna* he is a supreme *maheśvara*. Thus these ten are celebrated as the *bodhisattvabhūmis*...'. Subsequently the bodhisattva becomes a buddha (*ibid.*, 61-64).

The majority of Nāgārjuna's writings – MK, ŚS, VV, YṢ, CS, BV and VP – centre upon one single *pāramitā*, viz. that of *prajñā*.

This is above all an outcome of Nāgārjuna's innate philosophical inclination, but it is also a natural consequence of the fact that *prajñāpāramitā* is considered the most important of all the *pāramitās* (cf. BS, 5-7; RĀ, I, 5). It will therefore be reasonable to subject it to closer consideration.[234]

Traditionally *prajñā* is claimed to exhibit three degrees: one of *śruti,* one of *cintā* and one of *bhāvanā.* The first consists in the correct understanding of the scriptures (*āgama*). As far as the writings of Nāgārjuna are concerned SS, PK, SL etc. are designed to serve that need. The second is tantamount to well-reasoned appraisal of what one has learned from one's study of the scriptures. These two kinds of *prajñā* are thus of a discursive or rational order and serve a most practical purpose, i.e. a correct understanding of Buddhist dogma. The third mode of *prajñā* gradually unfolds itself by means of *bhāvanā* and is based on the former two. It consists in meditating upon the results of one's learning and understanding so as to realize them for oneself and integrate them in one's personality.[235]

Taking it for granted that his reader is conversant with this gradation Nāgārjuna does not spend many words discussing *prajñā* in the abstract but instead employs it in its current sense of analytical understanding, or 'intellect as conversant with general truths' (PED s.v. *paññā,* q.v.). However, his dialectical writings – especially MK, ŚS and VV, which may in fact be regarded as exercises in the application of this *pāramitā* – vividly display how he assigns a new and major role to *prajñā.* Now *prajñā* is not merely the analytical faculty which allows us to determine the *lakṣaṇas* and the *svabhāva* of dharmas at the *vyavahāra* level with certainty but it is the mediator which conveys its adept from a world of appearance (*saṃvṛti*) to one of absolute reality (*paramārtha*). Here the deep impact the Prajñāpāramitā texts exerted upon Nāgārjuna is unmistakable. So to Nāgārjuna *prajñā* is at the outset a critical faculty constantly engaged in analysing the more or less common-sense notions presented to it by tradition or experience. The more it penetrates them and 'loosens them up' the more their apparent nature vanishes and in the final analysis their true nature turns out to be 'empty', i.e. devoid of

234. On the relationship between *prajñā* and the other *pāramitās*, cf. Murti, *op.cit.*, p. 267 and pp. 209-227; *Traité,* pp. 2365-2371.

235. See n. 201 above; *Vimalakīrtinirdeśa*, pp. 420-425; *Bhāvanākrama* I (ed. Tucci), pp. 198-205; *Pañcaskandhaprakaraṇa* (my ed.), pp. 16-27; *Ratnapradīpa,* VII.

substance, or simply illusory as it cannot really be determined as A or, for that matter, non-A. At this stage *prajñā* has also brought its own raison d'être to an end: by analysing its objects away it has also deprived itself of an objective support (*ārambaṇa* etc.).[236]

At this moment the analytical understanding suddenly shifts into an intuitive *jñāna* which has *śūnyatā* as its 'object', i.e. which has no object. The culmination of *prajñā,* then, is *jñāna,* or intuitive insight into reality (*tattva*) beyond the duality of *asti* and *nāsti*. This *jñāna* is also the suspension of *avidyā* which, as we have seen, in the final analysis is based on the wrong assumption of existence and non-existence etc.[237]

Bodhisattvas who are still far from buddhahood may enjoy occasional glimpses of *tattva* since their *prajñā* has not yet achieved the perfectibility of a *pāramitā*. It is only a buddha who has perfected the *dhyāna-* and *prajñāpāramitā,* i.e. *jñānasaṃbhāra* so that he is in the unremitting possession of *tattvajñāna*. He is the only one to whom the epithet *sarvajña* applies for he experiences the *samatā* of all dharmas, their *śūnyatā*. He knows them all to be the same.[238]

The development of the *pāramitās* must in other words come about gradually. Again and again one must apply one's *prajñā* to the 'facts' of experience and tradition. This necessity accounts for the circumstance that Nāgārjuna's dialectical writings are so replete with 'repetitions' of what is essentially a very simple principle indeed. – Let us therefore turn our attention to the stage where *prajñā* plays the principal role.

All conscious beings find themselves living in an extended world

236. As Āryadeva puts it (*Catuḥśataka,* VIII, 5): *bhavaḥ saṃdehamātreṇa jāyate jarjarīkṛtaḥ*. ('... a bit of critical sense ...'). I cannot refrain from giving Dharmakīrti's celebrated verse to the same effect (*Pramāṇavārttika,* II, 209): *yathā yathārthāś cintyante viśīryante tathā tathā* (To the ref. given in Miyasaka's ed. may be added: *Madhyamakālaṃkāravṛtti,* TP, No. 5285, 65b; *Syādvādamañjarī* (ed. Dhruva), p. 117; *Siddhiviniścayaṭīkā* (ed. Jain), p. 92; *Nyāyāvatāravivṛti* (ed. Upadhye), p. 31 (printed as prose!).

237. Cf. on *jñāna* in Nāgārjuna: *samyagjñāna* (YṢ, 10; RĀ, II, 22); *jñānacakṣus* (YṢ, 54; CS, I, 1); *viviktajñāna* (CS, I, 1); *asamajñāna* (CS, III, 1); *tattvajñāna* (CS, III, 19; 47); *śūnyatājñāna* (BV, 90). See also MK, XXVI, 11; XVIII, 12; BS, 46. For *(a-)parijñāna,* YṢ, 4, 6, 47, 48; RĀ, I, 28, 39; II, 22 etc. – Hōbōgirin s.v. *Chie*.

238. *Traité,* pp. 1743-1755; Hōbōgirin s.v. *Byōdō* (*samatā*); *Vimalakīrtinirdeśa, passim*; RĀ, I, 74; II, 6, 8.

of plurality (*prapañca*). Only the Buddha is beyond *prapañca*.[239] Now, from the common Buddhist outlook we cannot really distinguish between an 'objective' and a 'subjective' world, we cannot really isolate 'facts' from 'judgments'. This is a most decisive point which should not be left out of account.[240] For this reason *prapañca* also means *our* expansion of the world, or, as one might say, the world presented to us in and by language. The very *modus operandi* of *prapañca* is *vikalpa,* usually to be translated as 'discursive or conceptual thinking' but occasionally also 'objectively' as 'distinctions, differences' and the like. *Vikalpas* differentiate the world of *prapañca* into something which is said to exist (*astīti*) and something which is said not to exist (*nāstīti*) and hypostatise these respectively as being (*bhāva*) and non-being (*abhāva*). These again entail the heresies of *śāśvata-* and *ucchedadarśana.* These are the basic conscious functions of mind. Subsequently we form ideas (*saṃkalpa*), assumptions (*parikalpa*), opinions (*kalpanā*), theories, or dogmas (*dṛṣṭi*) etc., and this in the end is tantamount to *duḥkha.* All of them are ultimately based on the uncritical acceptance of being (*bhāvābhyupagama,* cf. YṢ, 46).[241]

Now *prajñā* performs its task in the systematic intellectual endeavour to demonstrate that the *jāla* of *prapañca* is empty, that it lacks 'objective' foundation (cf. YṢ, 25-27 etc.). This is achieved by bringing to light that *asti* and *nāsti* hypostatised by the activity of *vikalpa* do not appertain to reality (*tattva*).

Before we see how *prajñā* faces its task the categories in which *vikalpa* operates must be ascertained. The things (*bhāva*) and conceptual phenomena (*dharma*) assumed to exist are necessarily conceived in terms of *hetu/phala, pūrva/apara/saha, kāraka/kriyā/karma/*

239. On *prapañca* May, *op. cit.,* p. 175, n. 562; L. Schmithausen, *Der Nirvāṇa-Abschnitt in der Viniścayasaṃgrahaṇī der Yogācārabhūmiḥ,* Wien 1969, pp. 137-142.

240. This ambiguity is decisive in key words such as *artha* ('object' or 'meaning'), *upalabdhi* ('exist' or 'perceive'), *prapañca* ('the universe' or 'language'), *satya* ('reality' or 'truth'), *sad* ('real' or 'good'), *saṃbhava* ('occurrence', 'possibility') etc. to mention only a few at random. – I think that, in a certain sense La Vallée Poussin was quite right when he claimed: 'Indians do not make a clear distinction between facts and ideas, between ideas and words, they never clearly recognized the principle of contradiction.' (quoted in de Jong's review in *JIP*, I, p. 401, q.v.). – On the other hand this need not always be a drawback! – Cf. also the most interesting book by the late R. E. A. Johansson, *The Dynamic Psychology of Early Buddhism,* London 1979.

241. On *pari-*, *vi-* and *saṃ-kalpayati* etc. see May, *op.cit.*, p. 64, n. 64.

karaṇa, lakṣya/lakṣaṇa, sva/para, dīrgha/hrasva, eka/aneka (i.e. *saṃkhyā*) etc. In short, human understanding invariably presupposes some kind of spatial, temporal or causal relationship.[242]

At the very base of any specific relationship lies the principle of identity (*ekatva*) and difference (*anyatva*). Without assuming this dichotomy no language, no rational discourse, no world – in a word, no *prapañca* is possible.[243]

Now, what Nāgārjuna simply wants to demonstrate is that strictly speaking (*i.e. paramārthataḥ*) not a single *bhāva* or *dharma* can be conceived either as 'one' (*eka*), i.e. as an independent unity, or as 'other' (*anya*), i.e. as absolutely independent of its correlate (cf. MK, II, 21). Why not? Because, obviously, the assumption that anything is *eka* or *anya* faces endless absurdities when confronted with the relentless demands of logic (*yukti*) or experience (*upapatti/saṃbhava*). It would be of little avail to depict how easy it is for Nāgārjuna to demonstrate the inherent conflict in discursive thinking ('reason') as none of the correlates in the above-mentioned categories can be taken as *eka* or *anya* – who would e.g. maintain that long and short were identical – or absolutely independent! MK, ŚS and VV show this at length and anyone could – and *should,* if he follows Nāgārjuna's advice about getting rid of all *vikalpas* – multiply the instances *ad infinitum.*[244] – From this it seems clear that the constructions of *vikalpa* do not point to any *tattva,* and I think that in this perspective the meaning of terms like *nirālamba, anālaya, nirāśraya, anāspada, śūnya, vivikta* etc. also becomes intelligible. It simply means that there really is no *dharma* or *bhāva* to fix one's mind upon as support. – By pointing out that nothing within the domain of experience can be conceived in and by itself independently of something else, Nāgārjuna merely intends to call attention to the fact that nothing has

242. This list is culled from MK, ŚS, *passim,* and the 'table of categories' given RĀ, I, 91-92, q.v.

243. Cf. MK, II, 21 (quoted below); also *Catuḥśataka*, XIV, 19: *tasya tasyaikatā nāsti yo yo bhavaḥ parīkṣyate* | *na santi tenāneke 'pi yenaiko 'pi na vidyate* ||. (Often cited in later literature). Similarly *Pramāṇavārttika*, II, 360: *bhāvā yena nirūpyante tadrūpaṃ nāsti tattvataḥ* | *yasmād ekam anekaṃ vā rūpaṃ teṣāṃ na vidyate* ||. – Ejima, *op.cit.*, p. 254.

244. See the exhortations occurring at intervals in MK (but not in any of the author's other works!): III, 8; IV, 7; VIII, 13; X, 15 and XIX, 4 (note that the verses *Prasannapadā*, p. 384 already appear in *Prajñāpradīpa ad loc.*!).

svabhāva (or, of course, *parabhāva* etc., cf. MK, XV, 3).[245] He displays the absurdities inherent in the assumption of *bhāva* of any kind whatsoever. Instead of taking things in terms of *asti* and *nāsti* one should become aware that all 'entities' are *pratītyasamutpanna*, without, however, committing the fallacy of conceiving *pratītyasamutpāda* as a fact in and by itself. Transcending *asti* and *nāsti* it is not apprehensible but elusive like phantoms, mirages and dreams, or, to use a term often employed in Mahāyānasutras: things are simply *anutpanna*.[246]

From later Madhyamaka sources we learn that there are four main arguments (*mahāhetu*) in support of *anutpāda*.[247] As each of these is already applied by Nāgārjuna himself it will be convenient to advance them here:

1. *catuṣkoṭyutpādapratiṣedha* – which demonstrates that there is *no subject* of origination. Examples of this are provided by ŚS, 4; CS, I, 13; III, 9; MK, XII, 1 and I, 6-7:

naivāsato naiva sataḥ pratyayo 'rthasya yujyate |
asataḥ pratyayaḥ kasya sataś ca pratyayena kim ||

na san nāsan na sadasan dharmo nirvartate yadā |
kathaṃ nirvartako hetur evaṃ sati hi yujyate ||

2. *vajrakaṇa* – which demonstrates that there is *no source* of origination. See MK, XXI, 12-13; CS, I, 13; III, 9. But MK, I, 1 affords the classical instance:

na svato nāpi parato na dvābhyāṃ nāpy ahetutaḥ |
utpannā jātu vidyante bhāvāḥ kva cana ke cana ||

3. *ekānekaviyoga* – showing that things cannot be established since they cannot be conceived as identical or different. See ŚS, 32; MK, XXI, 6 and, above all, II, 21:

245. On the interpretation of *svabhāva*, May, *op.cit.*, p. 124, n. 328; de Jong, *JIP*, II, p. 2-3. Cf. also Steinkellner, *WZKSO*, XV, pp. 179-211.

246. See e.g. *Vimalakīrtinirdeśa*, pp. 39-51.

247. They have been discussed by Atiśa in his *Pañjikā* to *Bodhipathapradīpa*, 189-208 and translated in my 'Atiśa's Introduction to the two Truths, and its sources', in *JIP*, IX, pp. 206-212. (The nomenclature is probably originally Bhavya's.)

ekībhāvena vā siddhir nānābhāvena vā yayoḥ |
na vidyate tayoḥ siddhiḥ kathaṃ nu khalu vidyate ||

4. *pratītyasamutpāda* – which points to the fact that 'things' only appear as they do in relation to a correlative and vice versa. See CS, III, 11-16. MK, XIV, 5-7 puts it tersely:

anyad anyat pratītyānyan nānyad anyad ṛte 'nyataḥ |
yat pratītya ca yat tasmāt tad anyan nopapadyate ||

yady anyad anyad anyasmād anyasmād apy ṛte bhavet |
tad anyad anyad anyasmad ṛte nāsti ca nāsty ataḥ ||

nānyasmin vidyate 'nyatvam ananyasmin na vidyate |
avidyamāne cānyatve nāsty anyad vā tad eva vā ||

Cf. also YṢ, 19 and MK, XVIII, 10:

pratītya yad yad bhavati na hi tāvat tad eva tat |
na cānyad api tat tasmān nocchinnaṃ nāpi śāśvatam ||

These proofs are of course conducted at the level of *cintāmayī prajñā* with the specific purpose of rendering support to the unsystematic statements of *anutpāda* found in the Prajñāpāramitā scriptures (~ *śrutamayī prajñā*). Needless to add, it must be left to the adept himself to attain *anutpādajñāna* by practising *bhāvanāmayī prajñā*. Being *aparapratyaya* (Tib.: *gźan las śes pa ma yin*) (cf. MK, XVIII, 9) it cannot be communicated by scriptures or arguments.[248]

Thus Nāgārjuna is able to argue – or at least to *suggest* – that all theories etc. generated through the operations of *vikalpa* are, in the final analysis, untenable as they impose absurd implications (*prasaṅga*) on the proponent of any kind of *bhāva*.[249]

But the *svabhāvavādin* is not prepared to succumb to such allegations. On the contrary, one may suspect the Prāsaṅgika of tacitly endorsing the existence of the very *svabhāva* he is negating, for how could anyone negate something unless he presupposes its existence as *negandum*? That would be a glaring inconsistency. But Nāgārjuna is

248. See also the ref. in CPD s.v. *apara(p)paccaya*. The Chinese version of *aparapratyaya* in MK, XVIII, 9 is quite explicit: *zì zhī*, 'personally known'.
249. For *prasaṅga*, Murti, *op.cit.*, pp. 131 sq.; Ramanan, *op.cit.*, p. 152.

convinced that this is an unwarranted accusation (*adhilaya,* cf. MK, XXIV, 13; VV, 63). Lack of *svabhāva* is universal and knows no exceptions. For this reason there is really no question of negating it (*pratiṣedha*). Nāgārjuna merely does his best to suggest its absence. He himself is not really negating – or affirming – anything at all. If he assumed *bhāva* at the outset and then negated it he might have to plead guilty of the alleged inconsistency. But, as said, everything is *śūnya* (= *anutpanna*) as it lacks *svabhāva* and his own arguments claim no exception to that rule. Similarly all the Buddhist *dharmas*; being *pratītyasamutpanna* they are certainly *śūnya.*[250]

In the terminology of the Vaiyākaraṇas Nāgārjuna's 'negations' of *svabhāva* may conveniently be classified as *prasajyapratiṣedhas* without any intended affirmation rather than *paryudāsas* implying an affirmative proposition.[251]

If the opponent, at this stage, has been persuaded to accept Nāgārjuna's arguments – *argumenta ad hominem,* in a sense – he should, as said, apply himself to *bhāvanā* in order gradually to become personally convinced of universal emptiness, i.e. in order to obtain what is technically termed the *anutpattikadharmakṣānti.*[252]

However, living beings who have fully realized universal emptiness – *sarvajñatā* – are rare indeed. This, as we have seen, presupposes that the practice of *dhyāna* and *prajñā* has been brought to complete perfection (*pāramitā*). Only Buddhas have gone that far.[253]

And this brings us to Nāgārjuna's celebrated doctrine of two truths (*satya*), or two levels of reality. The distinction between a *saṃvṛti-* and a *paramārthasatya* was not invented by Nāgārjuna: it is found, above all, in Mahāyānasūtras previous to him.[254] It is worthy of notice that even though the theory of *satyadvaya* has a cardinal func-

250. All this has been discussed at length in VV, q.v.

251. Cf. e.g. K. V. Abhyankar & J. M. Shukla, *A Dictionary of Sanskrit Grammar*, Baroda 1977, pp. 244 and 373. – In Madhyamaka, as known, the Svātantrikas argued *paramārthataḥ* by way of *prasajyapratiṣedha*, cf. especially Ejima, *op.cit.*, pp. 113-125; Y. Kajiyama, *An Introduction to Buddhist philosophy*, Kyoto 1966, n. 62. – Nāgārjuna never uses these terms but may have known them, cf. the fragment from **Lokaparīkṣā* above n. 27 and *Tarkajvālā*, 213a.

252. BS, 28-30, 47; *Śūraṃgamasamādhisūtra*, p. 160, n. 119 (*anutpattikadharmakṣānti* is obtained at the eighth *bhūmi* (*Acalā*)).

253. SL, 8 etc.

254. On this subject see my paper mentioned n. 247 which gives some of the most interesting Indian sources.

tion in his philosophy it does not play a very conspicuous role on the pages of his writings. The *locus classicus* is of course MK, XXIV, 8-10:

dve satye samupāśritya buddhānāṃ dharmadeśanā |
lokasaṃvṛtisatyaṃ ca satyaṃ ca paramārthataḥ ||

ye 'nayor na vijānanti vibhāgaṃ satyayor dvayoḥ |
te tattvaṃ na vijānanti gambhīraṃ buddhaśāsane ||

vyavahāram anāśritya paramārtho na deśyate |
paramārtham anāgamya nirvāṇaṃ nādhigamyate ||

Read along with the other pertinent passages, viz. ŚS, 1; 69-73; VV, 28, and YṢ, 30-33, q.v., these verses provide us with the following important information. In order to achieve Nirvāṇa one must understand *paramārtha*, i.e. *pratītyasamutpāda* = *niḥsvabhāvatā* = *śūnyatā*. But before this is feasible a beginner must as a *conditio sine qua non* receive instructions (*deśanā*) about the Dharma and practise accordingly. Unless his teacher resorts to the conventions of language (*vyavahāra*) he is unable to impart his instructions. Otherwise the pupil cannot form any correct idea about the *lakṣaṇas* and *svabhāva* of the *skandhas*, *dhātus* and *āyatanas* the true nature of which, viz. *śūnyatā*, he must gradually realize himself through the exertion of his own *prajñā*.

Thus the *lokasaṃvṛtisatya* is an indispensable pedagogical device for one's personal understanding of *paramārtha*. As Candrakīrti aptly puts it: *upāyabhūtaṃ vyavahārasatyam upeyabhūtaṃ paramārthasatyam*.[255]

The two truths cannot be claimed to express different levels of objective reality since all things always equally lack *svabhāva*. They are merely two ways of looking (*darśana*) at things, a provisional and a definite. The first is, in the unpretentious words of *Akutobhayā* ad MK, XXIV, 8-9, **sarvadharmotpādadarśana*, the second, **sarvadharmānutpādadarśana*.[256] This *vibhāga* must be clear. In his characteristic style Bhavya puts the same thing thus:

255. *Madhyamakāvatāra*, VI, 80 (some ref. in *AO*, XL, p. 89, n. 12).
256. TP, No. 5229, 102b.

tathyasaṃvṛtisopānam antareṇa vipaścitaḥ |
tattvaprāsādaśikharārohanaṃ na hi yujyate ||[257]

By adopting this *satyadvayavibhāga* and taking it as an *upāya-upeya* relationship Nāgārjuna is enabled, on one hand (= *paramārthataḥ*) to maintain that all things are empty, on the other (= *saṃvṛtitaḥ*), to advocate the practical value of all the various Buddhist teachings about *skandhas, pāramitās* etc. etc. – So while there is no ontological justification for *satyadvayavibhāga* there is most certainly a didactic (psychological) one, and as long as all living beings have not yet become Buddhas the need for *dharmadeśanā* will remain. But the day all *sattvas* have fulfilled *jñānasaṃbhāra* by realizing *pudgaladharmanairātmya,* and *puṇyasaṃbhāra* by perfecting *dāna, śīla* and *kṣānti* the manifold Buddhist teachings are rendered superfluous.

Let us finally recapitulate Nāgārjuna's soteriological system. Really the entire universe is nothing but emptiness beyond all conceptions and limitations. However, owing to *avidyā* we find ourselves confined in a manifold world of *duḥkha*. The beginning of *avidyā* cannot be accounted for, but fortunately, as the Buddha has pointed out, it can be abolished by *jñāna*.[258] Therefore we should strive to arouse ourselves, and – not to forget – all others from the nightmare of ignorance. But we shall not obtain 'enlightenment' before we have prepared ourselves morally and intellectually for *bodhi*. We must unremittingly collect an immense amount of *puṇyajñānasaṃbhāra* before we wake up as buddhas and recognize that all along we have been dreaming a life in *saṃsāra*. Now we see that (YṢ, 5): *na saṃsāraṃ na nirvāṇaṃ manyante tattvadarśinaḥ*.

Such are the simple frames of Mahāyāna's view of the world, and indeed, *mutatis mutandis* of several other major ancient Indian (Hindu) soteriologies.[259]

257. *Madhyamakahṛdayakārikā*, III, 12, see Ejima's ed. p. 271; my edition of Atiśa's *Satyadvayāvatāra*, 20 (in the paper ref. to n. 247).

258. MK, XXVI, 11; XI, 1: Being based on *avidyā saṃsāra* has no beginning (*anavarāgro hi* ...), but the attainment of *jñāna* brings it to an end.

259. Due to considerations of space I must abstain from drawing parallels to cognate Indian *darśanas* or to Western philosophers. See, however Conze's 'Buddhist Philosophy and its European Parallels', and 'Spurious Parallels to Buddhist Philosophy', *PEW*, XIII, pp. 9-23 and 105-115 (reprinted in his *Thirty Years of Buddhist Studies*, Oxford 1968). – Cf. recently N. Katz (ed.), *Buddhist and Western Philosophy*, New Delhi 1981 (not seen).

III. Vestiges of influence

It will be a very fascinating task to trace the impact of Nāgārjuna's writings on the subsequent development inside and outside the domain of Buddhist thinking, and if the present study has to some extent paved the way for such research it will have served a useful purpose.

Though it admittedly falls outside the limits imposed upon this work I cannot resist the temptation briefly to point out some instances where the influence of Nāgārjuna (or his school) must be assumed to account for the state of affairs.

I) Āryadeva was the first important and direct pupil of Nāgārjuna.[260] His works must always be read with a side-glance to those of his guru. The first four chapters of his *magnum opus, Catuḥśataka,* in sixteen chapters, deal with the means of abandoning the four *viparyāsas: nitya-, sukha-, śucigrāha* and *ahaṃkāra.*[261] Nāgārjuna also treats these 'perverted views' in MK, XXIII, and, with increasing attention to their basic significance as a source of *avidyā,* in ŚS (10; 62) written later than MK. Still, Nāgārjuna's discussion is not as extensive as the importance of the topic would warrant. It is therefore natural to regard *Catuḥśataka* I-IV as a deliberate continuation of the work initiated by Āryadeva's teacher. – *Catuḥśataka* IX-XVI seethes with arguments directed against various 'heretics', above all representatives of Sāṃkhya and Vaiśeṣika. Similarly Āryadeva's **Śataka* I-X (Taishō, No. 1569). As we have seen Nāgārjuna is aware of these and other *tīrthikas* (RĀ, I, 61) but for some reason he apparently only engaged in a debate with the Naiyāyikas. It is therefore a fair guess to say that he decided to leave the task of

260. For a bibliography of Āryadeva, v. *Traité,* III, pp. 1370-1375, and most recently J. May 'Āryadeva et Candrakīrti sur la permanence', in *Indianisme et bouddhisme. Mélanges offerts à Mgr Étienne Lamotte,* Louvain-la-Neuve 1980, pp. 215-232. – For three new fragments see my note 22 in *IIJ,* XXIII, p. 178. There are three more verses in Śāntarakṣita's *Madhyamakālaṃkāravṛtti,* TP, No. 5285, 61a, q.v. (I must postpone further remarks on Āryadeva and his works to my edition of *Catuḥśataka,* to appear in *Indiske Studier* VII.)

261. For the titles of the individual chapters v. V. Bhattacharya, *The Catuḥśataka of Āryadeva,* Calcutta 1931, pp. xx-xxi. – On the four *viparyāsas* cf. SL, 55 with ref.

refuting other non-Buddhist schools to a talented disciple he could rely on: Āryadeva. It may be added that though Āryadeva proves extremely faithful to the thought of his master the *style* in which he garbed his arguments was very much his own.

II) We have evidence to the effect that *Catuḥśataka* was studied by early Jaina philosophers.[262] An interesting instance is provided by Kundakunda's *Samayasāra,* I, 8:

jaha ṇavi sakkam aṇajjo aṇajjabhāsaṃ viṇā u gāheduṃ I
taha vavahāreṇa viṇā paramatthuvadesaṇam asakkaṃ II[263]

This recalls *Catuḥśataka,* VIII, 19:

nānyayā bhāṣayā mlecchaḥ śakyo grāhayituṃ yathā I
na laukikam ṛte lokaḥ śakyo grāhayituṃ tathā II

Similarly *Samayasāra,* I, 7, 11, 12 etc., q.v., betray an unmistakable influence from the Mādhyamika theory of *satyadvaya.*

III) I do not think that it is possible to name one single later Mādhyamika in India – Prāsaṅgika or Svātantrika – who does not expressly acknowledge, or at least indicate (through allusions, quotations etc.) Nāgārjuna as his authority par excellence, second only to Śākyamuni himself, of course. Whether future research decides to focus on issues such as the development of the philosophical prose style, the difference in presenting the *mārga,* the controversy between Prāsaṅgikas and Svātantrikas, or on the debates between Madhyamaka and Yogācāra – to mention only a few vital approaches – it will be imperative to take one's starting-point in the extant writings of Nāgārjuna.

IV) Though traces of Madhyamaka influence may now and then also be detected in Jaina and Cārvāka sources (see especially *Tattvo-*

262. *Catuḥśataka,* XI, 18 quoted in *Dvādaśāraṃ Nayacakram* (ed. Jambūvijayaji), p. 73; *Anekāntajayapatākā* (ed. Kāpadīā), I, p. 233; II, p. 202. *Hastavālaprakaraṇa,* 1 (if authentic) cited *Dvādaśāraṃ Nayacakram,* p. 93.
263. Cited from A. Chakravarti, *Samayasāra of Śrī Kundakunda,* New Delhi 1971, p. 17. (For Kundakunda's date, v. E. H. Johnston, *Early Sāṃkhya,* p. 14.)

paplavasiṃha, passim) it would be no exaggeration to claim that it penetrated deepest in early Advaita Vedānta, and subsequently in affiliated Hindu literature.

This is nowhere as manifest as in the *Gauḍapādīyakārikās*, a fact which has also already been noticed by several modern scholars.[264] But the close affinity between Madhyamaka and Vedānta was recognized by some of the ancient Buddhist authors too. The first to do so seems to have been Bhavya, the author of *Madhyamakahṛdaya-kārikā*.[265] In his *Madhyamakālaṃkāravṛtti* Śāntarakṣita (ca. 725-788) also quotes some stanzas from what is now known as *Gauḍapādīya-kārikās*.[266] It is not without a certain indignation that he cites II, 31-32, 35 exclaiming: 'What they state has already been said by the Tathāgata!' (*de dag gis gaṅ brjod pa de ni bde bar gśegs pas gsuṅs pa*). It is sheer plagiarism, so to say.

svapnamāye yathā dṛṣṭe gandharvanagaraṃ yathā |
tathā viśvam idaṃ dṛṣṭaṃ vedānteṣu vicakṣaṇaiḥ ||

| rig byed mtha' la ṅed (!) rnams kyis || rmi lam sgyu ma ci 'dra daṅ ||
| dri za'i groṅ khyer ci 'dra mthoṅ || de ltar 'jig rten 'di dag mthoṅ |

264. Cf. e.g. La Vallée Poussin, *MCB*, II, p. 35: 'Le bon interprète de la pensée de Nāgārjuna serait Gauḍapāda, le maître de Śaṃkara ... Armé des arguments et des expressions de Nāgārjuna, faisant sien tout le nihilisme de Nāgārjuna, Gauḍapāda introduisit dans l'archaïque Vedānta la doctrine de l'irréalité du contingent (*māyāvāda*), la doctrine rigoureuse de l'unité et du caractère 'impensable' de l'Être.' – More recently Murti, *op.cit.*, pp. 109-117; F. Whaling: Śaṅkara and Buddhism , *JIP*, VII, pp. 1-42; T. Vetter: 'Die Gauḍapādīya-Kārikās: Zur Entstehung und zur Bedeutung von (a)dvaita', *WZKS*, XXII, pp. 95-131; also T. Vetter, *Studien zur Lehre und Entwicklung Śaṅkaras*, Wien 1979, pp. 27-74. – Tuxen, *op.cit.*, pp. 22-24. – This is not the place to discuss the decisive impact the *satyadvaya*-theory has exerted upon the *śabdādvaitavāda* of Bhartṛhari, though this fact and its far-reaching implications seem to have escaped the notice of the modern interpreters of the *Vākyapadīya*. This point will be dealt with in a forthcoming work by Mr. Torvald Olsson (Lund).

265. Pointed out by M. Walleser, *Der ältere Vedānta. Geschichte, Kritik und Lehre*, Heidelberg 1910, p. 18. Cf. V. V. Gokhale: 'The Vedānta-Philosophy described by Bhavya in his *Madhyamakahṛdaya*', *IIJ*, II, p. 175.

266. Cf. Walleser, *op.cit.*, p. 20. – Walleser's list is not complete as Śāntarakṣita also cites III, 31-32. – His quotation of II, 31-32, 35 occurs *Madhyamakālaṃkāravṛtti*, TP, No. 5285, 81b.

na nirodho na cotpattir na baddho na ca sādhakaḥ |
na mumukṣur na vai mukta ity eṣā paramārthatā ||

|'gog pa med ciṅ skye ba med || bciṅs pa med ciṅ sgrub po med |
| thar 'dod med ciṅ thar pa med || 'di ni don dam ñid yin no |

vītarāgabhayakrodhair munibhir vedapāragaiḥ |
nirvikalpo hy ayaṃ dṛṣṭaḥ prapañcopaśamo 'dvayaḥ ||

| chags daṅ 'jigs daṅ khro bral ba || rig byed mthar phyin thub rnams kyis |
| spros pa ñer źi gñis med pa'i || rnam par mi rtog 'di mthoṅ ṅo |

Let these brief observations suffice to indicate that an extensive – and rewarding – task is awaiting future research within the field of Madhyamaka studies.

Bibliography

Note: This bibliography is selective. Usually it does not repeat a reference already given once or twice in full. It lists some standard works which have proved indispensable for Madhyamaka and allied studies. A few other books consulted have also been registered.

Extensive bibliographical information is provided e.g. by

Hanayama, S., *Bibliography of Buddhism*, Tokyo 1961.

Nakamura, H., *Indian Buddhism: A survey with Bibliographical Notes*, Osaka-fu 1980.

Potter, K.H., *The Encyclopedia of Indian philosophies*, Delhi 1970.

A good selective bibliography is given in

Regamey, C., *Buddhistische Philosophie*, Bern 1950.

Bibliographies with particular regard to Madhyamaka may be found in the works of May (1959); Murti (1960); Ramanan (1966); Streng (1967) and several others listed below. Also in D.S. Ruegg, *The Literature of the Madhyamaka School of Philosophy in India*, Wiesbaden 1981. (Reached me too late to be of any avail.)

References to *Pāli* are to the editions of the Pāli Text Society.

For the *Tibetan* texts I have referred to Suzuki, D.T. (ed.), *The Tibetan Tripiṭaka. Peking edition*, Kyōto 1955-1961 (abbreviated TP). In some cases also to the Narthang edition (TN) belonging to the Royal Library (Copenhagen). If modern critical editions exist I have referred to these. The recent Japanese reprint of the Derge edition (Madhyamaka section) reached me too late to come into full consideration.

All *Chinese* texts are quoted or translated from Takakusu, J. & Watanabe, K. (eds.), *Taishō Shinshū Daizōkyō*, Tokyo 1924-1929.

Edited *Sanskrit* texts have been listed below but Mahāyāna sūtras and śāstras are occasionally quoted from Vaidya, P.L. (ed.), *Buddhist Sanskrit Texts*, Darbhanga 1958 – unless otherwise noticed.

A few current abbreviations etc. have tacitly been adopted.

Abhyankar, K.V. & Shukla, J.M., *A Dictionary of Sanskrit grammar*, Baroda 1977.

Bendall, C. (ed.), *Śikṣāsamuccaya. A compendium of Buddhistic teaching, compiled by Śāntideva, chiefly from earlier Mahāyāna-Sūtras*, St. Petersburg 1897-1902.

Bendall, C. (ed.), 'Subhāṣitasaṃgraha', *Le Muséon*, IV-V, Louvain 1903-1904.

Broeck, J. van den, *La saveur de l'immortel (A-p'i-t'an Kan Lu Wei Lun)*, Louvain-la-Neuve 1977.

Carelli, M.E. (ed.), *Sekoddeśaṭīkā*, Baroda 1941.

Conze, E., *Materials for a Dictionary of the Prajñāpāramitā Literature*, Tokyo 1973.

Conze, E., *The Large Sūtra on Perfect Wisdom*, Berkeley 1975.

Conze, E., *The Prajñāpāramitā Literature*, Tokyo 1978.

Dayal, H., *The Bodhisattva doctrine in Buddhist Sanskrit Literature*, London 1932.

Edgerton, F.: *Buddhist Hybrid Sanskrit Dictionary*, New Haven 1953.

Eimer, H. (ed.), *Bodhipathapradīpa. Ein Lehrgedicht des Atiśa (Dīpaṃkaraśrījñāna) in der tibetischen Überlieferung*, Wiesbaden 1978.

Ejima, Y., *Chūgan-shisō no tenkai ... Bhāvaviveka kenkyū*, Tokyo 1980.

Frauwallner, E., *Geschichte der indischen Philosophie*, Salzburg 1953-1956.

Frauwallner, E., *Die Philosophie des Buddhismus*, Berlin 1969.

Guenther, H.V., *The Jewel Ornament of Liberation*, London 1959.

Hattori, M., *Dignāga, On Perception, being the Pratyakṣapariccheda of Dignāga's Pramāṇasamuccaya*, Cambridge, Massachusetts 1968.

Hikata, R. (ed.), *Suvikrāntavikrāmiparipṛcchā Prajñāpāramitā*, Fukuoka 1958.

Hirano, T., *An Index to the Bodhicaryāvatārapañjikā, chapter IX*, Tokyo 1966.

Jaini, P.S. (ed.), *Abhidharmadīpa with Vibhāṣāprabhāvṛtti*, Patna 1977.

Jhalakīkar, B., *Nyāyakośa or Dictionary of technical terms of Indian philosophy*, Poona 1978.

Jolly, J., *Indian Medicine*, New Delhi 1977.

Johnston, E.H. (ed.), *The Saundarananda of Aśvaghoṣa*, Lahore 1928.

Jong, J.W. de, *Cinq chapitres de la Prasannapadā*, Paris 1949.

Kajiyama, Y., *An Introduction to Buddhist Philosophy. An annotated translation of the Tarkabhāṣā of Mokṣākaragupta*, Kyoto 1966.

Kasawara, K. *et al.* (eds.), *Dharmasaṃgraha*, Oxford 1885.

Kiyota, M. (ed.), *Mahāyāna Buddhist Meditation: Theory and Practice*, Honolulu 1978.

Konow, S., *The two first Chapters of the Daśasāhasrikā Prajñāpāramitā, restoration of the Sanskrit text, Analysis and Index*, Oslo 1941.

Kunst, A., *Probleme der buddhistischen Logik in der Darstellung des Tattvasaṃgraha*, Kraków 1939.

Kværne, P. (ed.), *An Anthology of Buddhist Tantric Songs,* Oslo 1977.

Lamotte, É. (ed.), *Saṃdhinirmocanasūtra,* Louvain 1935.

Lamotte, É. (ed.), 'Karmasiddhiprakarana', *MCB,* IV, Bruxelles 1936.

Lamotte, É., *La Somme du Grand Véhicule d'Asaṅga (Mahāyānasaṃgraha),* I-II, Louvain 1938.

Lamotte, É., *Le Traité de la Grande Vertu de Sagesse de Nāgārjuna (Mahāprajñāpāramitāśāstra),* I-V, Louvain 1949-1980.

Lamotte, É., *Histoire de bouddhisme indien, des origines à l'ère Śaka,* Louvain 1958.

Lamotte, É., *L'Enseignement de Vimalakīrti (Vimalakīrtinirdeśa),* Louvain 1962.

Lamotte, É., *La concentration de la marche héroïque (Śūramgamasamādhisūtra),* Bruxelles 1965.

Lancaster, L. (ed.), *Prajñāpāramitā and related systems. Studies in honor of Edward Conze,* Berkeley 1977.

La Vallée Poussin, L. de, *Bouddhisme. Études et matériaux. Ādikarmapradīpa, Bodhicaryāvatāraṭīkā,* London 1898.

La Vallée Poussin, L. de (ed.), *Bodhicaryāvatārapañjikā. Commentary to the Bodhicaryāvatāra of Śāntideva,* Calcutta 1901-1914.

La Vallée Poussin, L. de (ed.), *Mūlamadhyamakakārikās de Nāgārjuna avec la Prasannapadā Commentaire de Candrakīrti,* St. Pétersbourg 1903-1913.

La Vallée Poussin, L. de (ed.), *Madhyamakāvatāra par Candrakīrti. Traduction tibétaine,* St. Pétersbourg, 1907-1912.

La Vallée Poussin, L. de, *Théorie des douze causes,* Gand 1913.

La Vallée Poussin, L. de, *L'Abhidharmakośa de Vasubandhu,* I-VI, Louvain 1923-1931.

La Vallée Poussin, L. de, *Vijñaptimātratāsiddhi. La Siddhi de Hiuan-tsang,* I-III, Paris 1928-1948.

La Vallée Poussin, L. de, 'Le Joyau dans la main', *MCB,* II, Bruxelles 1933.

Lévi, S. (ed.), *Vijñaptimātratāsiddhi: deux traités de Vasubandhu, Viṃśatikā et Triṃśikā,* Paris 1925.

Lévi, S., *Matériaux pour l'étude du système Vijñaptimātra,* Paris 1932.

Lindtner, C. (ed.), 'Candrakīrti's Pañcaskandhaprakaraṇa', *AO* XL, Hauniae 1979.

Malvania, D. (ed.), *Ācārya Jinabhadra's Viśeṣāvaśyakabhāṣya,* I-III, Ahmedabad 1966-1968.

Matsunami, S., *A Catalogue of the Sanskrit Manuscripts in the Tokyo University Library,* Tokyo 1965.

May, J., *Candrakīrti Prasannapadā Madhyamakavṛtti,* Paris 1959.

Mimaki, K., *La réfutation bouddhique de la permanence des choses (sthirasiddhidūṣaṇa) et la preuve de la momentanéité des choses (kṣaṇabhaṅgasiddhi),* Paris

1976.
Miyasaka, Y. (ed.), *Pramāṇavārttikakārikā (Sanskrit and Tibetan)*, Narita-shi Chiba-ken 1972.
Murti, T. R. V., *The Central Philosophy of Buddhism*, London 1960.
Nagao, G. M. (ed.), *Madhyāntavibhāga-Bhāṣya. A Buddhist philosophical treatise edited for the first time from a Sanskrit Manuscript*, Tokyo 1964.
Nakamura, H., 'A Survey of Mahāyāna Buddhism with bibliographical Notes', *The Journal of Intercultural Studies*, III-IV, Osaka-fu 1976-1978.
Nanjio, B. (ed.), *Laṅkāvatārasūtra*, Kyōto 1923.
Naudou, J., *Les bouddhistes kaśmīriens au Moyen Age*, Paris 1968.
Obermiller, E., *Bu-ston: History of Buddhism*, I-II, Heidelberg 1931-1933.
Obermiller, E. (ed.), *Ratnaguṇasaṃcaya*, The Hague 1960.
Pezzali, A., *Śāntideva, mystique bouddhiste des VIIe et VIIIe siècles*, Firenze 1968.
Pradhan, P. (ed.), *Abhidharmakośabhāṣyam of Vasubandhu*, Patna 1975.
Python, P. (ed.), *Vinaya-viniścaya-Upālipariprcchā*, Paris 1973.
Rahder, J. (ed.), *Daśabhūmikasūtra*, Louvain 1926.
Rahder, J., *Glossary of Sanskrit, Tibetan, Mongolian and Chinese versions of the Daśabhūmikasūtra*, Paris 1928.
Rahula, W., *Le compendium de la super-doctrine (philosophie) (Abhidharmasamuccaya) d'Asaṅga*, Paris 1971.
Ramanan, K. V., *Nāgārjuna's Philosophy as presented in the Mahāprajñāpāramitāśāstra*, Tokyo 1966.
Randle, H. N., *Indian Logic in the Early Schools*, Oxford 1930.
Ritter, J. *et al.* (eds.), *Historisches Wörterbuch der Philosophie*, Basel 1971.
Robinson, R. H., *Early Mādhyamika in India and China*, Madison 1967.
Ruben, W., *Die Nyāyasūtra's. Text, Übersetzung, Erläuterung und Glossar*, Leipzig 1928.
Rubow, P., *Den kritiske Kunst. En afhandling om filologisk litteraturforskning*, København 1938.
Ruegg, D. S., *La théorie du Tathāgatagarbha et du Gotra*, Paris 1969.
Samtani, N. H. (ed.), *The Arthaviniścaya-sūtra & its commentary (Nibandhana)*, Patna 1971.
Sakaki, R., *Mahāvyutpatti*, Kyōto 1916-1925.
Sastri, N. A. (ed.), *Śālistamba Sūtra*, Adyar 1950.
Schiefner, A. (ed.), *Tāranāthae de doctrinae buddhicae in India propagatione*, Petropoli 1868.
Schmithausen, L., *Der Nirvāṇa-Abschnitt in der Viniścayasaṃgrahaṇī der Yogācārabhūmiḥ*, Wien 1969.
Shackleton Bailey, D. R., *The Śatapañcāśatkastotra of Mātṛceṭa*, Cambridge 1951.
Staël-Holstein, A. v. (ed.), *Kāśyapaparivarta*, Shanghai 1926.

Streng, F., *Emptiness, A study in religious meaning,* Nashville 1967.
Suali, L. (ed.), *Ṣaḍdarśanasamuccaya by Haribhadra with Guṇaratna's commentary Tarkarahasyadīpikā,* Calcutta 1905.
Suzuki, D. T., *An index to the Laṅkāvatārasūtra,* Kyoto 1934.
Takakusu, J., *The essentials of Buddhist philosophy,* Honolulu 1956.
Takasaki, J., *A study on the Ratnagotravibhāga (Uttaratantra),* Roma 1966.
Thakur, A. (ed.), *Jñānaśrīmitranibandhāvali,* Patna 1959.
Tripāthī, C. (ed.), *Fünfundzwanzig Sūtras des Nidānasaṃyukta,* Berlin 1962.
Tucci, G., 'Studi Mahāyānici, I: La versione cinese del Catuḥśataka de Āryadeva confrontato col testo sanscrito e la traduzione tibetana', *Rivista degli Studi Orientali,* X, Roma 1925.
Tucci, G., *Pre-Diṅnaga Buddhist texts on Logic from Chinese sources,* Baroda 1929.
Tucci, G. (ed.), *Minor Buddhist Texts,* I-III, Roma 1956-1971.
Tucci, G., *Opera Minora,* I-II, Roma 1971.
Tuxen, P., *Yoga,* København 1911.
Tuxen, P., *Indledende Bemærkninger til buddhistisk Relativisme,* København 1936.
Ui, H., *Vaiśeṣika Philosophy, according to the Daśapadārthaśāstra, Chinese text, with introduction, translation and notes,* London 1917.
Vetter, T., *Studien zur Lehre und Entwicklung Śaṅkaras,* Wien 1979.
Walleser, M., *Die Mittlere Lehre des Nāgārjuna. Nach der chinesischen Version übertragen,* Heidelberg 1912.
Wayman, A., *Calming the Mind and discerning the Real. Buddhist Meditation and the Middle View. From the Lam rim chen mo of Tsoṅ-kha-pa,* New York 1978.
Weller, F., *Zum Kāśyapaparivarta, Verdeutschung des sanskrit-tibetischen Textes,* Leipzig 1965.
Yamaguchi, S., *Chūkan Bukkyō Ronkō,* Tokyo 1965.
Yamaguchi, S., *Index to the Prasannapadā Madhyamaka-vṛtti,* I-II, Kyoto 1974.

Dansk resumé

Det har længe været forskningen bekendt, at den buddhistiske tænker Nāgārjuna (2.-3. årh. e.K.) gennem sit forfatterskab har udøvet en umådelig indflydelse på den filosofiske og religiøse udvikling både inden for og uden for den såkaldte Mahāyāna-buddhismes egentlige domæne.

Men klart har det også stået, at den dag endnu er fjern hvor hans værk og dets betydning kan betragtes som endeligt udforsket.

Det står dog allerede nu fast at Nāgārjuna er mere end blot en historisk central skikkelse. Hans filosofiske tanker har krav på opmærksomhed for deres egen skyld. Om en almindelig og tiltagende interesse herfor vidner ikke mindst den efterhånden uoverskuelige mængde artikler, monografier, oversættelser osv. der skyldes såvel europæiske som asiatiske forskere.

Alligevel befinder forskningen sig her i den penible situation at forudsætningerne for den videnskabelige bearbejdelse af Nāgārjunas tanker og deres indflydelse endnu ikke er skabt: Traditionen tilskriver ham forfatterskabet af mere end ét hundrede af de hvad form og indhold angår yderst forskelligartede skrifter. Kun få er overleveret i deres originalaffatning på sanskrit medens hovedparten kun er tilgængelig i tibetanske og kinesiske oversættelser, der tilmed ofte byder forståelsen store vanskeligheder, bl.a. grundet manglende leksikografiske og litteraturhistoriske forarbejder. Den moderne forskning har bl.a. derfor i reglen henholdt sig til tre-fire vigtige værker hvis ægthed gerne stiltiende blev taget for givet som udgangspunkt for indholdsmæssig behandling.

Nærværende afhandling – der for sin fremgangsmåde og sine resultater forudsætter og viderefører forfatterens tidligere arbejde: *Nāgārjuna – Ægte og Uægte. En analyse og sammenfatning af Nāgārjunas autentiske værker og fragmenter udskilt blandt samtlige på sanskrit, tibetansk og kinesisk under hans navn overleverede skrifter* (upubliceret speciale) – rejser derfor i første omgang spørgsmålet: Er det muligt at udskille en genuin kerne i denne mængde værker der traditionelt tillægges forfatteren? Med henblik på ægthedsbestemmelsen opstilles dels nogle indre kriterier, dels nogle ydre. Til de første hører stilistiske, filosofiske og kompositionelle overensstemmelser mellem *Mūlamadhyamakakārikā*, der i henhold til den samstemmende overlevering aksiomatisk betegnes som forfatterens hovedværk, og de øvrige ham tillagte værker. De ydre kriterier leveres af »troværdige vidner«. Der tænkes her fremfor alt på en række kommentatorer der står i Nāgārjunas tradition, den såkaldte Madhyamaka. Såfremt en eller flere af disse kilder udtrykkeligt tillægger Nāgārjuna forfatterskabet af et værk der *samtidigt* sandsynliggør sin autenticitet i lyset af de nævnte indre kriterier, da accepteres traditionens vidnesbyrd og værket anerkendes som ægte.

Som det fremgår heraf har det ikke blot været påkrævet at gennemlæse alle de værker der tillægges Nāgārjuna, men det har desuden været uomgængeligt at konsultere den langt mere omfattende kommentarlitteratur, hvis tydning i øvrigt ikke bekvemmeliggøres af den omstændighed at størsteparten endnu ikke er udforsket og kun foreligger i ældre tibetanske bloktryk. – Imidlertid har studiet af kommentarlitteraturen i flere henseender vist sig overraskende udbytterigt. Ad disse veje er således et stort antal fragmenter bragt for dagens lys, bl.a. fra værker der ansås for tabte.

Afhandlingen er disponeret således at der indledningsvis gives et overblik over de værker som i ovenfornævnte arbejde grupperedes som *enten* afgjort uægte (fx derved at de kompromitterede sig ved at anføre en forfatter der må sættes senere end Nāgārjuna, idet muligheden for interpolation naturligvis ikke overses), *eller* tvivlsomme (nogle dog med større sandsynlighed for at være ægte, andre med mindre). Dernæst behandles de tretten værker der tidligere er bestemt som ægte, ét for ét men efter omstændighederne på forskellig vis: κατὰ τὴν ὕλην οἱ λόγοι ἀπαιτητέοι. I enkelte tilfælde hvor de pågældende tekster allerede er eller forventes udgivet eller oversat til et hovedsprog, har jeg begrænset mig til en indholds- eller argumentationsanalyse eller på anden vis søgt at bidrage med supplerende materiale. Hvad de øvrige værker angår har jeg enten udarbejdet en kommenteret oversættelse (især fra tibetansk og kinesisk) eller kritiske udgaver (sanskrit og tibetansk) med tilhørende filologisk apparat osv., så vidt muligt ud fra devisen: Ὅμηρον ἐξ Ὁμήρου σαφηνίζειν. Ofte er det, som nævnt, takket være citatforekomster i kommentarlitteraturen lykkedes at identificere sanskritfragmenter fra værker der i øvrigt er gået tabt eller måske kun kendes i tibetansk eller kinesisk oversættelse.

Afhandlingen afrundes med på grundlag af de indvundne forskningsresultater at give en sammenfattende skildring af Nāgārjunas filosofiske system i lyset af dets historiske forudsætninger.

Til slut gives nogle vink om i hvilken retning den kommende forskning med særlig fordel kunne rette sin indsats inden for et arbejdsfelt hvor videnskaben i mangt og meget endnu må træde sine børnesko.

Appendix

The Nepalese MS of *Catuḥstava* with *Akāriṭīkā:*

CS, I: *Lokātītastava, fol.* 1b3-8b4
CS, II: *Niraupamyastava, fol.* 9a3-16b6
CS, III: *Acintyastava, fol.* 17a4-32b7
CS, IV: *Paramārthastava, fol.* 33a2-35b9

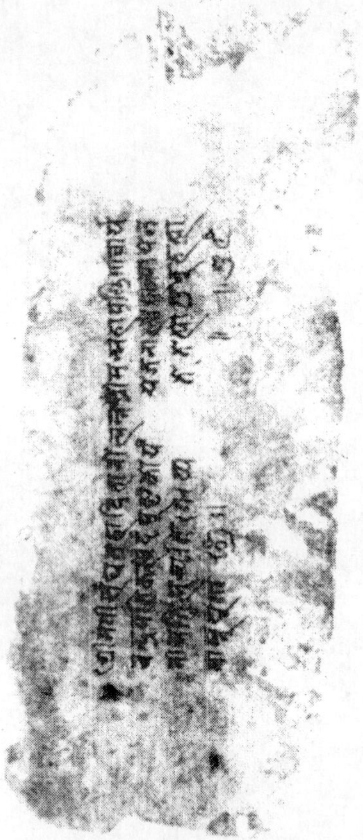

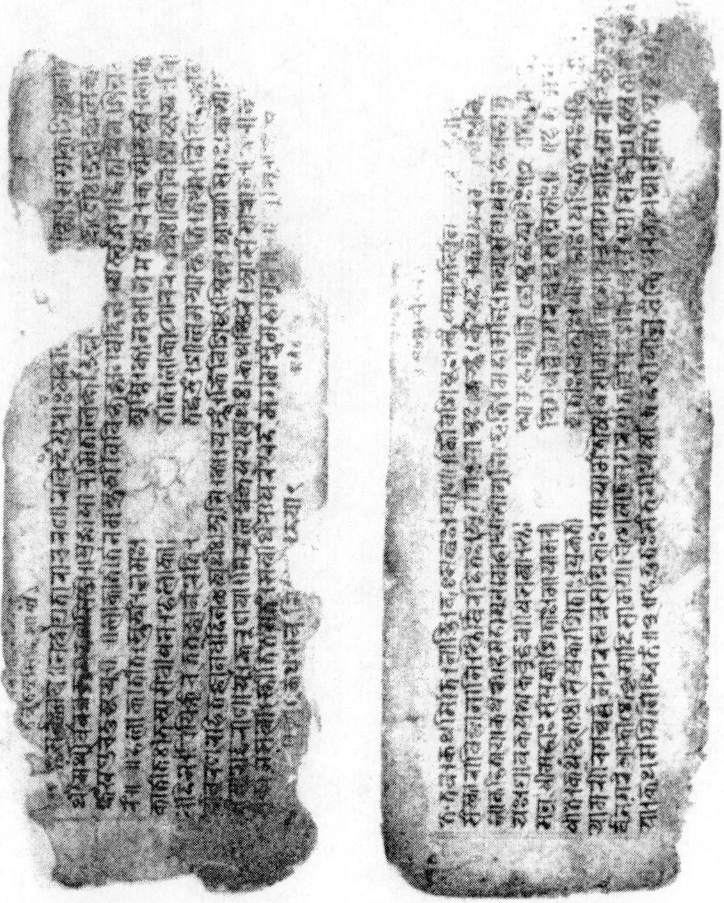

1 2 3 4

CS, I

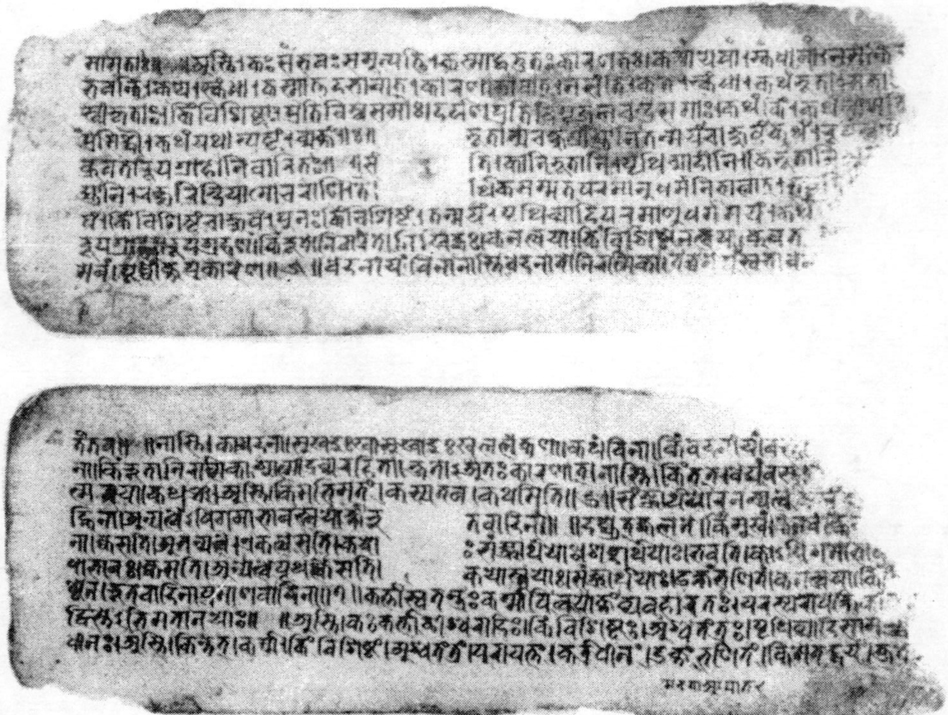

5

6

7

8

CS, I

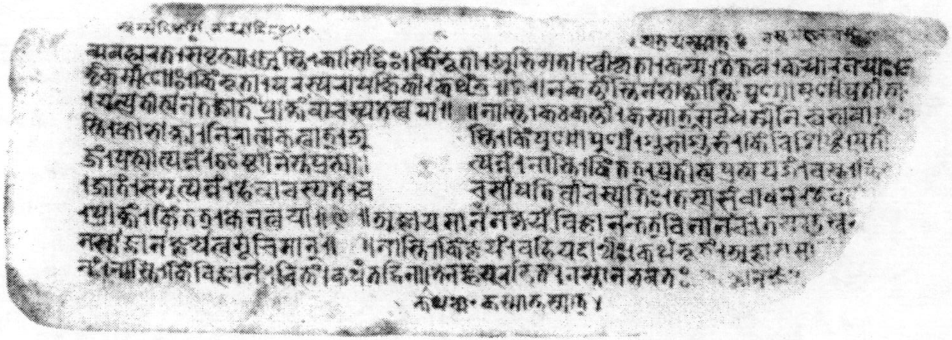

9

10

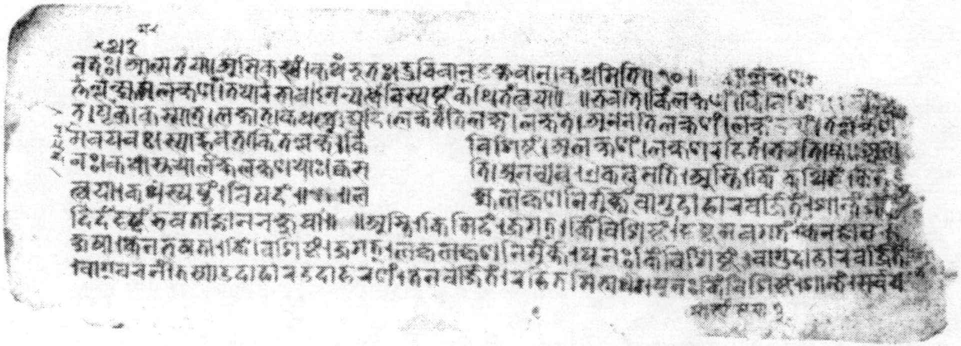

11

12

CS, I

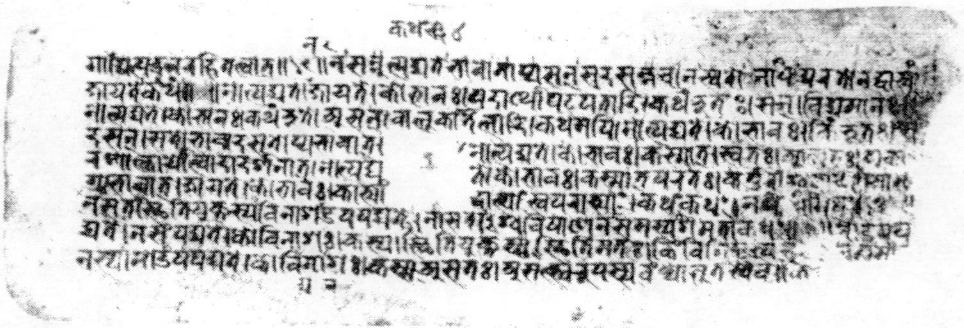

13

14

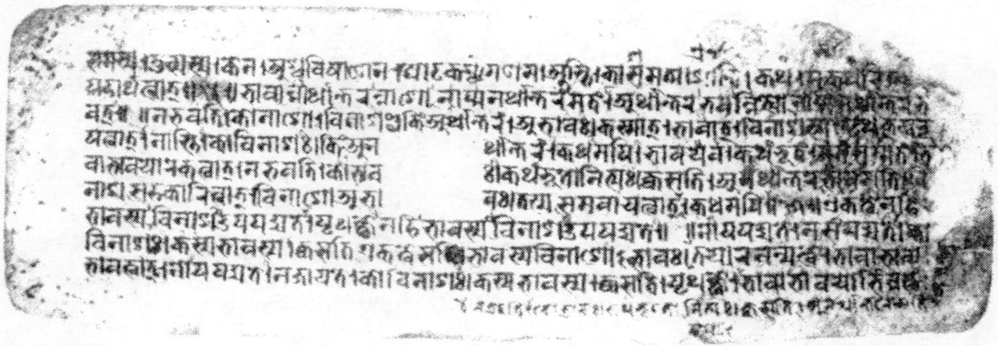

15

16

CS, I

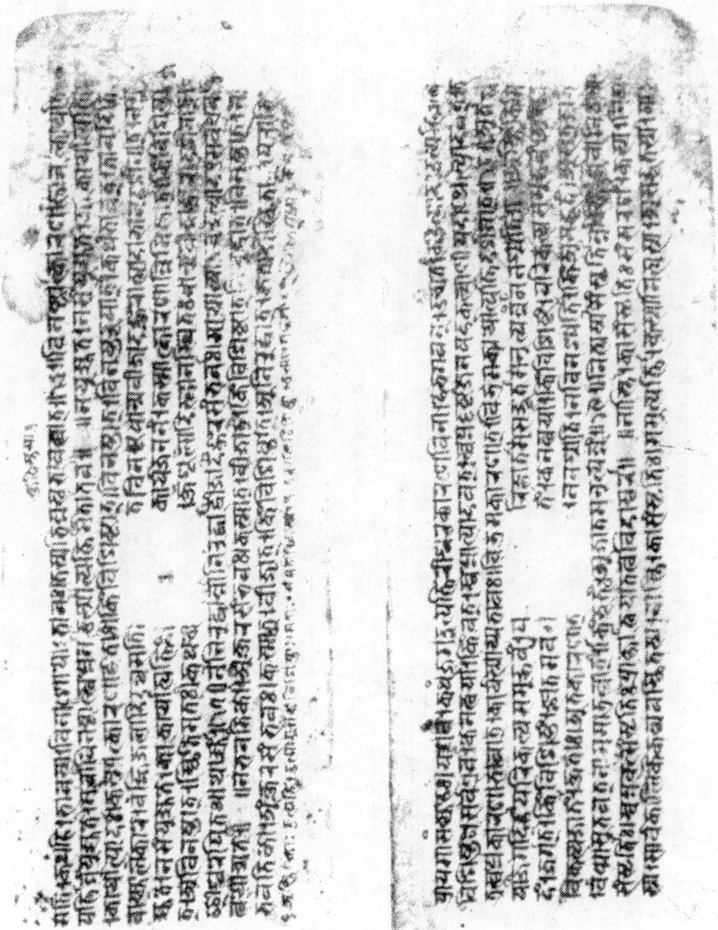

7

8

9

20

CS. I

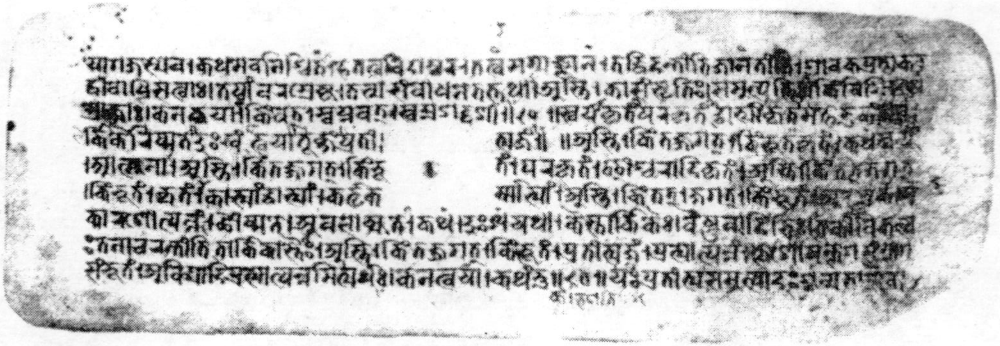

21

22

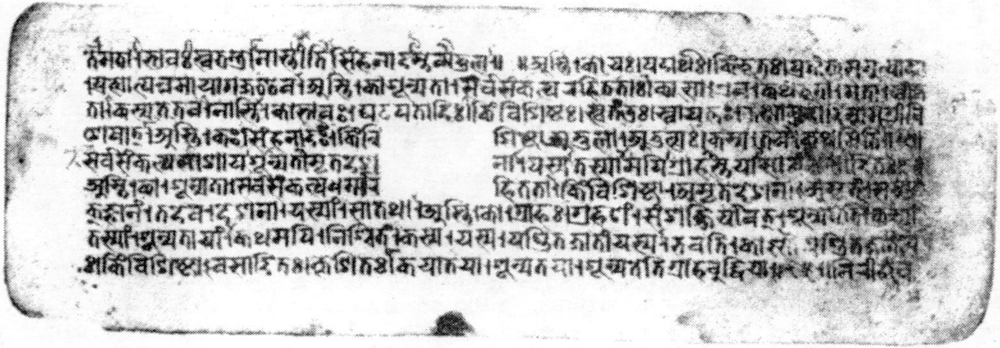

23

24

CS, I

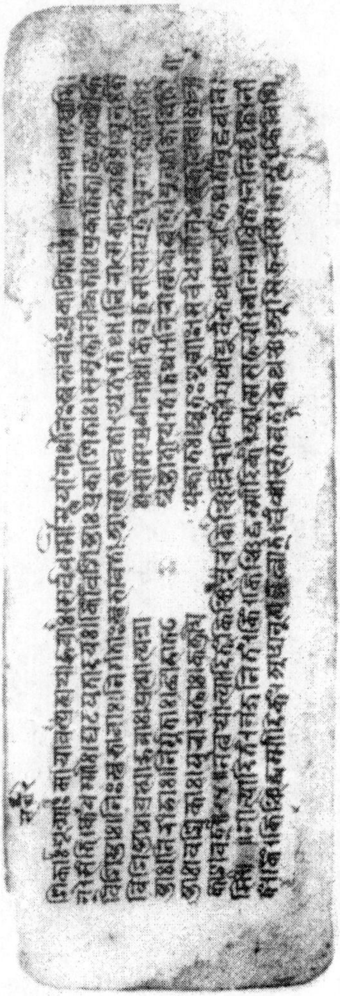

25

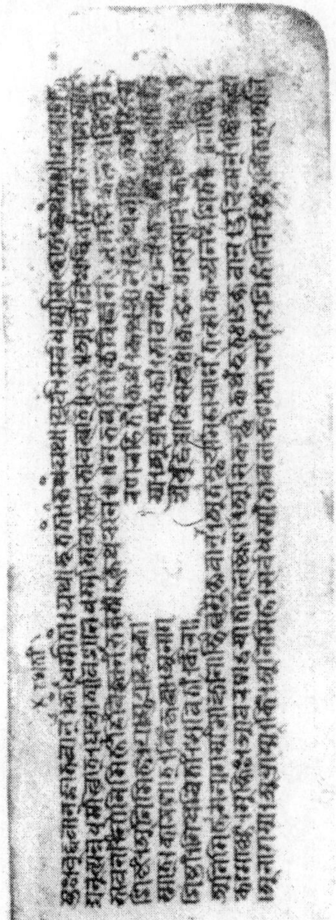

26

27

CS, 1

28

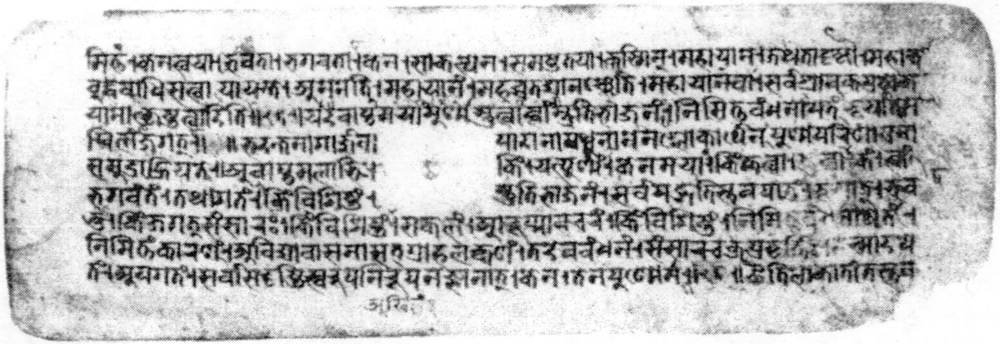

1

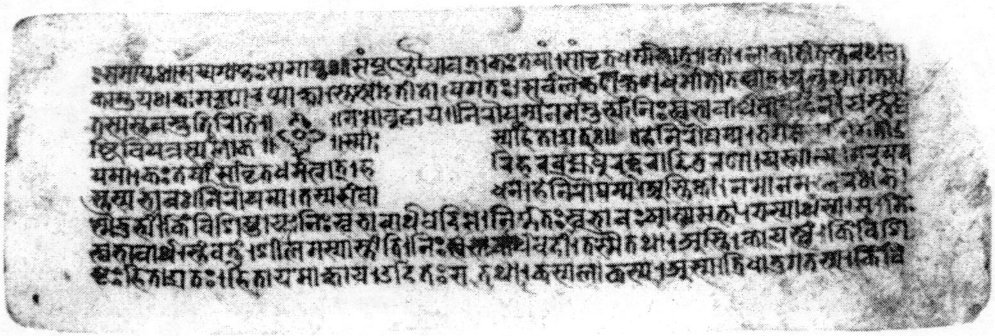

CS, II

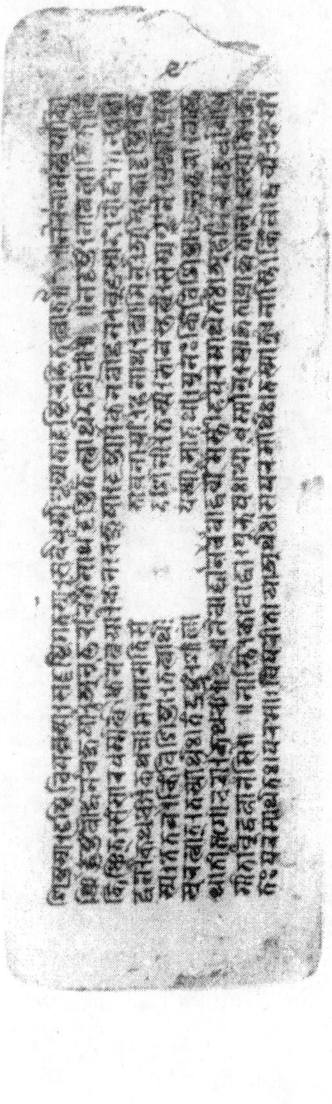

2

3

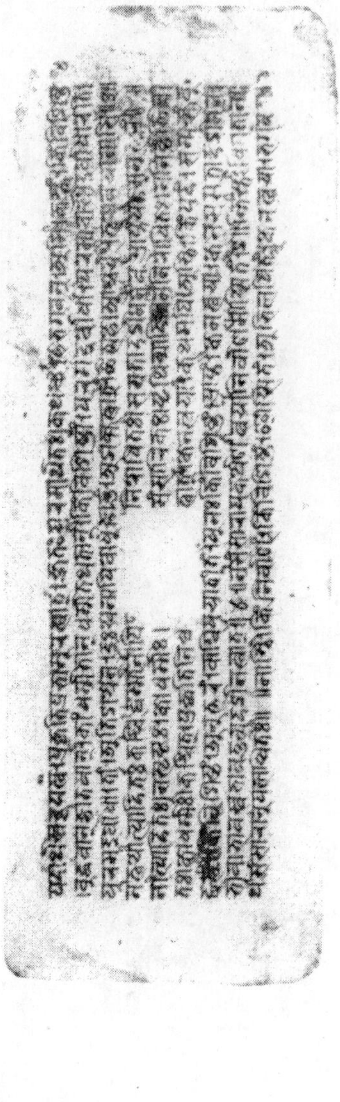

4

5

CS, II

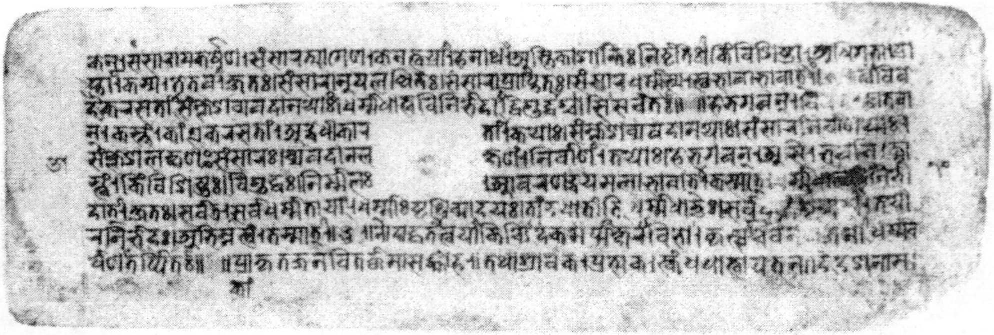

6

7

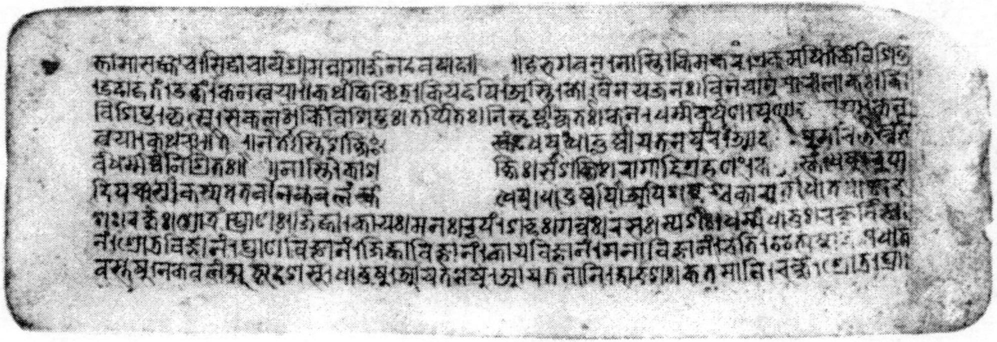

8

CS, II

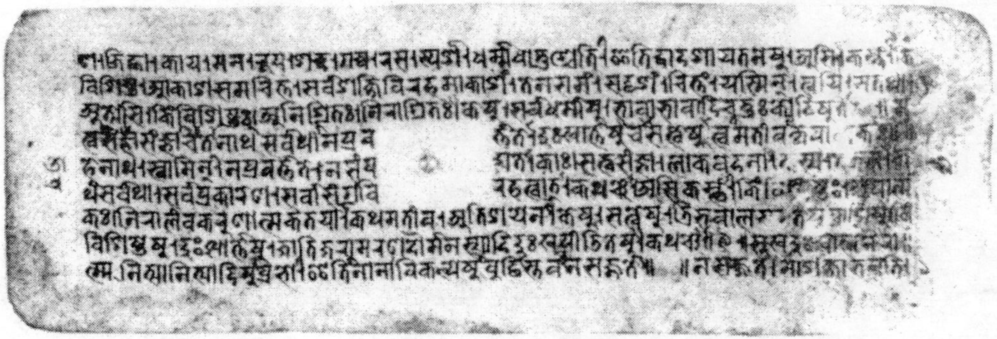

9

10

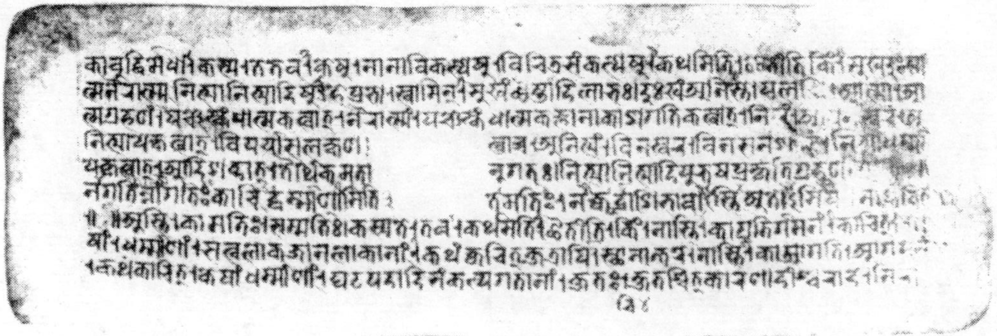

11

CS, II

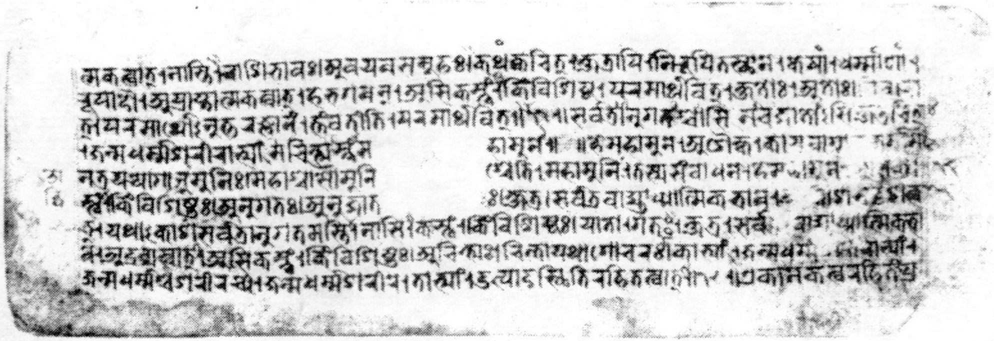

12

13

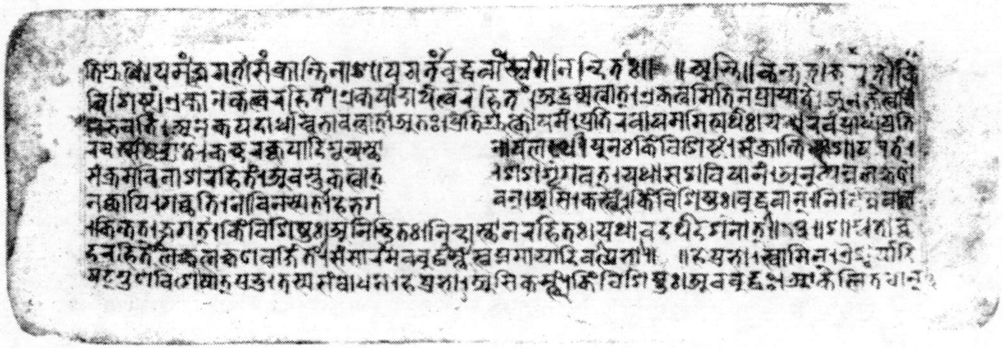

14

CS, II

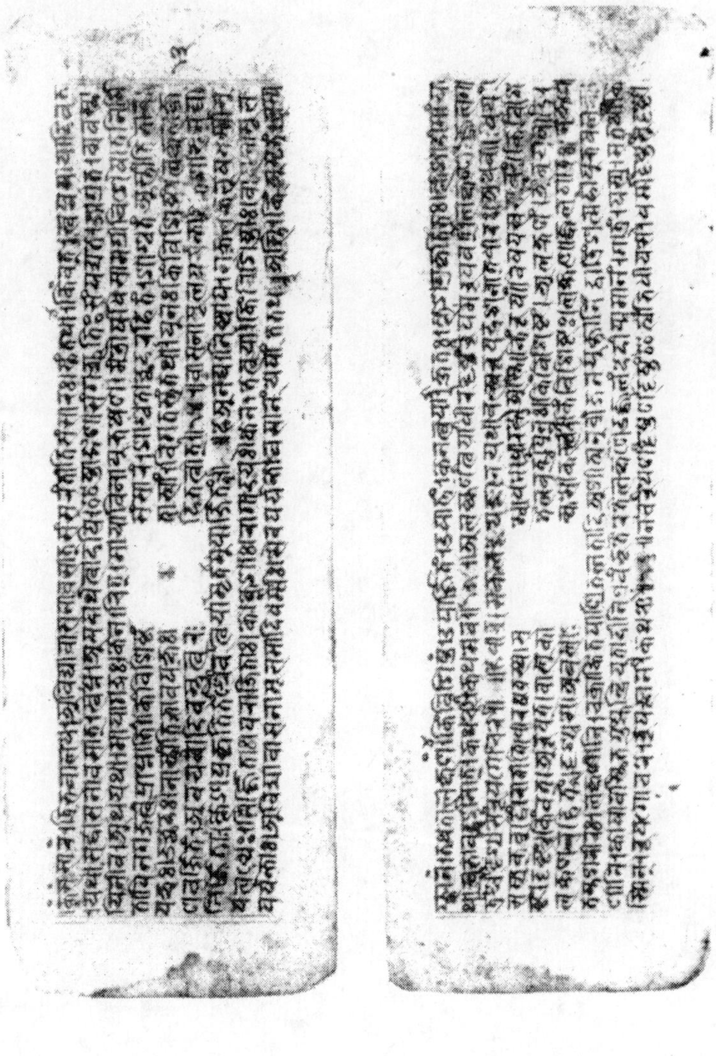

15 16 17

CS. II

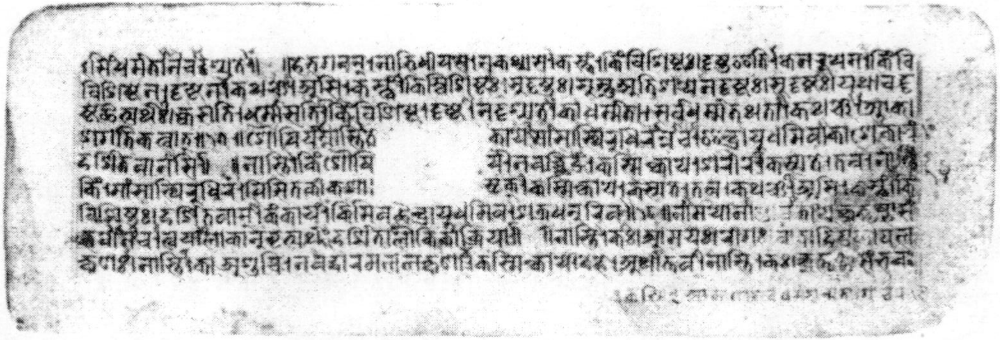

18

19

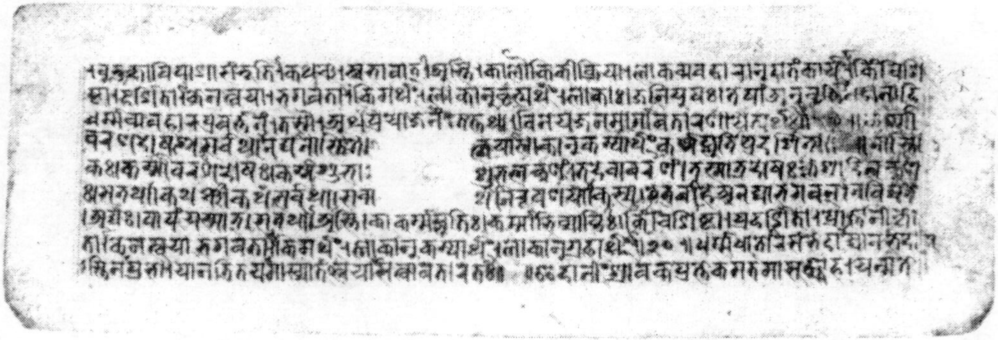

20

21

CS, II

22

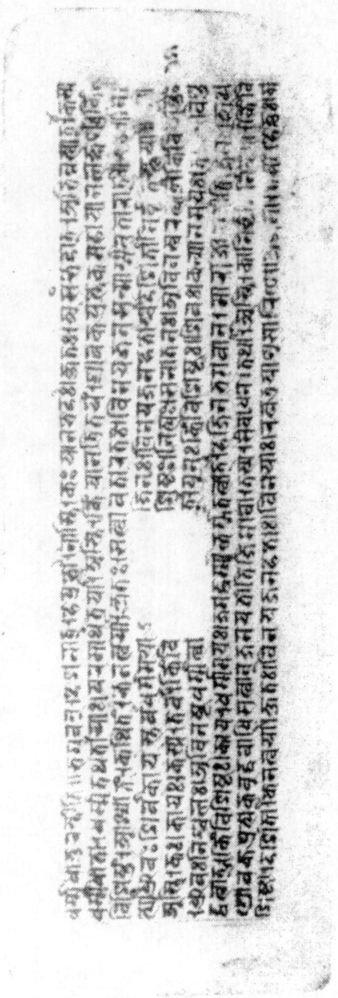

23

24

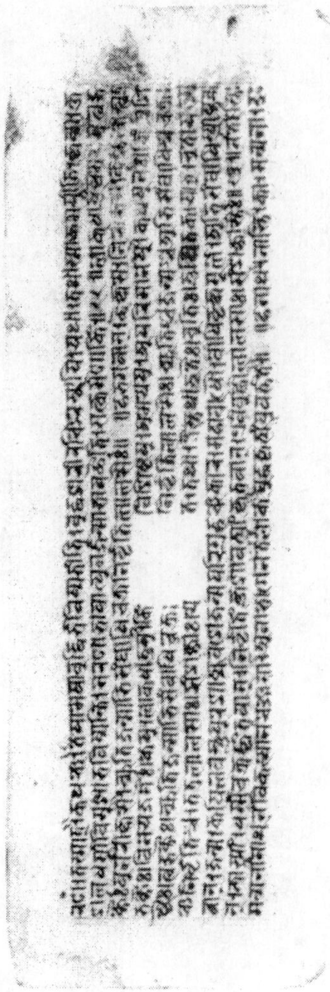

CS. II

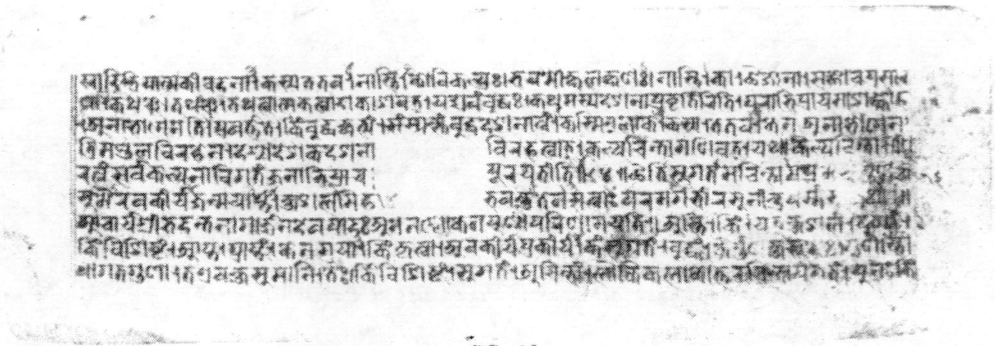

25

CS, II

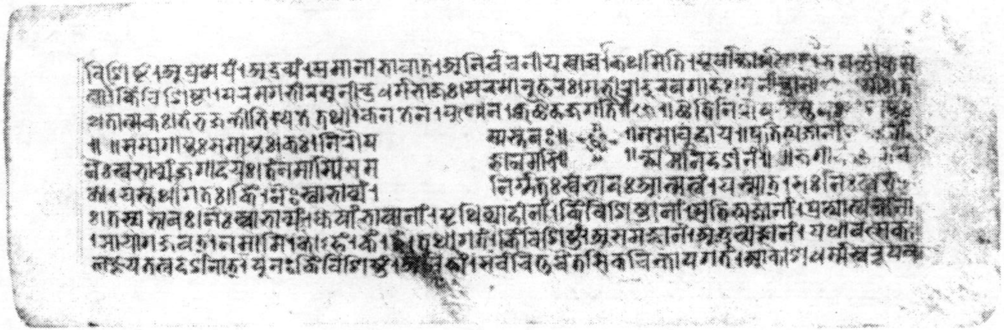

1

CS, III

2

3

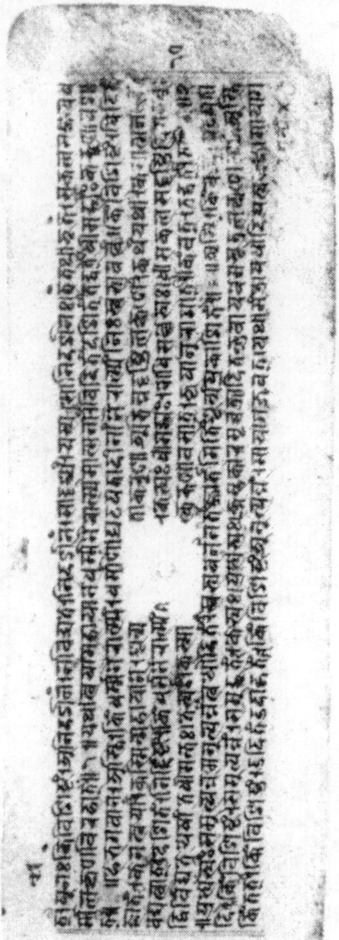

4

5

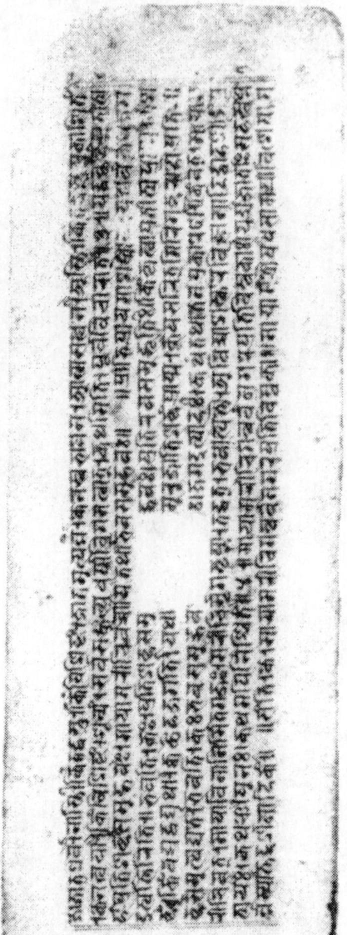

CS, III

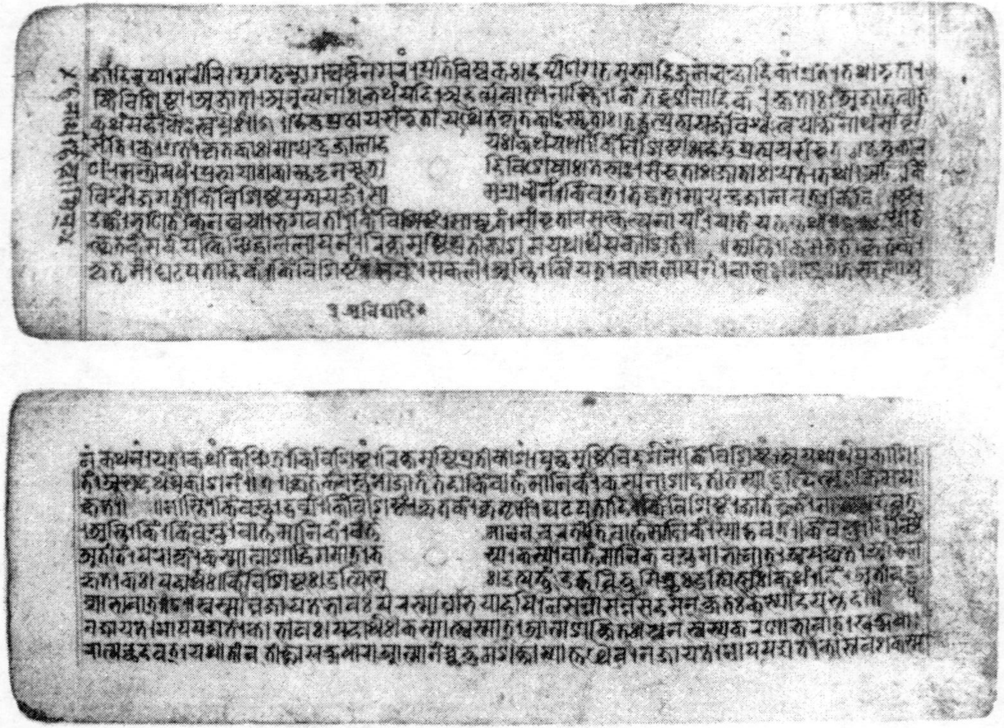

6

7

8

9

CS, III

10

11

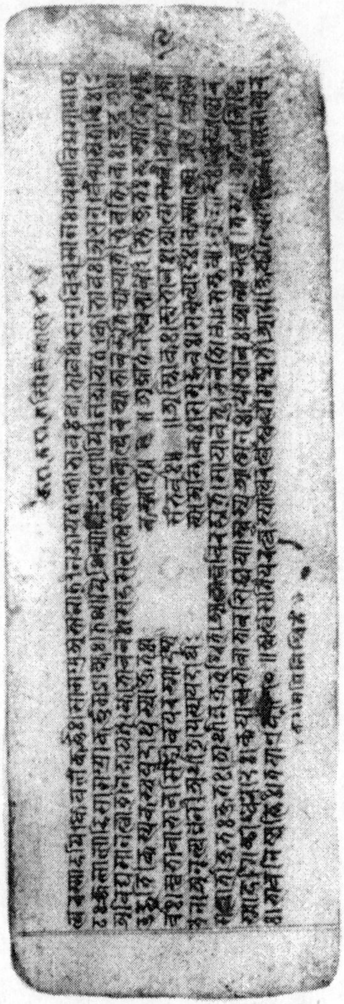

12

13

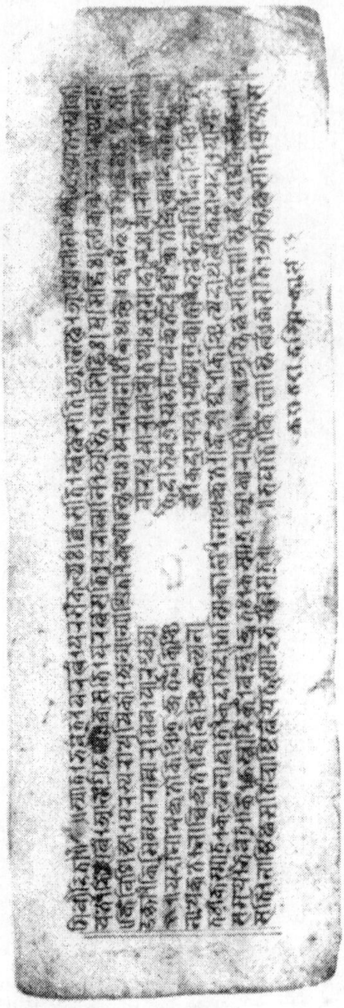

CS. III

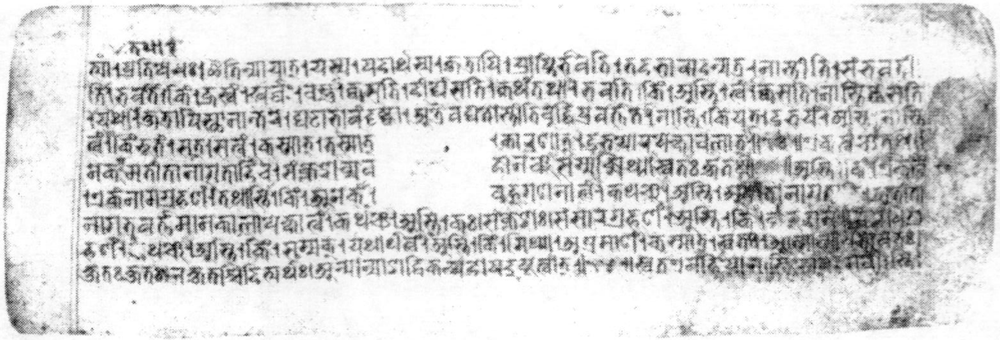

14

15

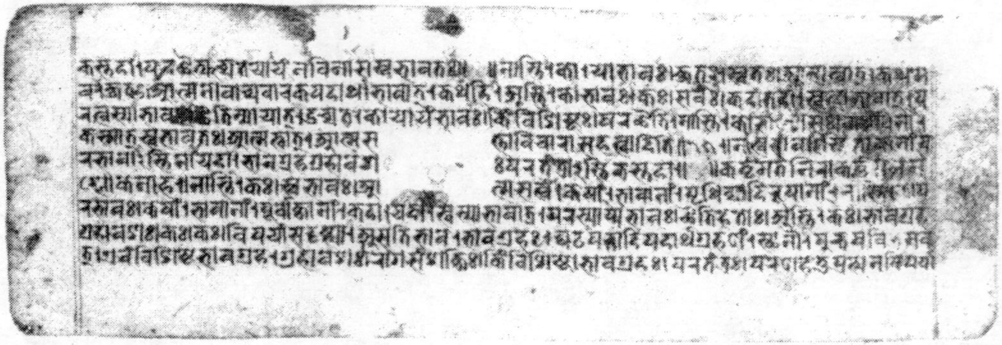

16

CS, III

17 18 19 20

CS, III

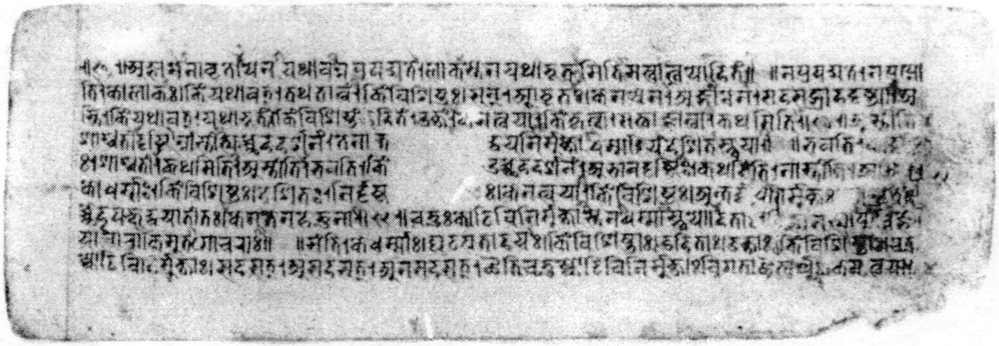

21

22

23

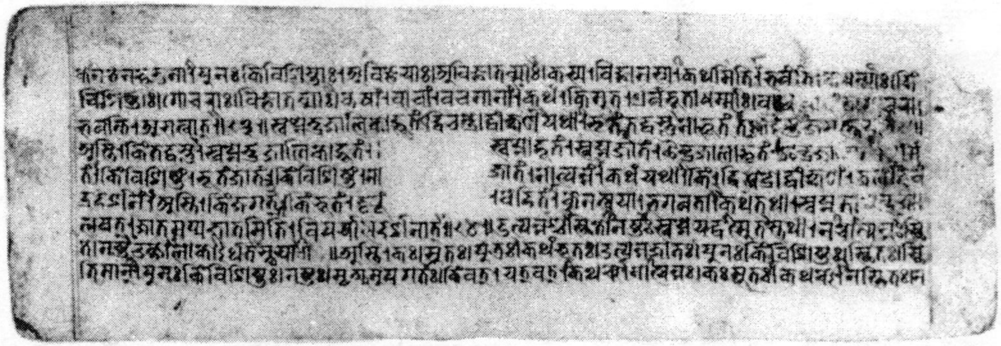

24

25

CS, III

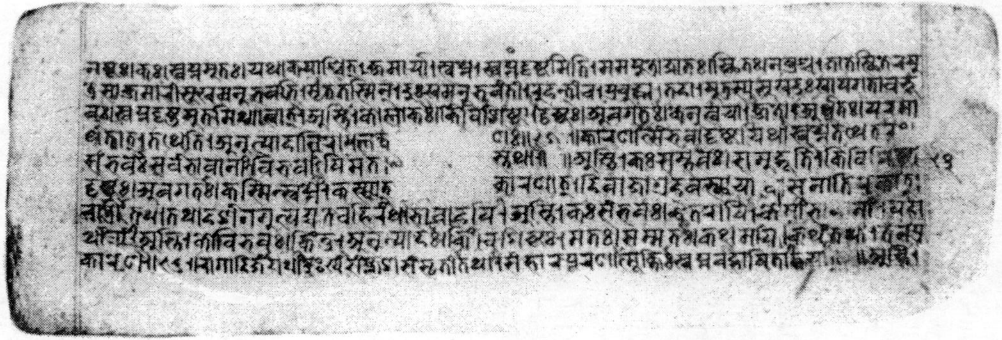

26

27

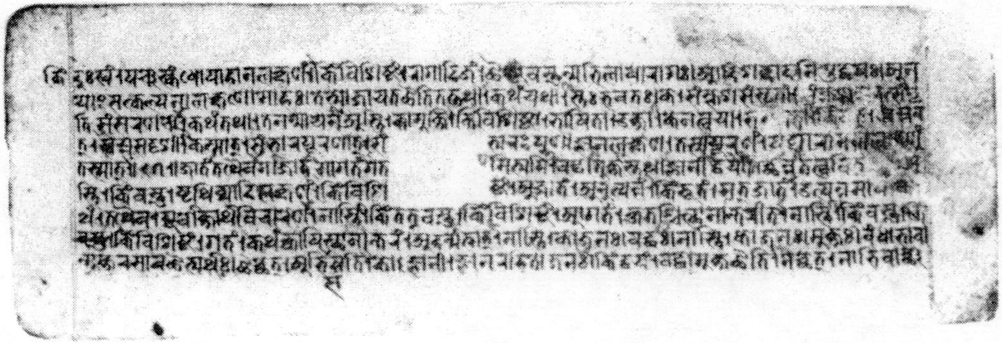

28

CS, III

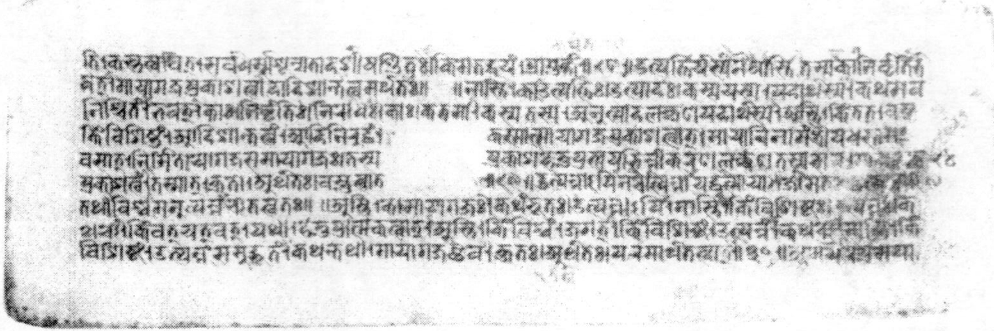

29

30

31

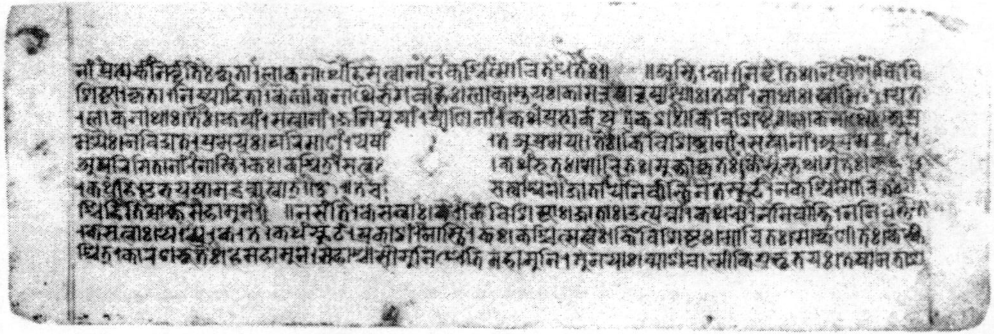

32

CS, III

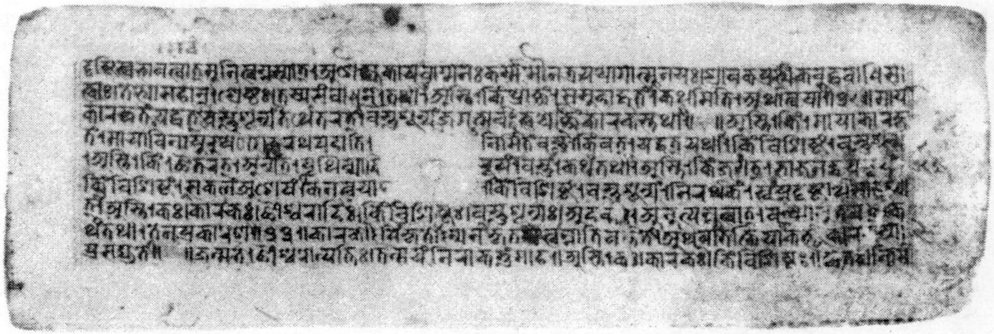

33

34

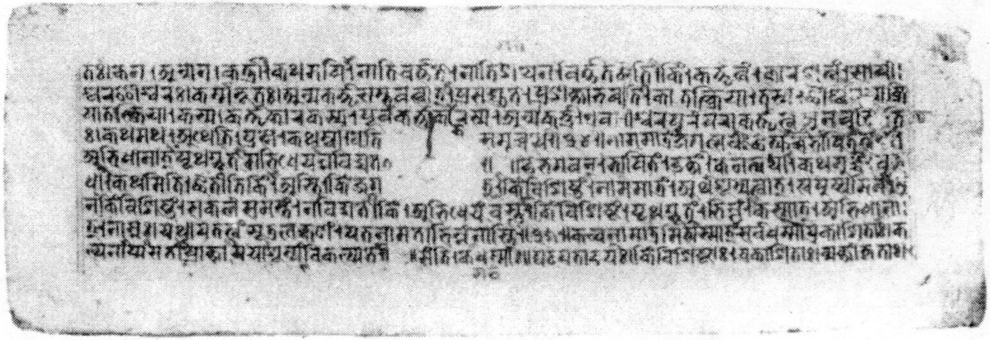

35

36

CS, III

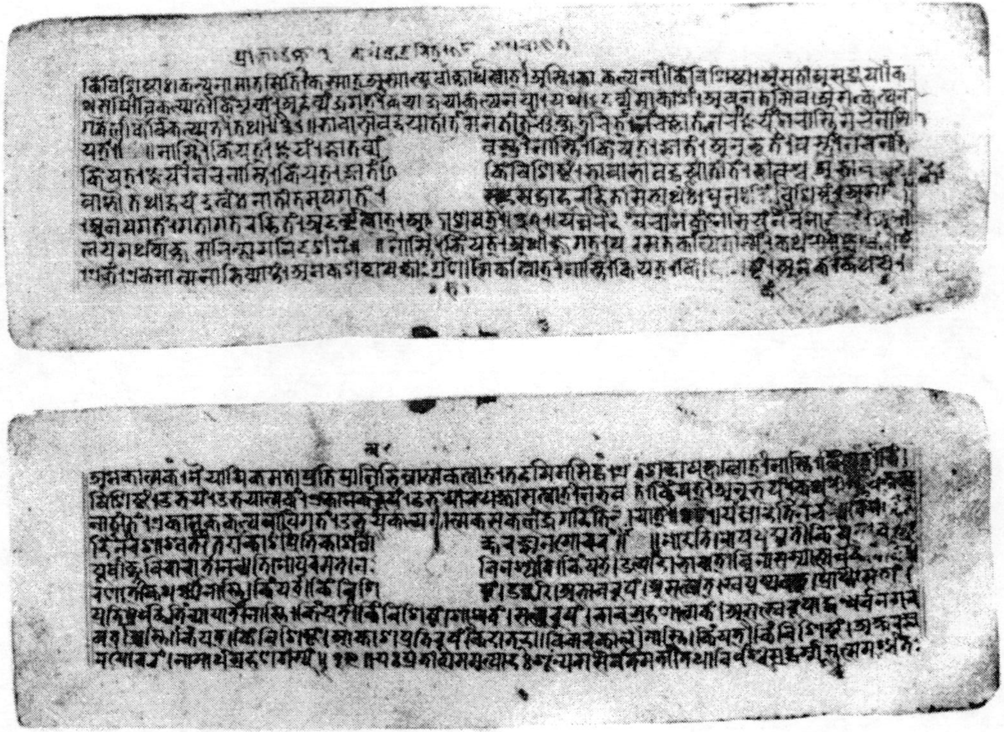

37

38

39

40

CS, 111

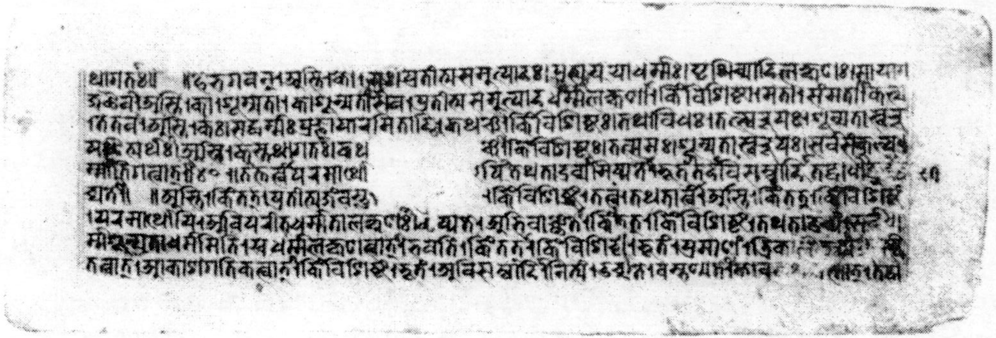

41

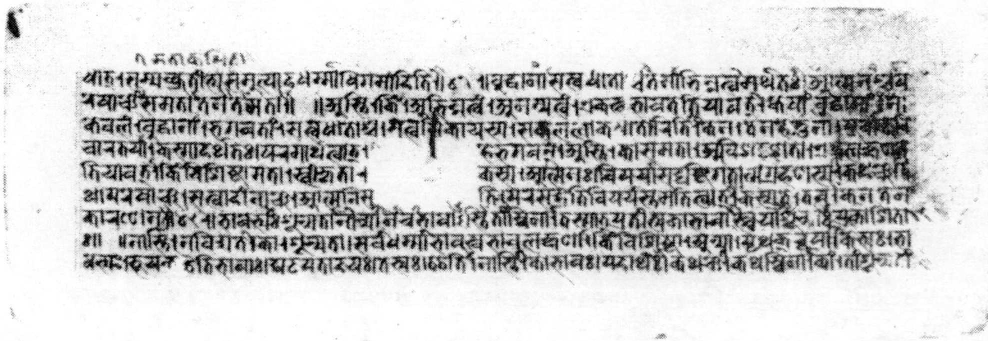

42

43

CS, III

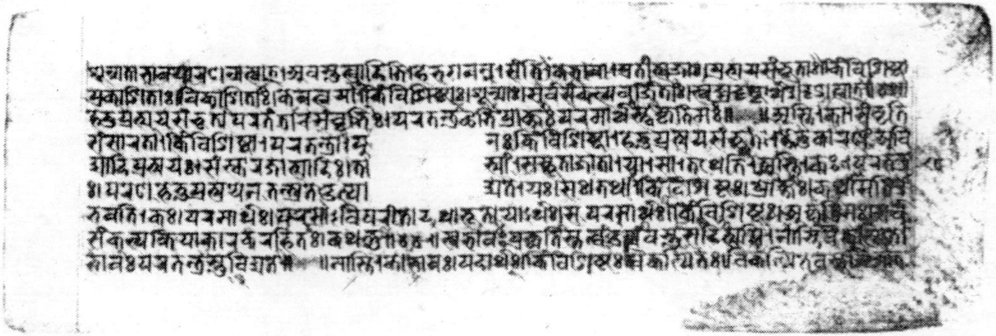

44

45

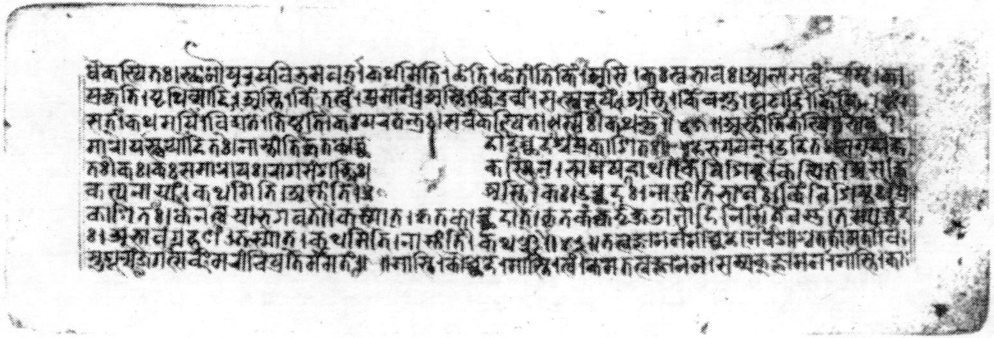

46

47

CS, III

48

49

50

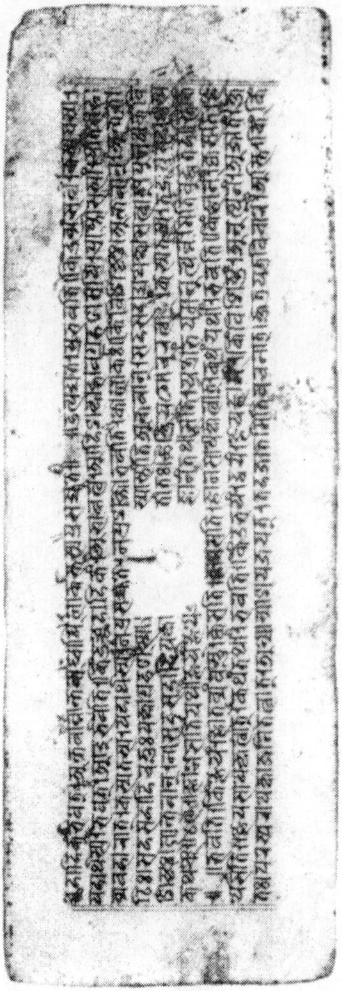

CS. III

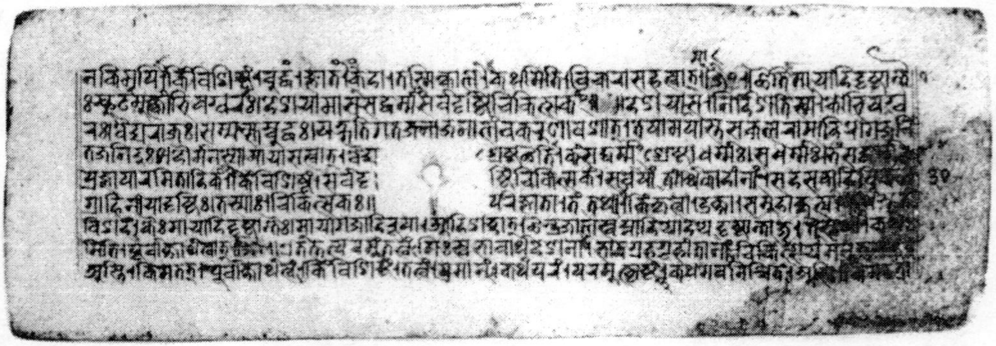

51

52

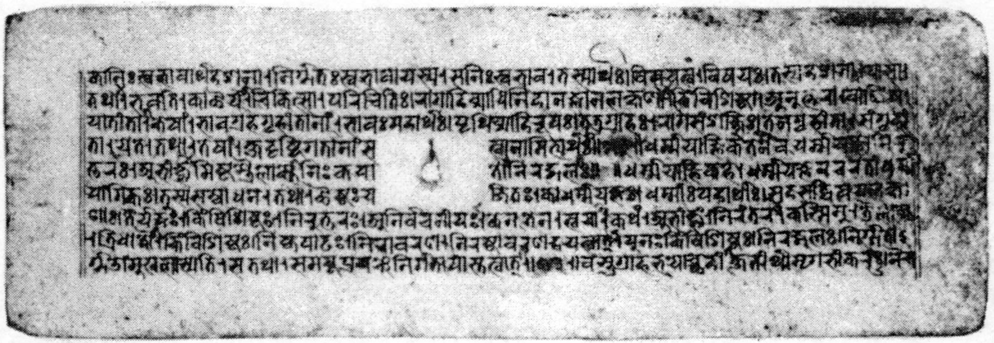

53

54

CS, III

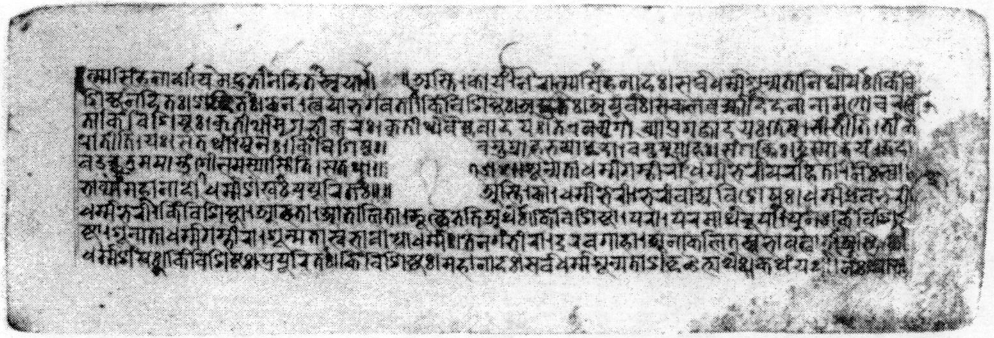

55

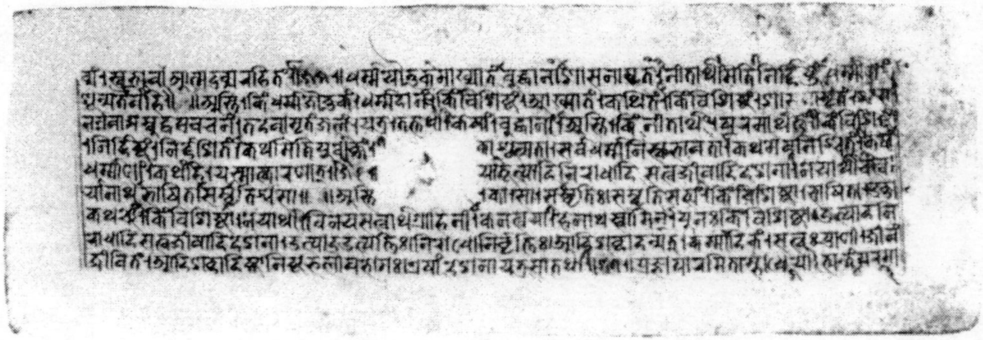

56

57

58

CS, III

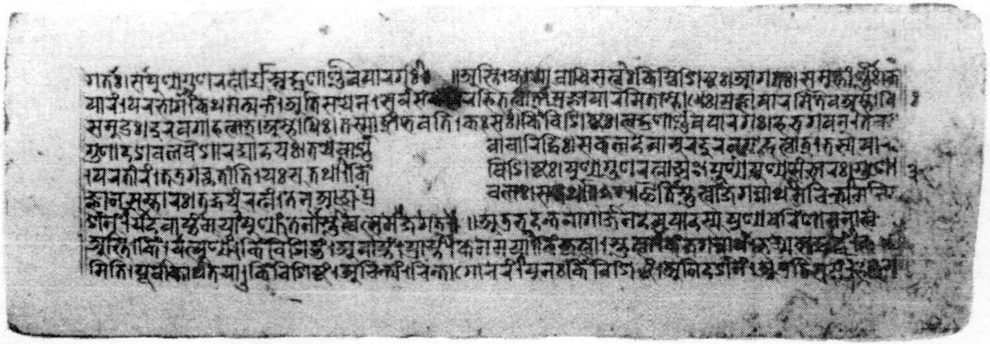

59

CS, III

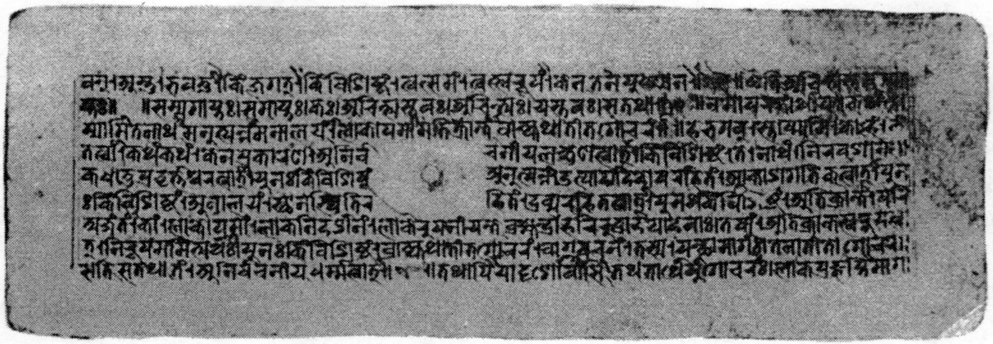

1

2

CS, IV

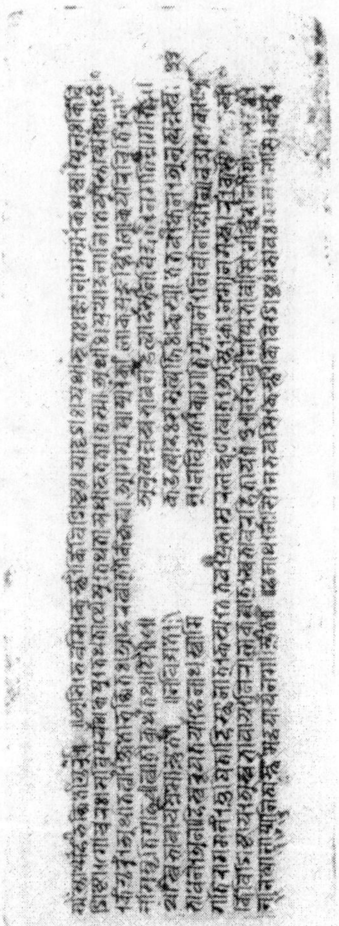

5

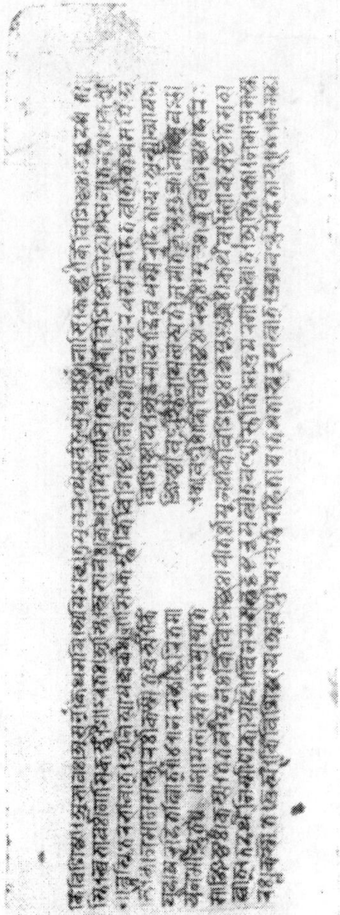

6

CS, IV

7

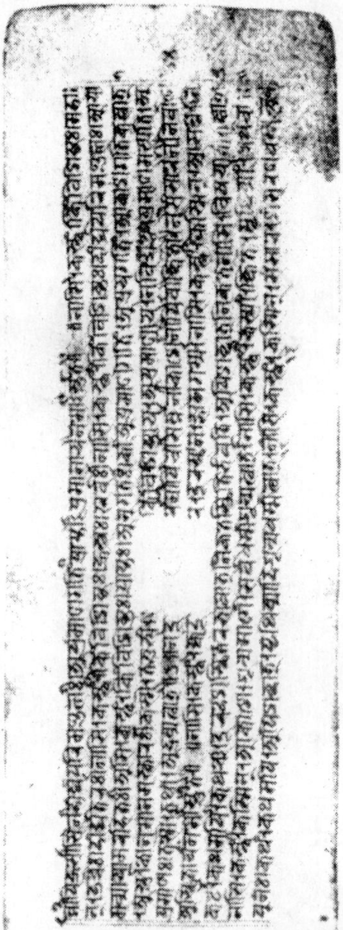

8

9

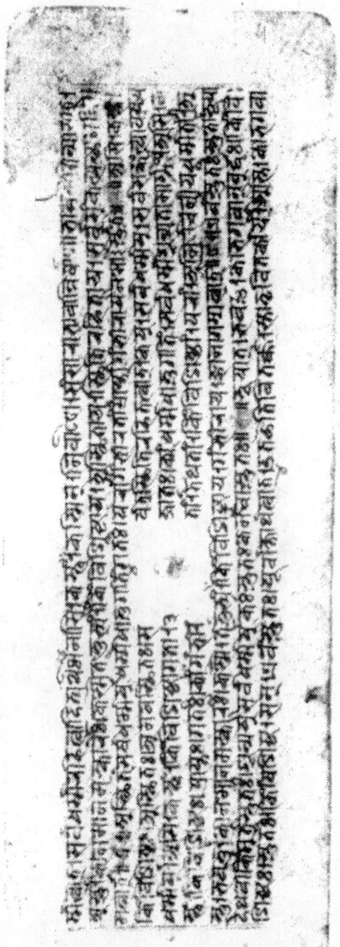

CS, IV

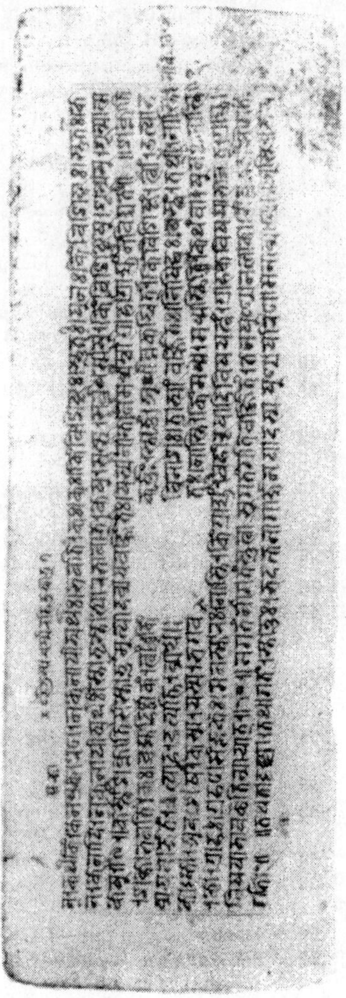

10

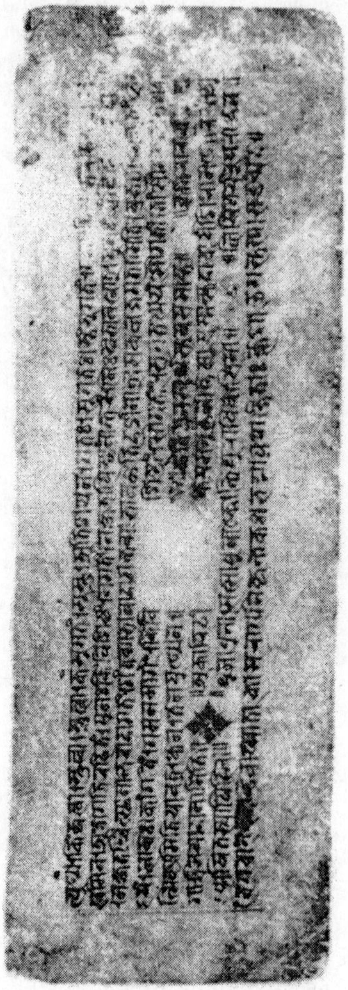

11

CS, IV

BUDDHIST TRADITION SERIES

General Editor: ERNST STEINKELLNER
Joint General Editor: ALEXANDER VON ROSPATT
Founder Editor: Late ALEX WAYMAN

1 Indian Buddhism—*Hajime Nakamura*
2 Nagarjuniana—*Chr. Lindtner*
3 Chinese Monks in India—*Latika Lahiri*
4 Buddhism in Central Asia—*B.N. Puri*
5 Dharmakīrti's Theory of Hetu-Centricity of Anumāna—*M. R. Chinchore*
6 The Legend of King Aśoka—*John S. Strong*
7 Buddhist Insight—*George R. Elder*
8 Buddhism Transformed—*Richard Gombrich* and *Gananath Obeyesekere*
9 The Buddhist Tantras—*Alex Wayman*
10 The Lion's Roar of Queen Śrīmālā —*Alex Wayman* and *Hideko Wayman*
11 The Buddha Nature—*Brian E. Brown*
12 Evolution of Stupas in Burma —*Sujata Soni*
13 Buddhist Parables—*E. W. Burlingame*
14 The Debate of King Milinda —*Bhikkhu Pesala*
15 The Chinese Madhyama Āgama and the Pāli Majjhima Nikāya—*Bhikṣu Thich Minh Chau*
16 Sudden and Gradual—*Peter N. Gregory*
17 Yoga of the Guhyasamājatantra—*Alex Wayman*
18 The Enlightenment of Vairocana —*Alex Wayman* and *R. Tajima*
19 A History of Indian Buddhism—Tr. *Hirakawa Akira*, Ed. *Paul Groner*
20 Introduction to the Buddhist Tantric Systems—*F.D. Lessing* and *Alex Wayman*
21 Anāgatavaṃsa Desanā—Tr. *Udaya Meddegama*, Ed. *John Clifford Holt*
22 Chinnamastā—*Elisabeth Anne Benard*
23 On Voidness—*Fernando Tola* and *Carmen Dragonetti*
24 Nāgārjuna's Refutation of Logic (Nyāya) Vaidalyaprakaraṇa—*Fernando Tola* and *Carmen Dragonetti*
25 The Buddhist Art of Nāgārjunakoṇḍa —*Elizabeth Rosen Stone*
26 Discipline—*John C. Holt*
27 Philosophy and its Development in the Nikāyas and Abhidhamma —*Fumimaro Watanabe*
28 Untying the Knots in Buddhism —*Alex Wayman*
29 Early Buddhist Theory of Knowledge —*K. N. Jayatilleke*
30 Calming the Mind and Discerning the Real—Tr. *Alex Wayman*
31 A Comparative Study of the Prātimokṣa—*W. Pachow*
32 The Rise of Esoteric Buddhism in the Tibet—*Eva M. Dargyay*
33-35 Saṃyuktābhidharmahṛdaya (3 Parts) —*Bart Dessein*
36 A Millennium of Buddhist Logic —*Alex Wayman*
37 The Buddhist Pilgrimage—*Duncan Forbes*
38 Chanting the Names of Mañjuśrī —*Alex Wayman*
39 The Literature of the Personalists of Early Buddhism—*Bhikshu Thich Thien Chau*
40 The Laṅkāvatāra Sūtra—*D. T. Suzuki*
41 Studies in the Laṅkāvatāra Sūtra —*D.T. Suzuki*
42 The Vimalakīrti Sūtra—*Burton Watson*
43 The Gāndhārī Dharmapada—*John Brough*
44 Imaging Wisdom—*Jacob N. Kinnard*
45 Pain and Its Ending—*Carol S. Anderson*
46 Apparitions of the Self—*Janet Gyatso*
47-49 Rules for Nuns according to the Dharma-guptakavinaya (3 Parts) —*Ann Heirman*
50 The Chinese Hevajratantra—*Ch. Willemen*
51 The Historical Buddha—*H. W. Schumann*
52 Dana—*Ellison Banks Findly*
53 Hermeneutics & Tradition in the *Saṃdhinirmocana-sūtra—John Powers*
54 Skillful Means—*John W. Schroeder*
55 The Two Truths in Chinese Buddhism —*Chang-Qing Shih*
56 The Bodhisattva Path—*Jan Nattier*
57 Becoming the Buddha—*Donald K. Swearer*
58 Approaching the Land of Bliss —*Richard K. Payne* & *Kenneth K. Tanaka*
59 Indian Monastic Buddhism: Collected papers on Textual, Inscriptional and Archaeological Evidence— *Gregory Schopen*